PROTEST CITY

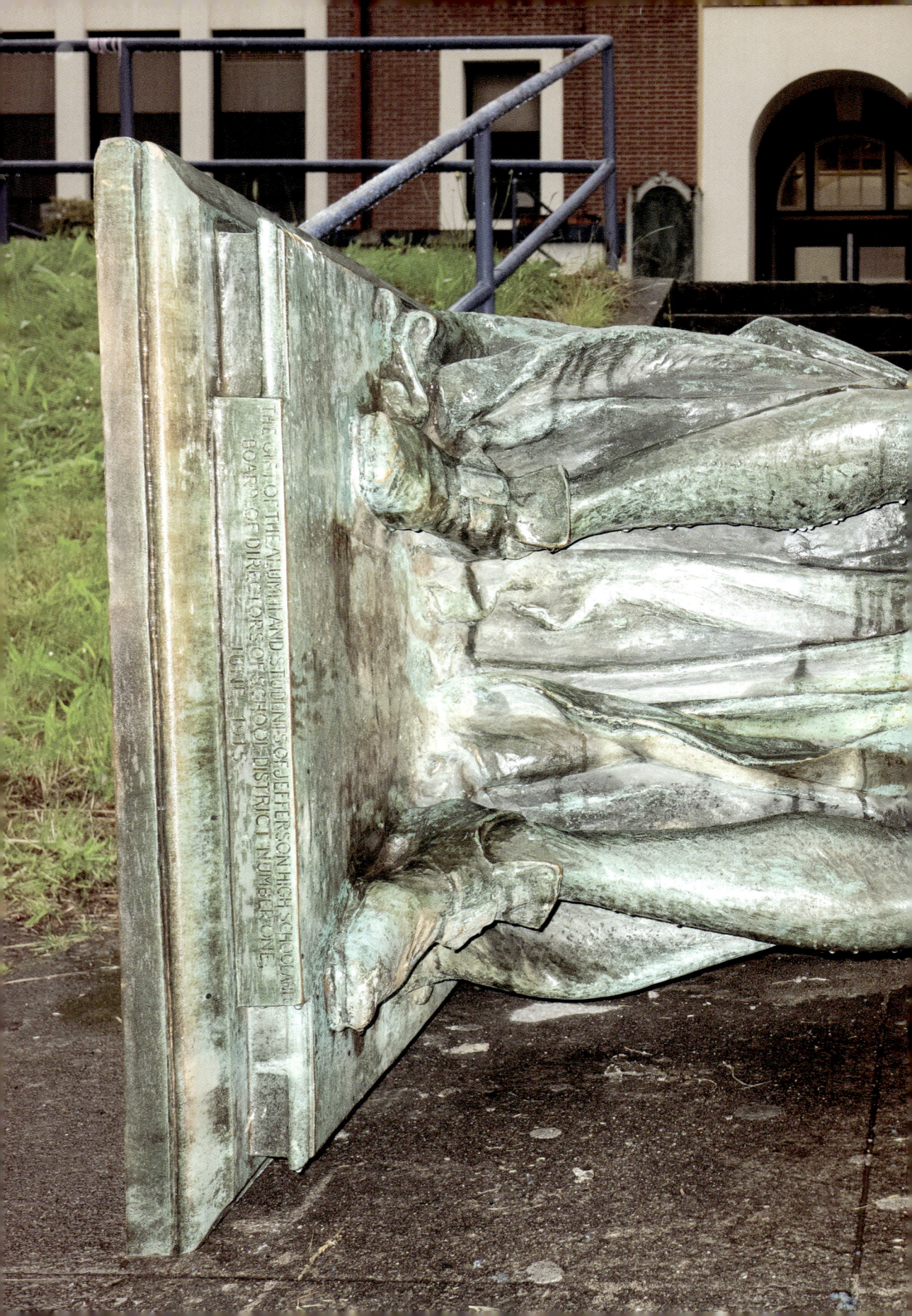

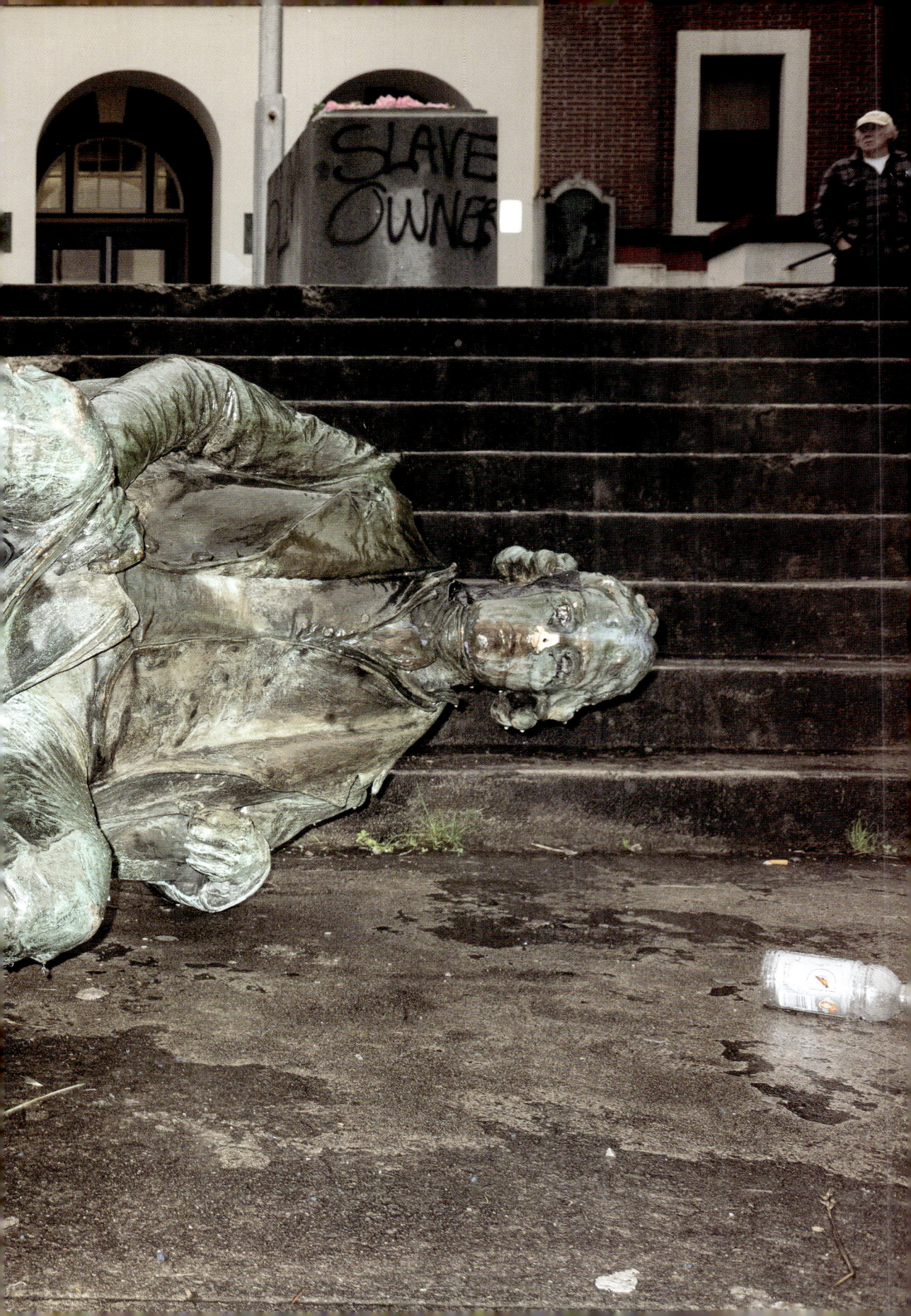

PROTEST

RIAN DUNDON

FOREWORD BY DONNELL ALEXANDER INTRODUCTION BY CARMEN P. THOMPSON

CITY

PORTLAND'S SUMMER OF RAGE

OREGON STATE UNIVERSITY PRESS   CORVALLIS

The publisher and author would like to thank the Magnum Foundation, Documentary Arts, and the Economic Hardship Reporting Project for their generous support of this publication. Additional funding has been provided by Furthermore: a program of the J. M. Kaplan Fund.

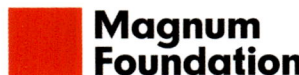 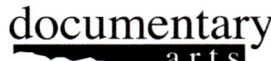

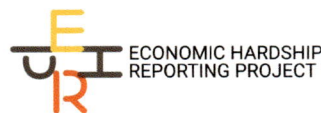 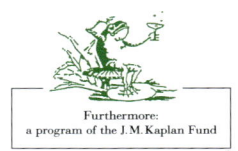

Library of Congress Cataloging-in-Publication Data

Names: Dundon, Rian, author, photographer. | Alexander, Donnell, writer of foreword. | Thompson, Carmen P, writer of introduction.
Title: Protest city : Portland's Summer of Rage / Rian Dundon ; foreword by Donnell Alexander ; introduction by Carmen P Thompson.
Other titles: Portland's Summer of Rage
Description: Corvallis : Oregon State University Press, 2023. | Includes bibliographical references.
Identifiers: LCCN 2023003761 | ISBN 9780870712265 (paperback) | ISBN 9780870712272 (ebook)
Subjects: LCSH: Portland (Or.)—History—21st century—Pictorial works. | Protest movements—Oregon—Portland—History—21st century—Pictorial works. | Black lives matter movement—Oregon—Portland—Pictorial works. Right-wing extremists—Oregon—Portland—History—21st century—Pictorial works. | Riots—Oregon—Portland—History—21st century—Pictorial works.
Classification: LCC F884.P857 D86 2023 | DDC 305.800979549—dc23/eng/20230203
LC record available at https://lccn.loc.gov/2023003761

♾ This paper meets the requirements of ANSI/NISO Z39.48-1992 (Permanence of Paper).

© 2023 Rian Dundon
All rights reserved.
First published in 2023 by Oregon State University Press
Printed in South Korea

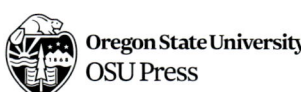

Oregon State University Press
121 The Valley Library
Corvallis OR 97331-4501
541-737-3166 • fax 541-737-3170
www.osupress.oregonstate.edu

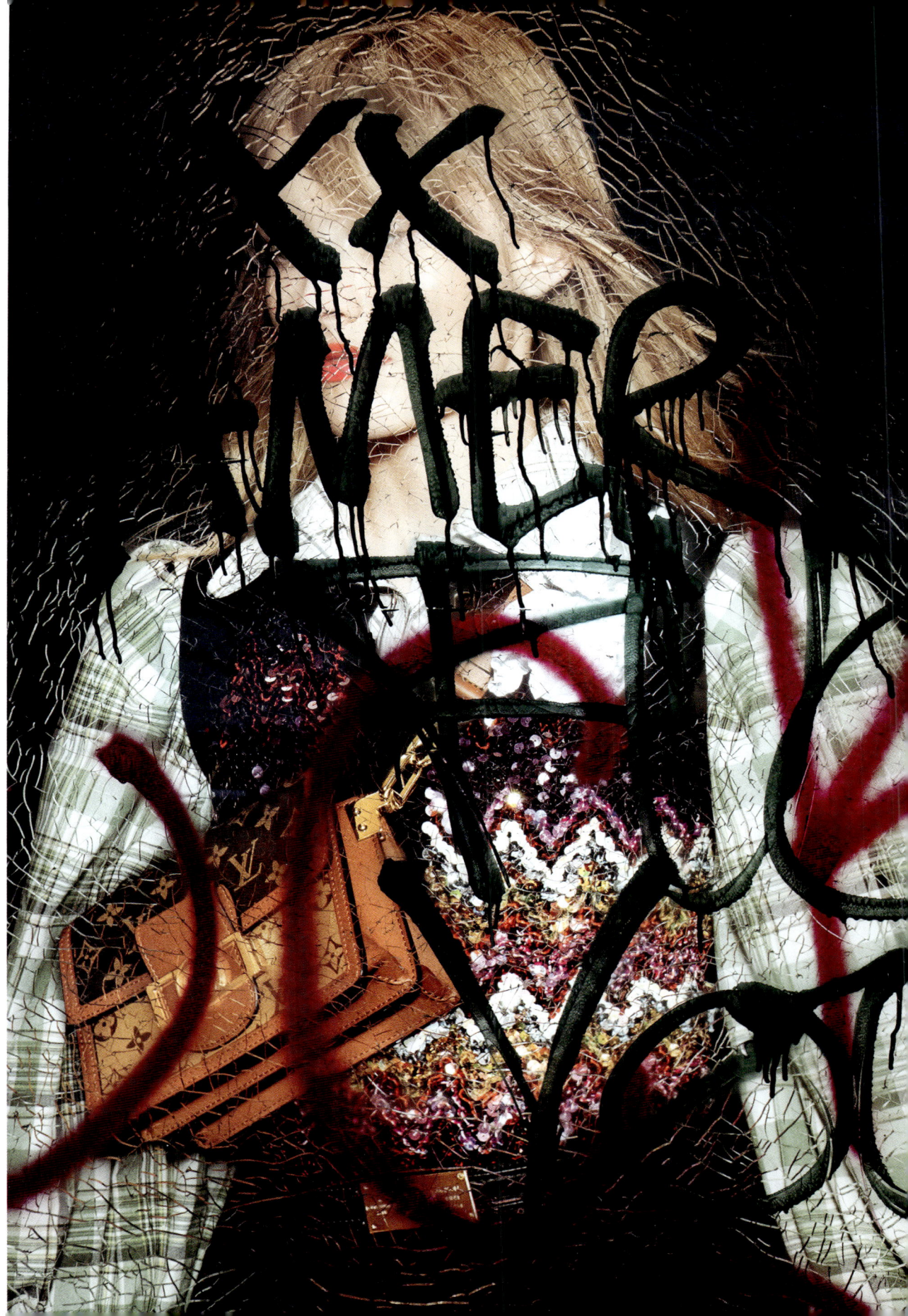

CONTENTS

FOREWORD BY DONNELL ALEXANDER — xi

INTRODUCTION BY CARMEN P. THOMPSON — xv

AUTHOR'S NOTE — xix

CHRONOLOGY — xxiii

PHOTOGRAPHS — 1

IMAGE CAPTIONS — 171

ACKNOWLEDGMENTS — 185

SUGGESTED READING — 187

FOREWORD

> "I would like to thank all of the advocates, the activists, I'd like to thank the people who stayed in these streets, marching night and day. The people of Portland *stayed* in the streets—for 83 days, I think."
> —RODNEY FLOYD, April 2021

In 2017, photojournalist Rian Dundon was in Oakland, documenting local anti-Trump protests. I was in Portland, putting a wrap on my seven-year stint of watching the city come to terms with itself. Rip City was receiving the last of its flowers for being America's Most Desirable. Whenever I asked local left-leaning friends if they knew Oregon's origins as a whites-only state, some still claimed blissful ignorance.

I first got here in 2010, right before the civic brand found its *Portlandia*-liberal-oasis peak. The dearth of diversity was an unspoken attribute. I happened to be dwelling in The Numbers, a diverse and working-class section of the city's deep east side. Straight away, Portland played more white than its boundaries actually allowed. To friends I referred to Portland as The City of Ill-Gotten Booty; urban American idylls sans the rough wrasslin' of integration.

There's a photograph in Rian Dundon's riveting photographic document *Protest City* that makes me think of that funny and racially blinkered show. The image is a 2020 summer shield line, five humans in downtown Portland, standing between the courthouse and Chapman Square. They're preparing to confront actual, state-sanctioned law enforcement whilst wearing homemade protection. One activist covers his mouth and nose with a handkerchief, another protects his head with a bike helmet.

Real cop shields are made of transparent polycarbonate. Among these protesters' shields appear to be an outdoor patio table top and one cabinet door. Hogging all of the attention is a protester decked out as a crusader, complete with metal helmet.

The get-ups register to me as a bit extra, but I feel the photo. Black Bloc and other such offshoot chaos makers were familiar to me from numerous protests. They annoyed me far more than my inability to pump my own gas. And they almost certainly weren't the same folks I'd see in the seminal Don't Shoot Portland meetings.

At those gatherings of unquestionably concerned citizens, politicians, and law enforcement, organizers "were trying to build direct engagement between elected officials and the community to expose how tightly tangled the corruption in the city was," recalls Glenn Waco. "We always carried the banner that said community action plan. The community has always been that action plan."

This coalition that met and strategized for years sits at the heart of the 2020 protests against a policing model rooted in slave patrols. But the freelancers in the aforementioned image were a part of it, too. They gave the protest oxygen on par with the NBA finals not being on. The wild-card fighters were a reflection of the setting and—perhaps more significantly—the time.

"As they became more entrenched that tendency toward spectacle embedded itself in the culture," Dundon told me. "And it was a culture, at least for those summer months. COVID still had the city shuttered, so protests were a space for expression and release even as they remained a dangerous and at times deadly serious enterprise."

What I've always loved about the Pacific Northwest is its within-the-country faintly foreign feel—Vaguely Canadian, I call it. Oregon's place in the American imagination is largely made of speculation. America never really knew Portland, but no one predicted Keep Portland Weird would yield to the Protest City.

Calling Portland "City of Ill-Gotten Booty" feels longer ago than the act was in fact; *Portlandia* premiered in January 2011. Feels like forever ago. Network executives would not greenlight that TV show as I write this. The place doesn't exist anymore, even as a state of mind.

One last note on the city's singular blending of protest and pleasure:

On the Thursday after 2016's presidential election I hosted the first of two cultural engagements put on by Portland's NAACP. This timing was a challenge. The most bummed-out audience of my twenty years of telling stories publicly sat in Northeast Portland, Billy Webb Elks Lodge, for History Night. Racially mixed and super, *super* sad.

But the audience offered a very legit laugh in response to a joke about white people fleeing to Canada and reversing the impacts of gentrification. It was telling.

Come Saturday night, later, the lodge got looser. On its walls was visual art celebrating this specific, culturally rich spot on the Oregon map, on the American map: Northeast Portland, America. Earth. And on this night the people danced and rapped and sang as only Black Americans can and some white people got swept up in the joyful noise. White membership in the NAACP spiked.

Outside, rioters were tearing it up. Ever since I skipped town in the summer of 2017, there's been new perspective on Portland and how the place is coming to be seen. Now, I understand clearly not only how the pure protests and performance protests are related, but how in one transcendent summer they functioned in league, however awkwardly.

DONNELL ALEXANDER
OAKLAND, 2021

INTRODUCTION *Carmen P. Thompson*

When George Floyd was murdered on May 25, 2020, in Minneapolis, Minnesota, by police officer Derek Chauvin while three other officers watched Chauvin kneel on Floyd's neck for nine minutes and twenty-nine seconds, it set off a fury of protests around the nation and the world. His dying words, "I can't breathe," were a rallying cry for millions of people protesting the regular murder of unarmed Black women, men, and children at the hands of police or self-proclaimed White vigilantes. Unfortunately, occurrences like this were not new in America.

For centuries police and vigilante violence against Black people at the hands of Whites has been used to intimidate and literally beat back Black advancement in American society such as what occurred in the aftermath of the passage of the thirteenth, fourteenth, and fifteenth amendments that resulted in the birth of the Ku Klux Klan as well as with the civil rights activism and legislation of the 1960s that birthed the modern Conservative Movement. Such state sanctioned, wanton violence against Black people by Whites has left innumerable unexplained, murdered, and mutilated Black bodies in its wake, including Emmitt Till, Medgar Evers, and other civil rights activists. And recently the unprovoked killings of Trayvon Martin, Michael Brown, Tamir Rice, Breonna Taylor, Sandra Bland, Amad Aubrey, and numerous others illustrate America's continued lack of regard for Black life.

These cases sadly represent a phenomenon in American society that scholar Frank Wilderson III describes as gratuitous violence against Black people and White indifference to Black suffering dating back to this nation's founding. In this context, Rian Dundon's prescient book, *Protest City*, asks us to question not only why did the murder of Floyd hit such a nerve in the nation, but more specifically, why did it hit such a nerve in Portland, Oregon, with protests lasting over 365 days?

Protest City deftly chronicles—in stark, shocking, and sometimes gruesome detail—the protests in Portland over George Floyd's murder. That Portland, Oregon, the Whitest city in the United States with a population of more than five hundred thousand, would protest the police killing of another unarmed Black person was befuddling to many. Some wrote off the length of Portland's protests as part of the left-wing liberalism and quirkiness epitomized in the city's moniker, "Keep Portland Weird," which was brought to life in the sketch comedy television series *Portlandia* that spoofed the city's far-left eccentricities. Others explain the anomaly as part of Portland's long history of protest and activism; the city was ground zero in the United States for the Occupy movement in 2011, which shined light on rampant corporate greed and wealth inequality in America and around the world.

All of these explanations for why the Whitest city in America would protest for over one year the murder of an unarmed Black man fails to get at why this particular police murder would cause such a long-lasting uproar. I suggest that the protesting was not as much about Floyd, the police, or liberalism run amok as it was about White people's anxiety about their own precarious social position relative to Blacks and the state's authority to use lethal force to maintain the social and racial order. In other words, the gratuitous murder of George Floyd was representative of the racial order of White over Black, which is the defining relational dynamic in American society that all Whites, especially poor and working-class ones, are expected to uphold. And George Floyd's Black body represents what would/could be happening to poor and working-class Whites if there were no "Black" people. This stark reality undergirded the length and fervor of protests in Portland that expressed the varying degrees of comfort Whites have with this part of the social contract.

Blackness and Black bodies—and the concomitant gratuitous violence used against them—have historically been a galvanizing symbol that telegraphed White people's conception of their place and rank in civil society. The violence against Floyd's Black body was a check and balance for Whites, Blacks, and other racialized groups, affirming America's racial pecking order of Whites on top and Blacks on the bottom and all others situated between these two groups. Thus, those more than 365 days of protest were an expression of White Portlanders' reconciliation of the meaning of their Whiteness vis-à-vis the gratuitous violence against this unarmed Black man.

Those more than 365 days of protest also revealed the angst felt by Whites at the state's bludgeoning reminder of the quid pro quo between Whites that Floyd's body represents. And what better place than Portland, Oregon, the Whitest city in America, to observe the breadth of that angst, revealing what I call the "spectrum of Whiteness" that spanned from liberal White allies of all classes to anarchists, White nationalists, and extremists. For differing and varying reasons, Whites along the spectrum of Whiteness were expressing in their protests their nervousness about their vulnerability to federal, state, and local government and to the elite classes of Whites who control the institutions that order their lives and civil society.

The protests that occurred in Portland reflect the fears, demands, and frustrations of Whites at the government over the tenuousness of their social position even though Floyd's murder should symbolically have assuaged their concerns. It is as if the murder of George Floyd was a perverted message from the state to all Whites that in spite of Black progress and optimism, the state has not forgotten its commitment to uphold their top spot in the racial pecking order. And Floyd was the human sacrifice that made this point manifest.

The protests in Portland thereby reflect White people's simultaneous unease with and expectation for the government to uphold the racial hierarchy that the murder of an unarmed Black man highlights, i.e., that White people are ranked above Black people, even as they protest the grotesqueness of Floyd's murder. And yet in the centuries since America's founding, there is still much to be learned about the evolution of Whiteness from the fears and demands expressed in the protests, rebellions, wars, and revolutions of its White participants. Namely, that race and/or Black people are often at the center of these events. That said, *Protest City* provides a rarely seen look into the world of Whiteness. It is ugly; it is violent and often hidden; it is a snapshot of America.

AUTHOR'S NOTE *Photographing Portland's Summer of Rage*

Portland, Oregon, spent the summer of 2020 uncomfortably thrust into the national spotlight. After the killing of George Floyd, protests erupted here just as they did across the country, with thousands of people flooding the streets, demanding police accountability and racial justice. But when federal police began clearing the area around a US district courthouse downtown in July, making arrests and shooting off wave after wave of tear-gas canisters, Portland became an epicenter in a battle over freedom of protest and government might, with the whole country's attention turned to its streets.

That summer, the main protest site in Portland was only about a mile from my home. I would leave my quiet southeast Portland neighborhood on foot, crossing the Hawthorne bridge at dusk to find myself transported into another universe. On the other side, under chemical clouds, I found a twisted vision of twenty-first century urban warfare. Protesters carried homemade shields and paint respirators for protection, used leaf blowers to expel tear gas, and lobbed bottle rockets at officers who responded with high velocity impact munitions and deafening flashbang grenades. Federal agents in fatigues were snatching people from the park and packing them into unmarked vans while the barricades erected to protect government buildings were relentlessly pressed upon by a furious sea of bodies. I had been photographing political clashes on the West Coast since Trump took office, and this leftist surge felt like a counterpoint to the displays of right-wing militancy we'd grown accustomed to during his tenure. World events were happening in my hometown and not even a pandemic could keep me away.

And then they came for me. In the early hours of July 22, I was set upon by US Marshals while covering a protest outside the Mark O. Hatfield United States Courthouse. Photos of the incident shot by reporters from the *New York Times* and Associated Press ran in newspapers around the world, and a video spread online showing me getting thrown to the ground as a group of officers bullrush across the sidewalk, casually dropping smoke bombs and canisters of tear gas as they go. One of the marshals rips the press ID from around my neck; another pins me under the gas with his nightstick for ten excruciating seconds. I walked home with third-degree burns that night, bedraggled but buzzing on residual adrenaline.

This was one of the many times—the worst time—that the protests felt like a medieval siege.

Though protesters were effectively unified under the banner of Black Lives Matter, many were motivated by more personalized concerns. A lot of people were there to stand against the Trump administration's aggressive intervention in local policing. Others focused their rage on Portland mayor Ted Wheeler, whose deafness to protesters' demands had been palpable from the start, or rallied more generally against systemic racism, capitalism, the patriarchy. Some just wanted to fight cops. Many were in it to document it—they were filming, photographing, and live streaming for the parallel conflict taking place online and in the media.

Weeks passed and the protests kept going, downtown at first, then outside various precinct houses, sheriff's headquarters, and an Immigration and Customs Enforcement facility in South Portland. The police union offices on North Lombard were set on fire multiple times. After one hundred consecutive days there was still no sign of things letting up—until Mother Nature intervened. On Labor Day, September 7, wildfires blanketed the region in thick smoke for several weeks, halting most outdoor activity. I remember watching the skies go from yellow to orange to red as I drove home from a rally in Salem that day, where a caravan of Proud Boys had just unfurled an enormous American flag outside the Oregon statehouse. A small band of counter-protesters had gathered there too, swiftly outnumbered by the dozens of heavily armed right-wingers in attendance. It was the most guns I had seen all summer, and as skirmishes broke out across the Capitol Mall, the encroaching firestorm bathed those unruly proceedings in an ominous golden glow. It was the end of Portland's summer of protest, but it felt like the beginning of something much worse.

A lot of people ask me about the goals of the protests. What do they really hope to accomplish? To me the feasibility of protester demands is beside the point. Protest is spontaneous; protest is spiritual. It's an imperfect response to our biggest problems, but it means confronting the past and a threat to the status quo, both of which are powerful tools for change.

On New Year's Eve, 2020, activists staged another downtown rally outside the Multnomah County Justice Center. It was the biggest demonstration since Election Day, and the mood was celebratory as the first riot of 2021 was declared. "We did this to remind them that we still can," a smiling protester told me as the police line retreated from a barrage of paint balloons and fireworks. "We can do this anytime we want."

RIAN DUNDON
PORTLAND, 2022

CHRONOLOGY

2020

MAY 28 — Protests begin in Portland, Oregon, three days after the death of George Floyd, a Black man killed by police in Minneapolis, Minnesota. A viral video of Floyd's death sparks similar protests in cities across the country.

MAY 29 — Thousands of people gather at Peninsula Park in North Portland and march downtown to the Multnomah County Justice Center. Windows are smashed and a fire is briefly set inside. Downtown businesses are looted.

MAY 30 — Mayor Ted Wheeler declares a state of emergency and enacts an 8 p.m. curfew. Throngs of protesters gather outside the justice center and are dispersed with tear gas.

MAY 31 — President Donald J. Trump tweets, "The United States of America will be designating ANTIFA as a Terrorist Organization." Protesters march from Laurelhurst Park to be met with tear gas outside the justice center.

JUNE 1 — In defiance of the citywide curfew, thousands of people rally at Pioneer Courthouse Square.

JUNE 2 — Demonstrators hold a "die in" on the Burnside Bridge, lying prostrate for eight minutes and forty-six seconds—the length of time police held George Floyd to the ground before he passed.

JUNE 4 — Portland Public Schools announces they will cease to employ school resource police officers on campus.

JUNE 5 — After a week of nightly protests, Mayor Wheeler makes an impromptu appeal for peace outside City Hall, speaking to press and protesters through a bullhorn. He is drowned out with booing.

JUNE 6	Portland Police officers are permitted to cover their name tags while working protests.
JUNE 8	Portland Police chief Jami Resch resigns. She is replaced by Chuck Lovell.
JUNE 9	A temporary restraining order against the city of Portland and Multnomah County prohibits the use of tear gas unless lives are at risk.
JUNE 17	Portland City Council votes to cut $15 million from the police bureau. Protesters erect an overnight "autonomous zone" outside Mayor Wheeler's home in the Pearl District.
JUNE 24	Sentencing hearing for MAX train killer Jeremy Christian, a local right-wing affiliate found guilty for the double murder of Ricky John Best and Taliesin Myrddin Namkai-Meche in 2017.
JUNE 25	Protesters gather outside the Portland Police Bureau's North Precinct, barricading the building and occupying the intersection of Martin Luther King Jr. Boulevard and NE Killingsworth.
JUNE 26	President Trump issues Executive Order 13933, "On Protecting American Monuments, Memorials, and Statues and Combatting Recent Criminal Violence." Agents with the Federal Protective Service of the Department of Homeland Security (DHS) are deployed to Portland.
JUNE 29	Protesters hold vigil at Portland State University to commemorate the second anniversary of the killing of Jason Washington by campus police.
JUNE 30	Protesters target the Portland Police Association, a law enforcement union with offices on NE Lombard Street. Fire is set to the building and demonstrators are dispersed with tear gas and arrests.
JULY 2	City removes the "Thompson Elk" sculpture, a 1900 bronze that became a rallying point for protesters outside the justice center.

JULY 7	Federal agents break up a candlelight vigil for Summer Taylor in Chapman Square. Taylor, a twenty-four-year-old activist, was killed while participating in a Black Lives Matter demonstration in Seattle on July 4.
JULY 12	Pro-cop "back the blue" activists begin holding daytime rallies outside the justice center.
JULY 14	Protesters barricade the intersections around Lownsdale Square, occupying the park and establishing a short-lived "Chinook Lands Autonomous Territory."
JULY 15	Federal police are filmed using unmarked minivans to snatch protesters off the streets.
JULY 16	Fiftieth consecutive day of protest. Department of Homeland Security acting secretary Chad Wolf makes an unannounced visit to Portland to tour federal facilities impacted by protests. Wolf meets with federal officers and Portland Police Association president Daryl Turner.
JULY 17	Community leaders and activists hold a press conference outside the Mark O. Hatfield United States Courthouse demanding the removal of federal agents from protests. Skirmishes break out with suspected right-wing infiltrators in the crowd.
JULY 18	Federal authorities erect an eight-foot-high steel mesh fence around the Hatfield courthouse. Protesters quickly dismantle it and use its panels to barricade the building's doors. Fifty-three-year-old Navy veteran Christopher David is filmed being beaten and maced by federal agents.
JULY 22	Contractors reinforce the fence with concrete barriers. Mayor Wheeler attends a protest and retreats after being tear-gassed by federal officers.
JULY 29	Oregon governor Kate Brown announces the phased withdrawal of federal officers from protests, describing "an occupying force" that has "refused accountability and brought strife to our community."

AUGUST 5	Protesters begin targeting the Portland Police Bureau's East Precinct.
AUGUST 8	A Christian prayer concert and mass baptism dubbed "riots to revival" is held a few blocks from the justice center at Waterfront Park.
AUGUST 11	Multnomah County district attorney Mike Schmidt announces his office will drop most charges against protesters.
AUGUST 15	Gunfire erupts during skirmishes between right-wing activists and leftist counter-protesters at a downtown "back the blue" rally.
AUGUST 19	Activists clash with DHS agents outside the Immigration and Customs Enforcement (ICE) facility on S Macadam Avenue.
AUGUST 22	Right-wing activists and militants gather outside the justice center for a "No to Marxism in America" rally. Open brawling with counter-protesters goes unchecked by law enforcement; bricks, mace, and homemade explosive devices are among the weapons used.
AUGUST 29	Trump supporters hold a "cruise rally" of flag-waving vehicles caravaning through the city. They are met downtown by counter-protesters and street brawling ensues. Michael Forest Reinoehl, an avowed antifascist, shoots and kills Patriot Prayer affiliate Aaron "Jay" Danielson.
SEPTEMBER 1	Mayor Wheeler announces he will move out of his Pearl District condo, a regular target for protesters.
SEPTEMBER 3	Michael Reinoehl is shot to death by a US Marshals fugitive task force in Lacey, Washington.
SEPTEMBER 5	One hundredth consecutive day of protest. Thousands gather in East Portland's Ventura Park to be dispersed after a protester lobs a Molotov cocktail at police. Neighborhood residents suffer the effects of tear gas inside their homes.
SEPTEMBER 7	Trump supporters caravan from the parking lot of Clackamas Community College to the State Capitol in Salem. Armed militants and Proud Boys in attendance clash with a small number of counter-protesters. Wildfires begin to inundate the region in smoke.

SEPTEMBER 10	Mayor Wheeler bans the Portland Police Bureau from using tear gas at protests.
SEPTEMBER 21	The Department of Justice identifies Portland, Seattle, and New York City as jurisdictions "permitting anarchy, violence, and destruction in American cities."
SEPTEMBER 23	Protesters rally outside the justice center in reaction to the Breonna Taylor grand jury decision in Louisville, Kentucky.
SEPTEMBER 26	A Proud Boys demonstration in Delta Park attracts national media attention and sparks counter-protests across the city.
OCTOBER 11	"Indigenous day of rage" protesters topple statues of Teddy Roosevelt and Abraham Lincoln and vandalize the Oregon Historical Society.
OCTOBER 29	Kevin Petersen Jr., a twenty-one-year-old Black man, is shot to death by Clark County sheriffs during a prescription drug sting in the Portland suburb of Hazel Dell, Washington.
OCTOBER 30	Hundreds gather for a candlelight vigil in the bank parking lot where Kevin Petersen Jr. was killed. Armed right-wing counter-protesters assemble nearby, waving pro-Trump flags and provoking skirmishes with mourners. At least one person fires a gun. Protesters in downtown Vancouver, Washington, smash windows and light fires.
NOVEMBER 2	Governor Brown declares a state of emergency in anticipation of 2020 presidential elections.
NOVEMBER 3	Election Day protesters march through Southeast Portland, chanting and challenging neighborhood residents to join them.
NOVEMBER 4	Oregon National Guard are deployed to post-election protests downtown.
NOVEMBER 7	Democrat Joe Biden is declared the forty-sixth president of the United States. Spontaneous celebrations break out at Pioneer Courthouse Square.

DECEMBER 8 — Red House eviction blockade begins. Activists erect barricades and take up arms to protect the Kinney family, residents of a North Portland home threatened with removal by Multnomah County sheriff's deputies. A five-day standoff with law enforcement ensues, successfully preventing the eviction.

2021

JANUARY 6 — Trump supporters rally outside the Oregon State Capitol in Salem to contest the presidential election results. Clashes break out between Proud Boys and antifascists.

JANUARY 20 — On Inauguration Day, left-wing activists gather outside Revolution Hall for a "Fuck Biden" rally. Protesters vandalize the Democratic Party headquarters and skirmish with police. A nighttime protest at the ICE building leads to multiple days of clashes with federal law enforcement.

MARCH 12 — Police detain over one hundred protesters on NW Marshall between Thirteenth and Fourteenth Avenues. Demonstrators are identified and photographed by Portland Police Bureau before being released.

APRIL 20 — Mayor Wheeler declares a state of emergency in response to ongoing protest-related vandalism. Wheeler asks residents to note the license plates of people dressed in black and report them to the police, vowing to "unmask" protesters.

MAY 25 — On the one-year anniversary of George Floyd's death, protesters march through downtown Portland, smashing windows and vandalizing government buildings and businesses, with minimal police intervention.

AUGUST 22 — After Portland Police Bureau states they will not intervene in political violence, a right-wing "Summer of Love" rally leads to open brawling and gunfire between far-right attendees and leftist counter-protesters.

PORTLAND, OREGON 2020

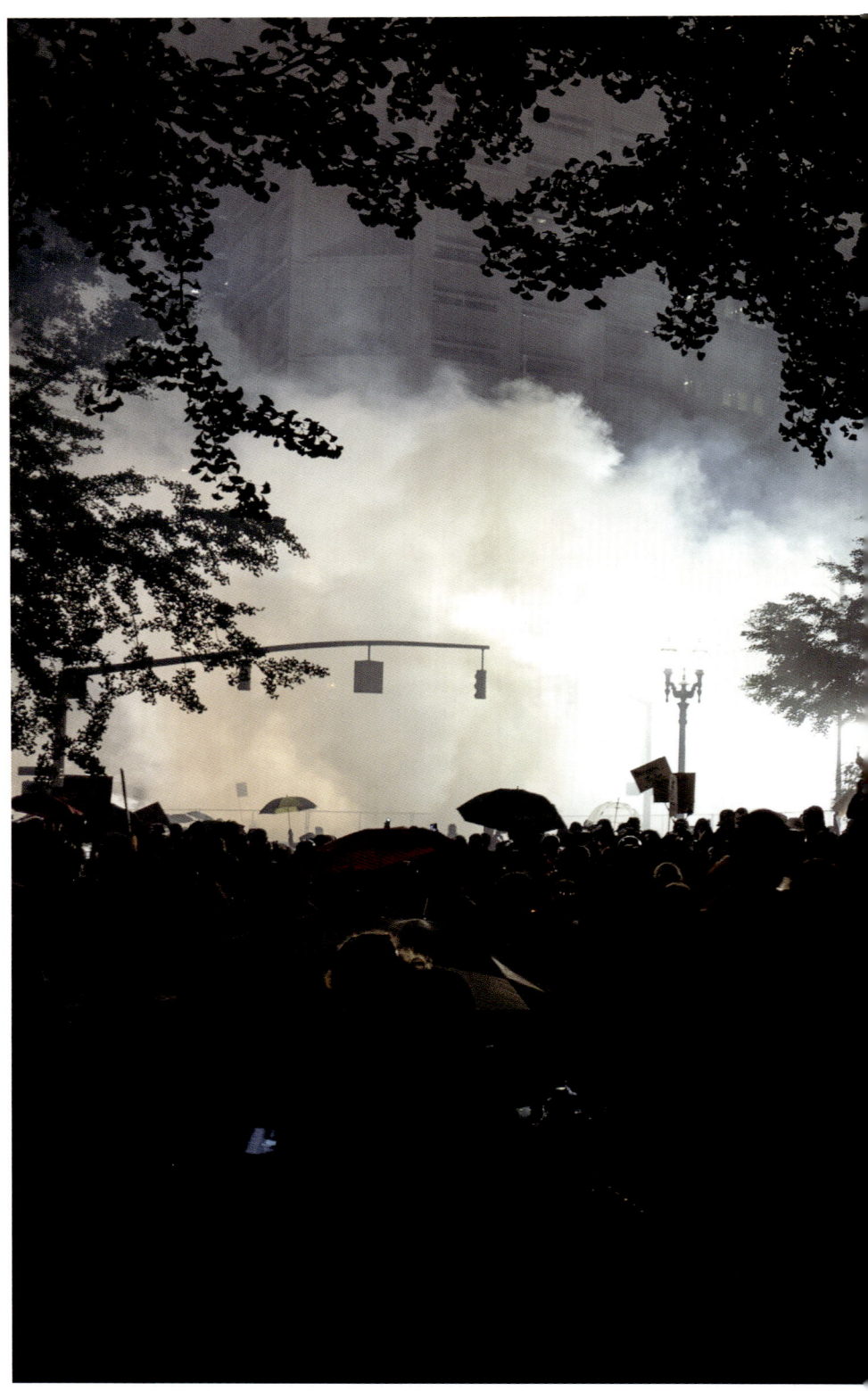

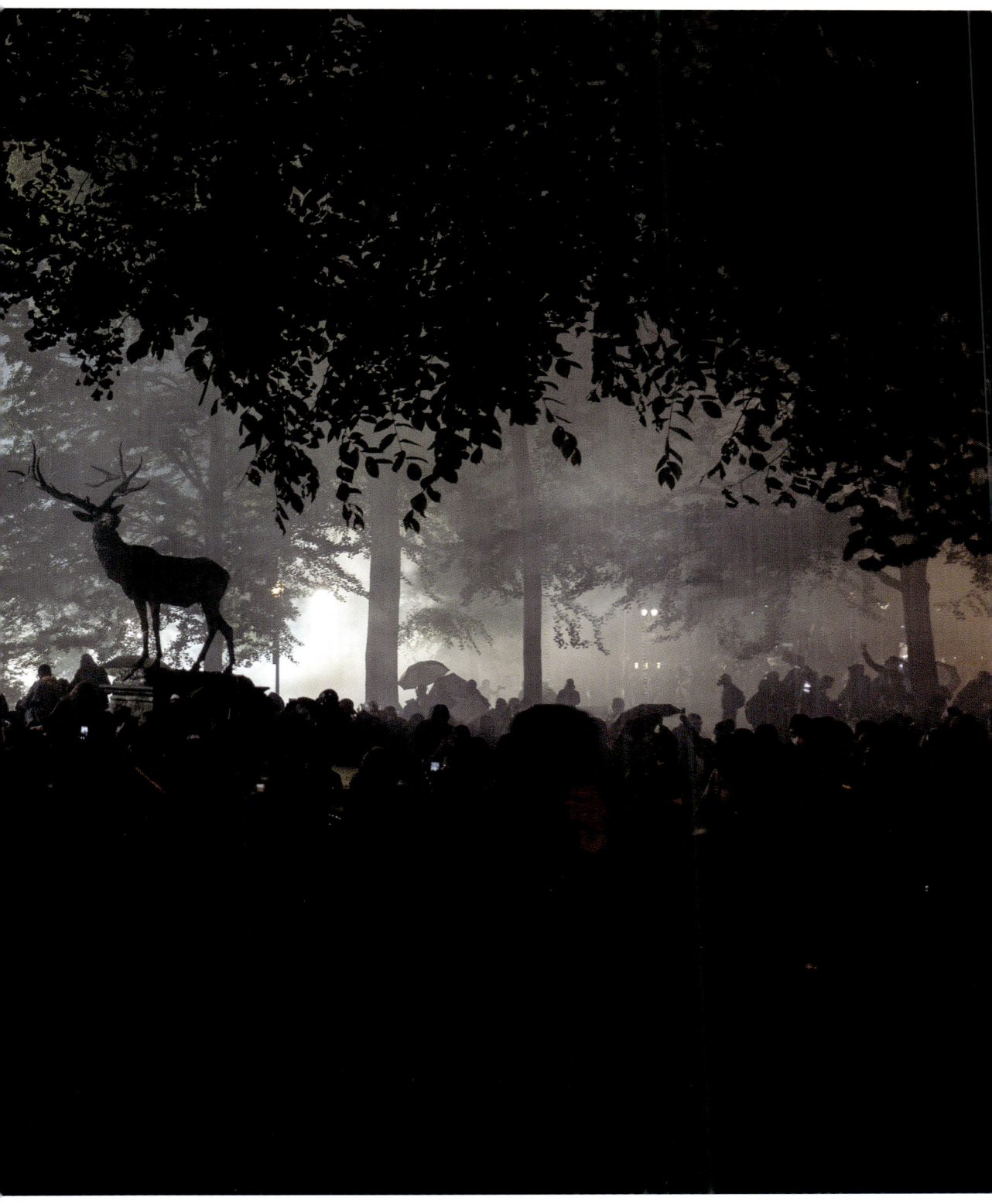

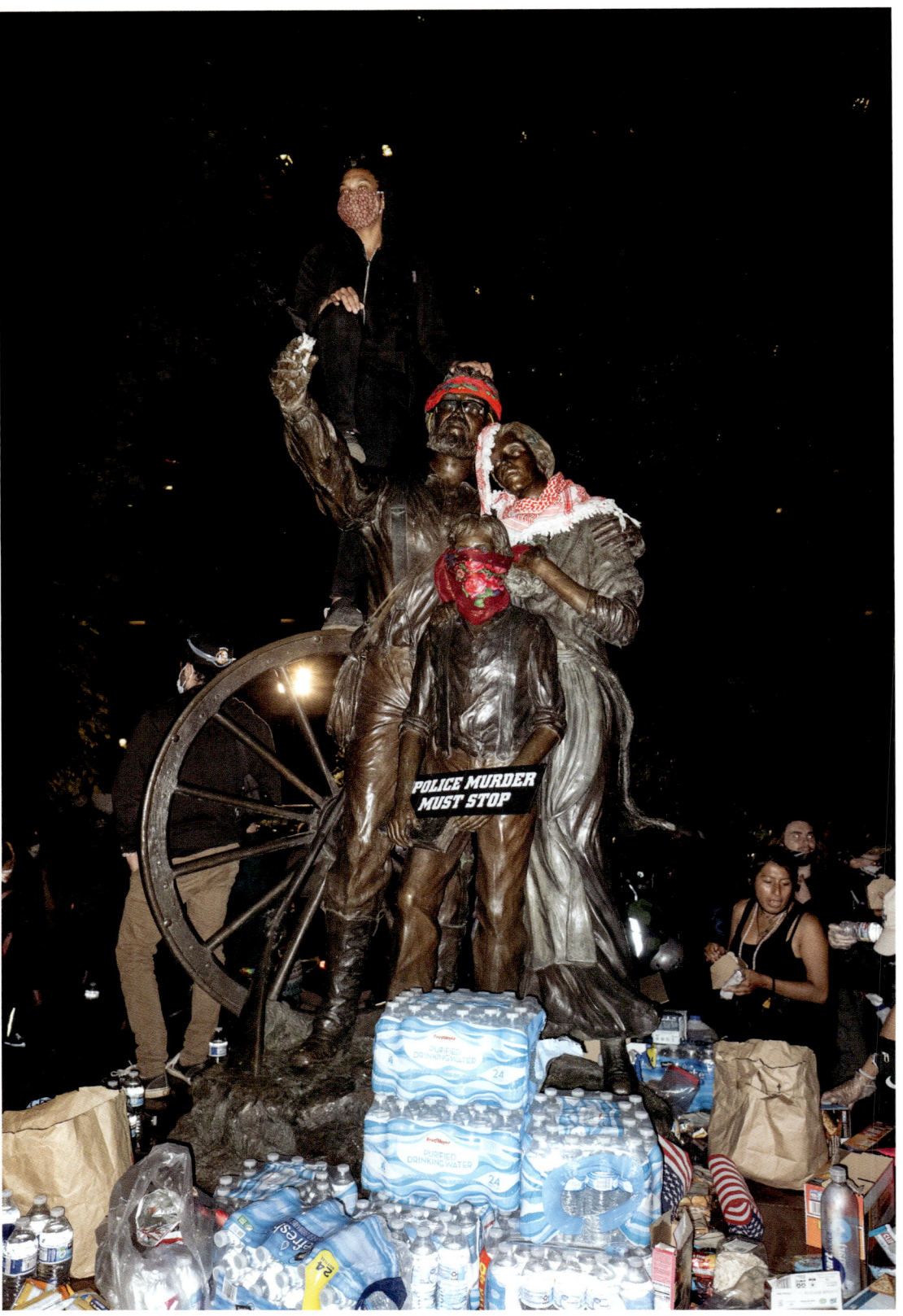

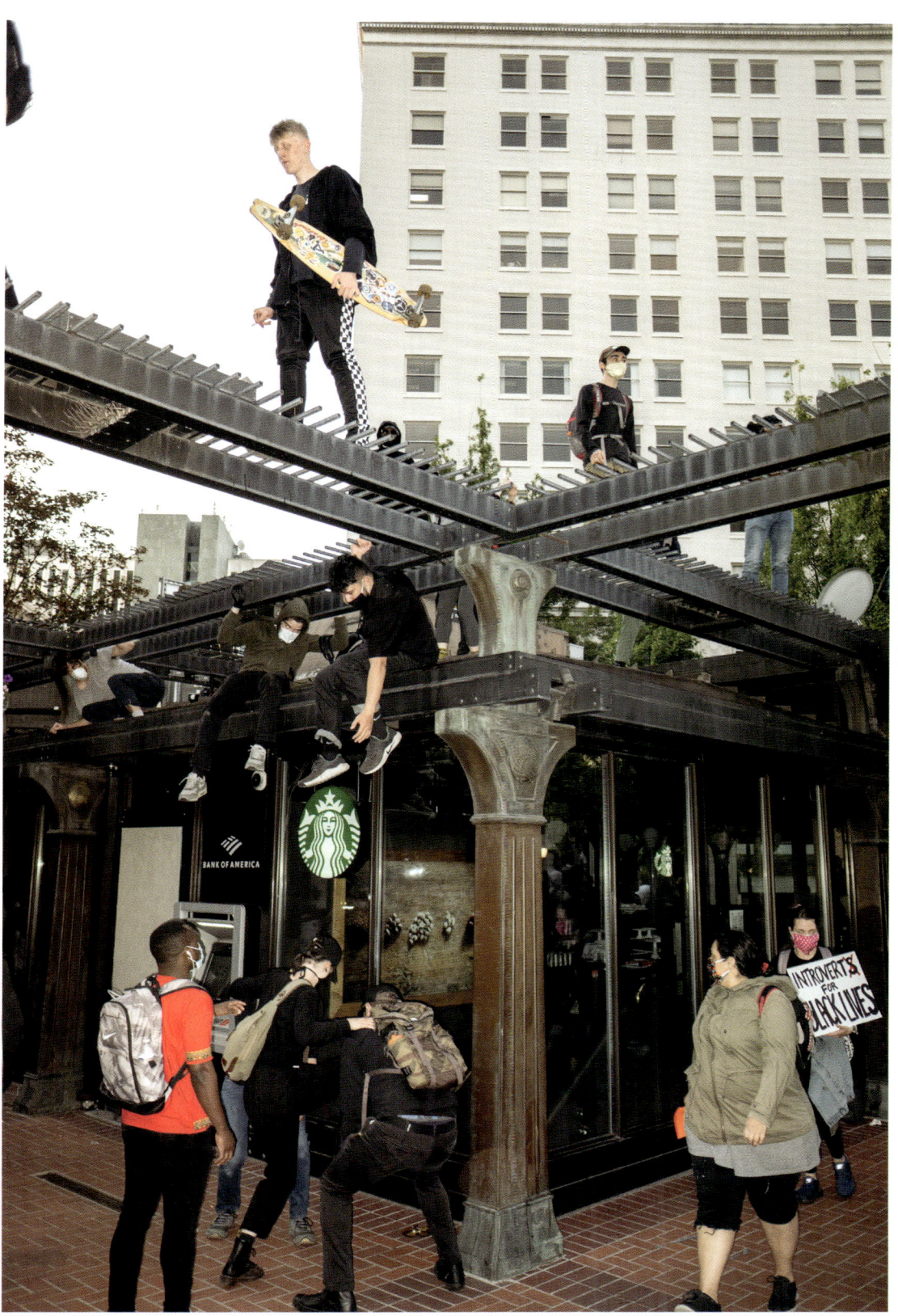

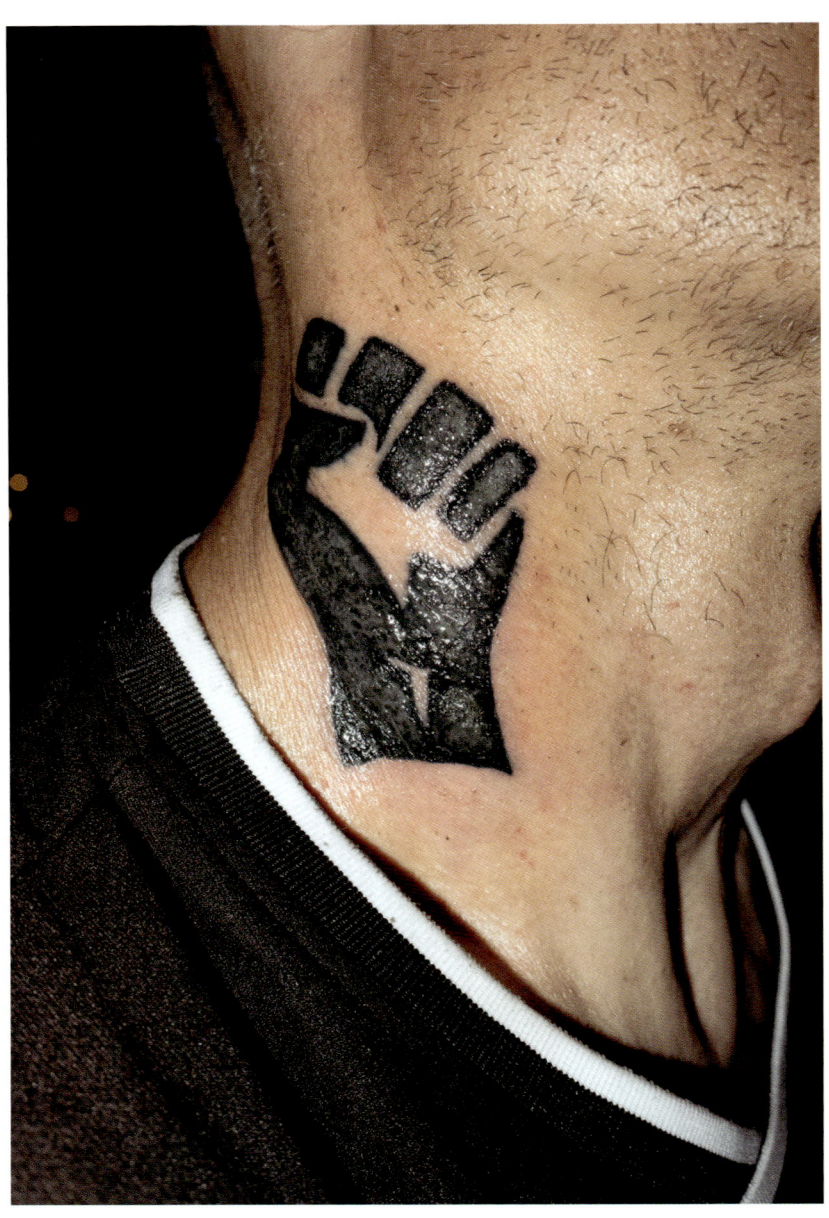

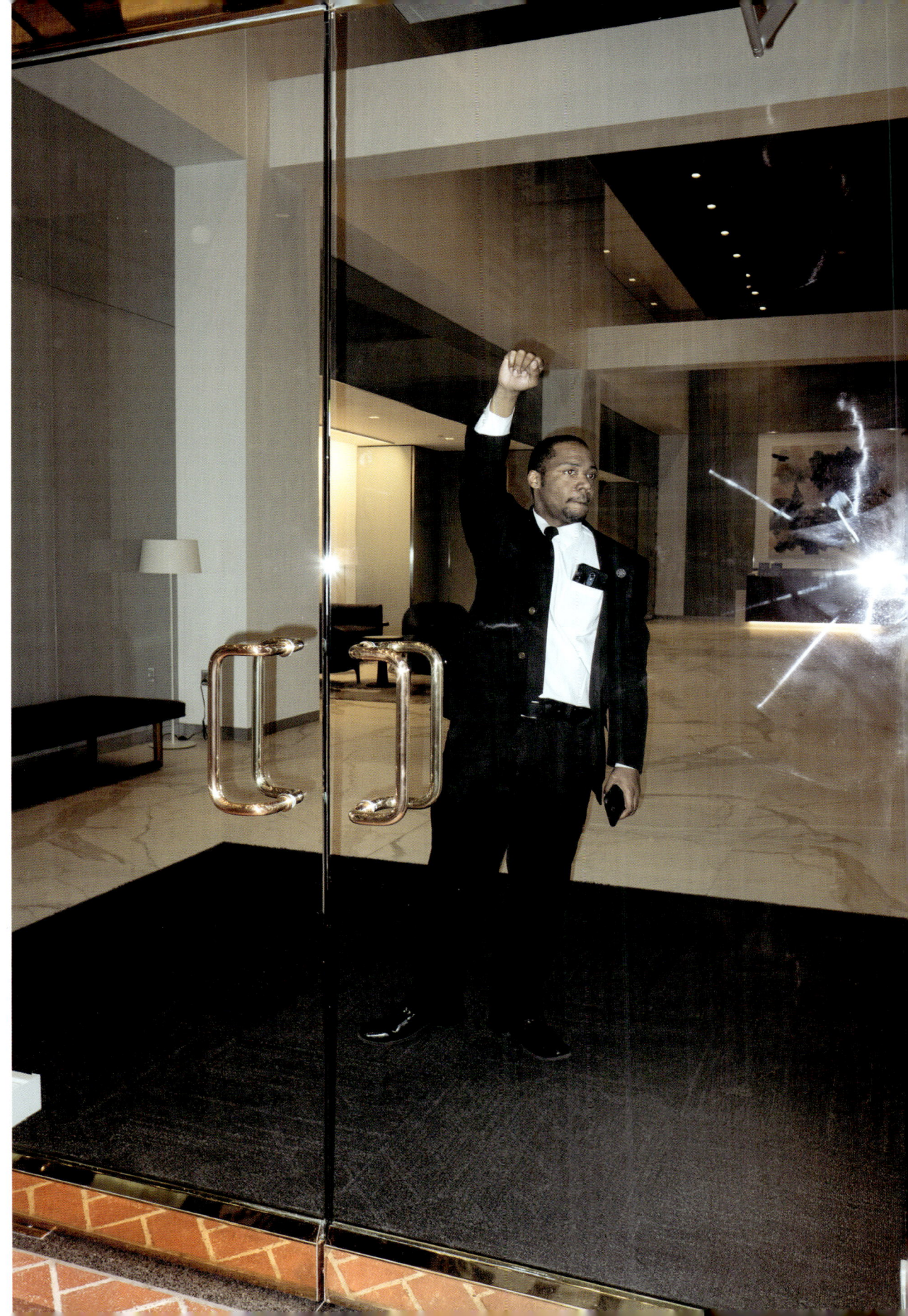

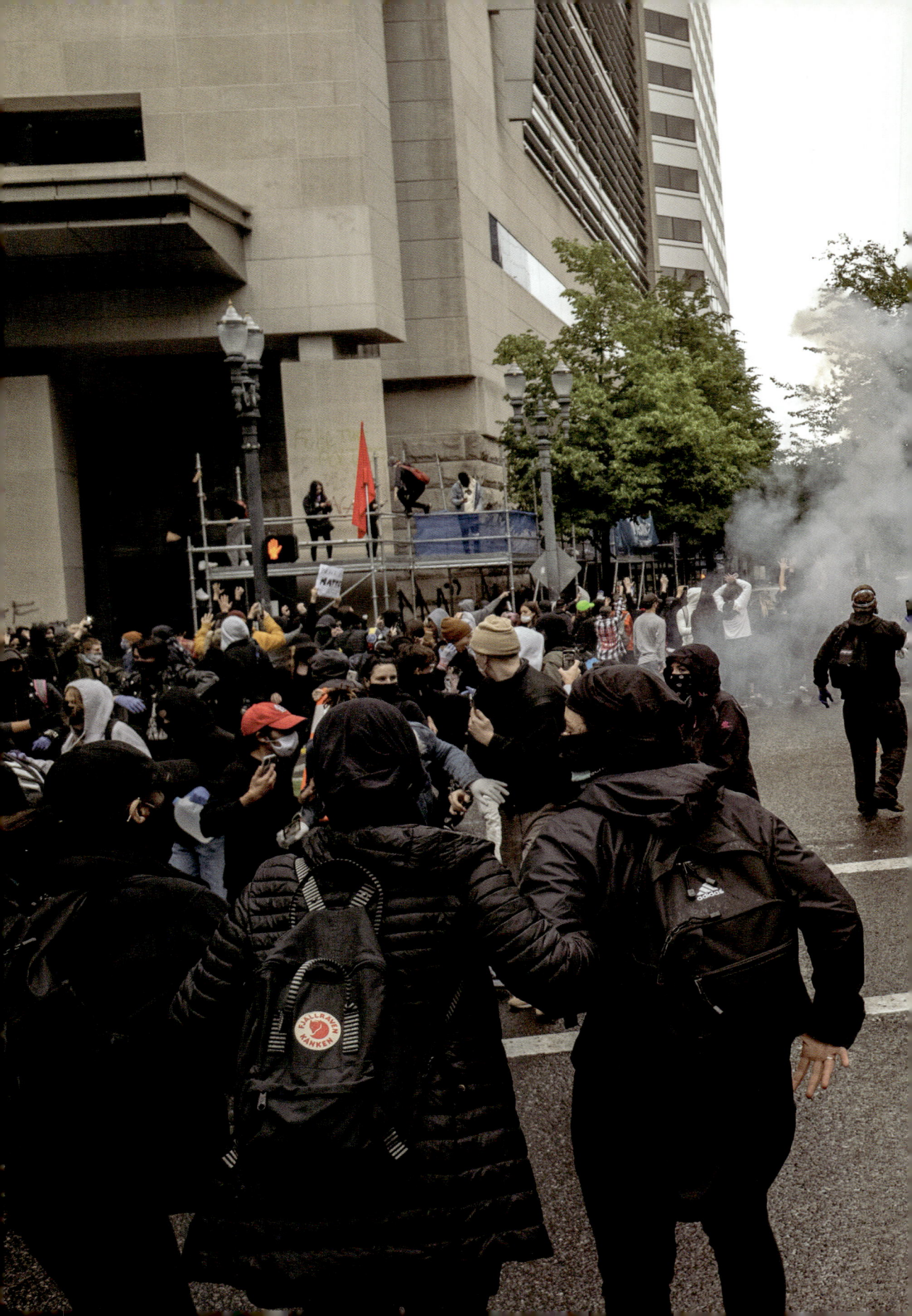

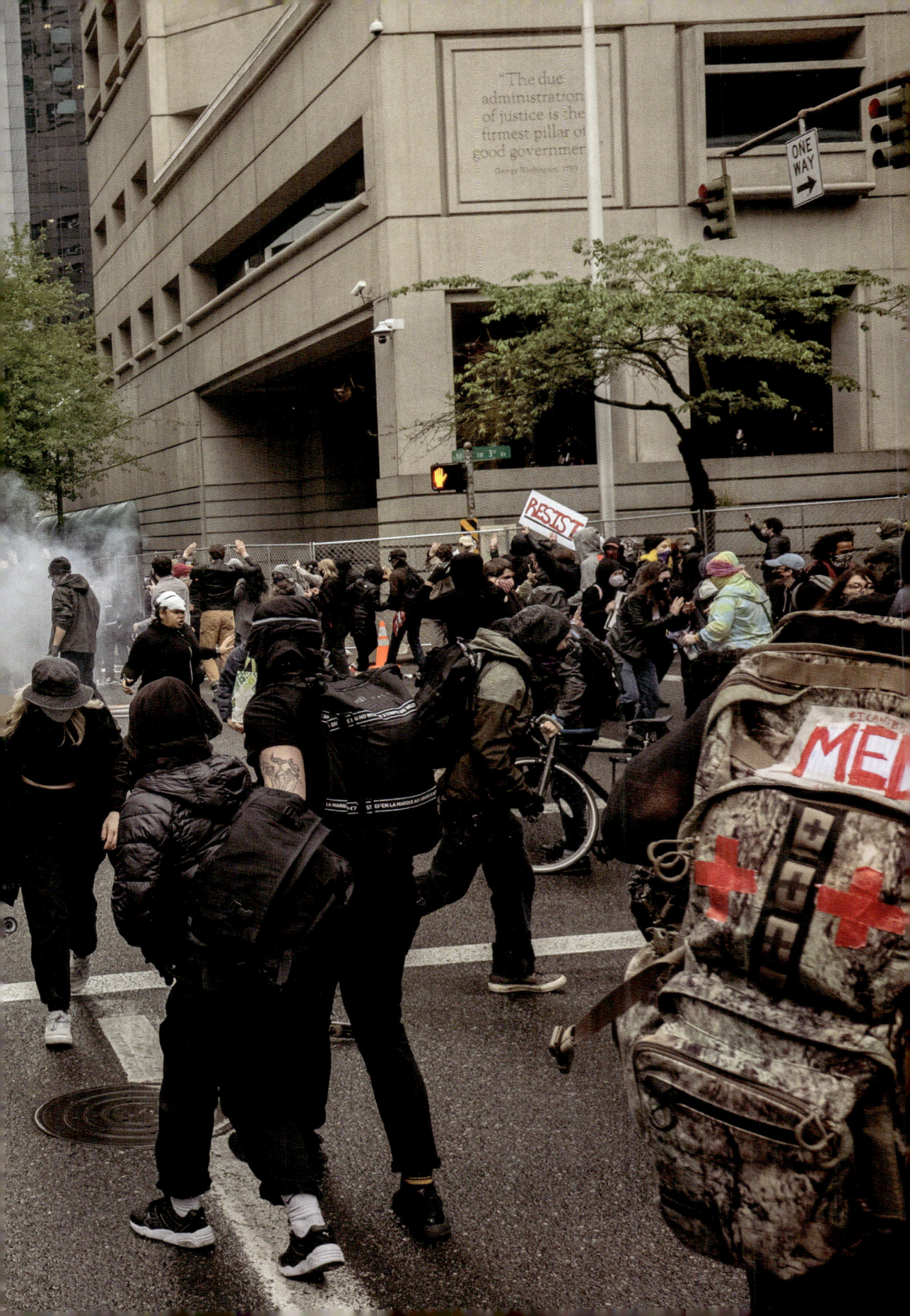

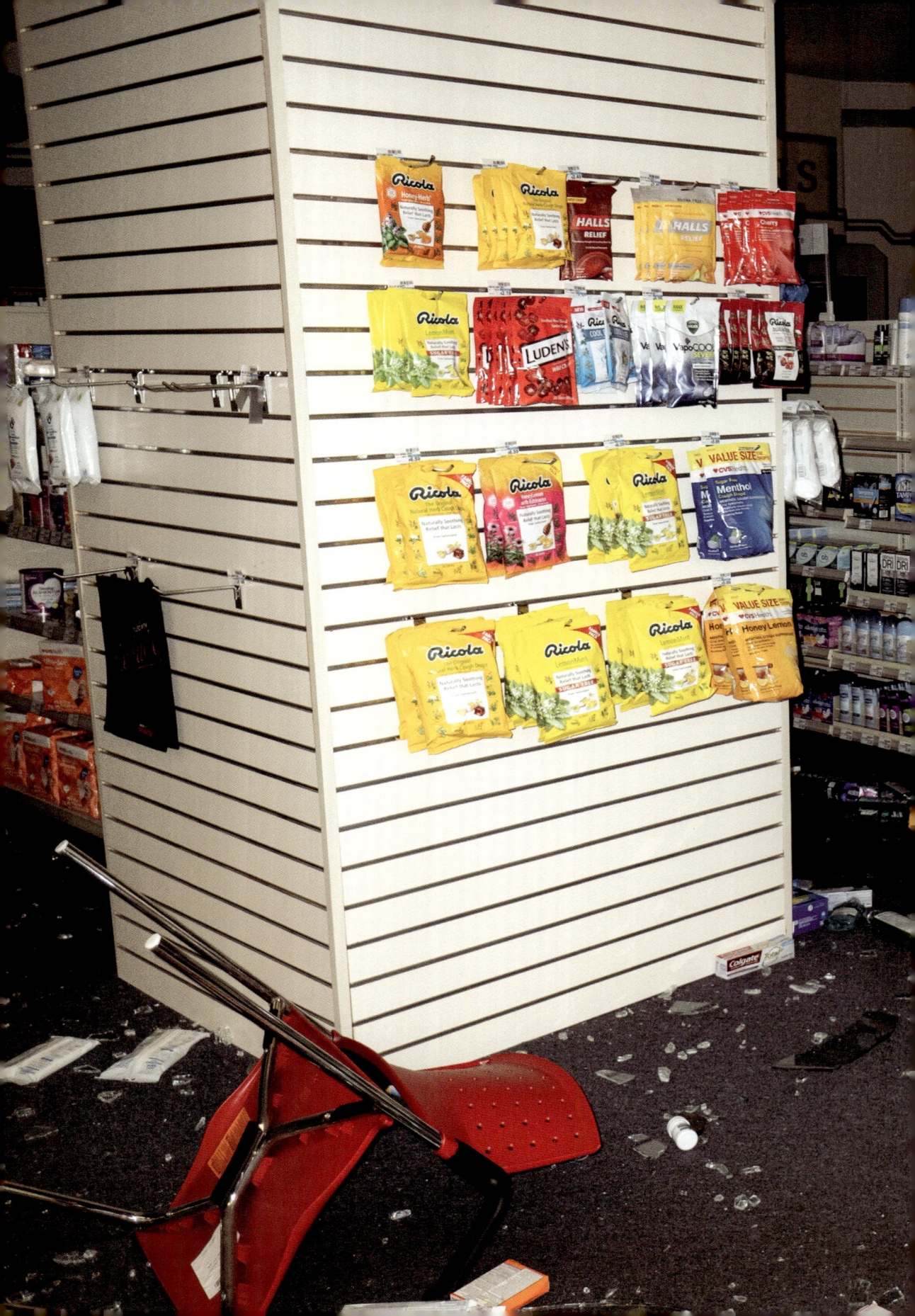

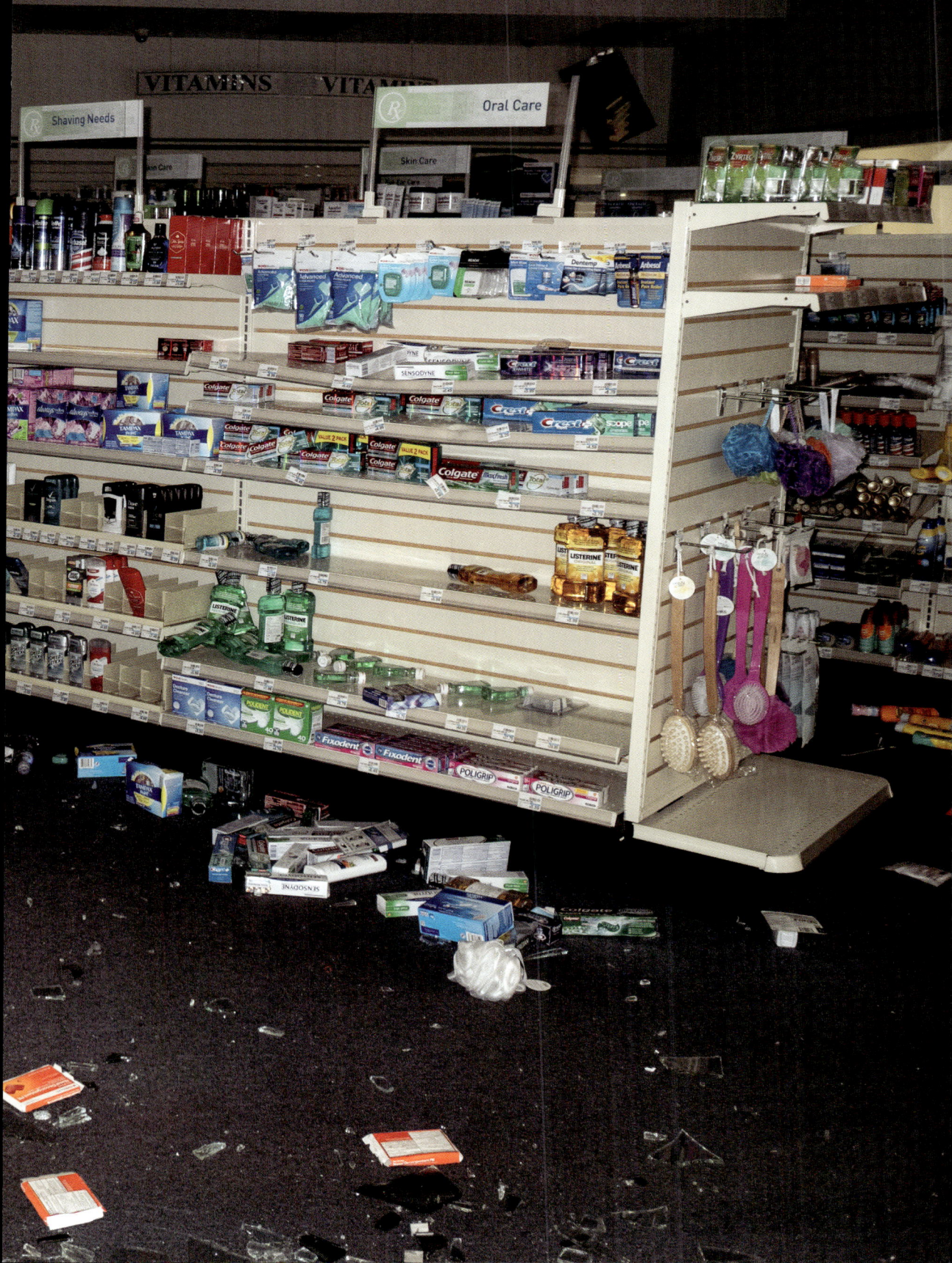

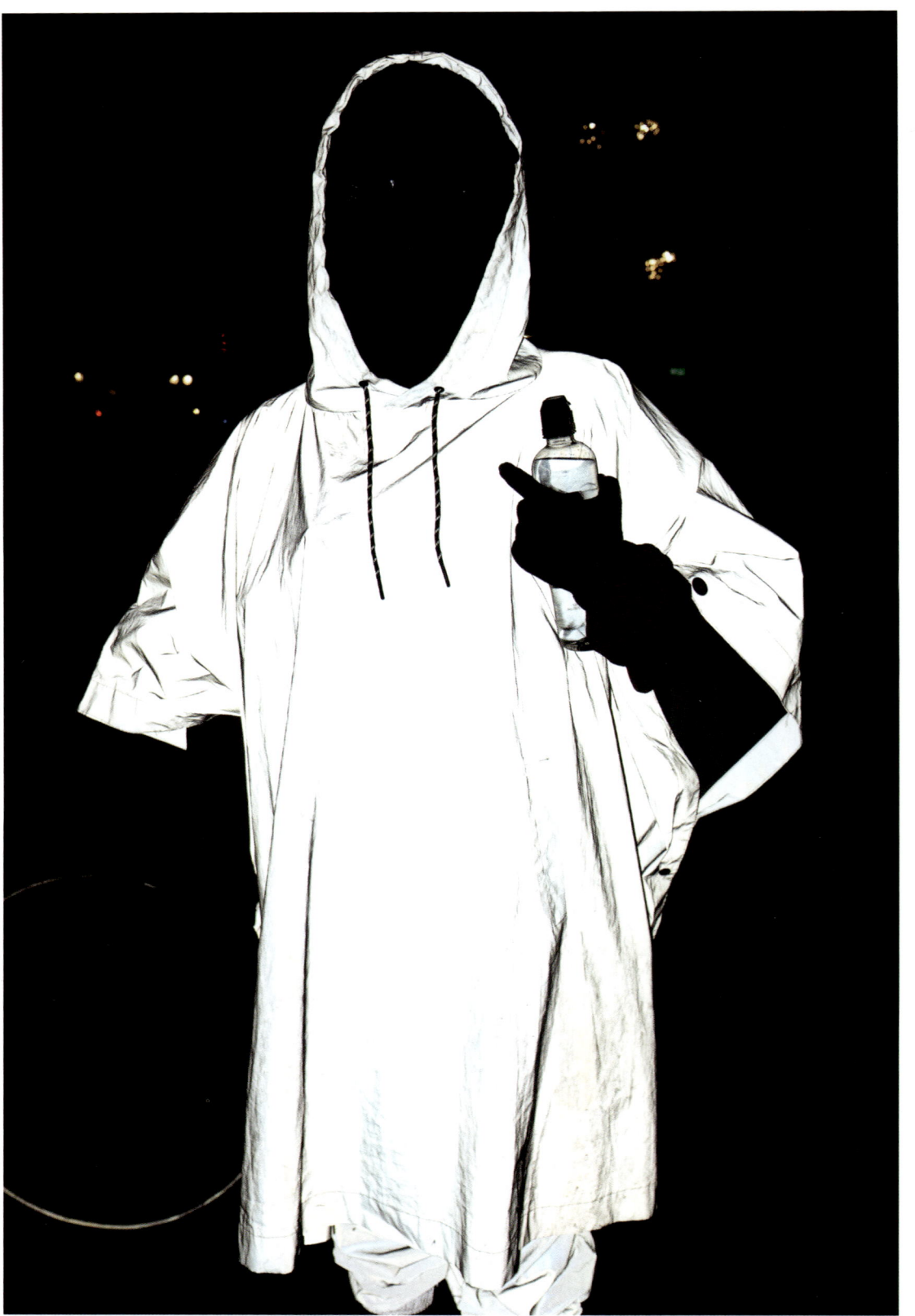

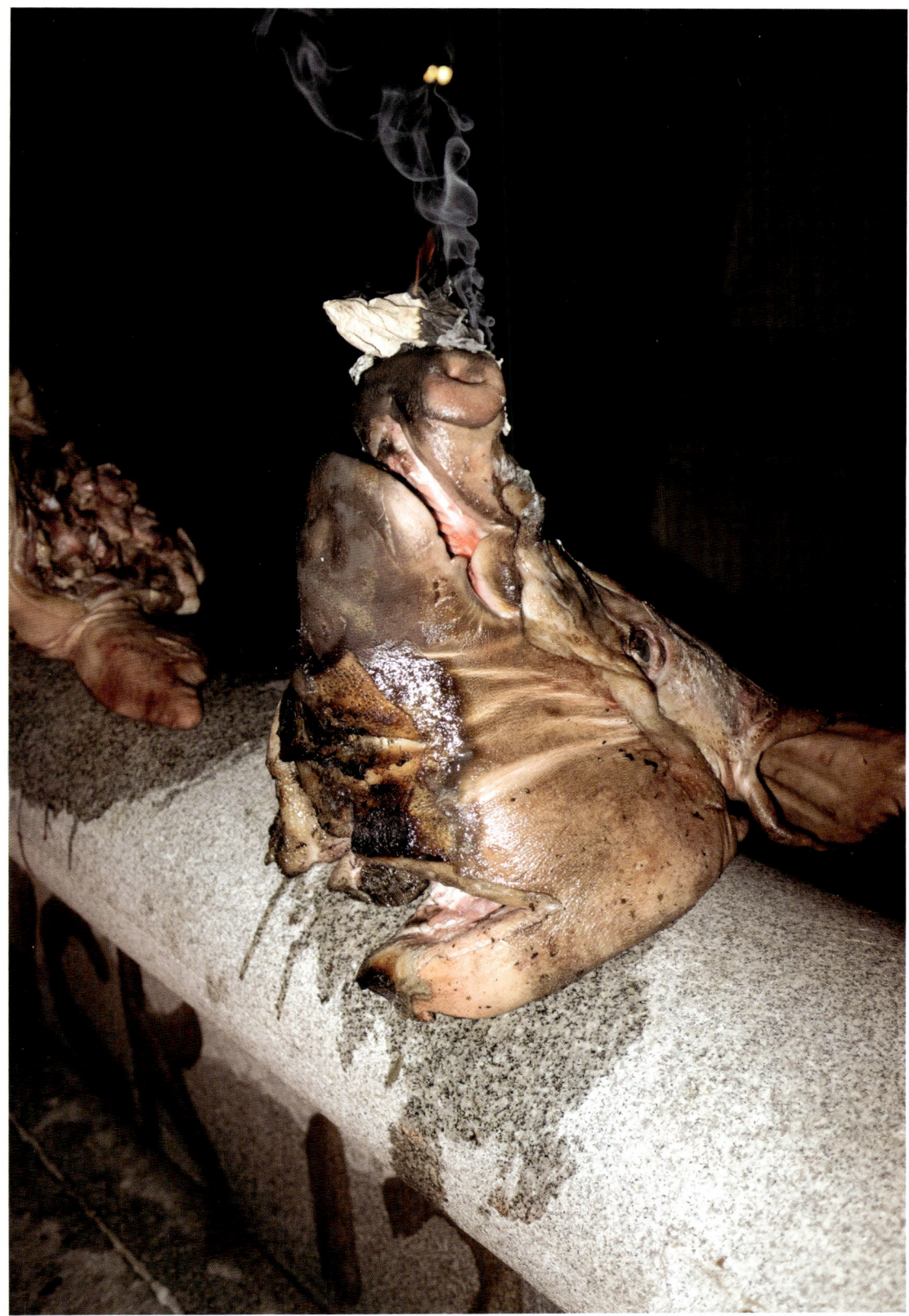

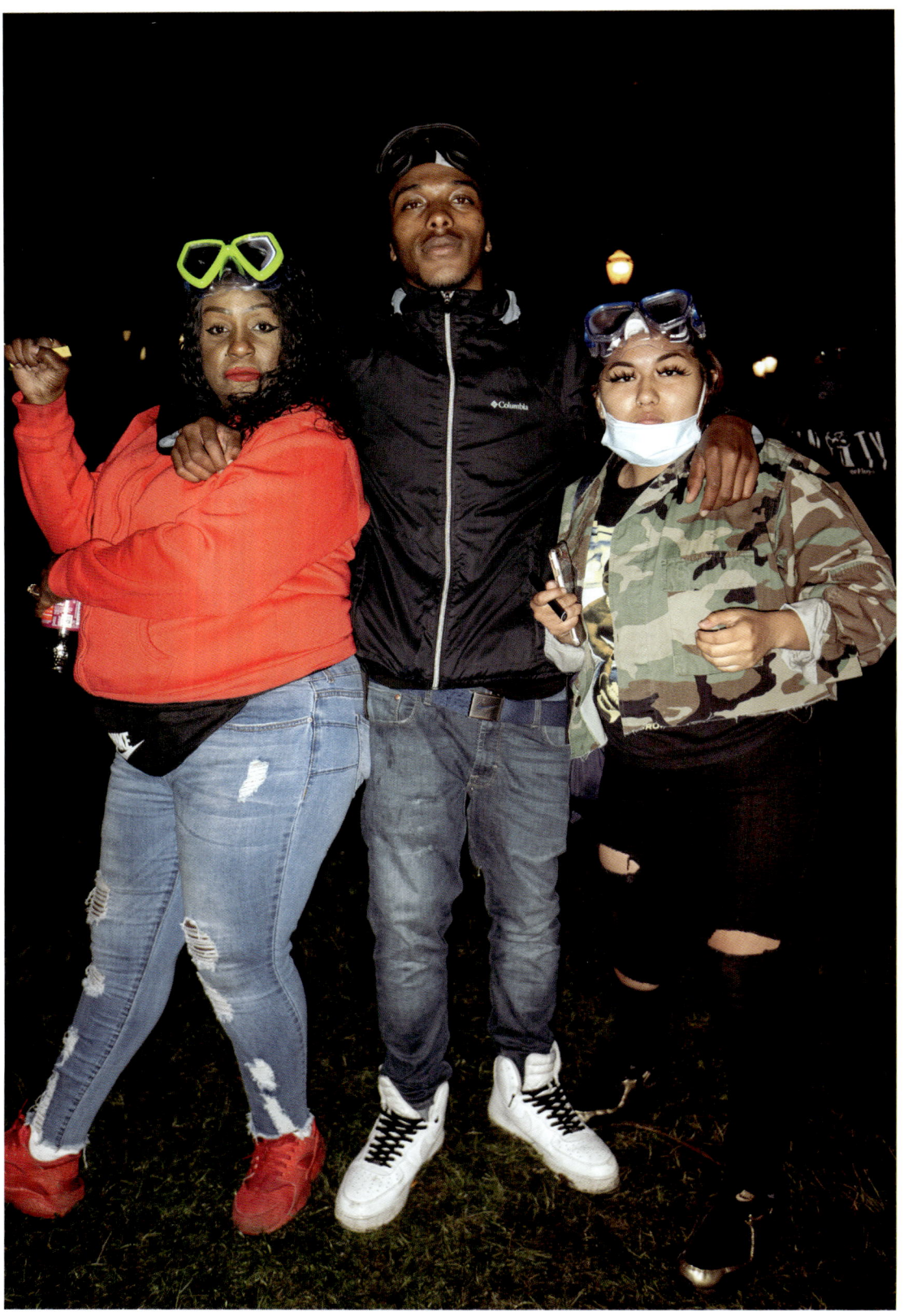

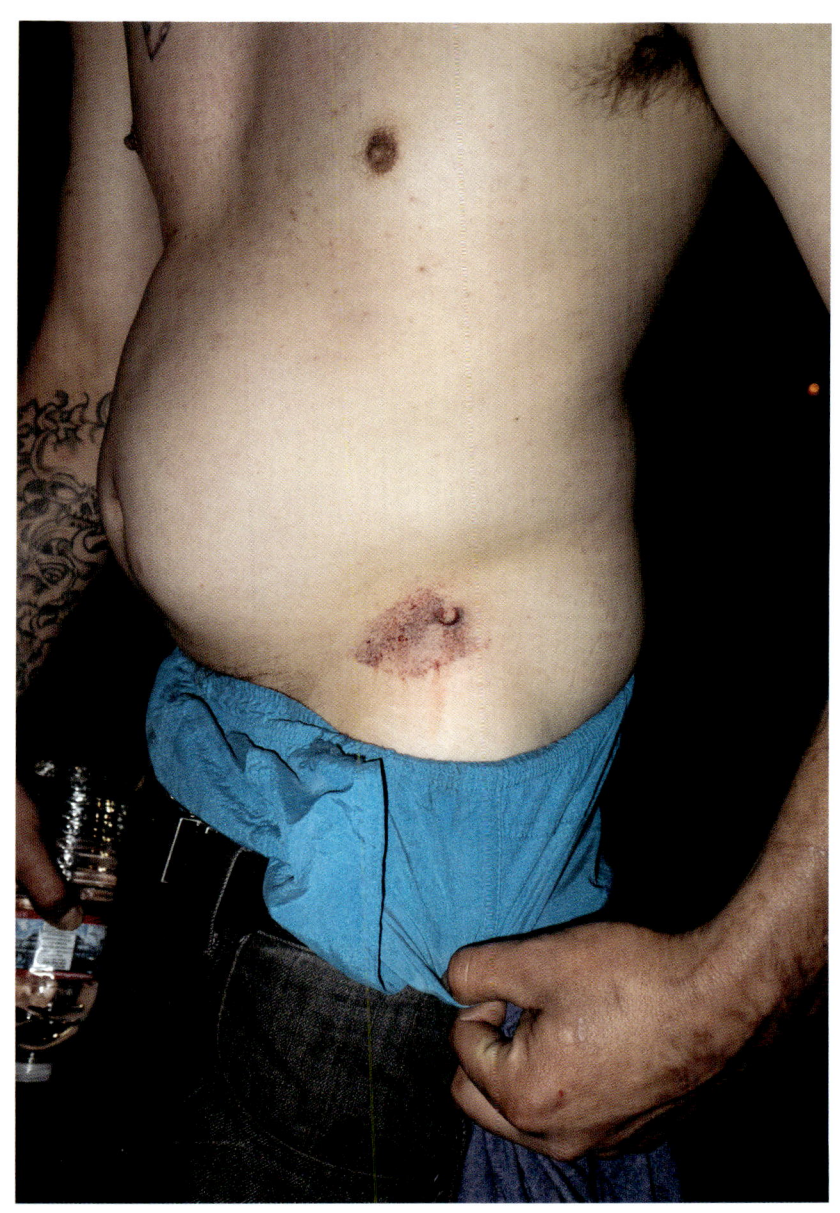

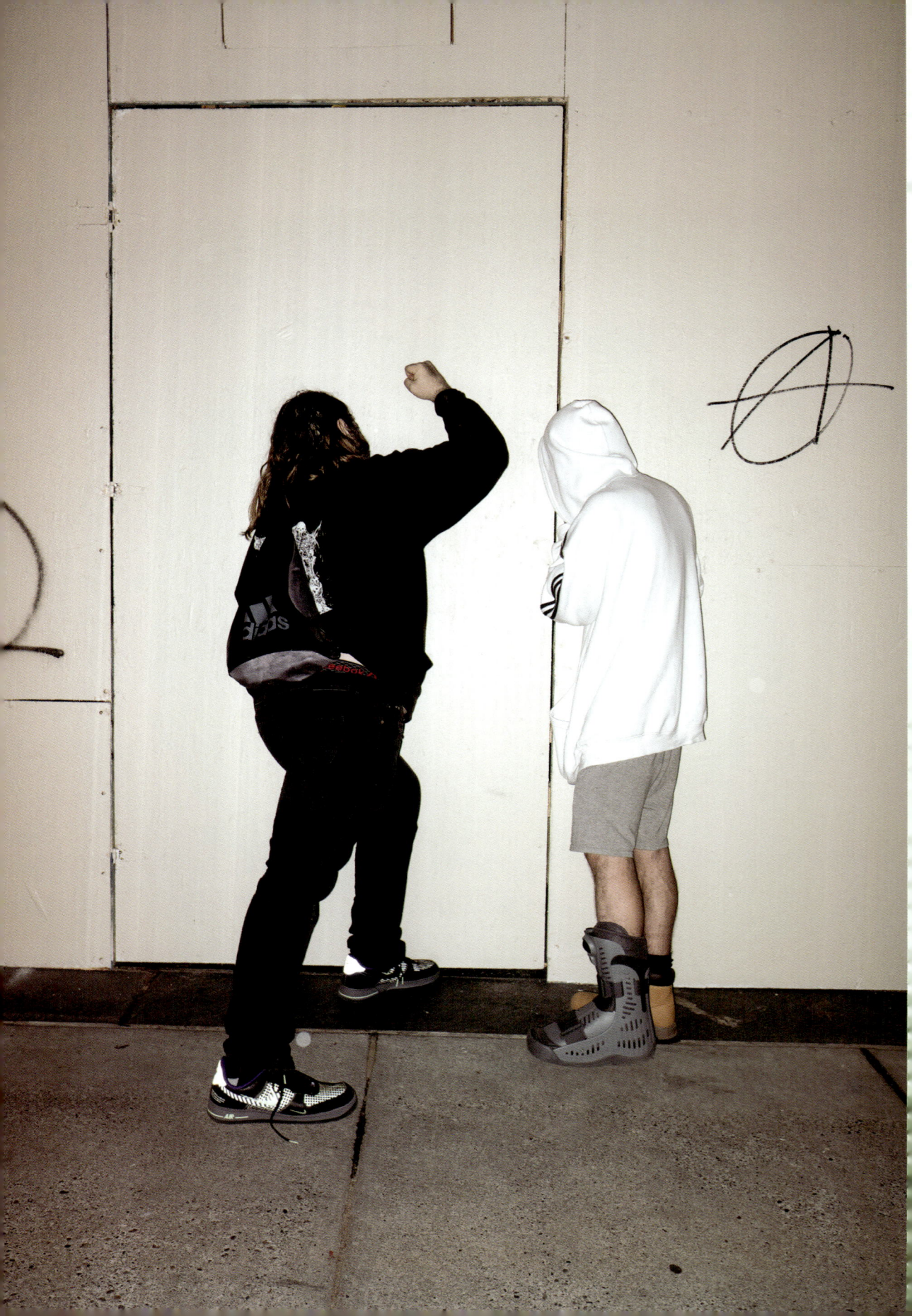

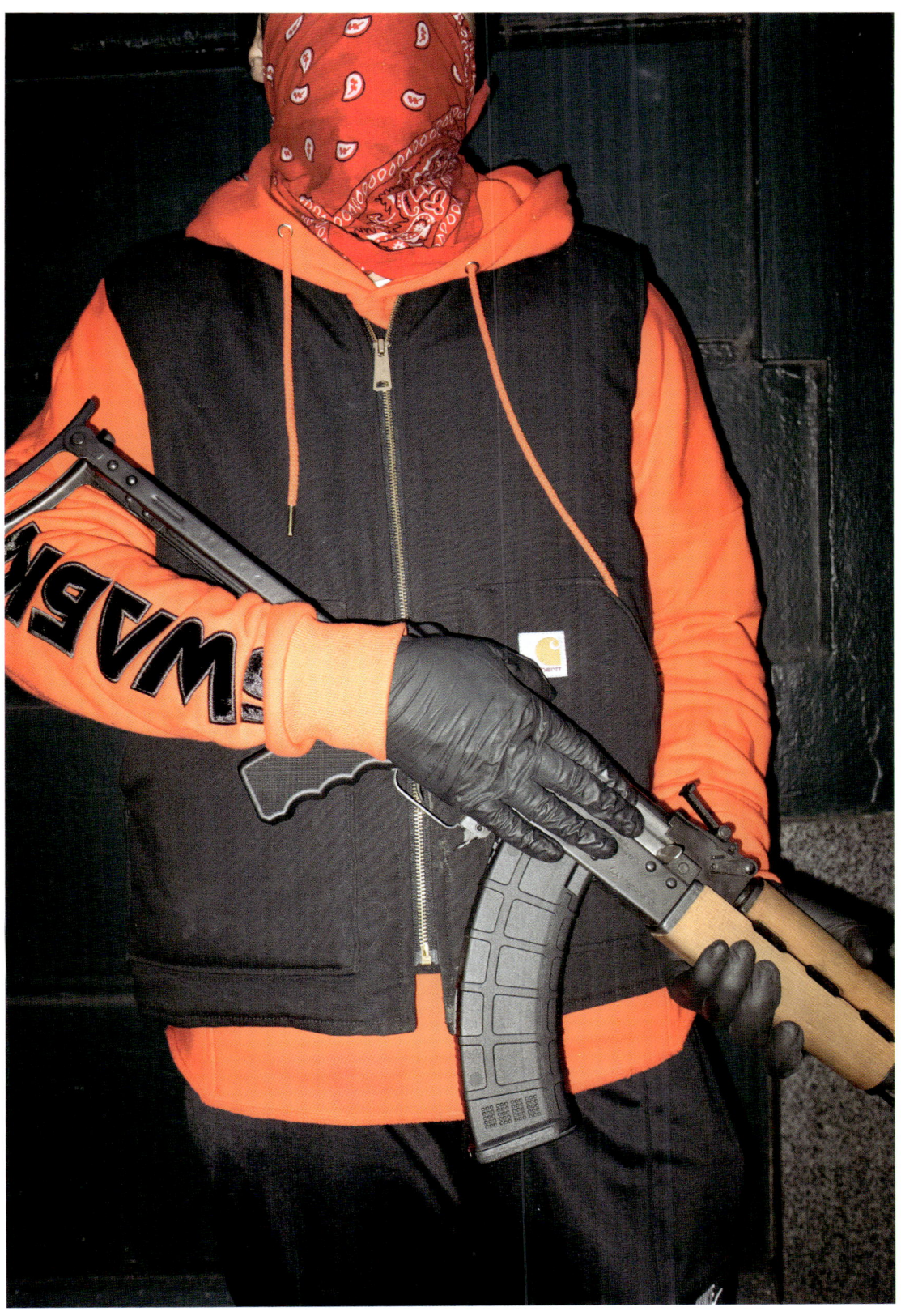

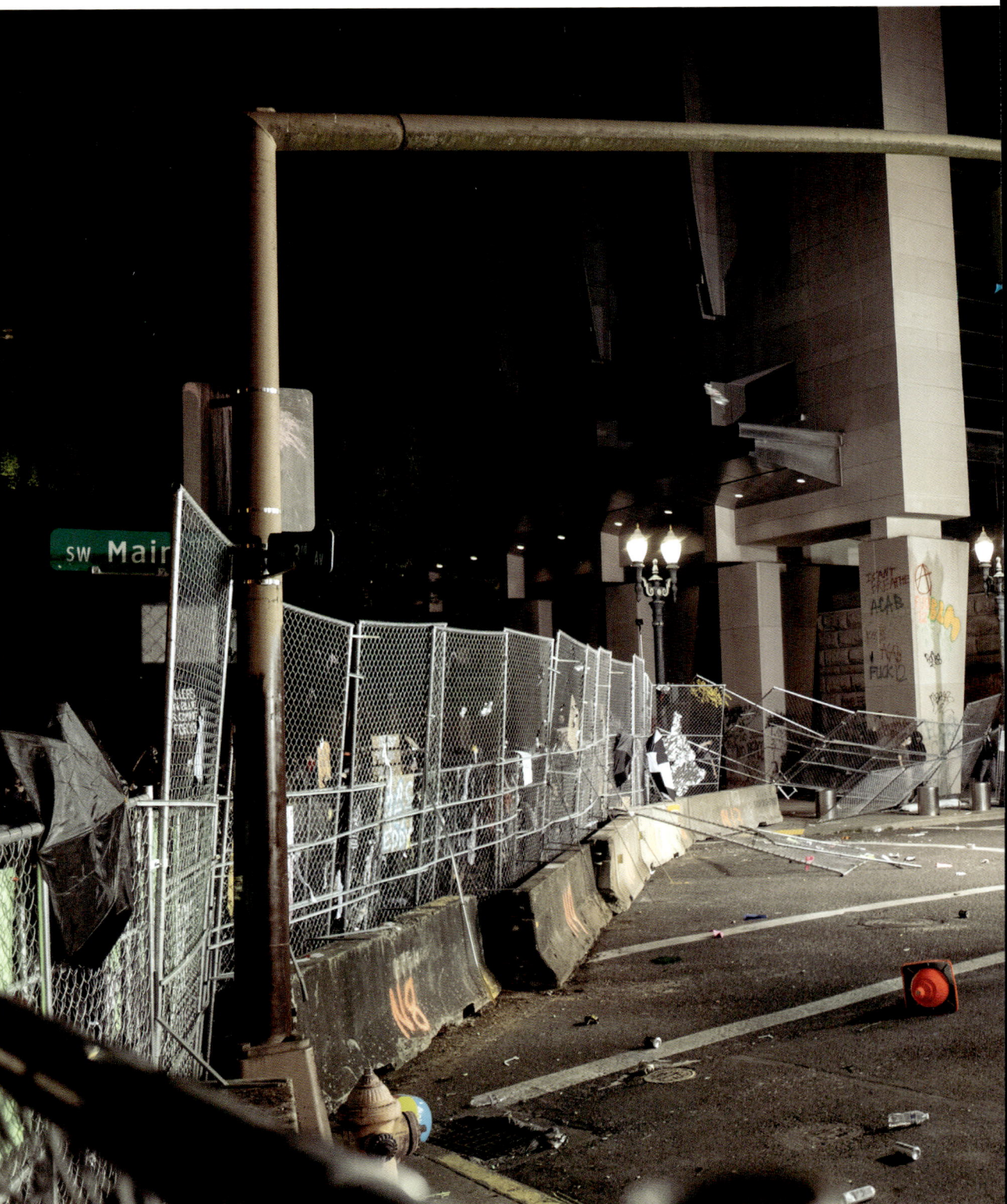

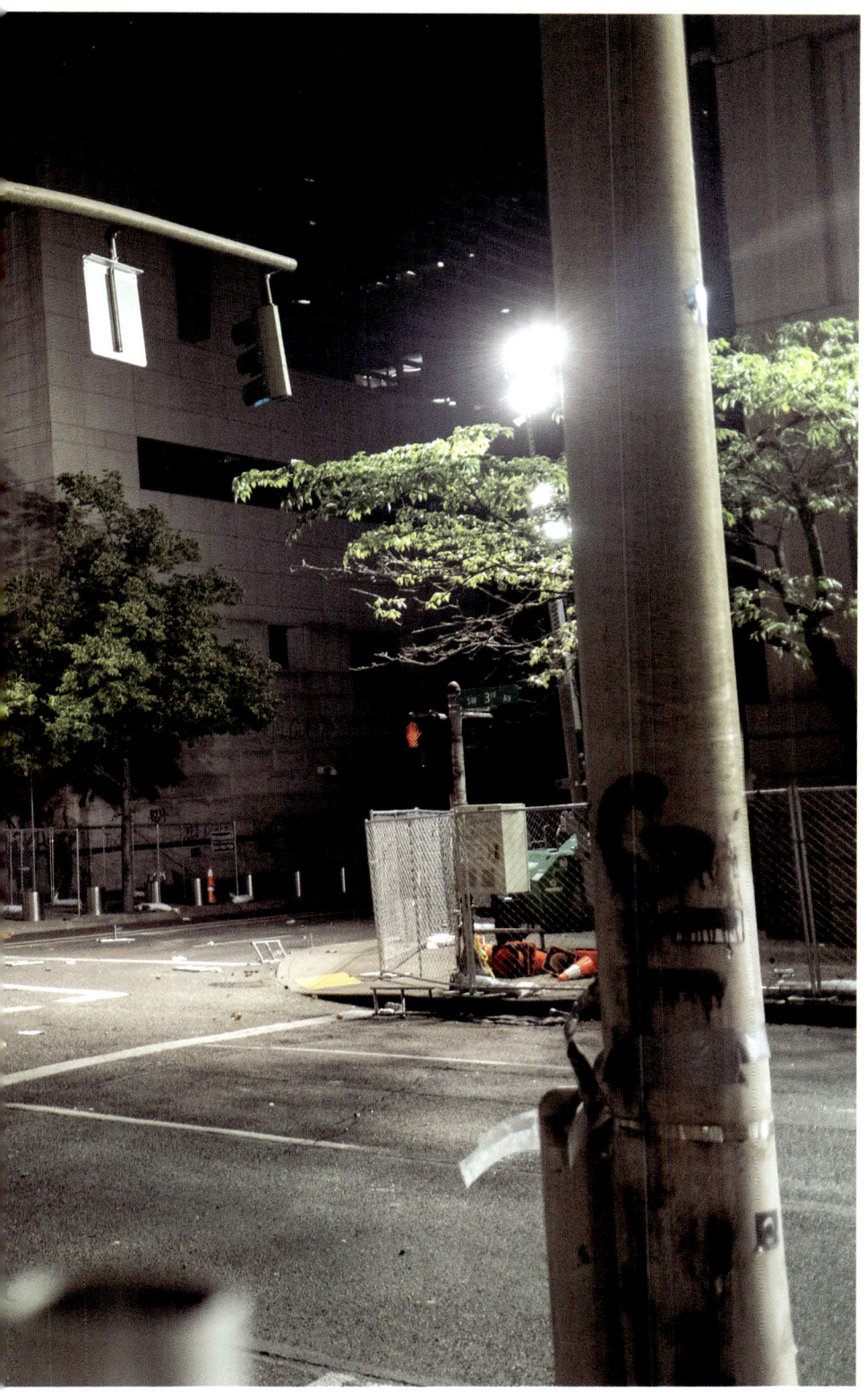

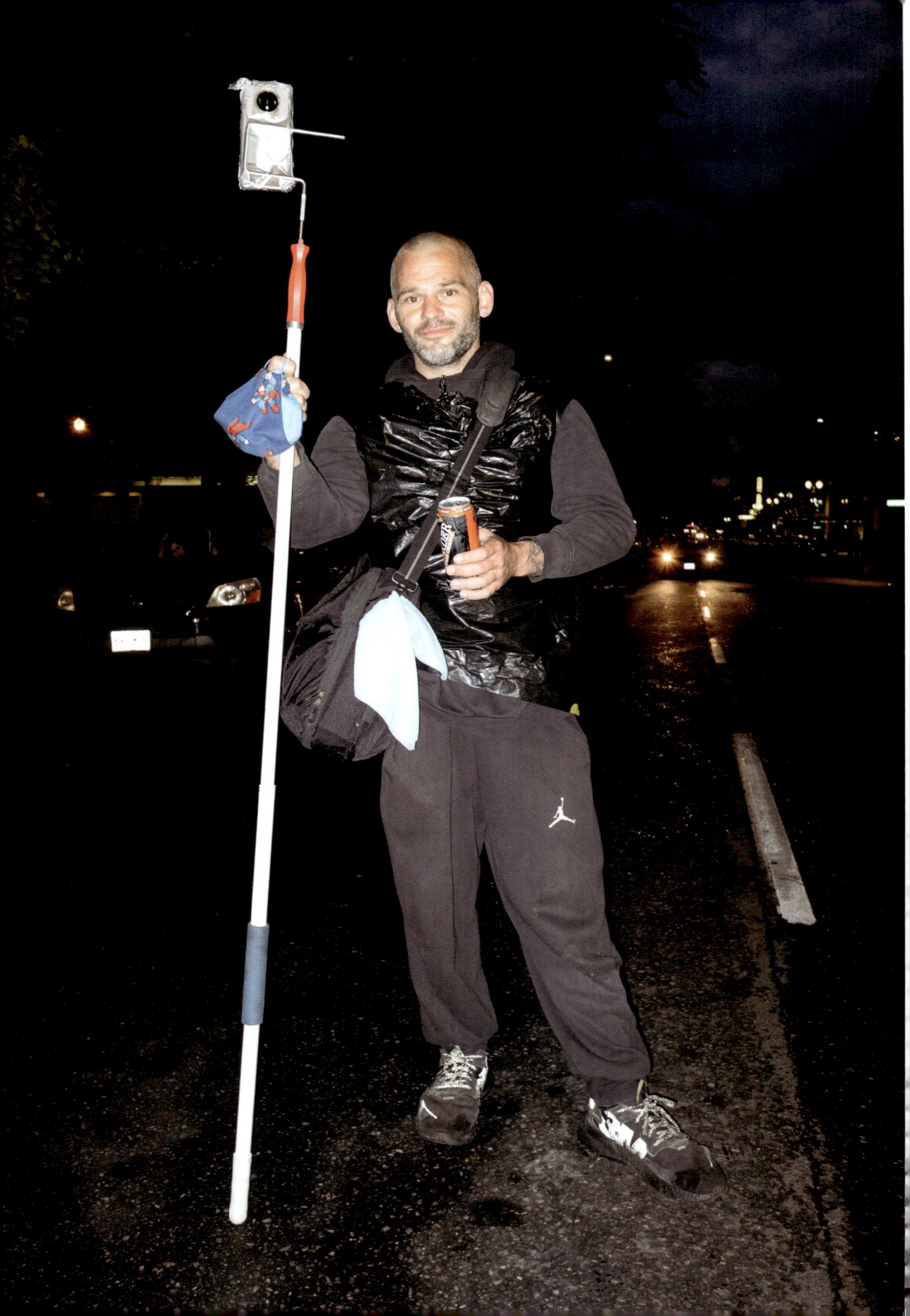

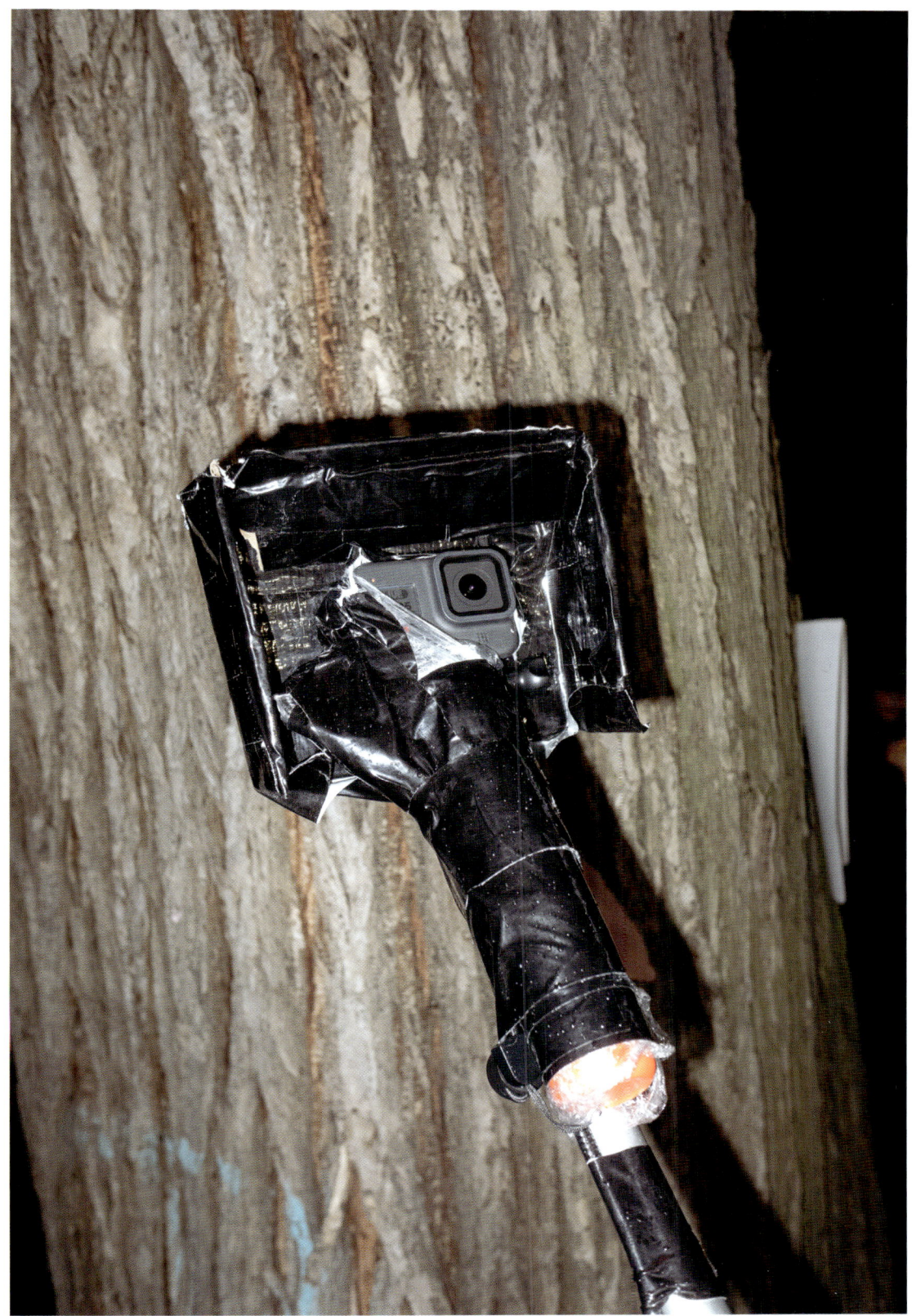

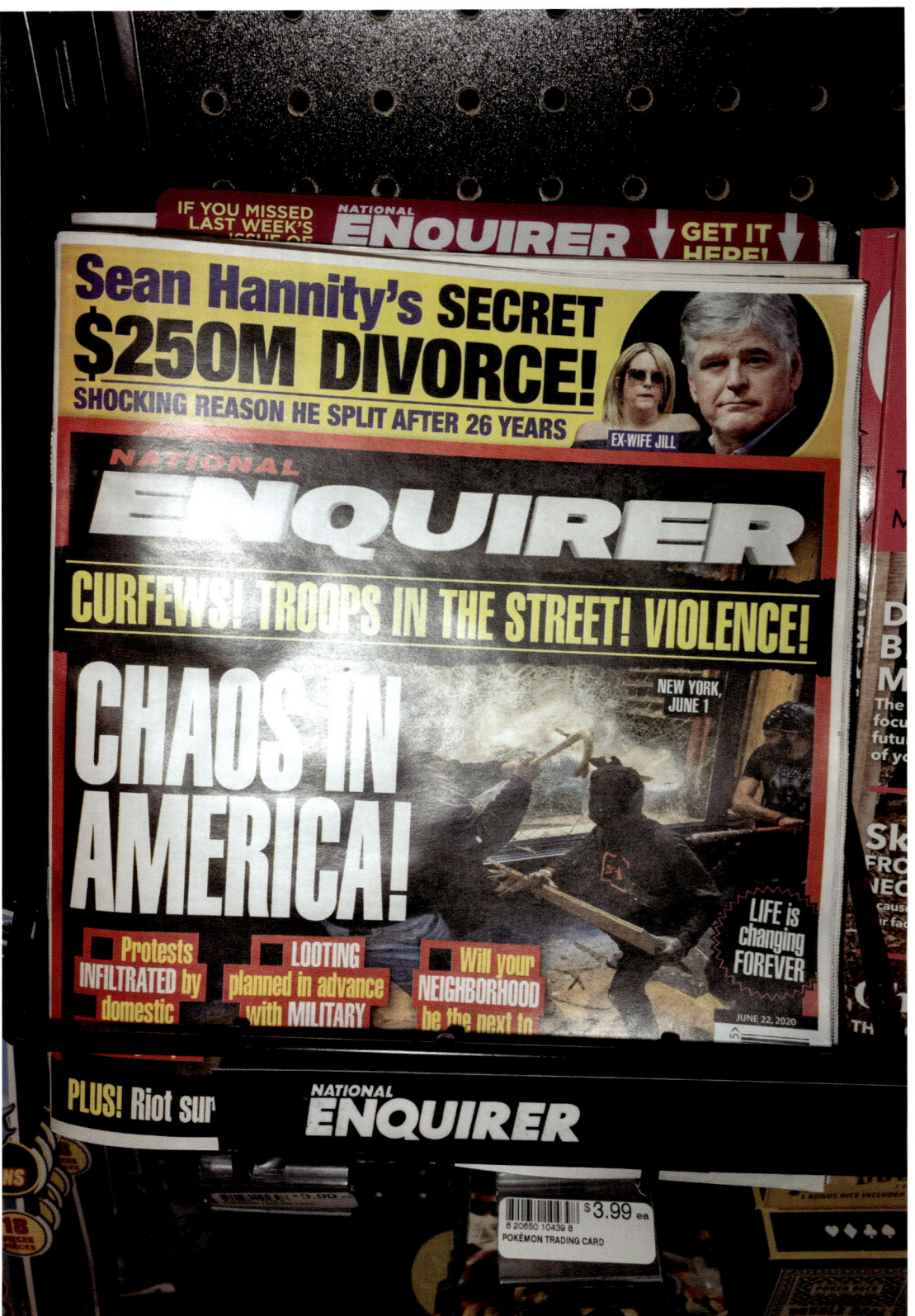

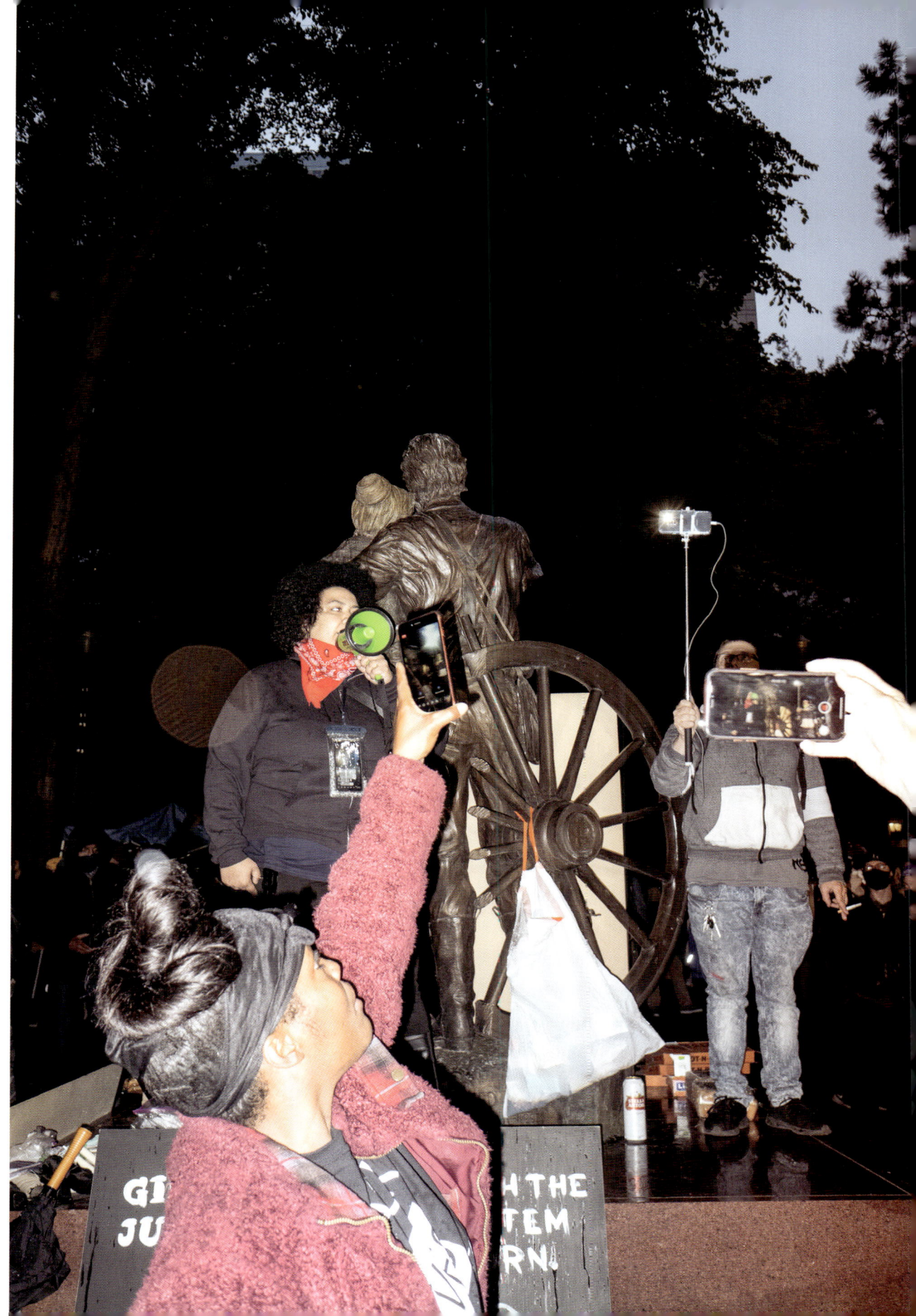

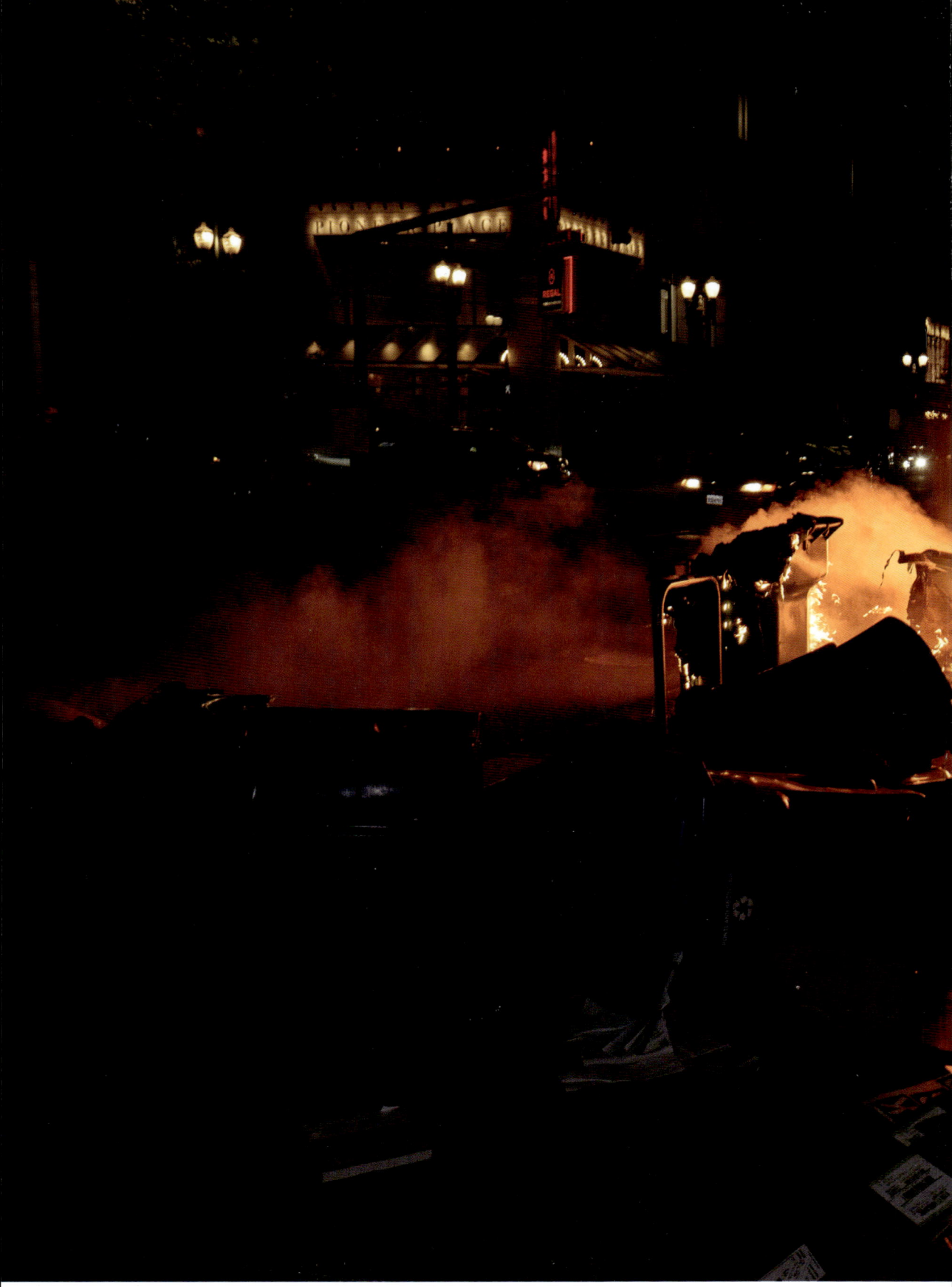

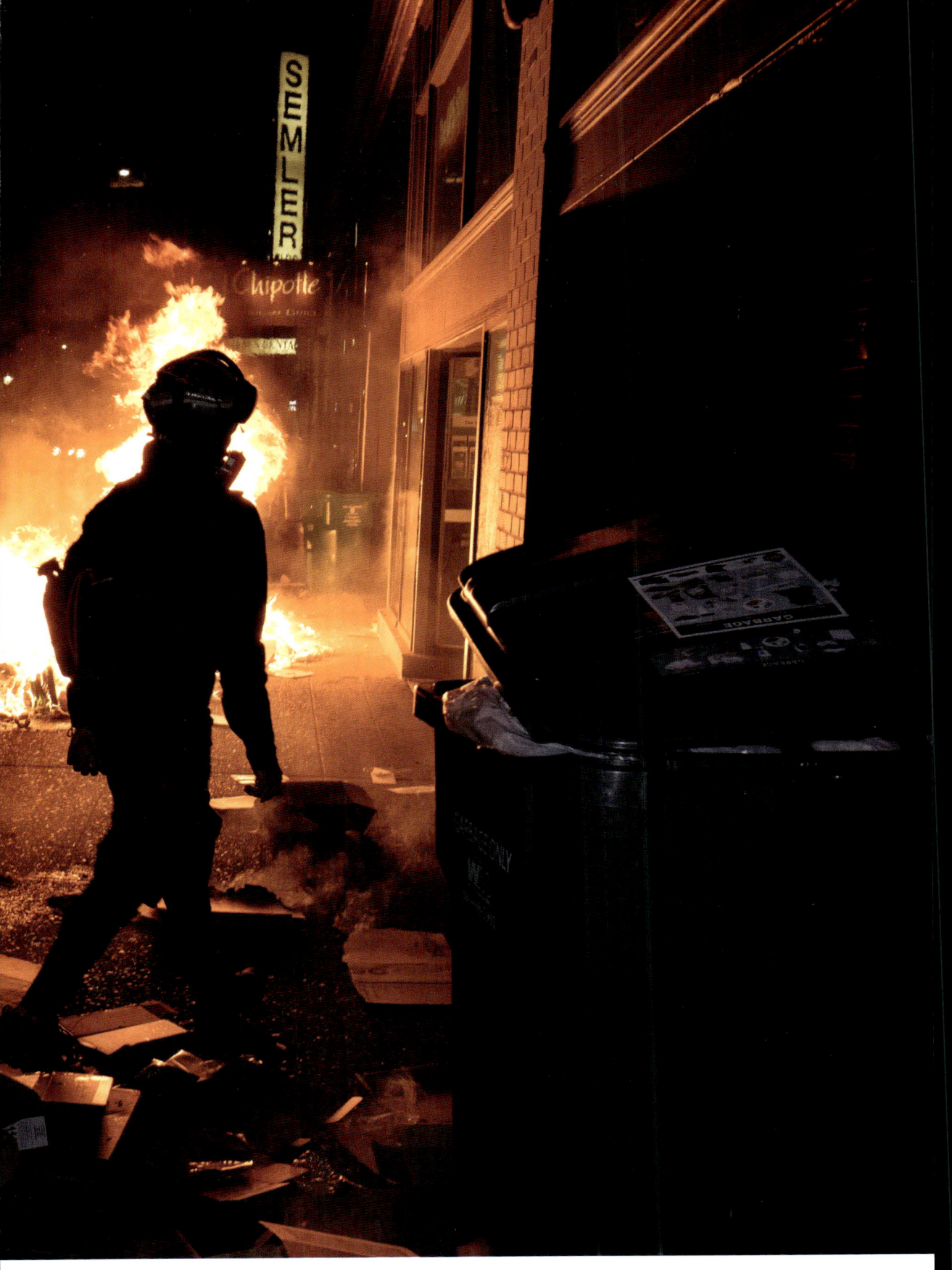

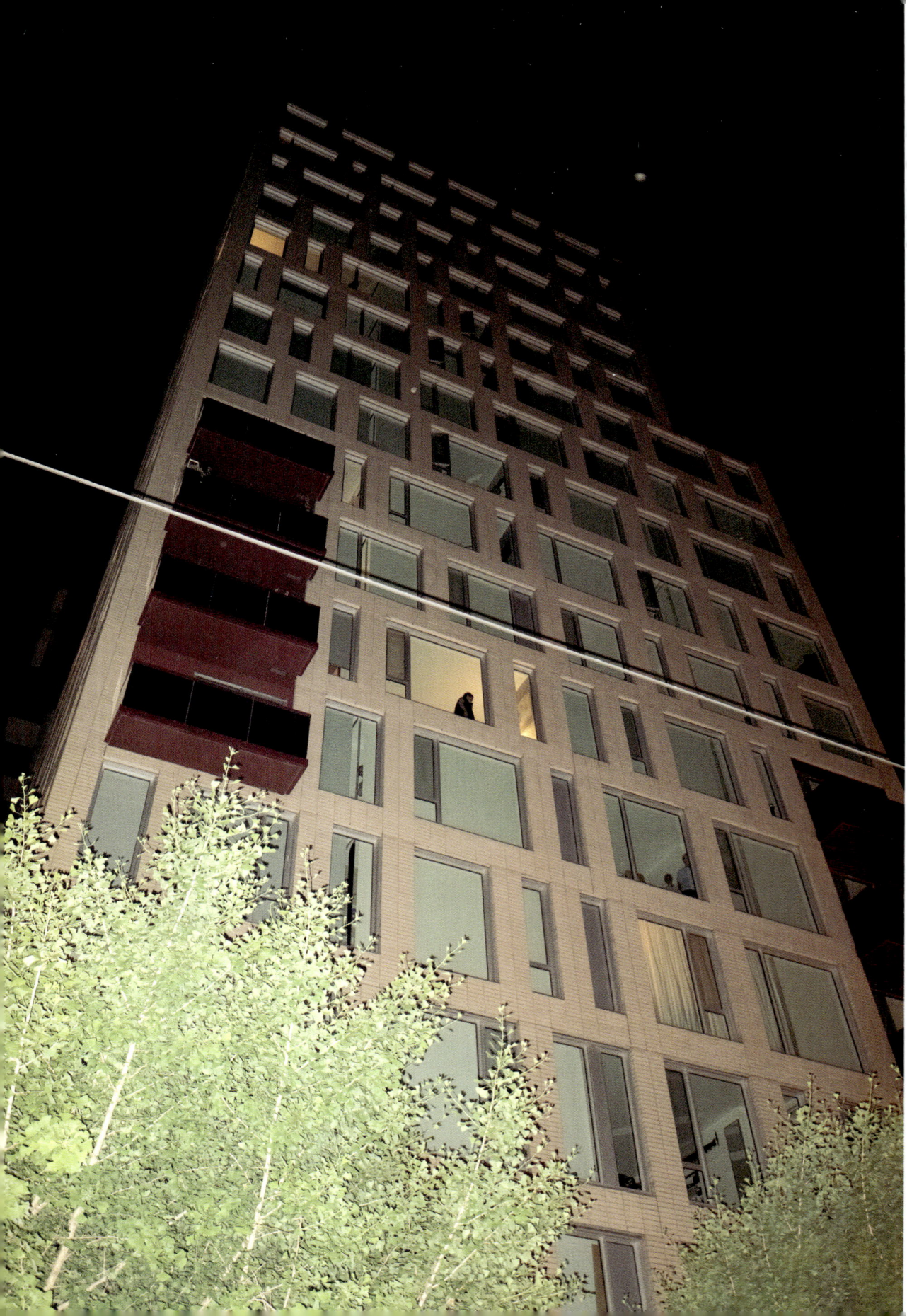

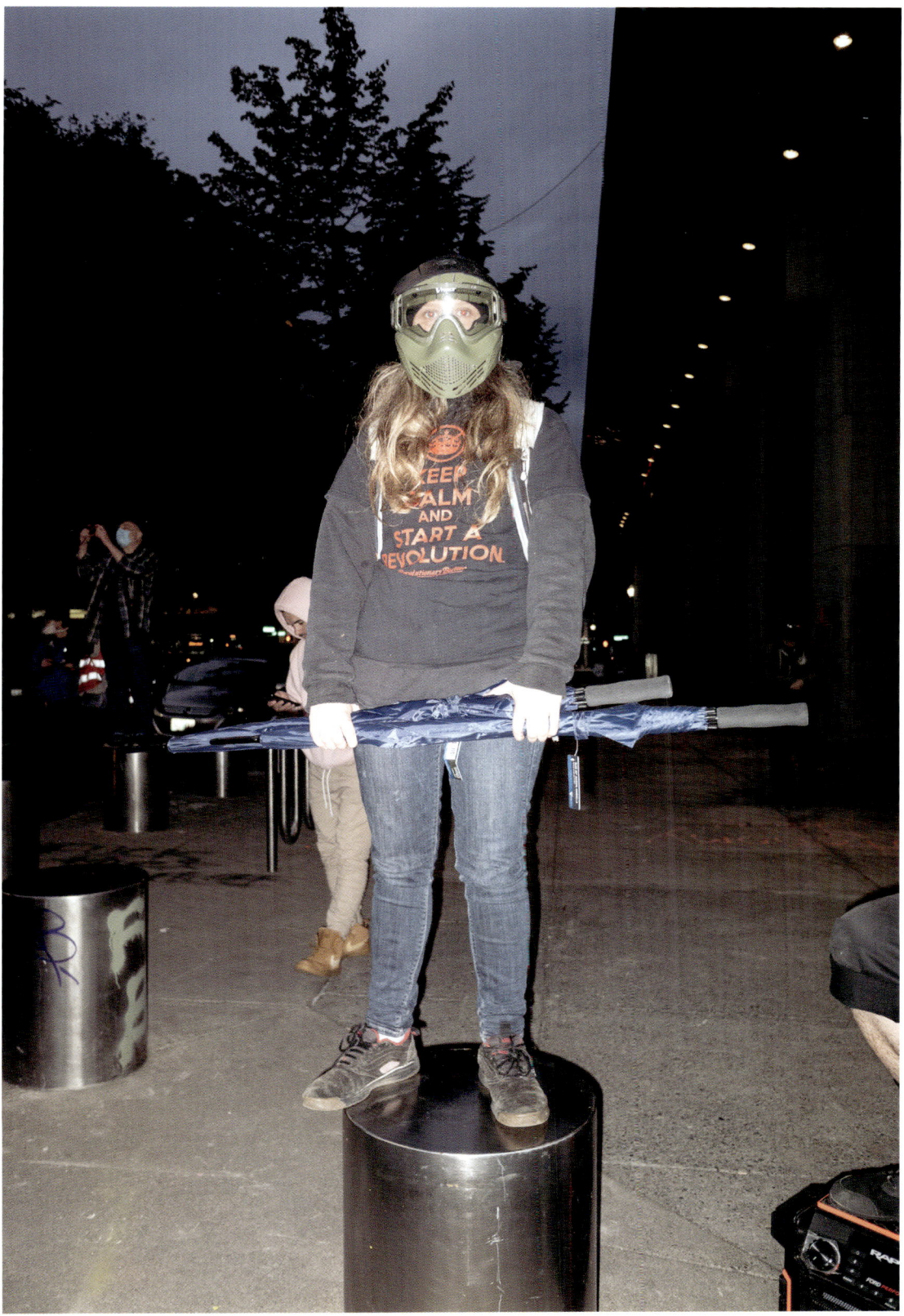

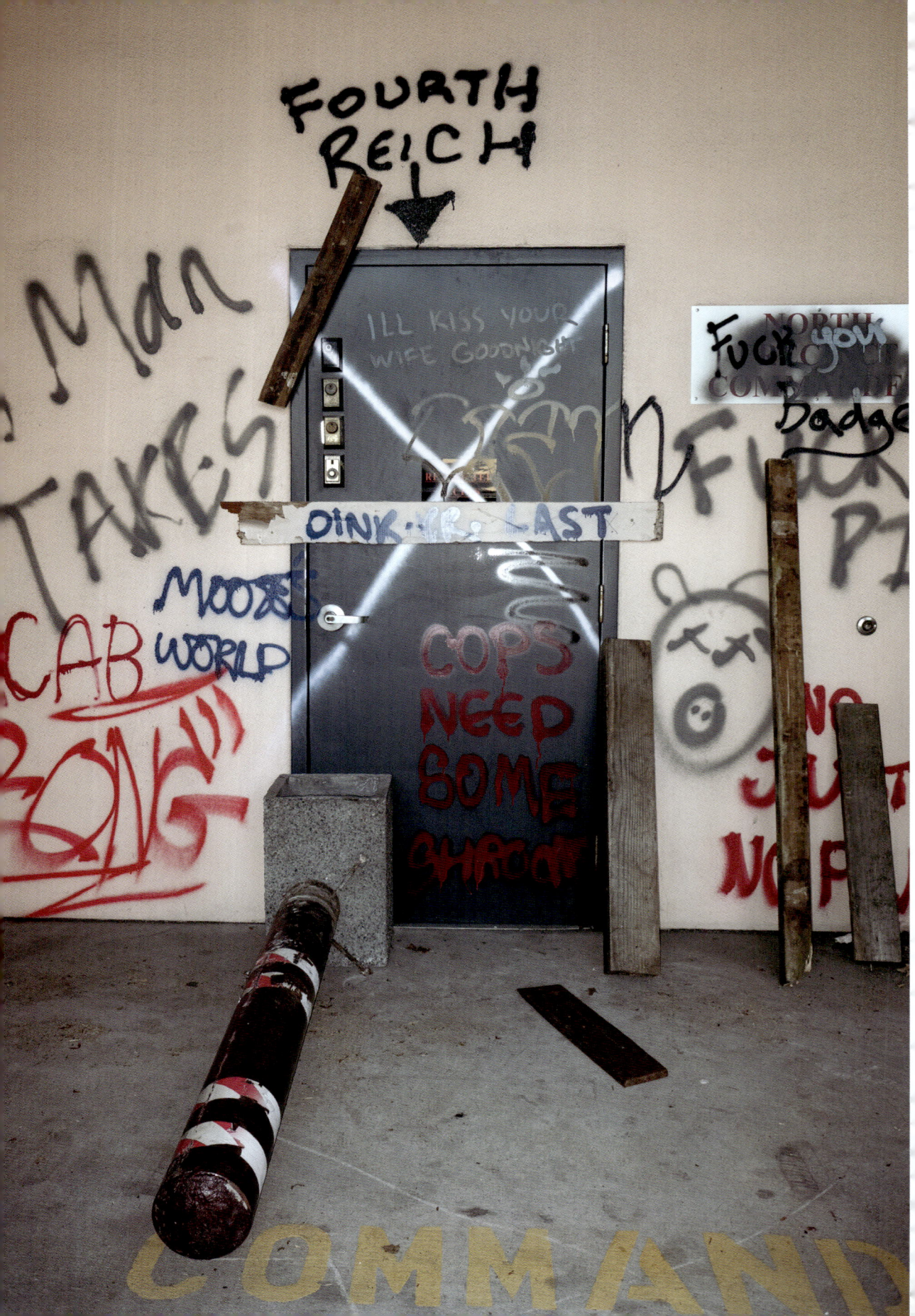

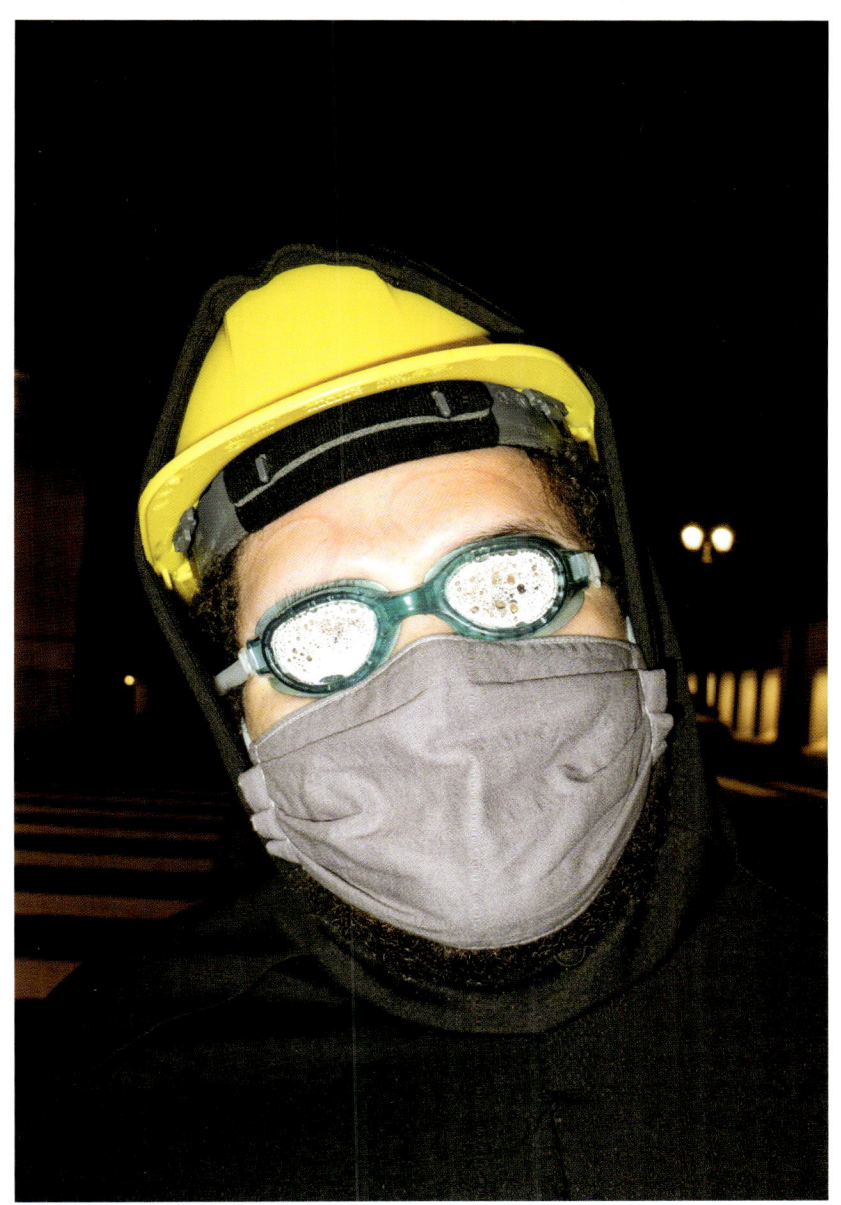

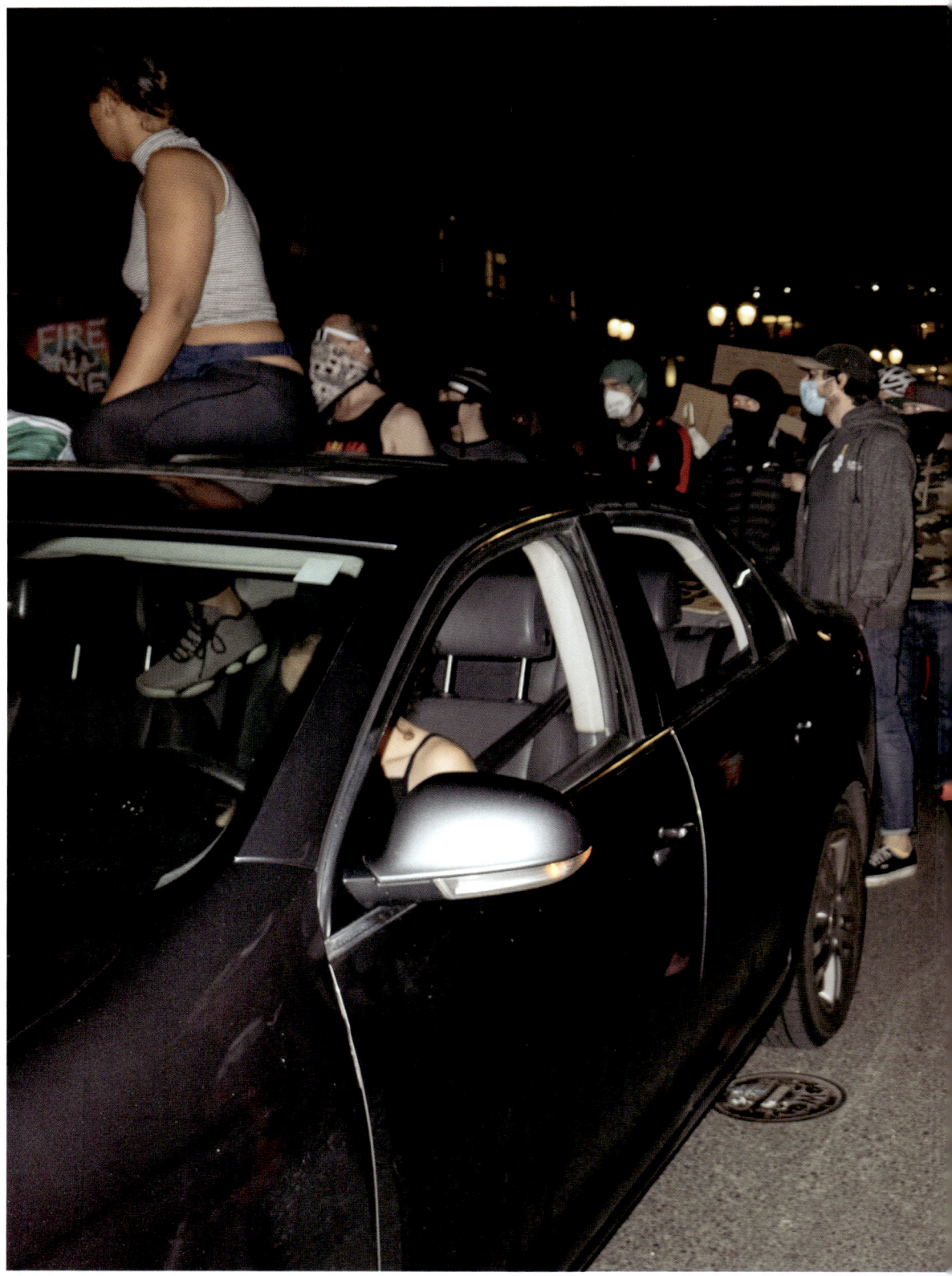

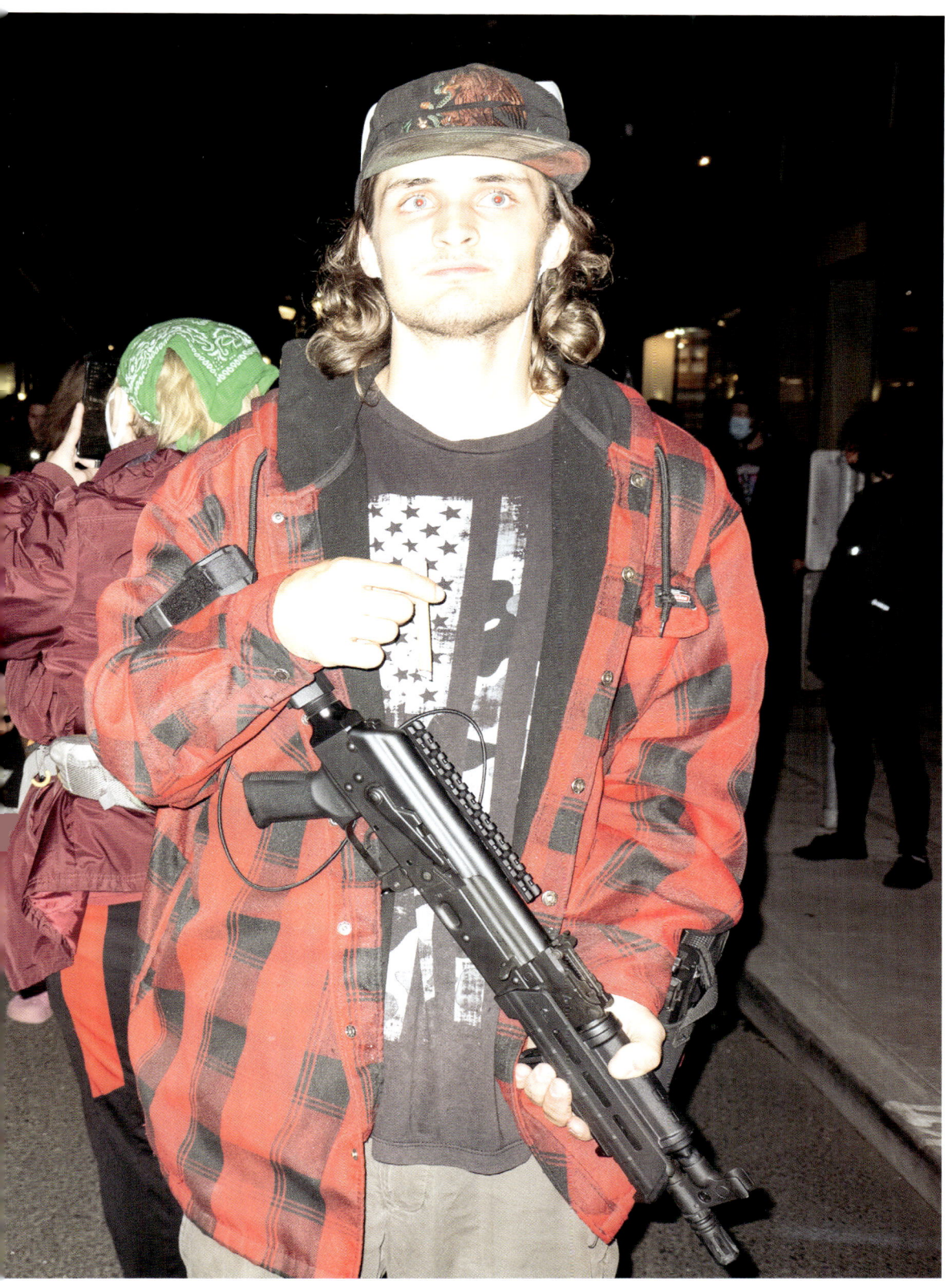

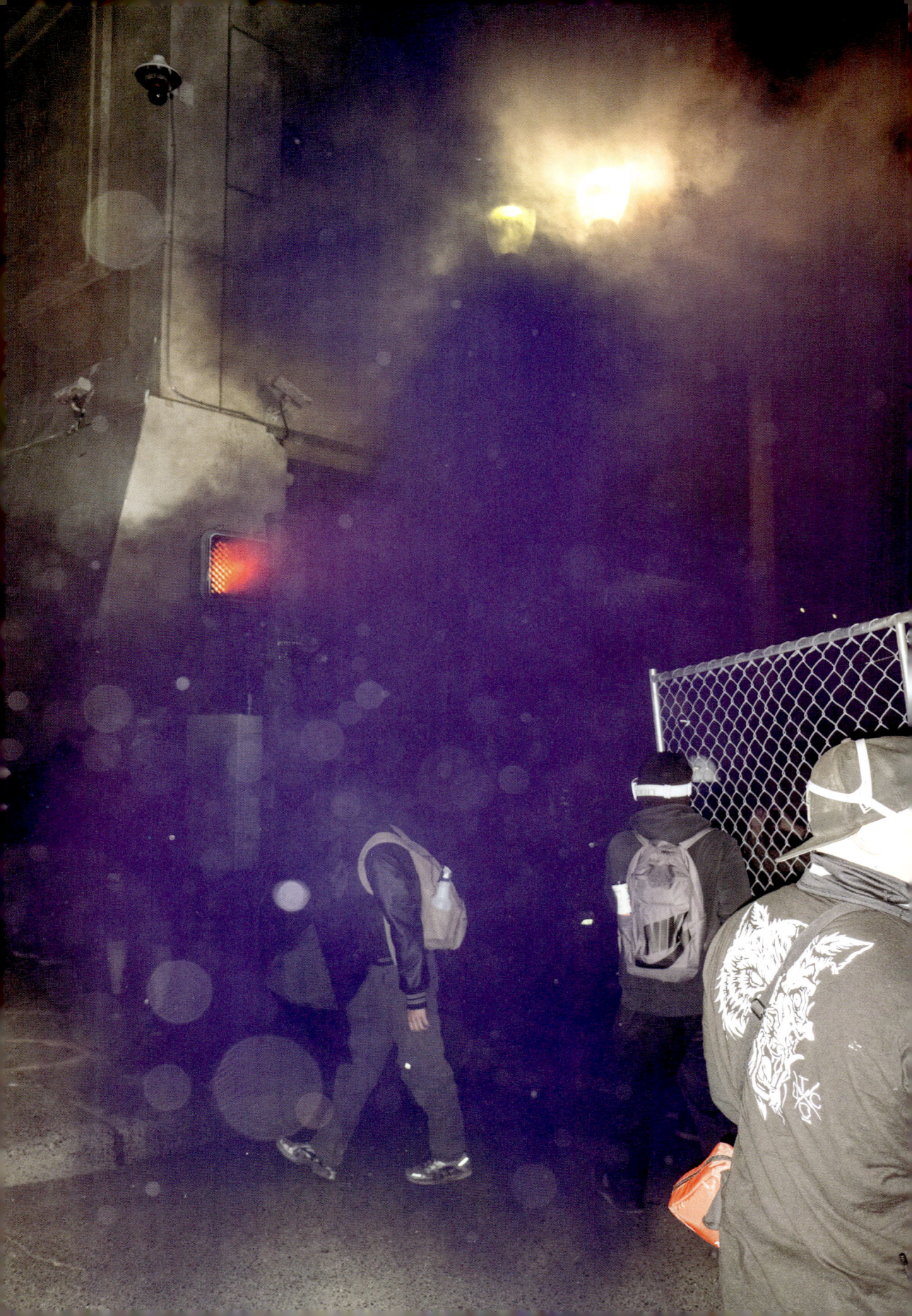

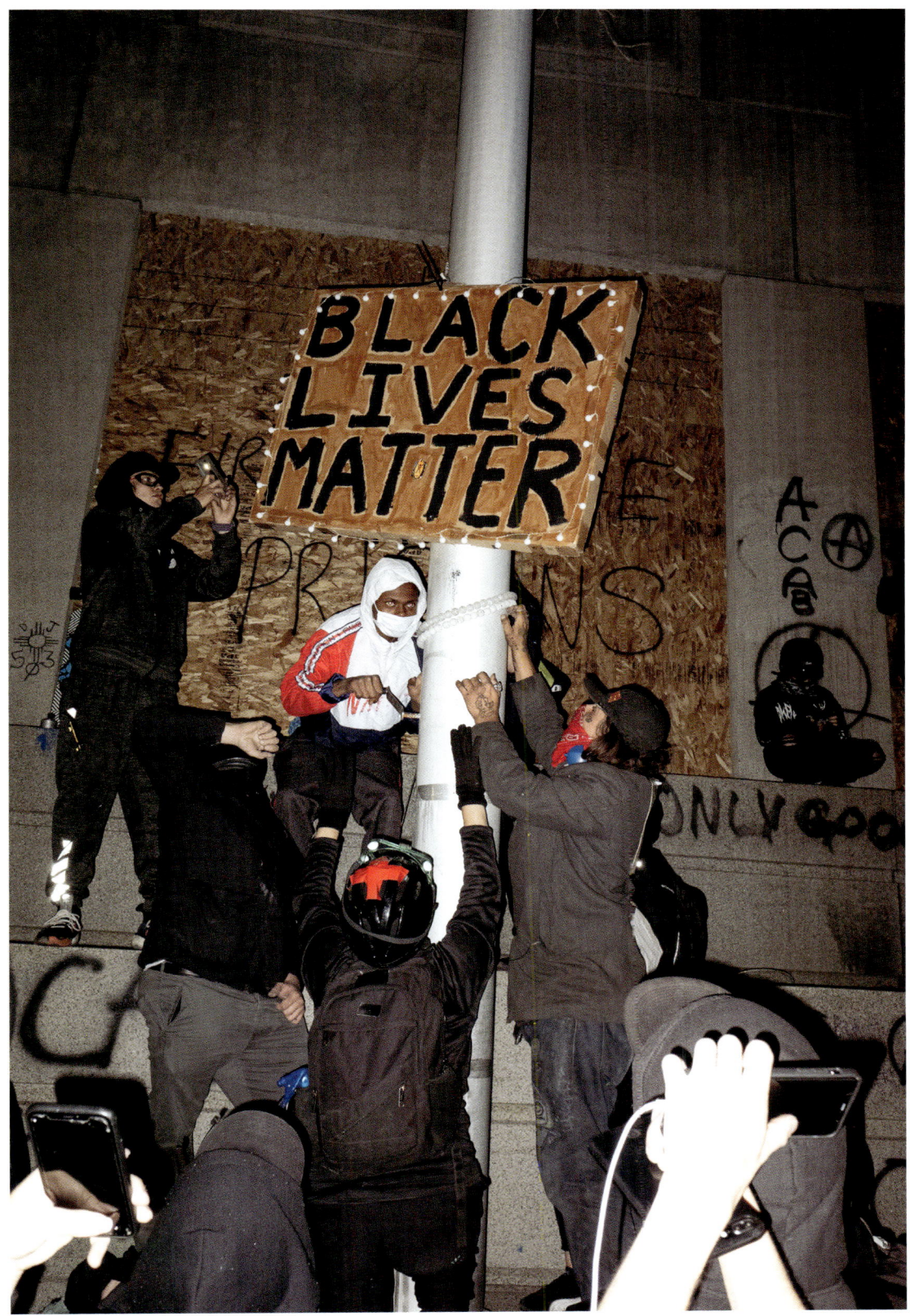

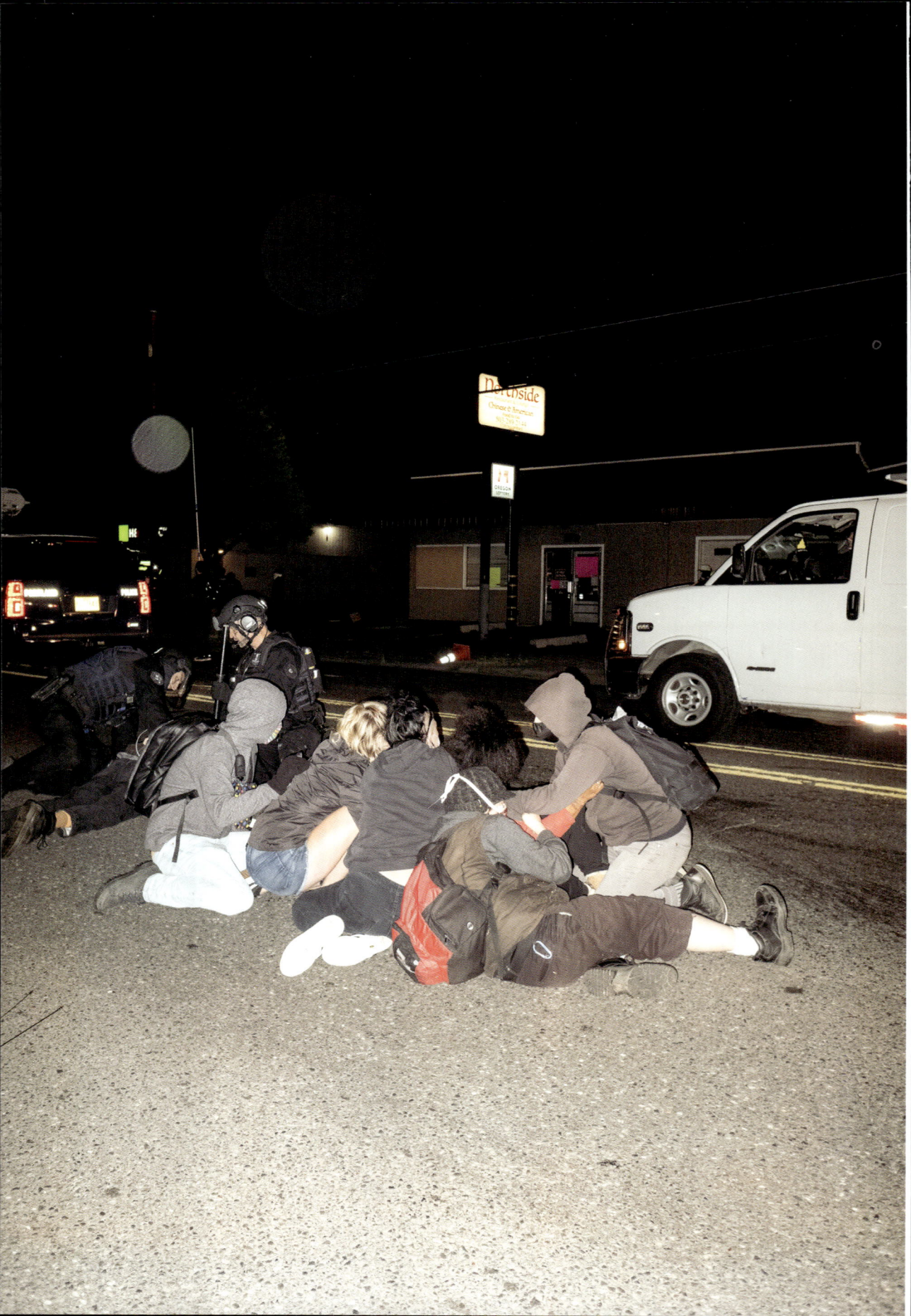

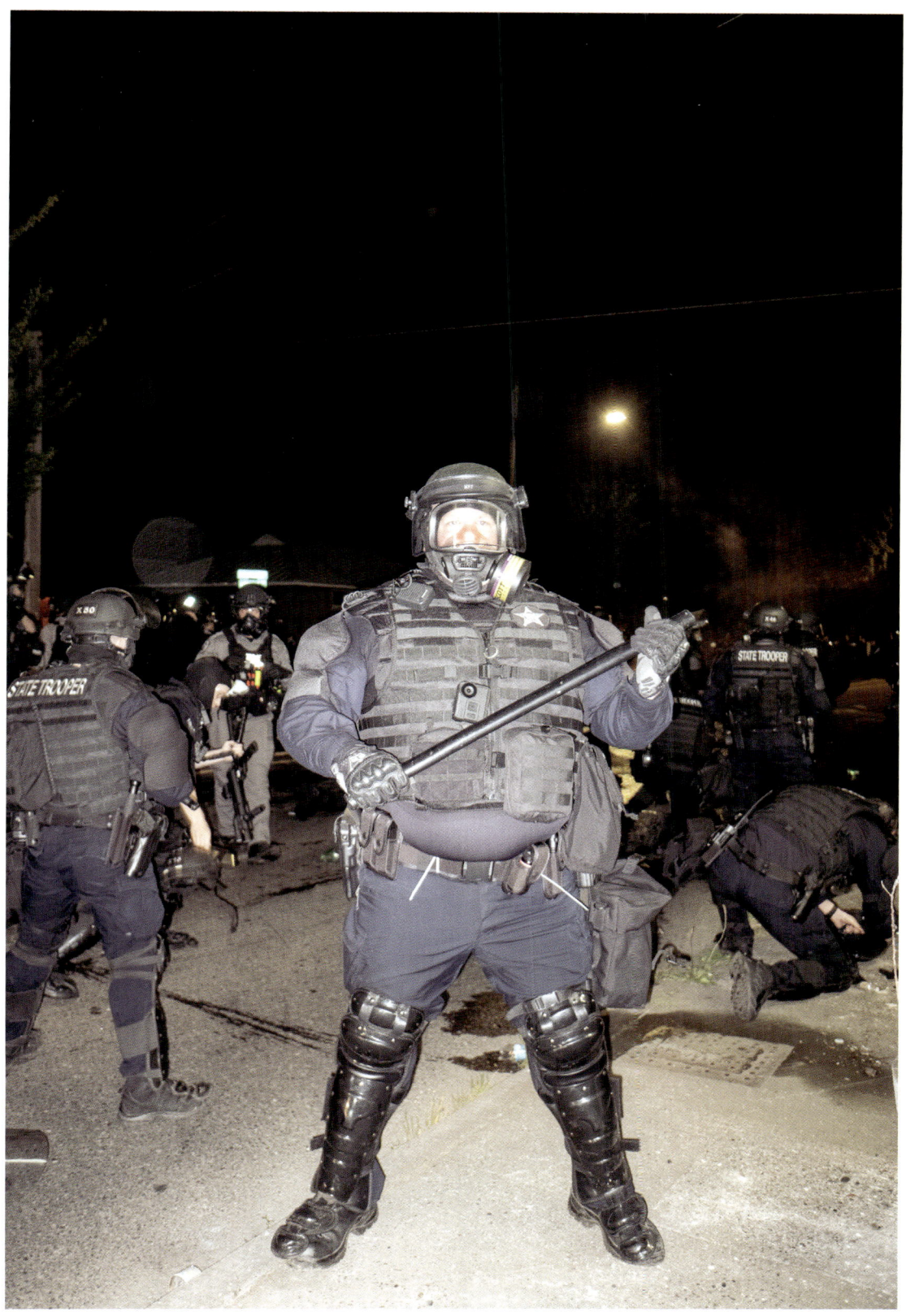

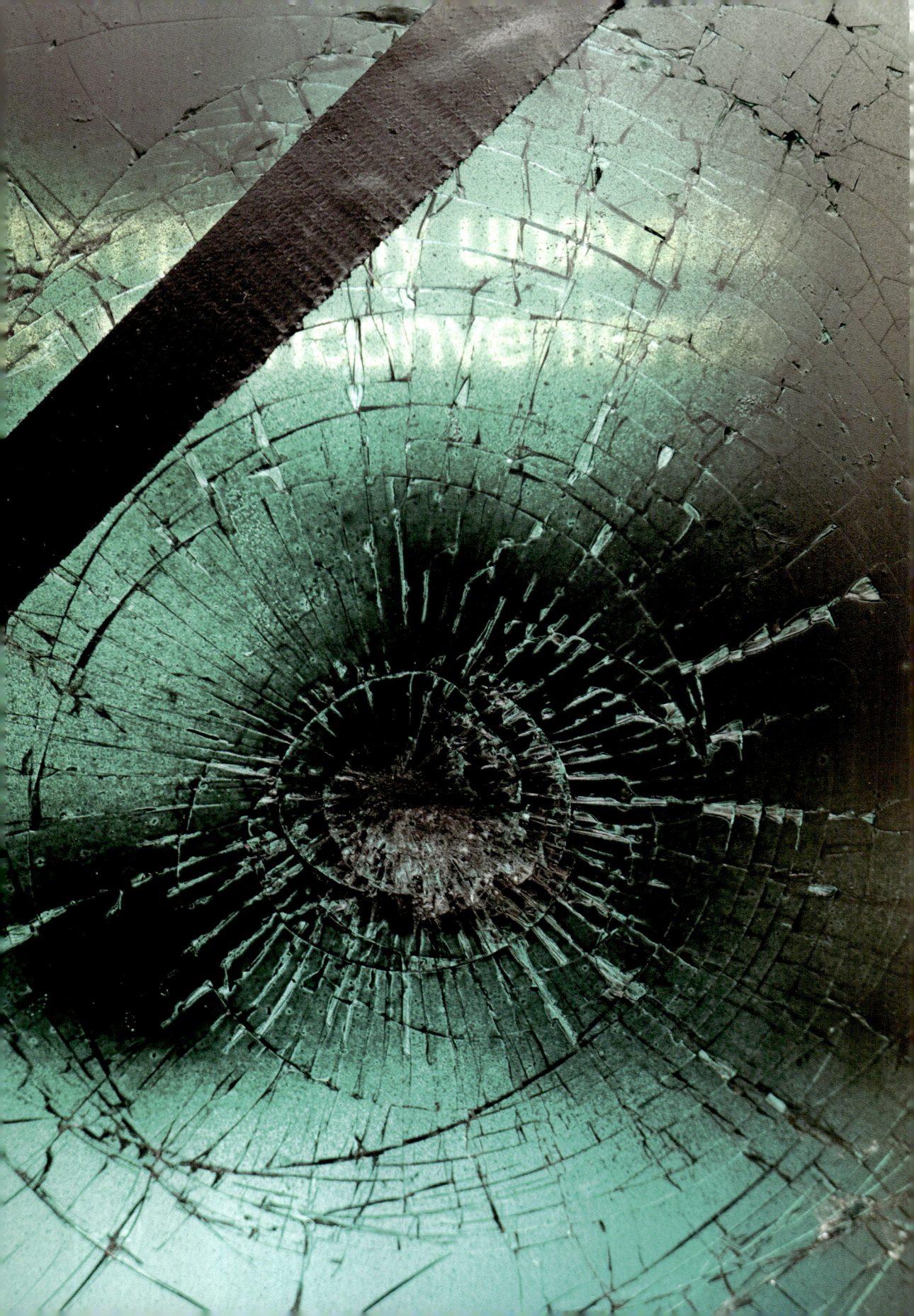

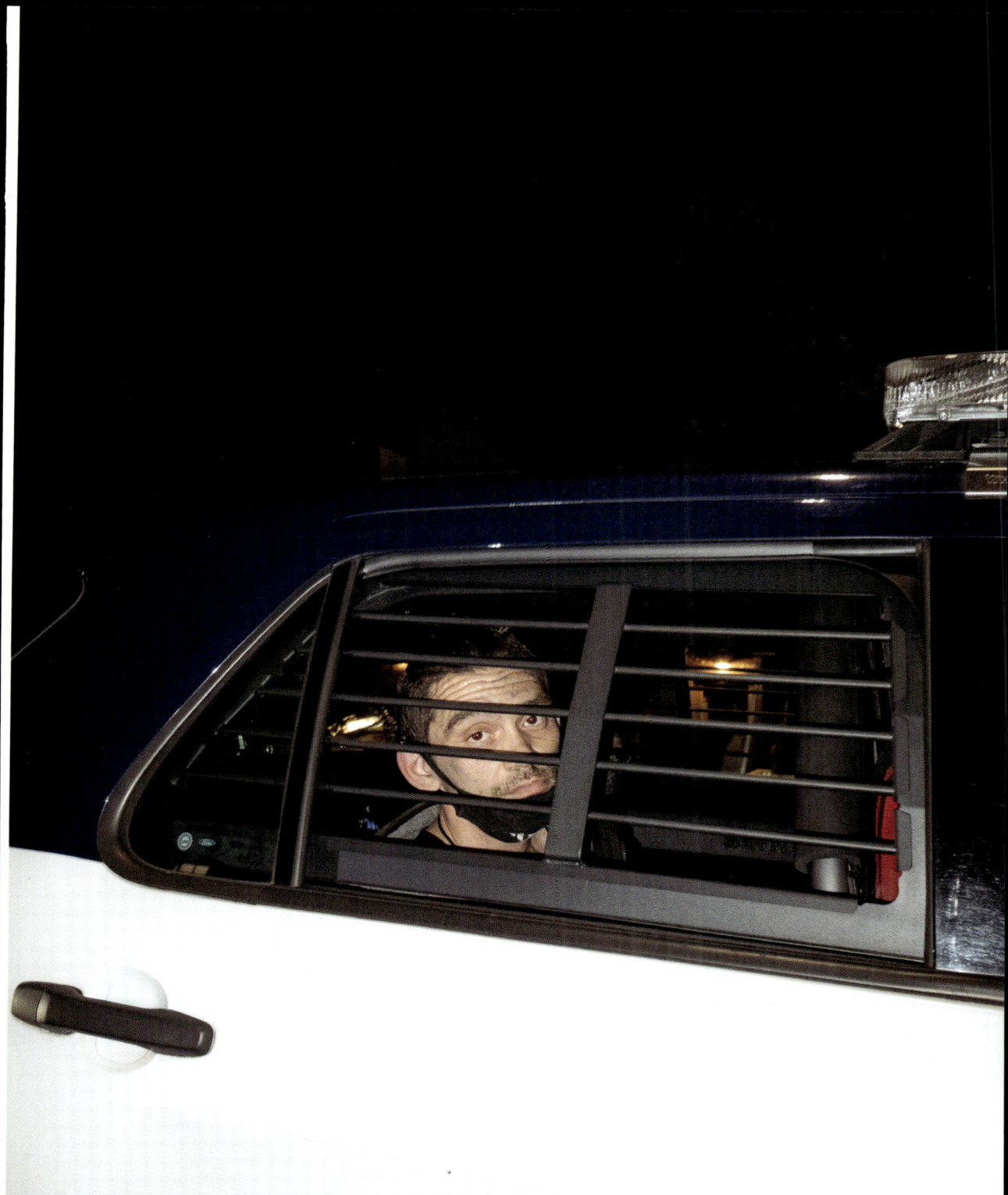

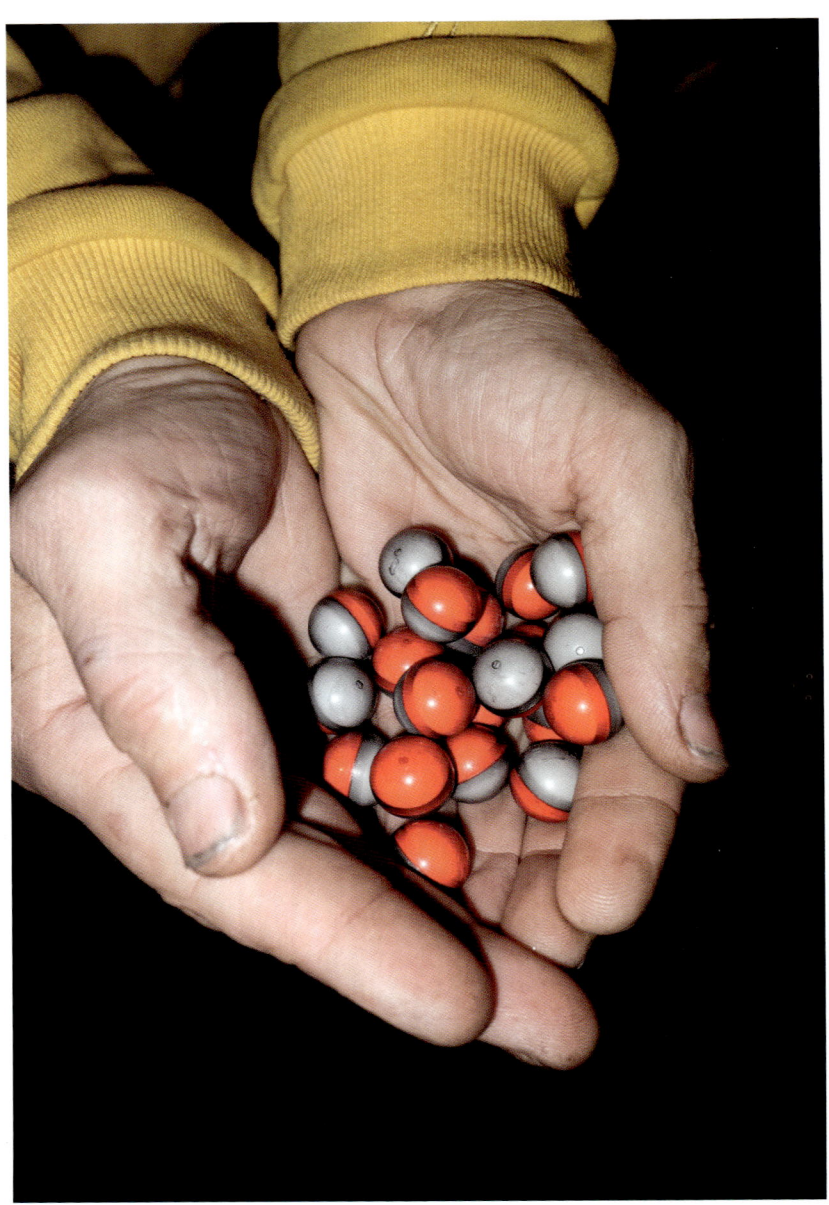

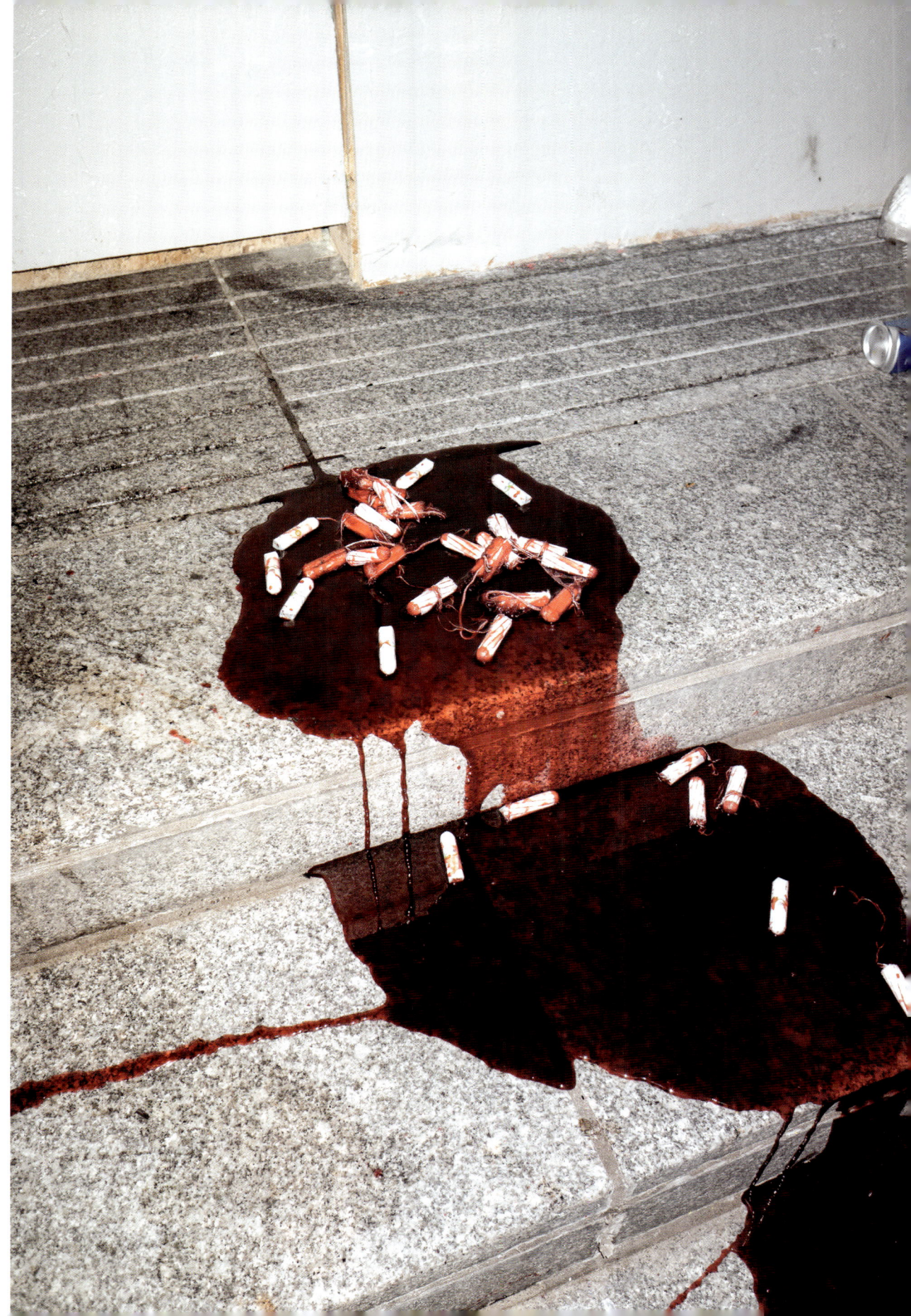

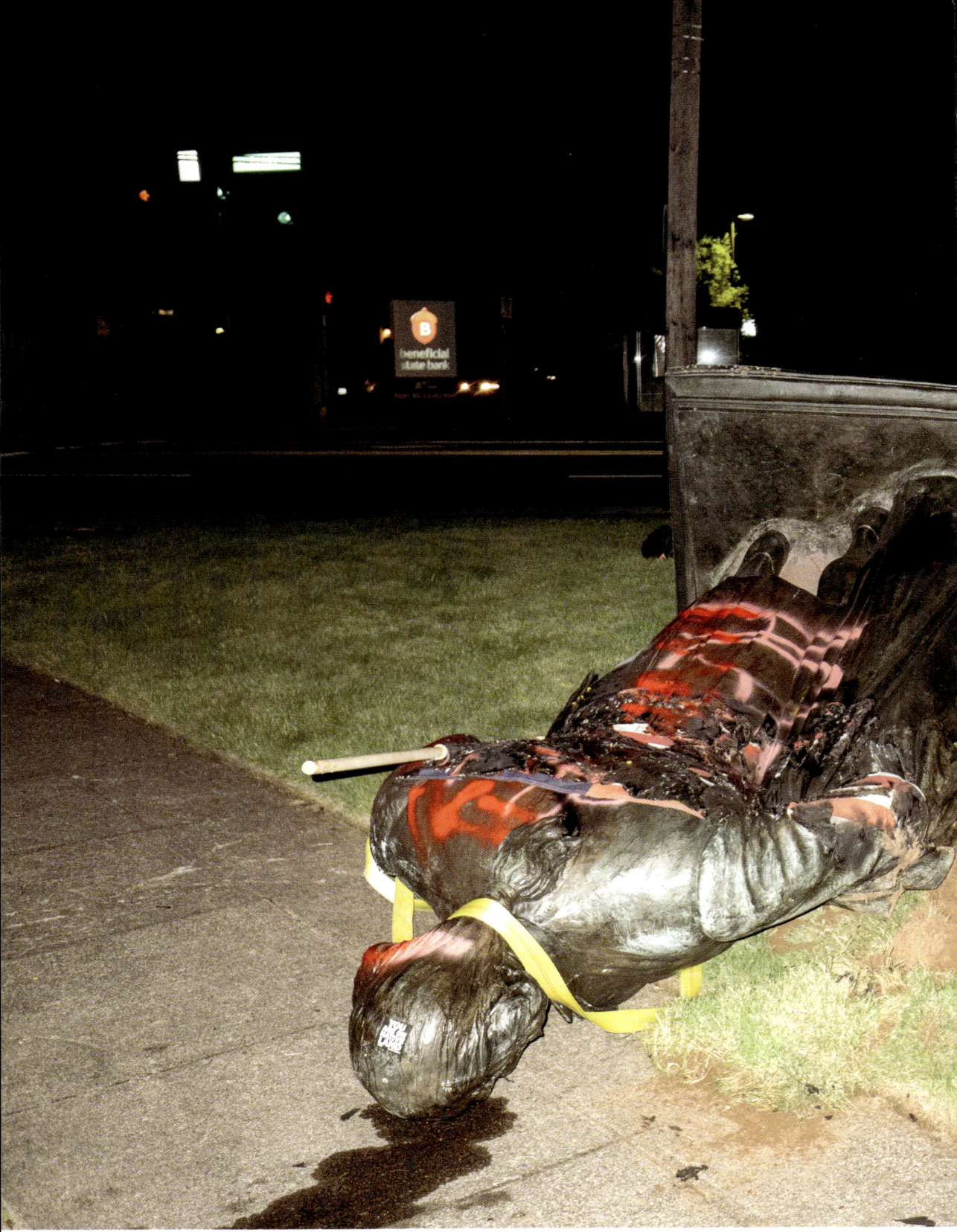

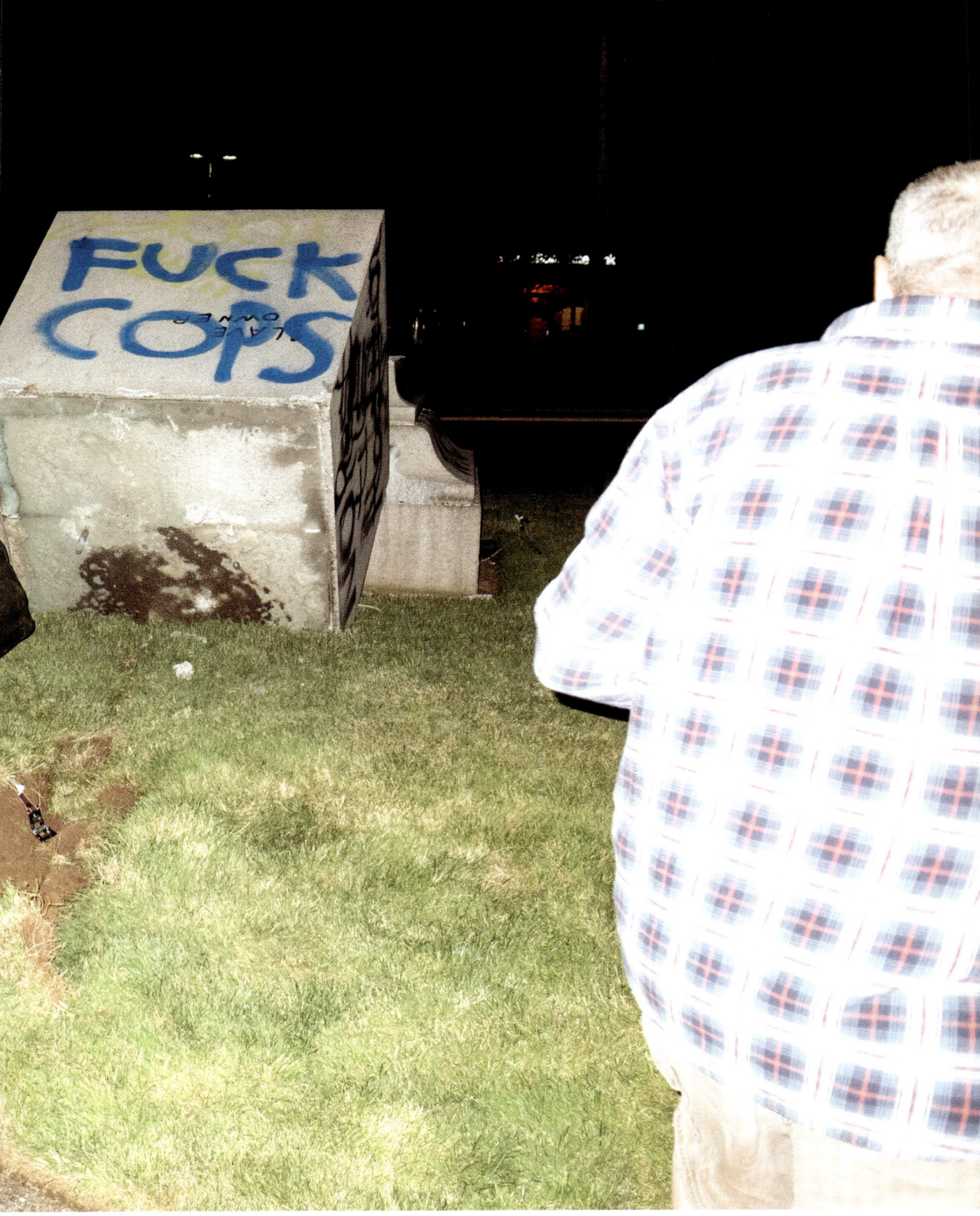

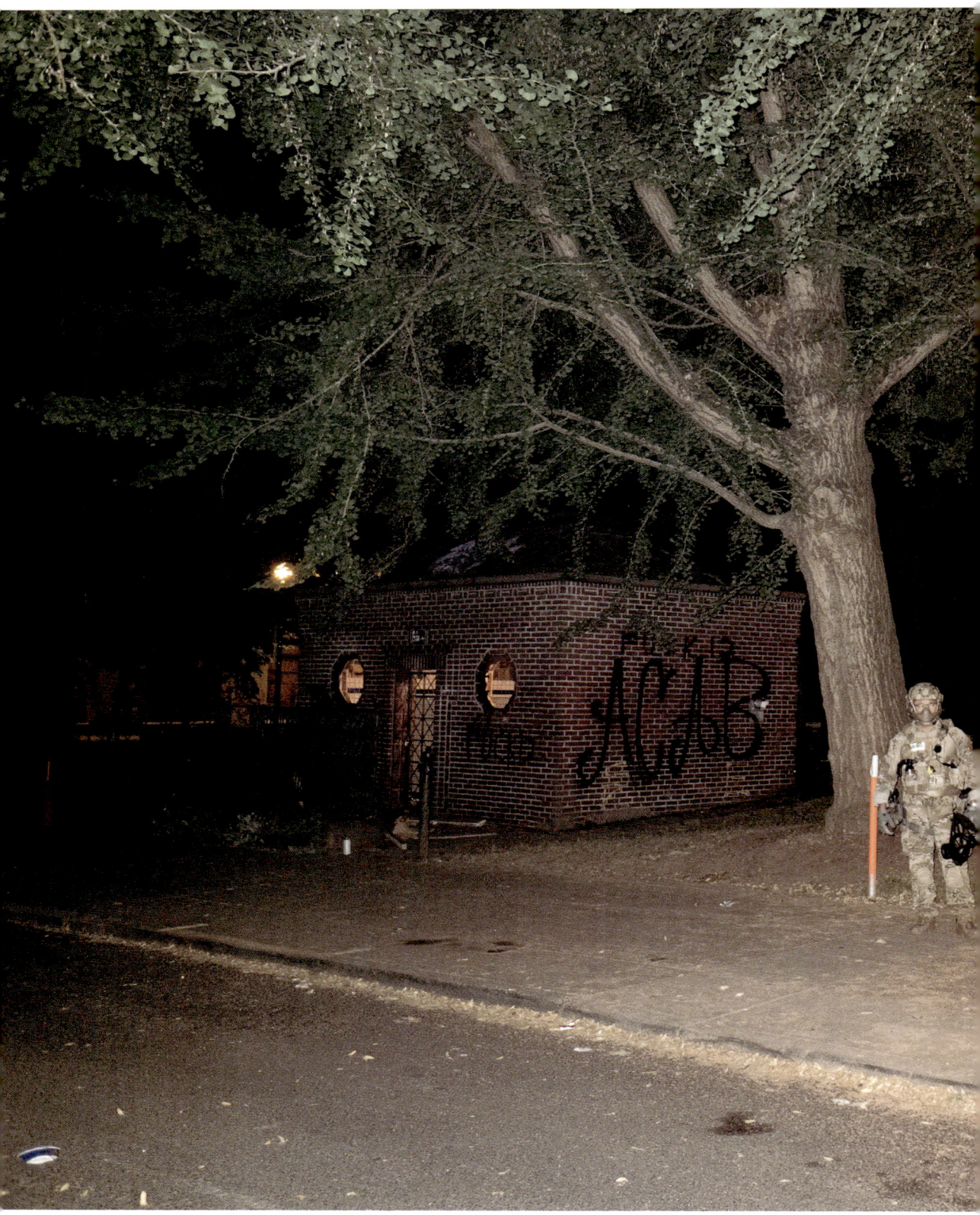

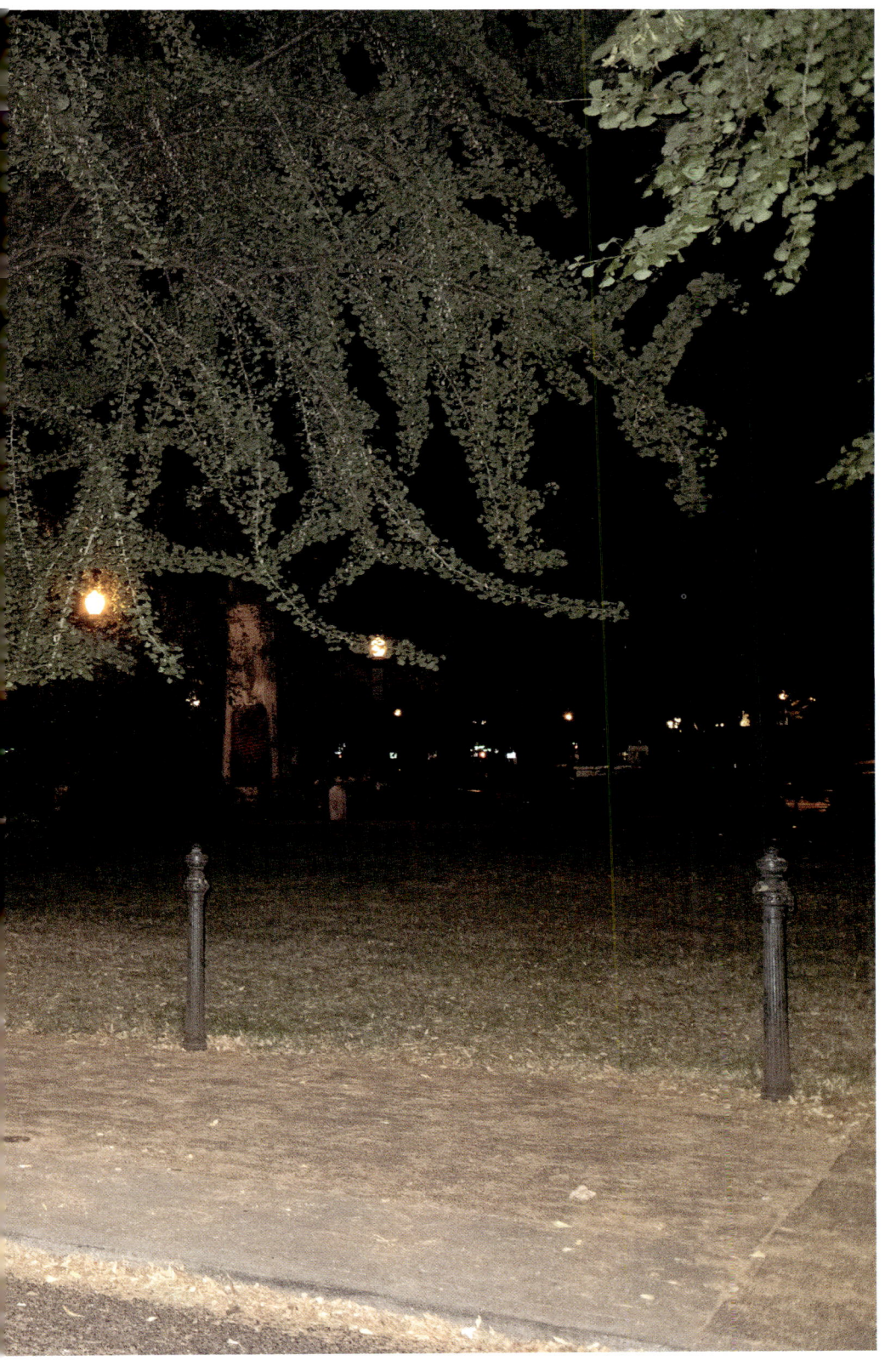

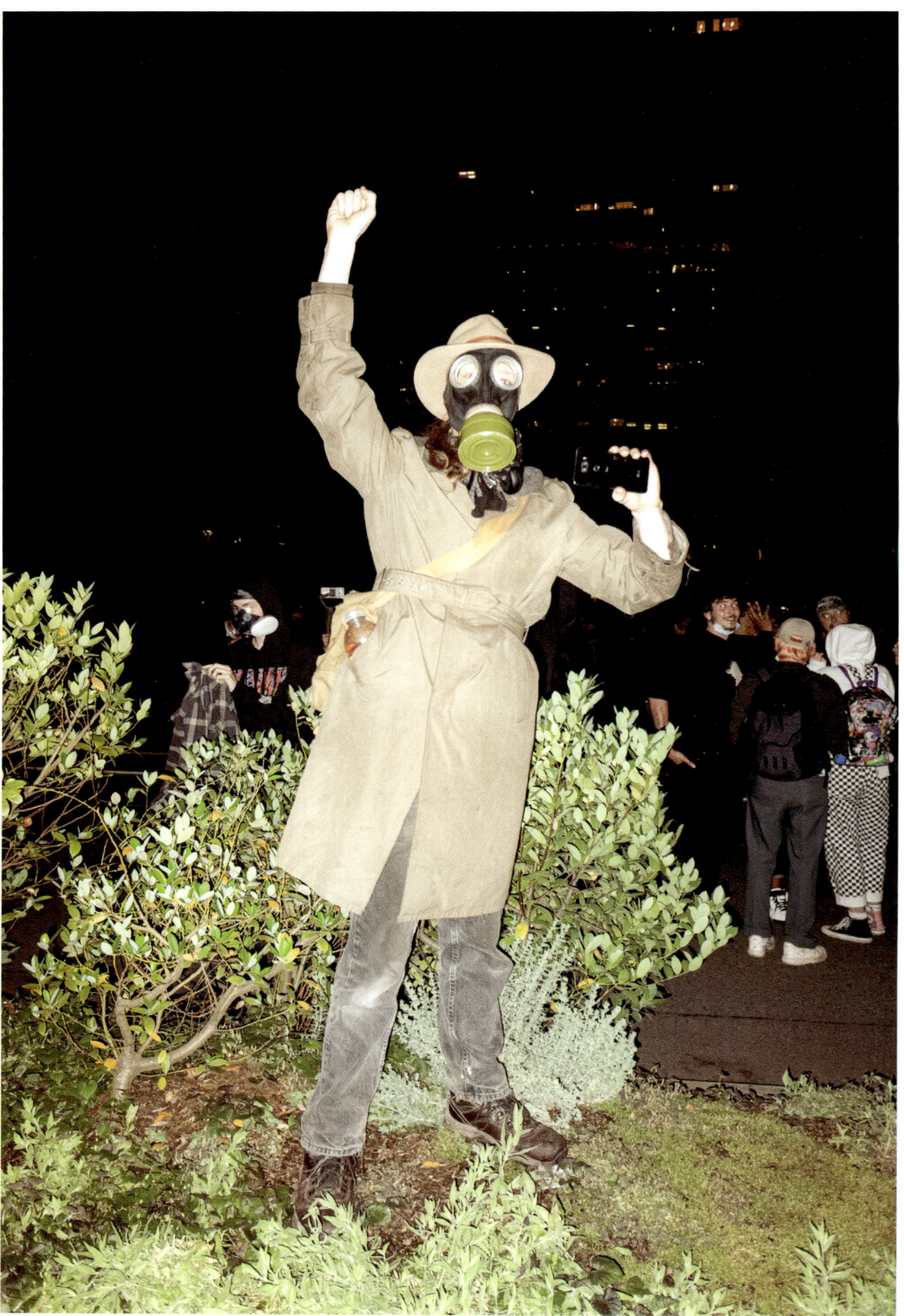

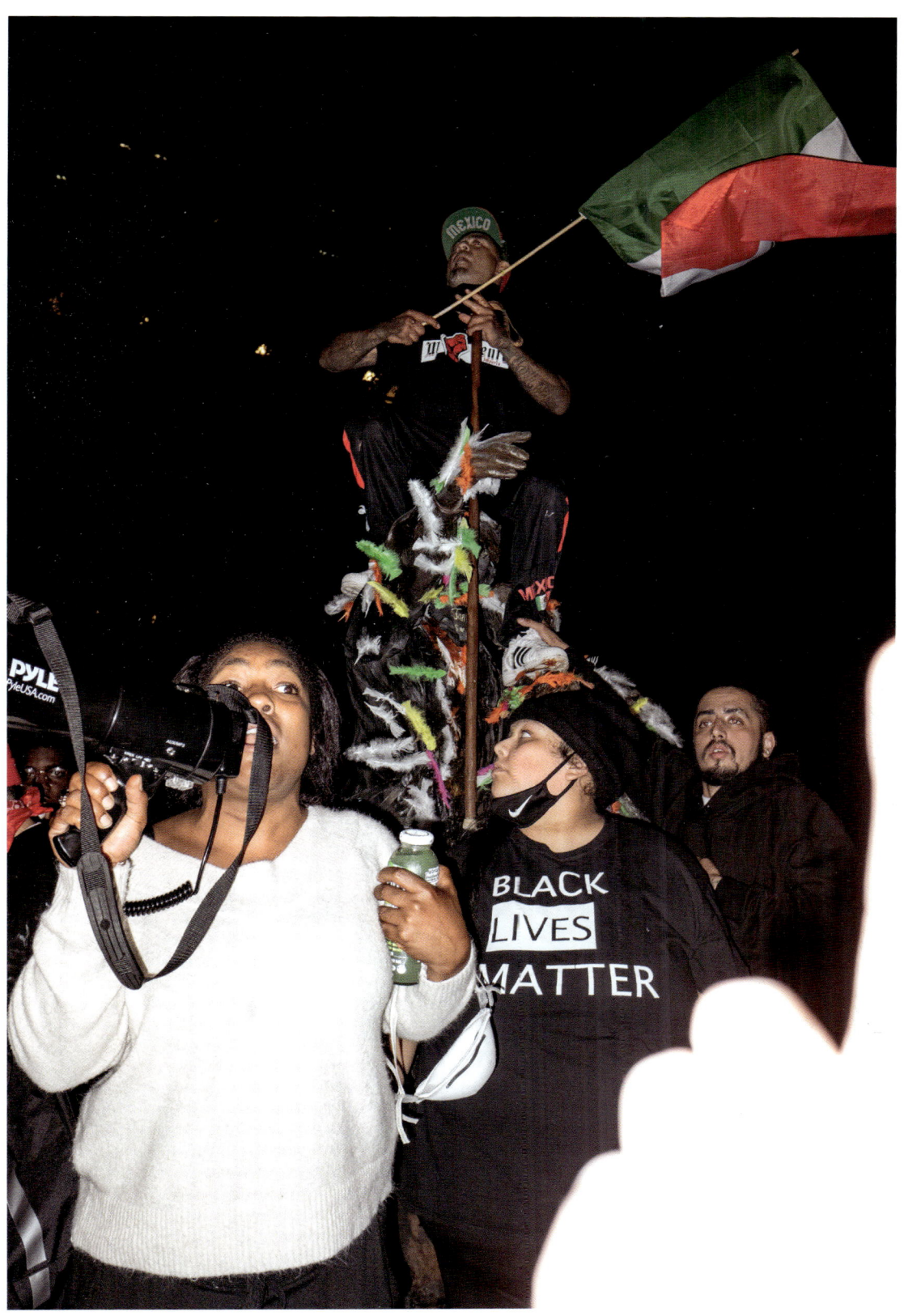

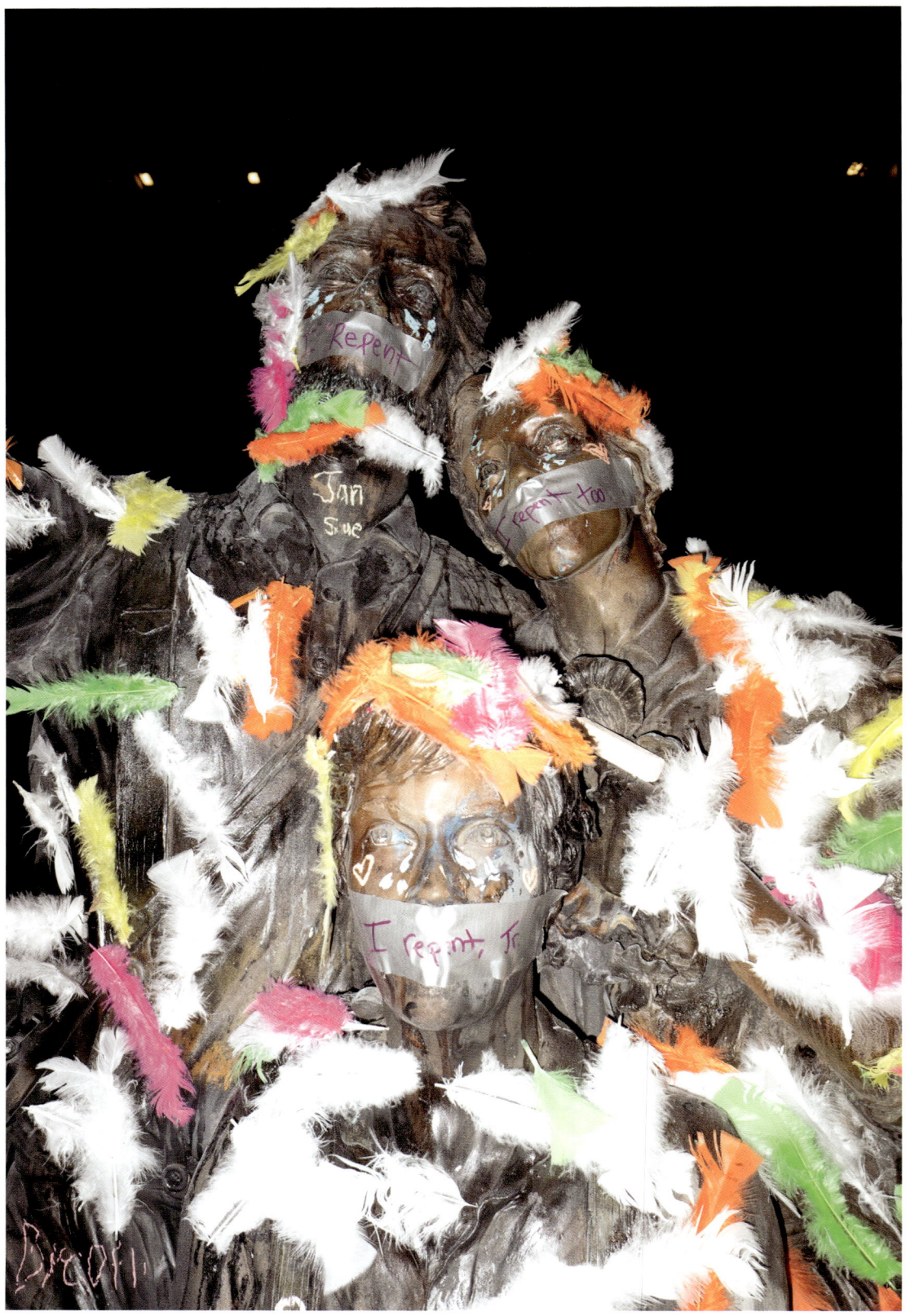

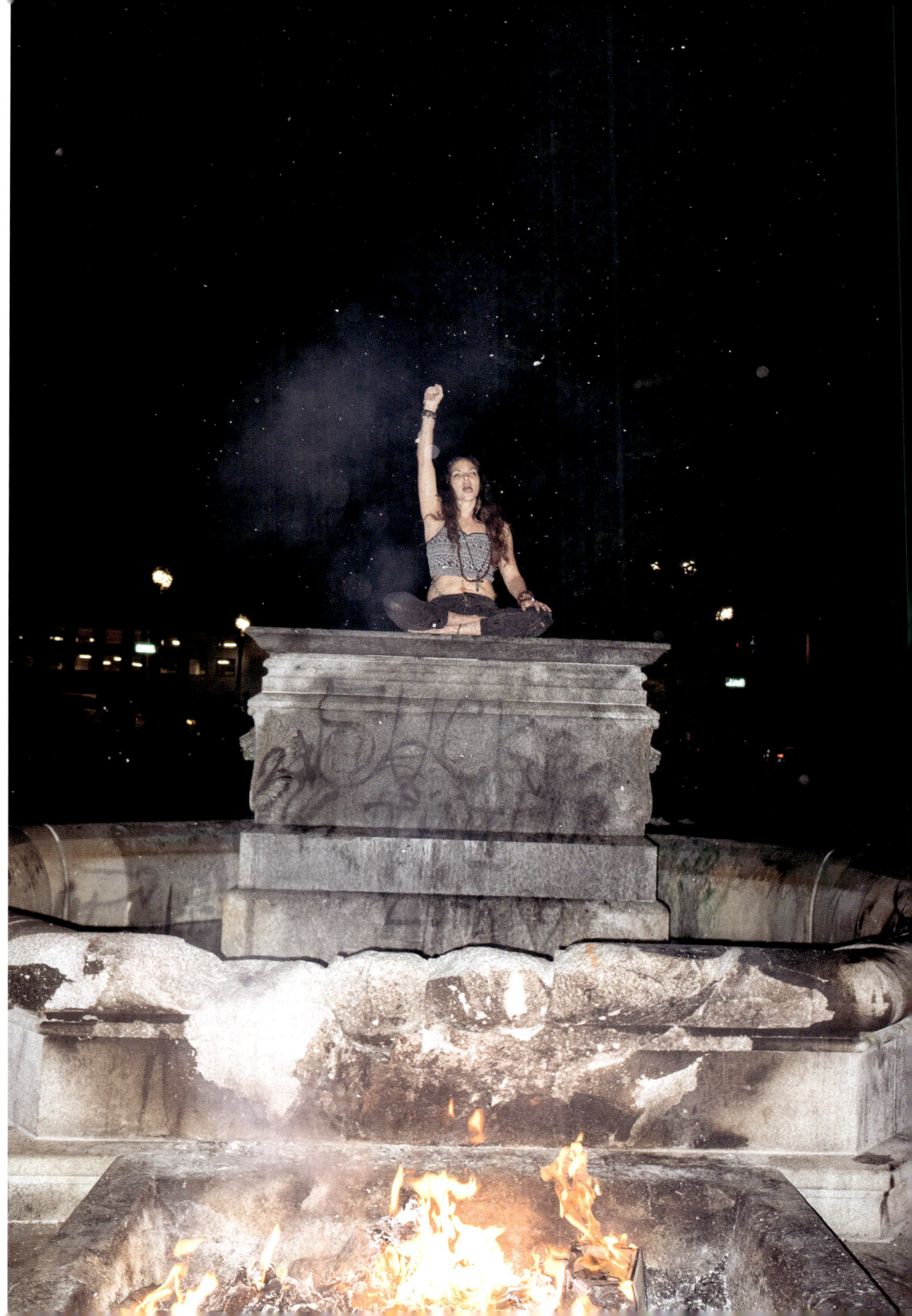

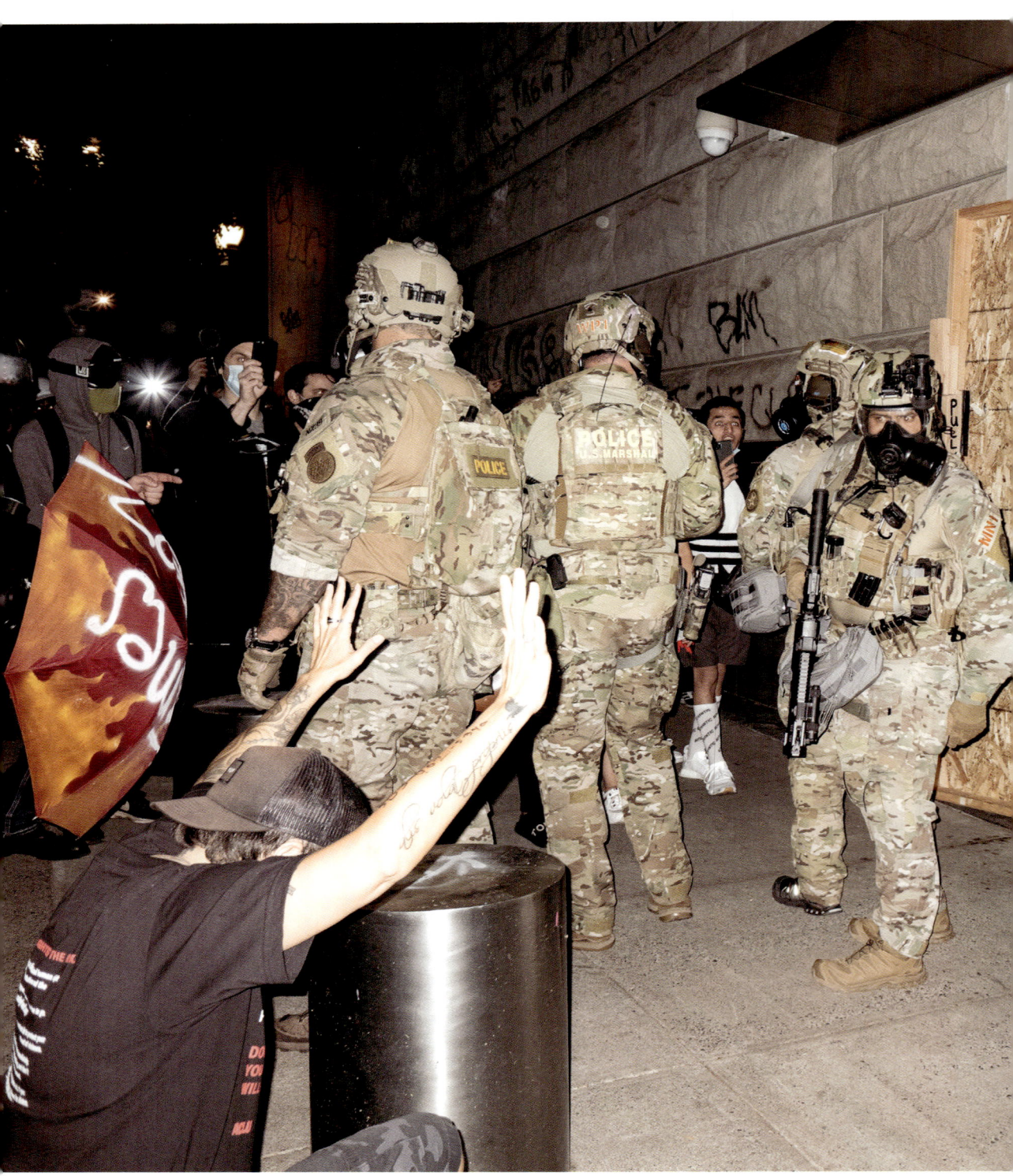

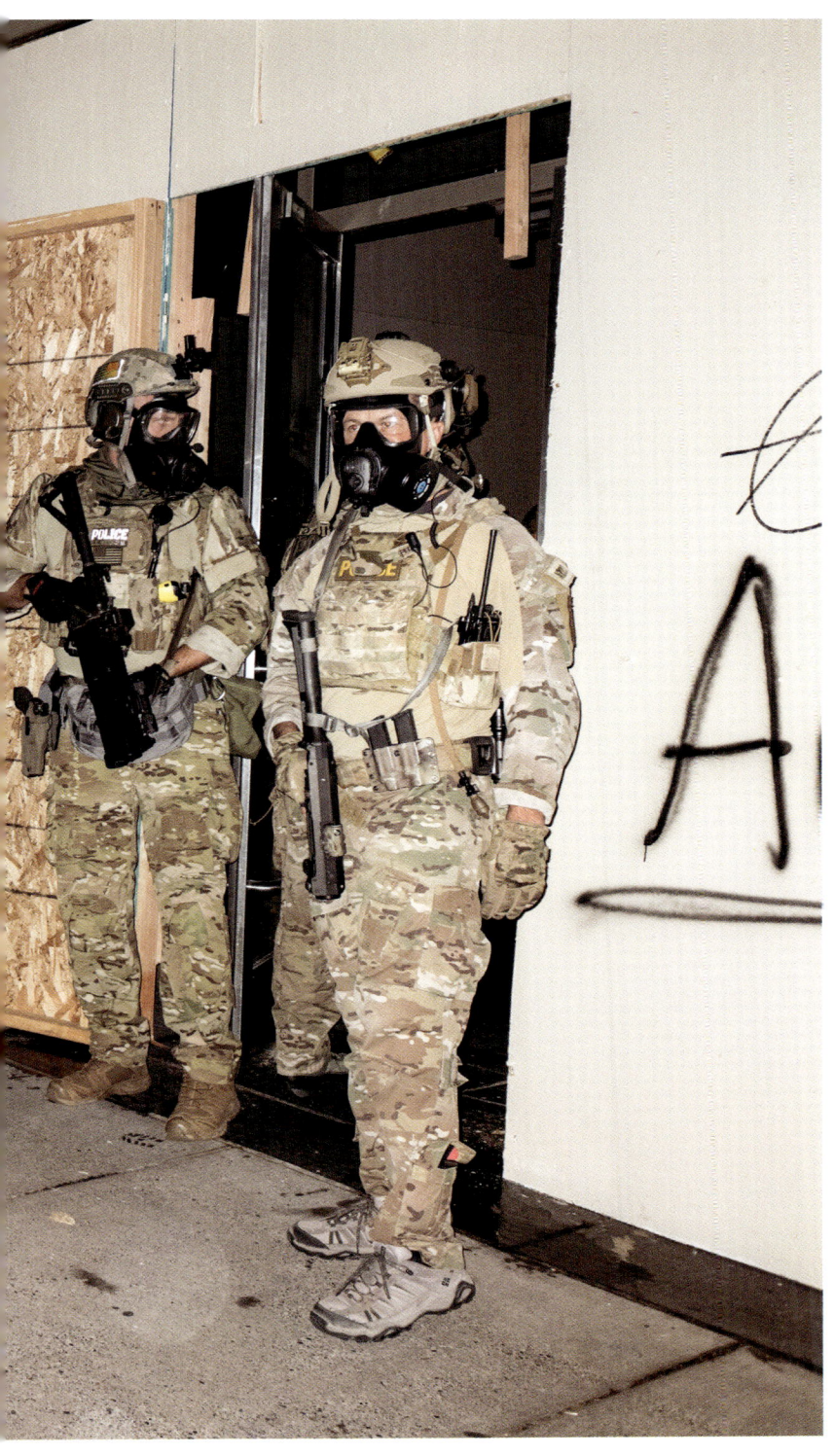

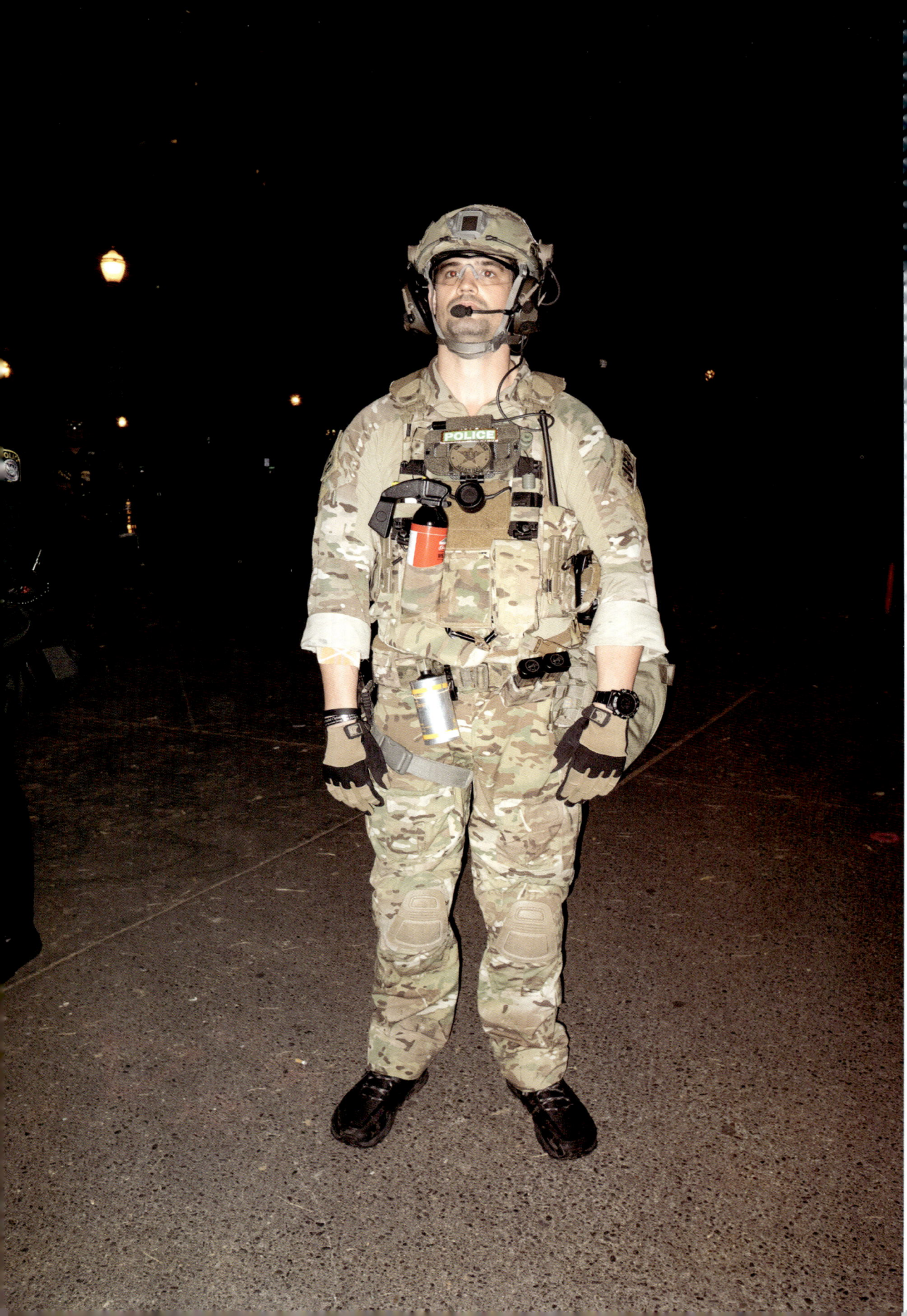

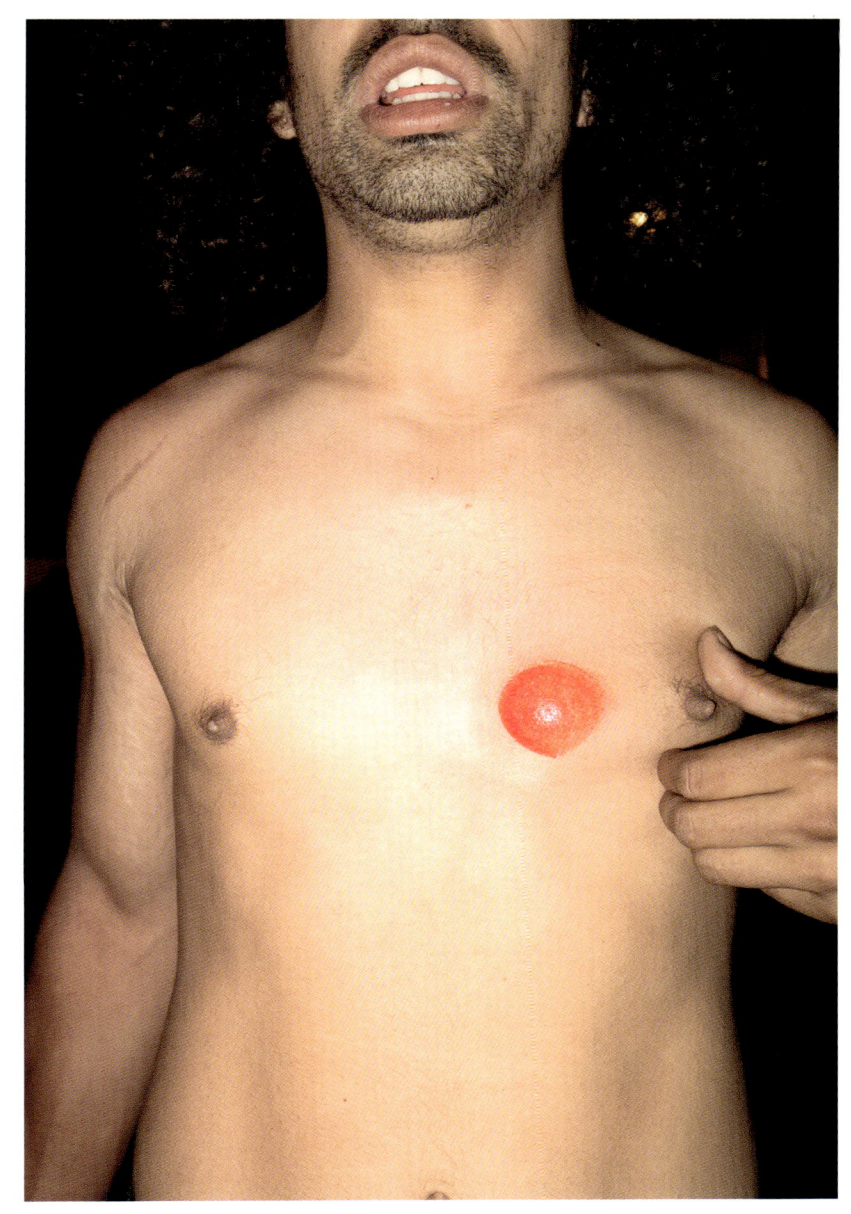

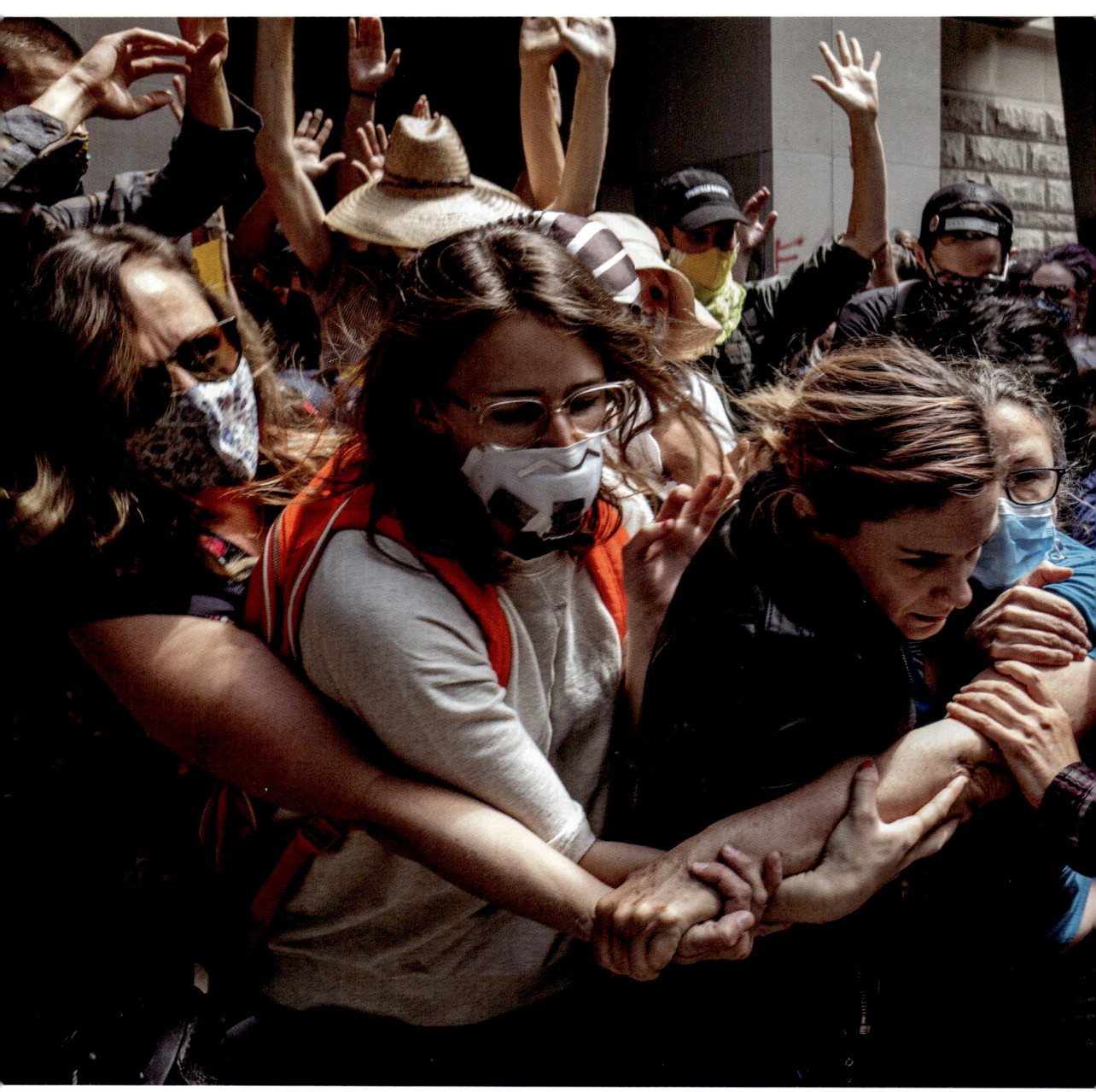

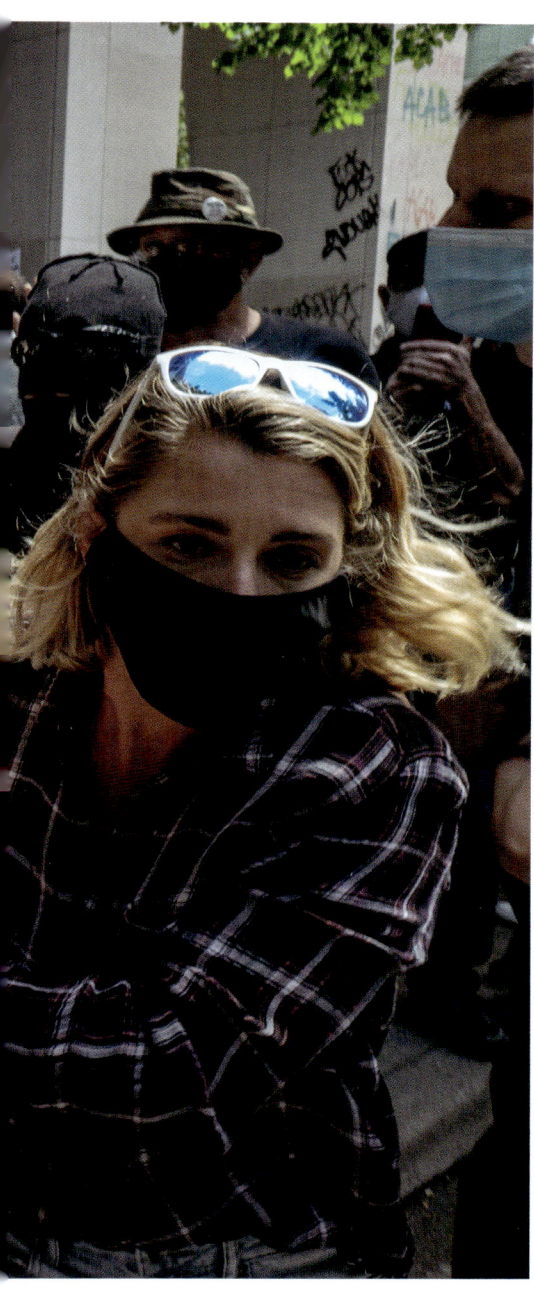

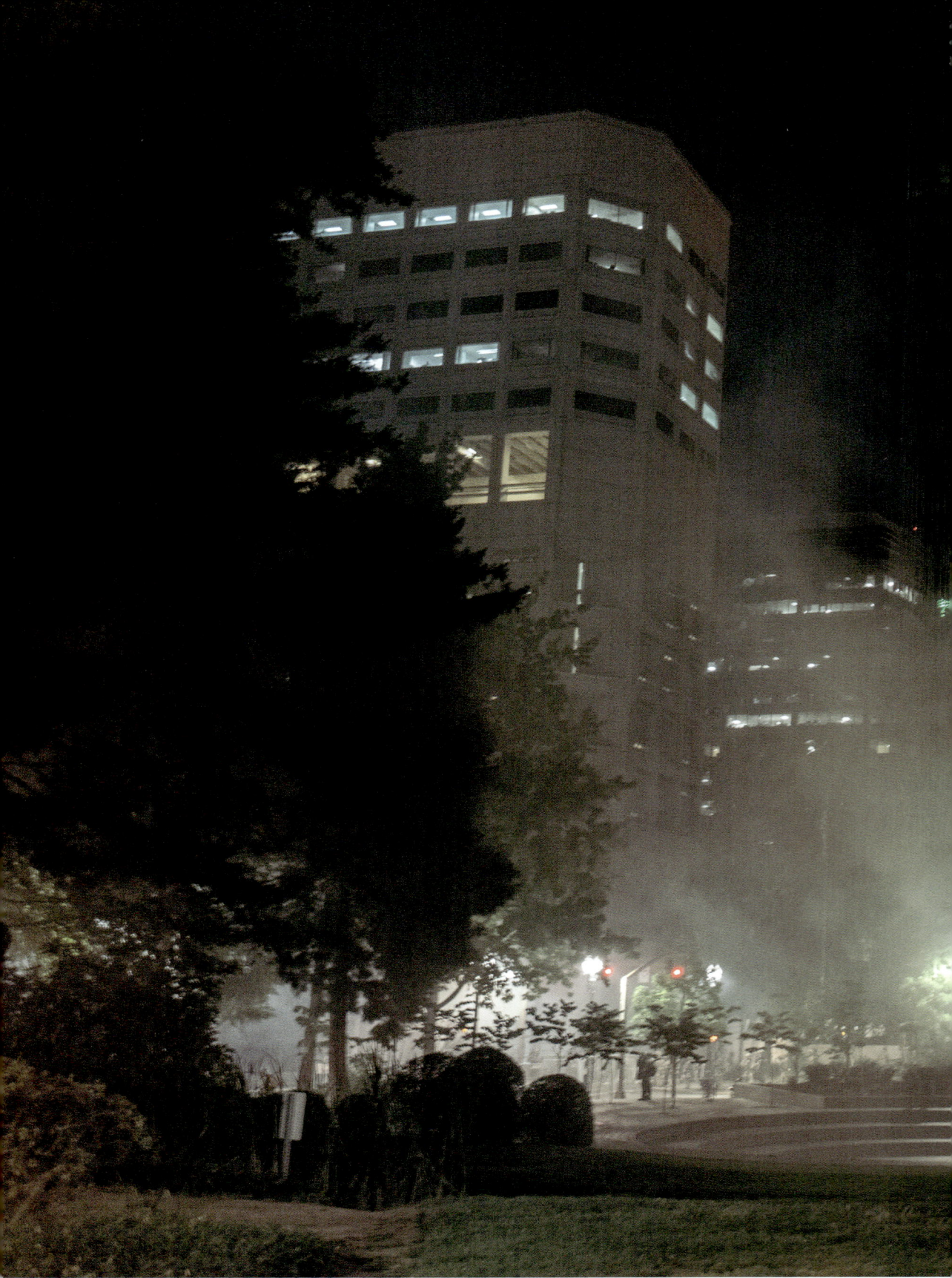

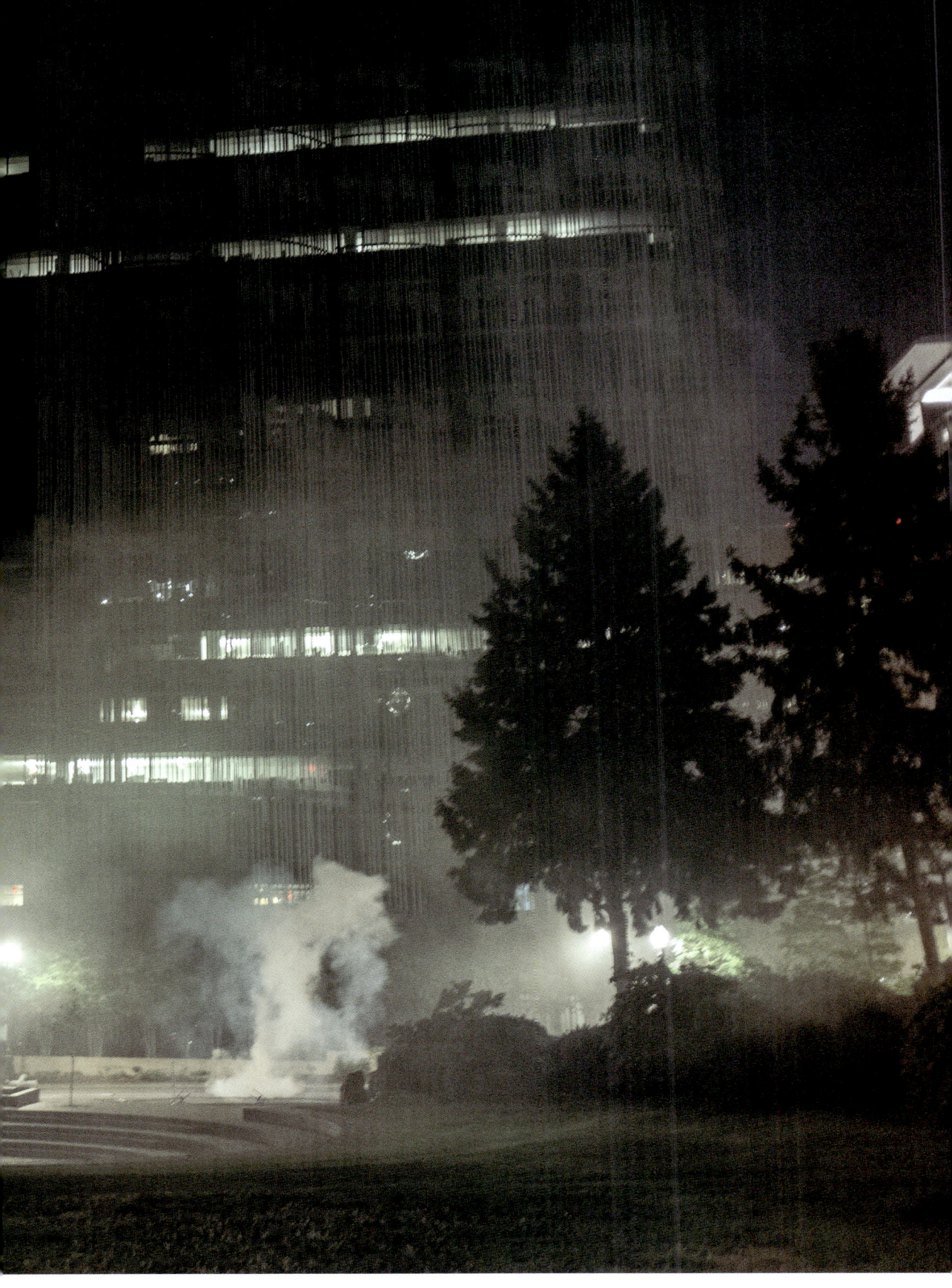

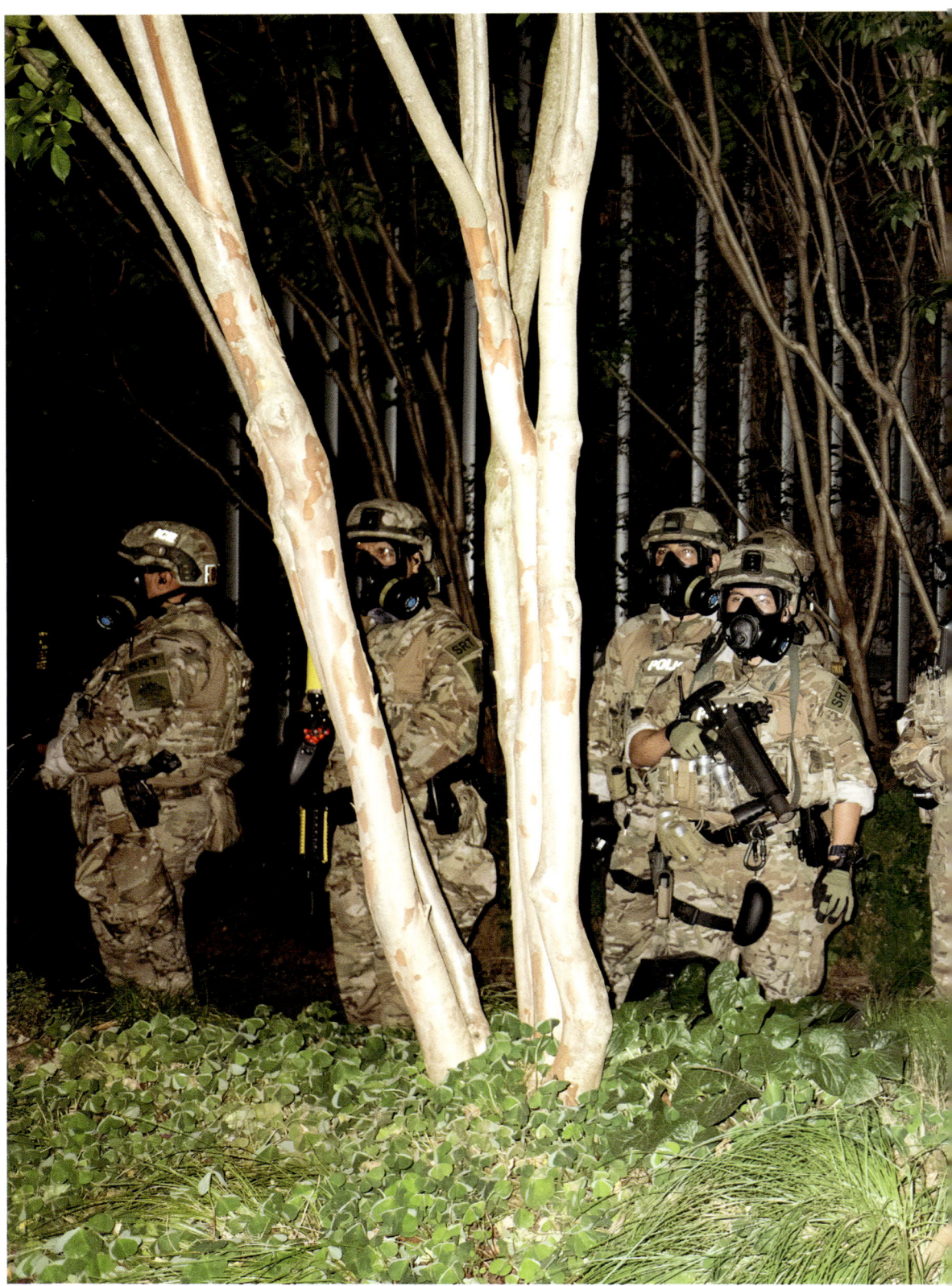

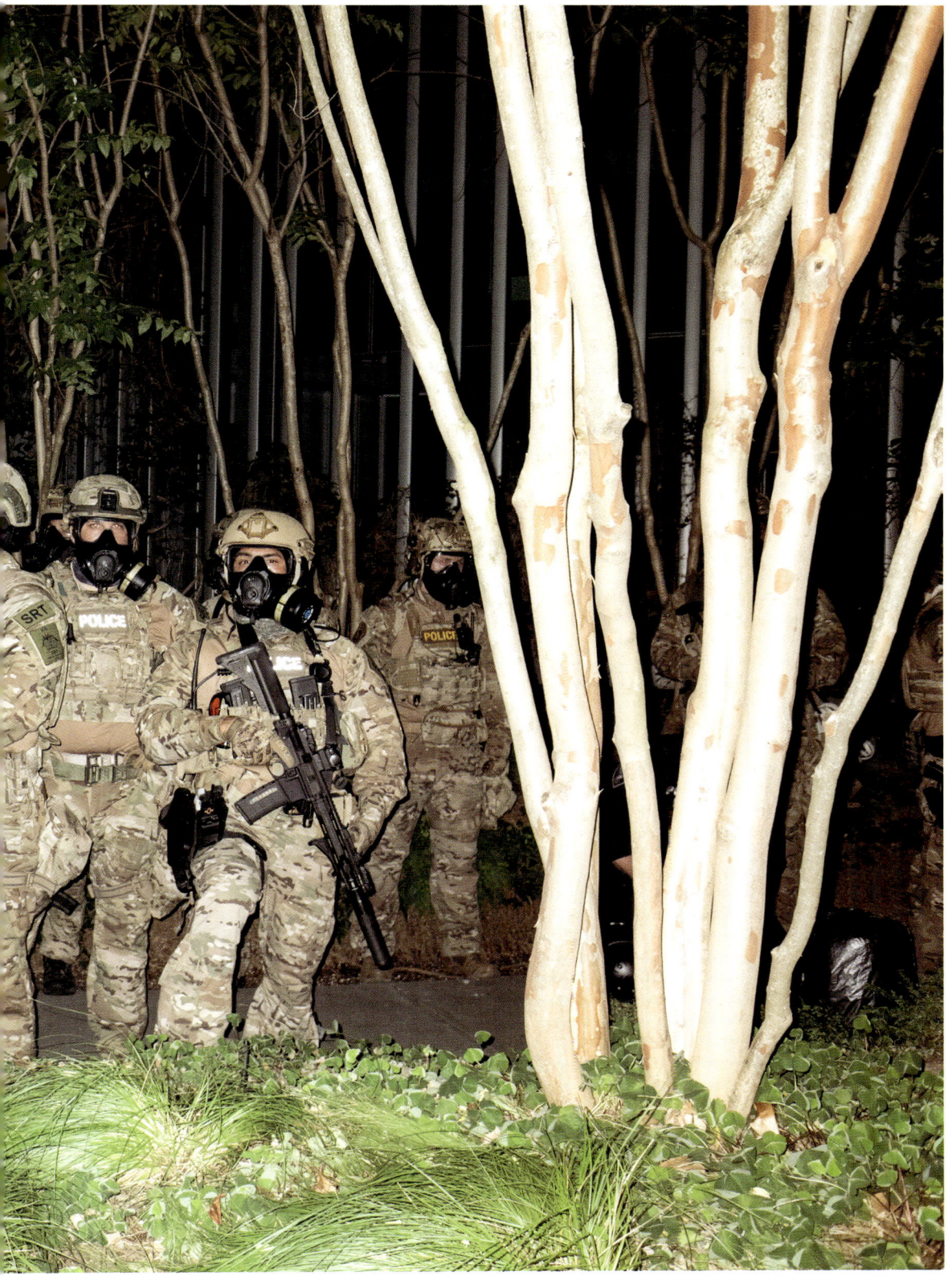

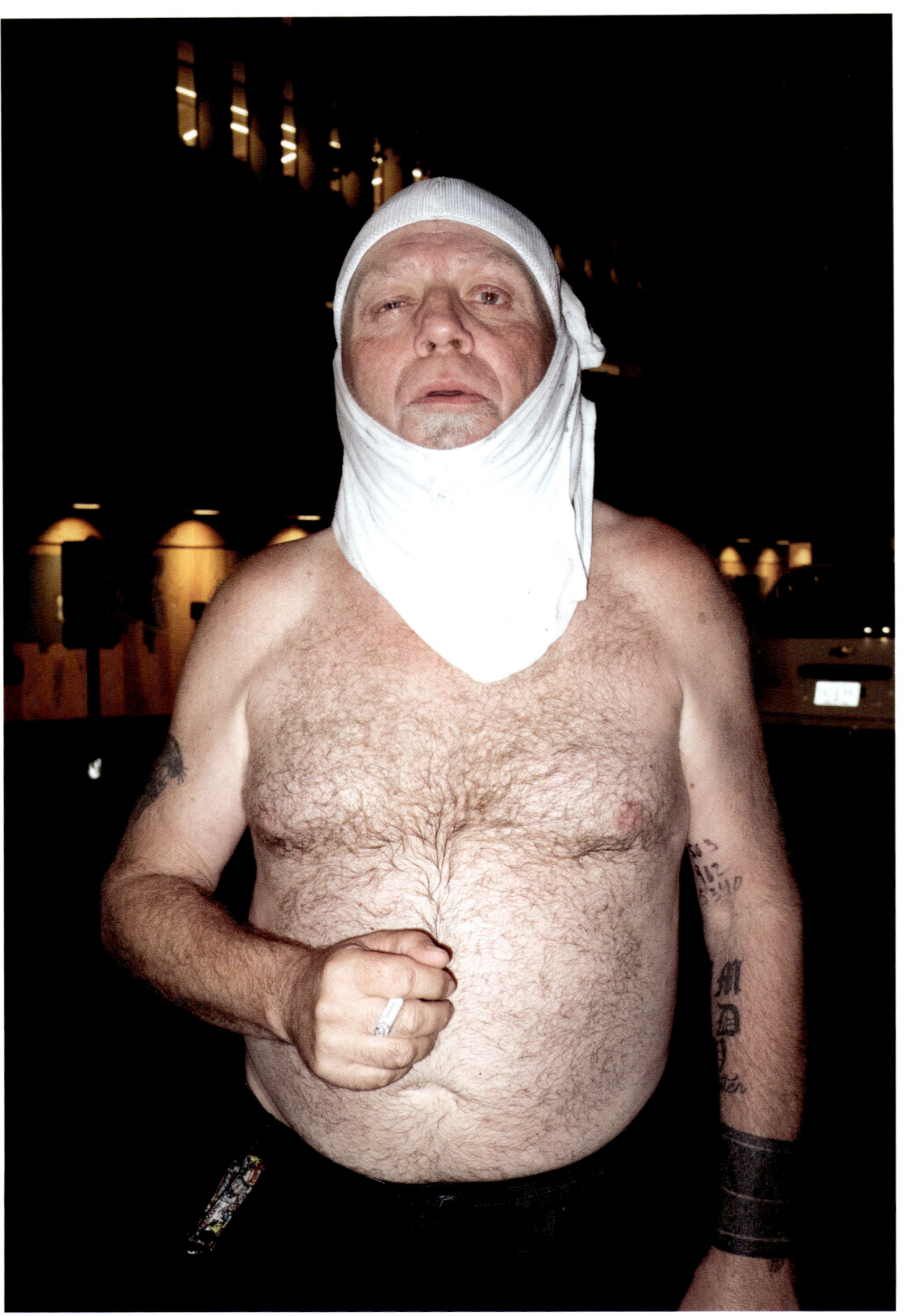

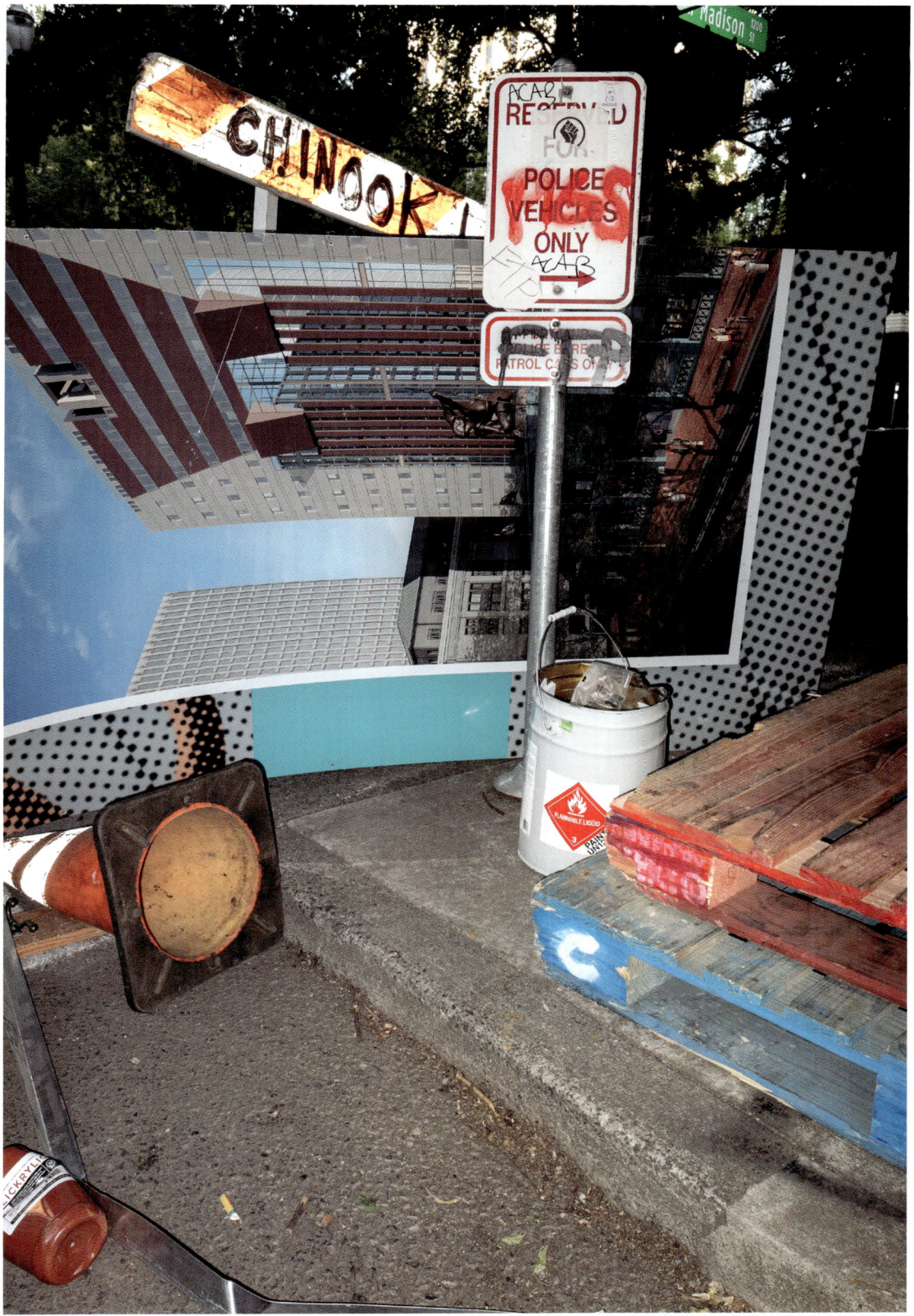

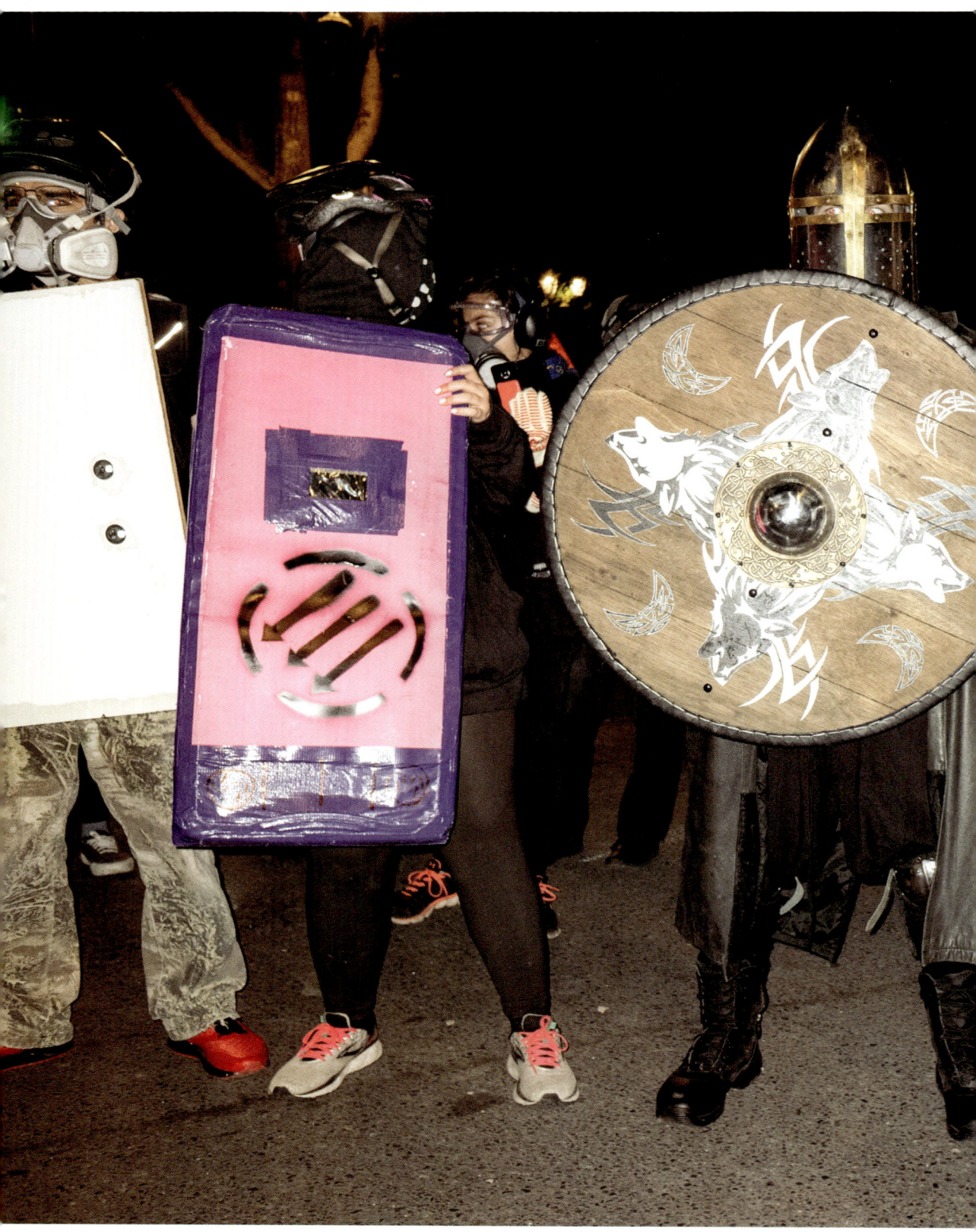

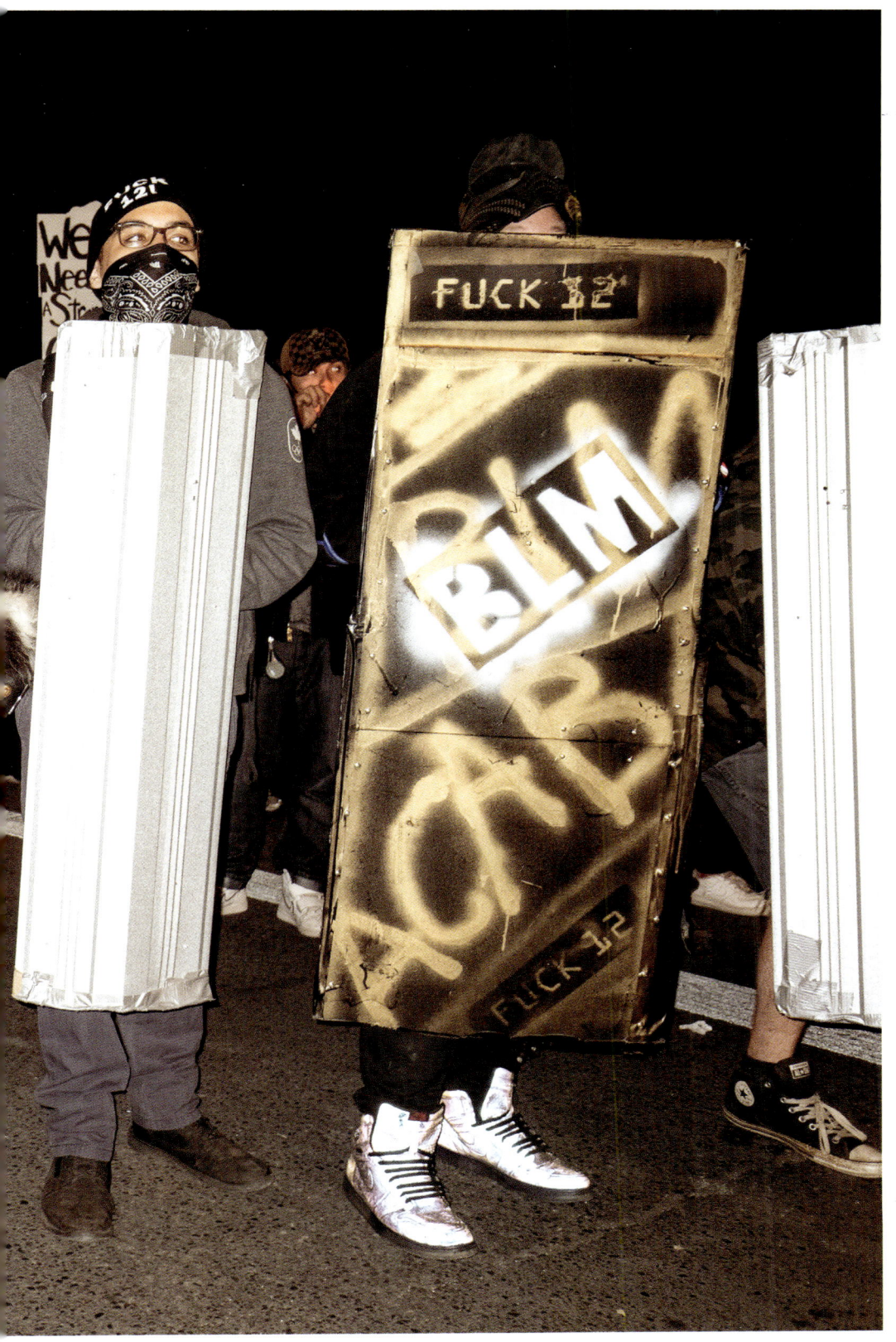

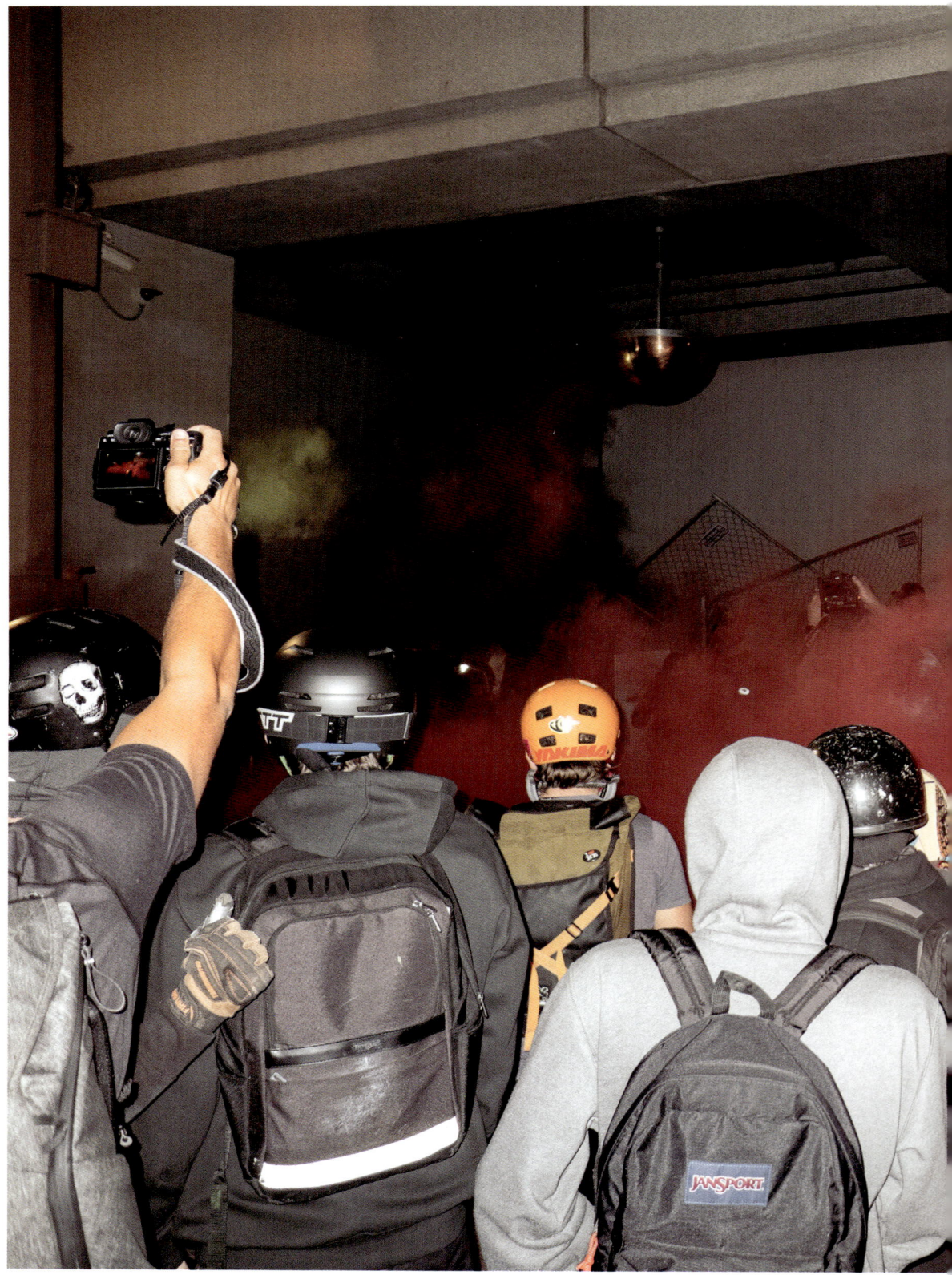

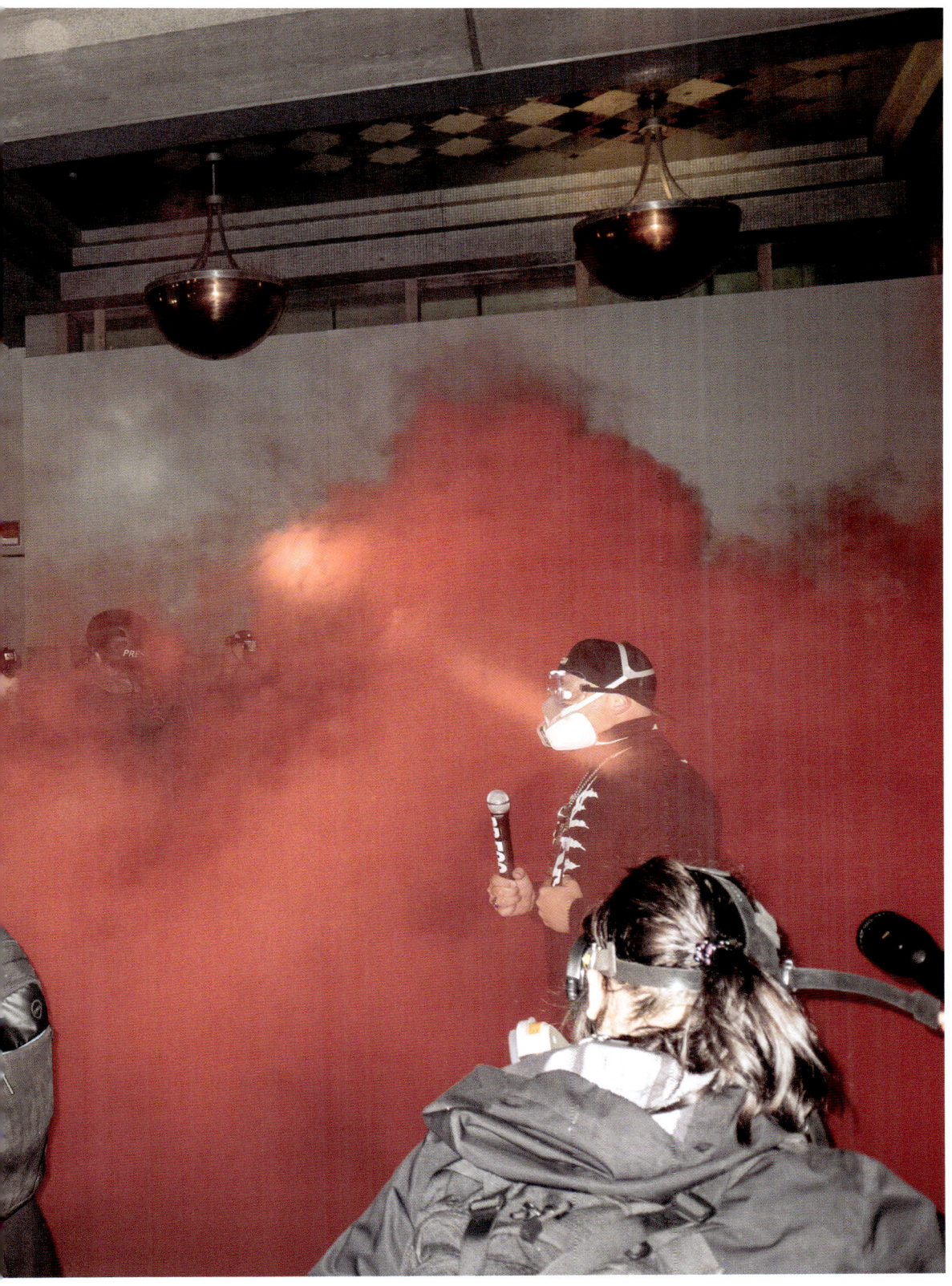

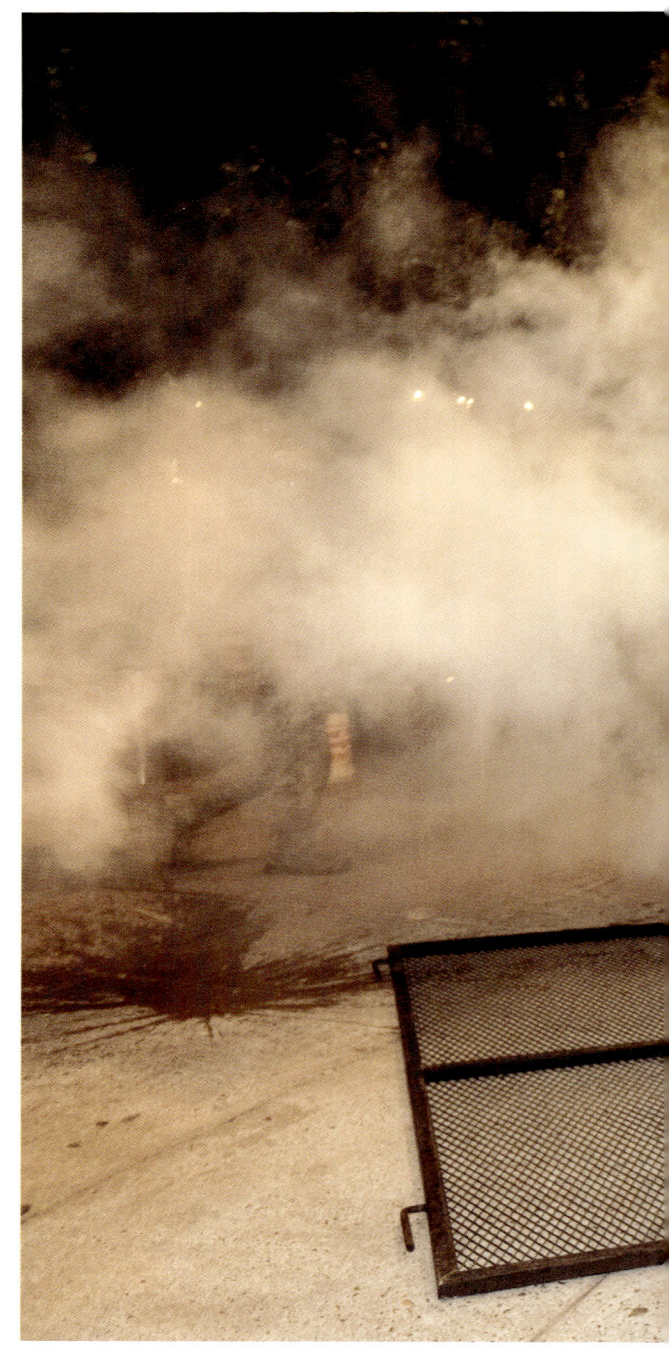

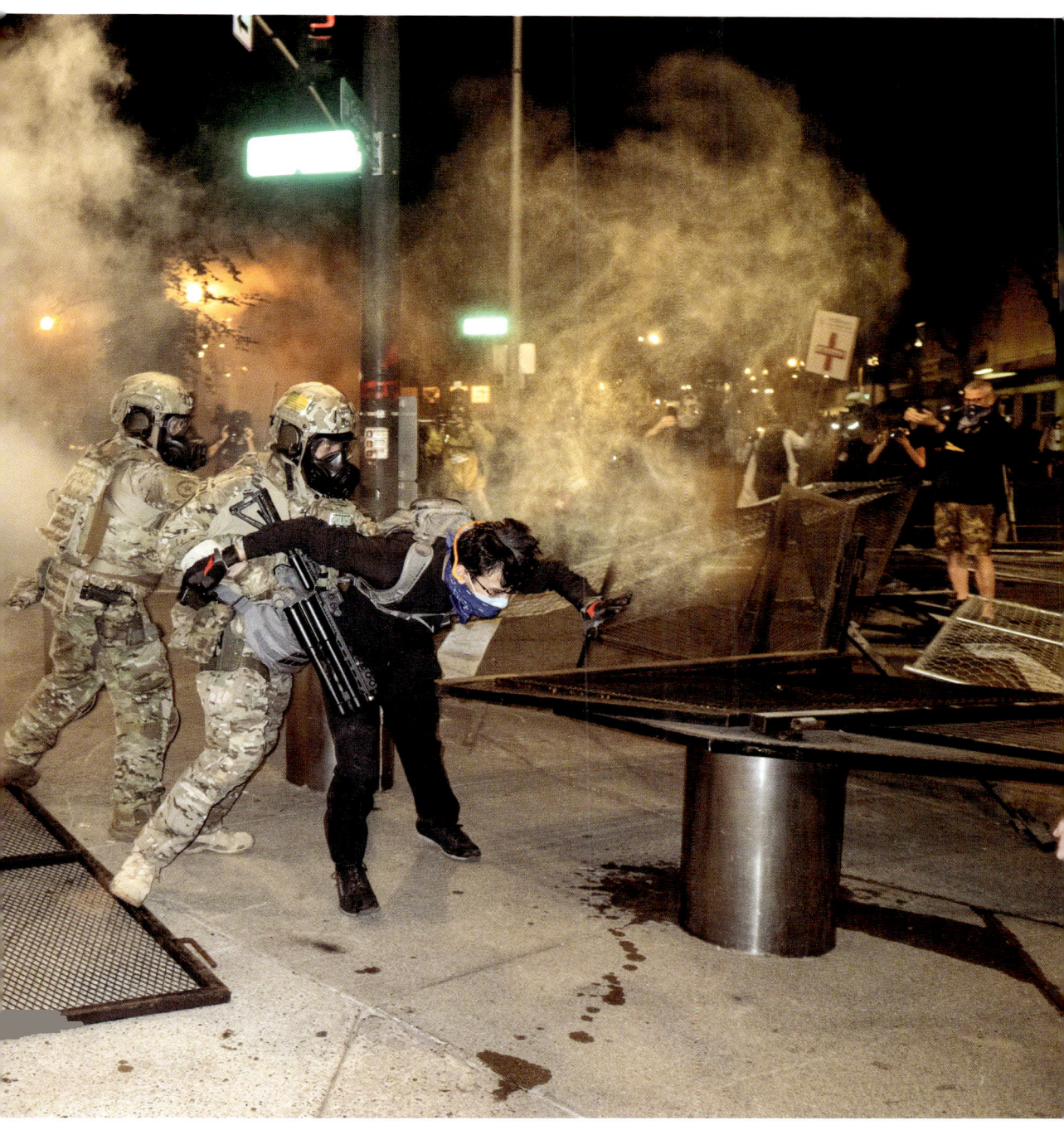

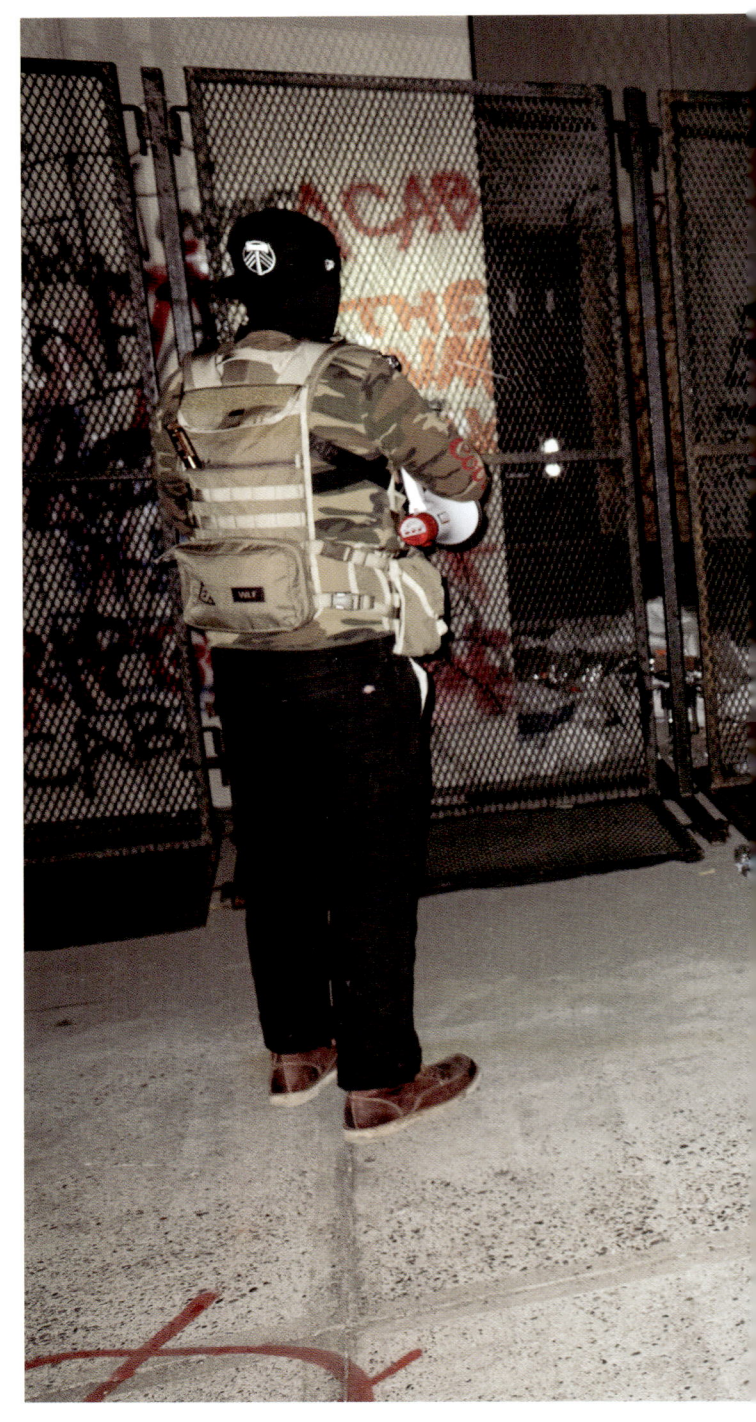

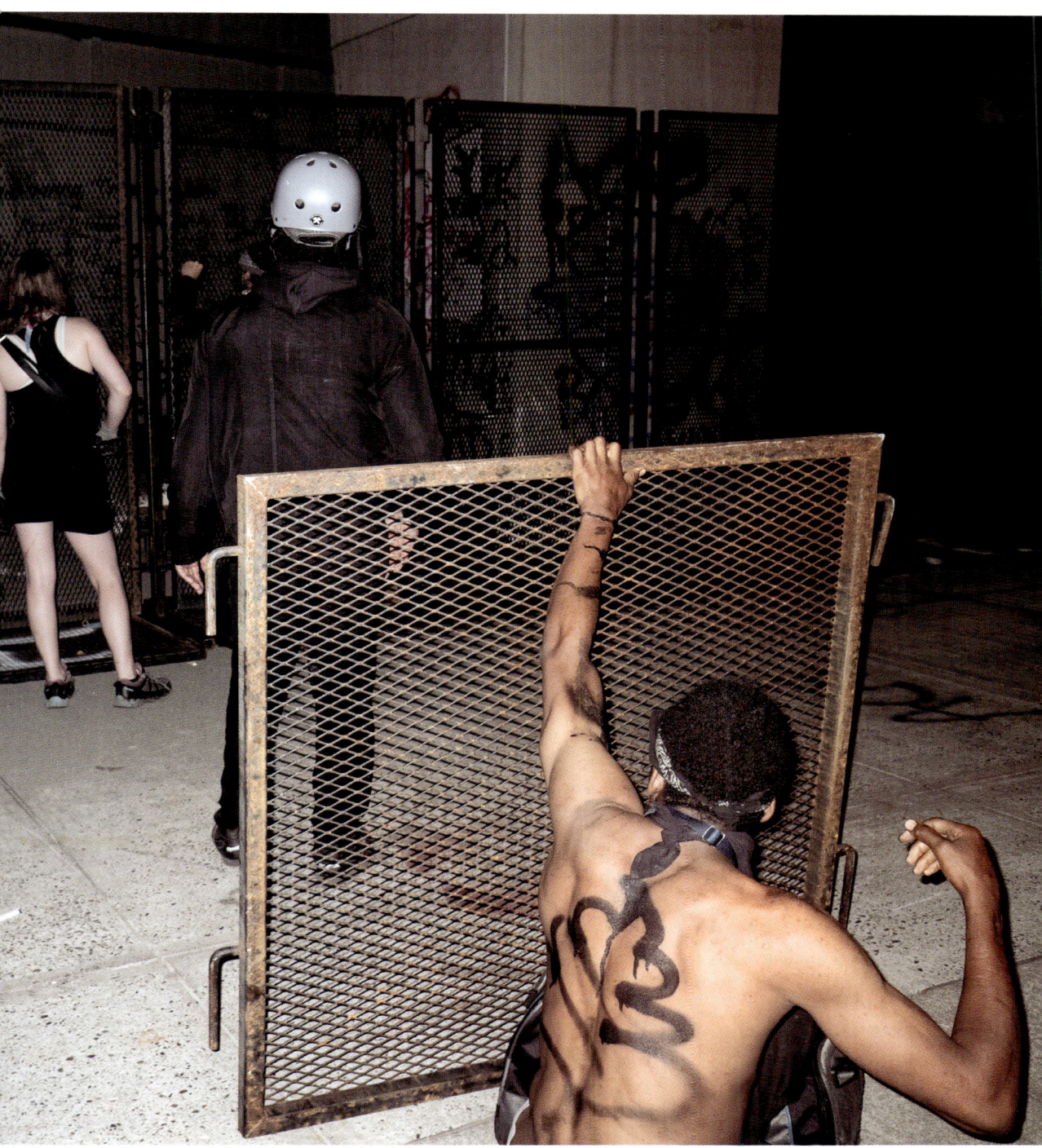

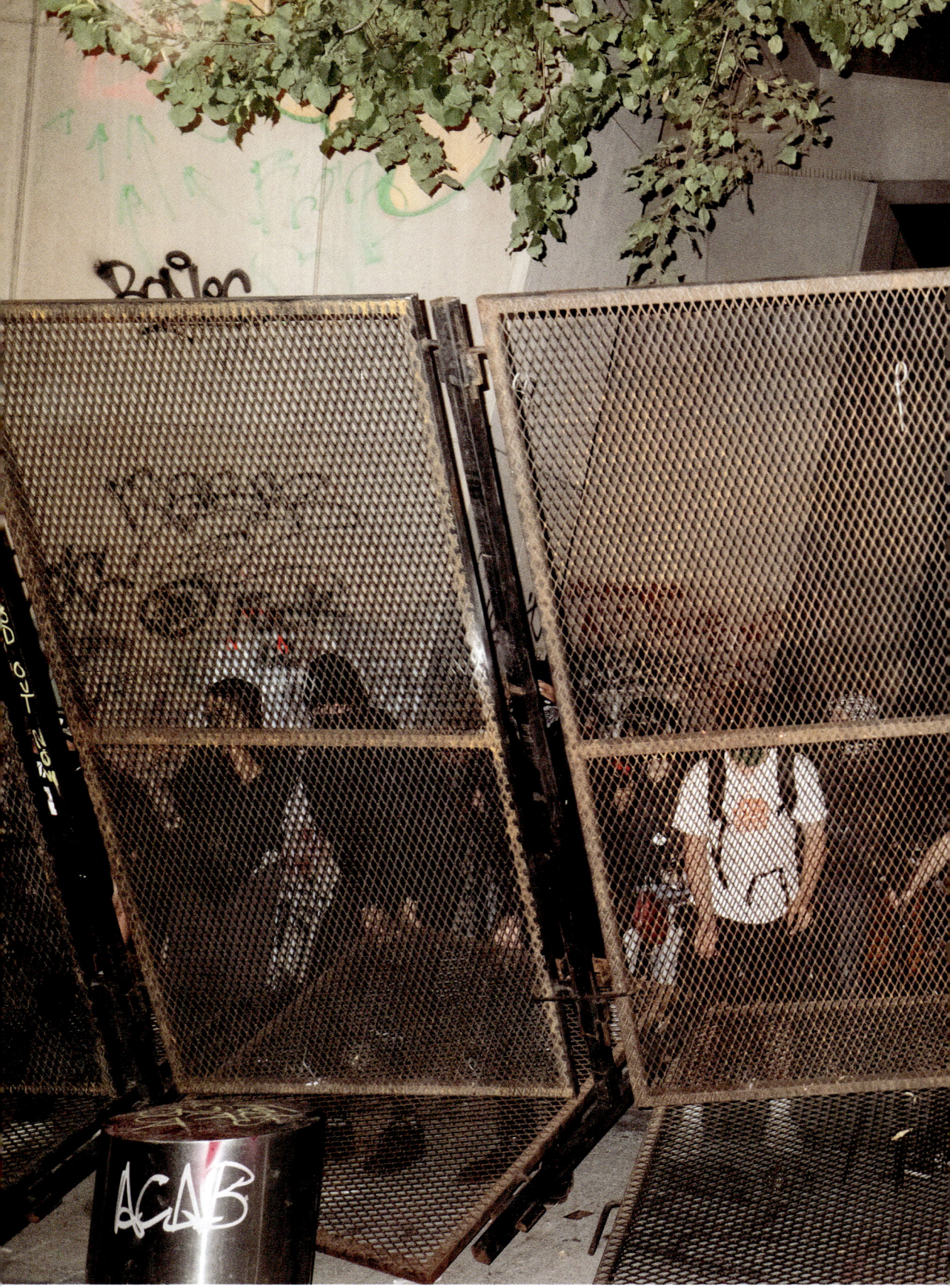

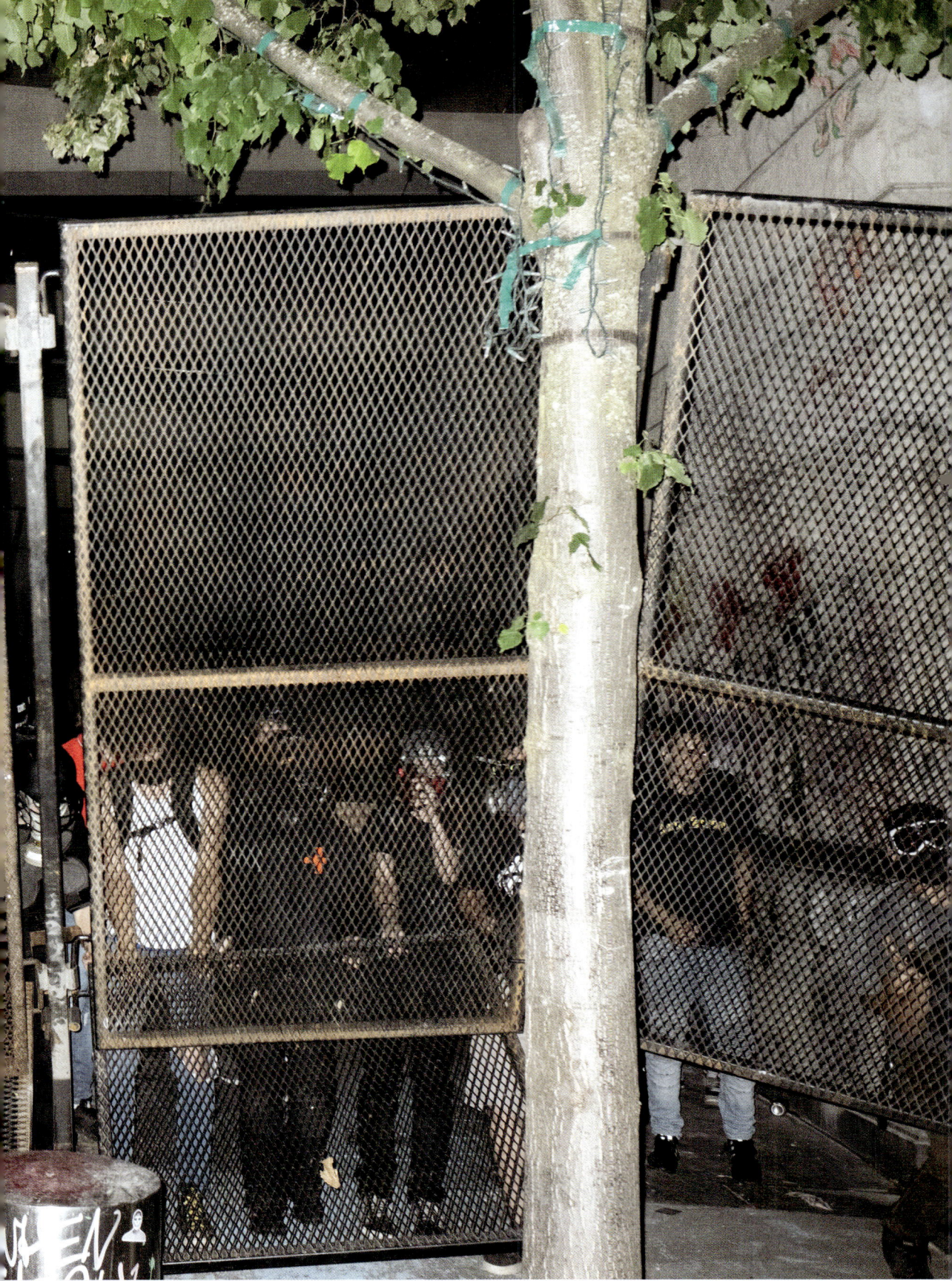

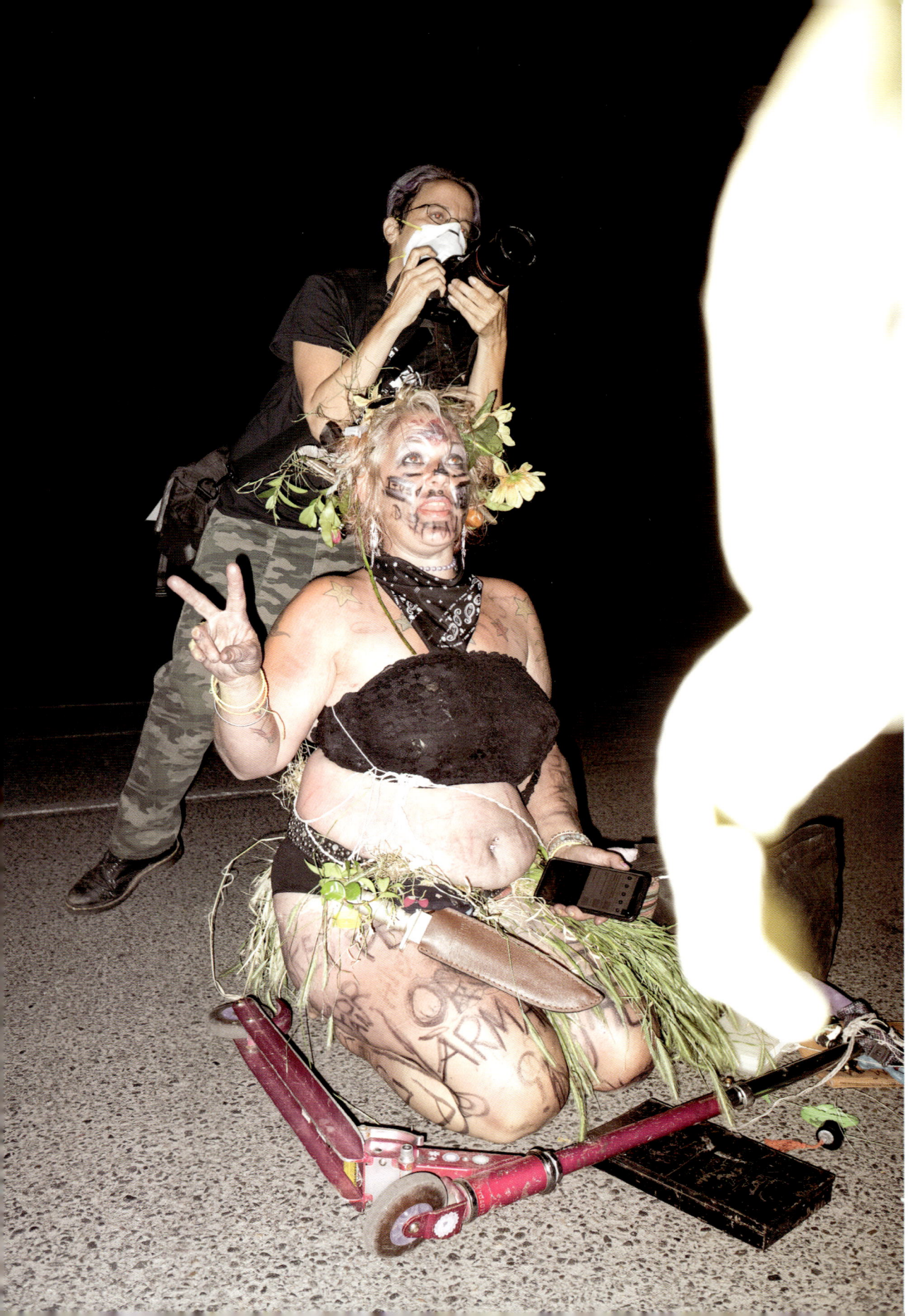

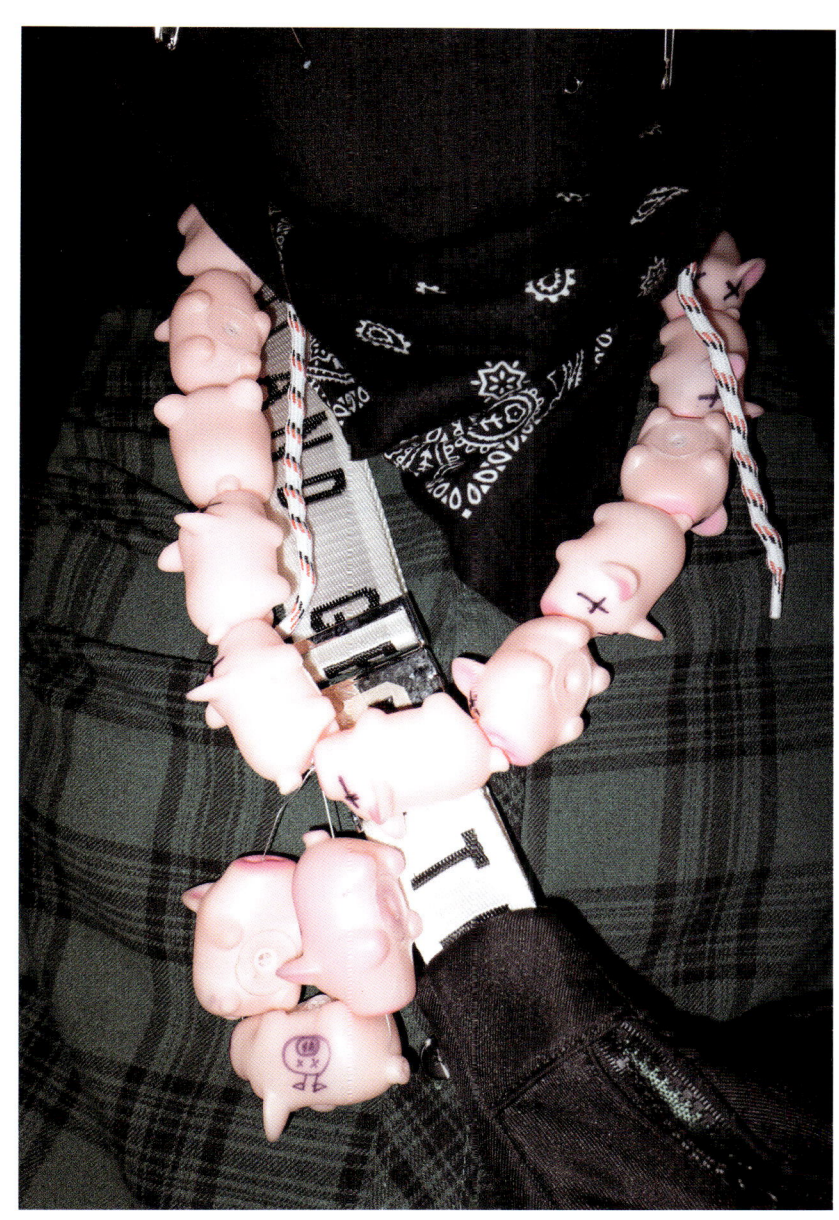

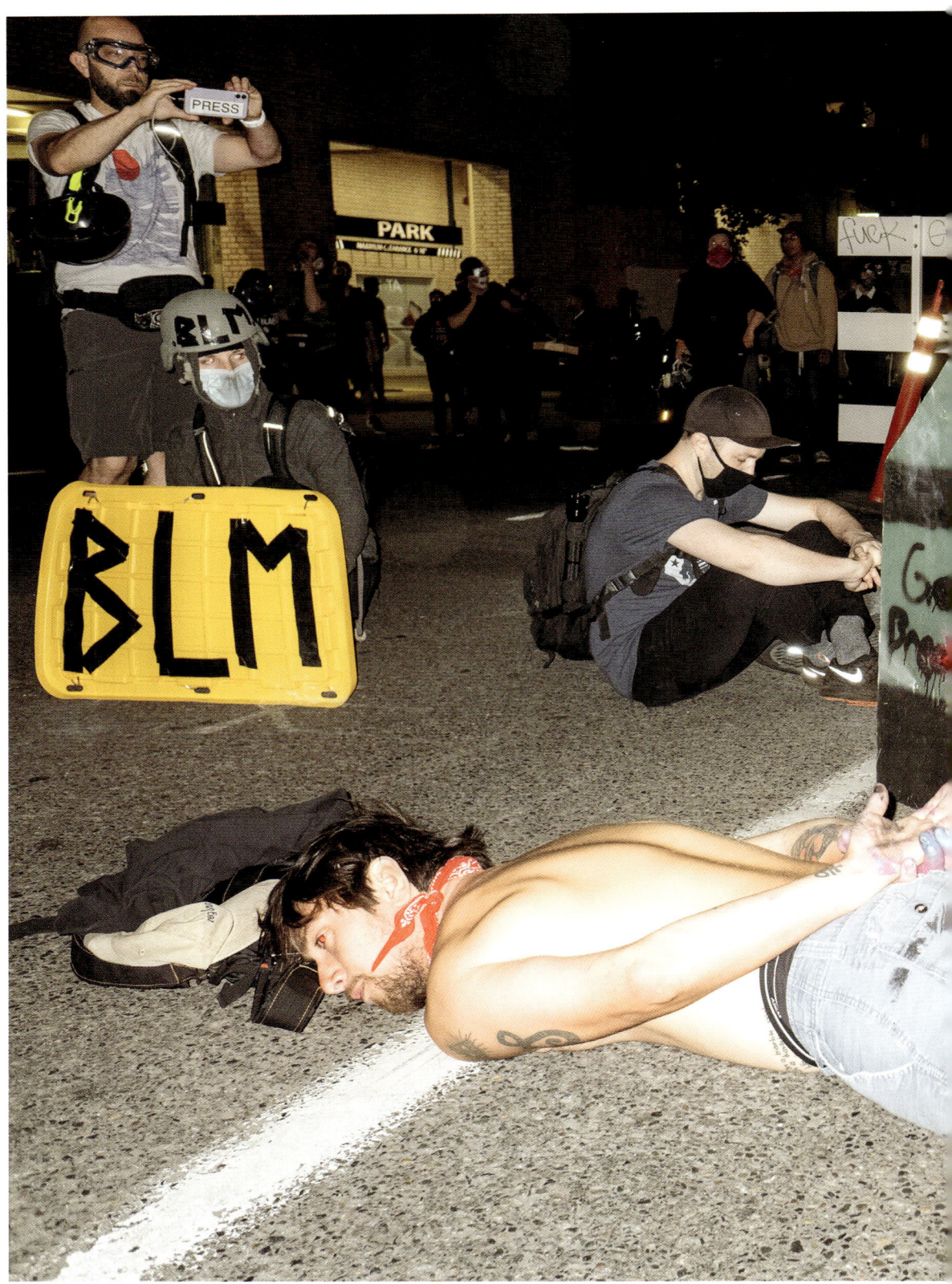

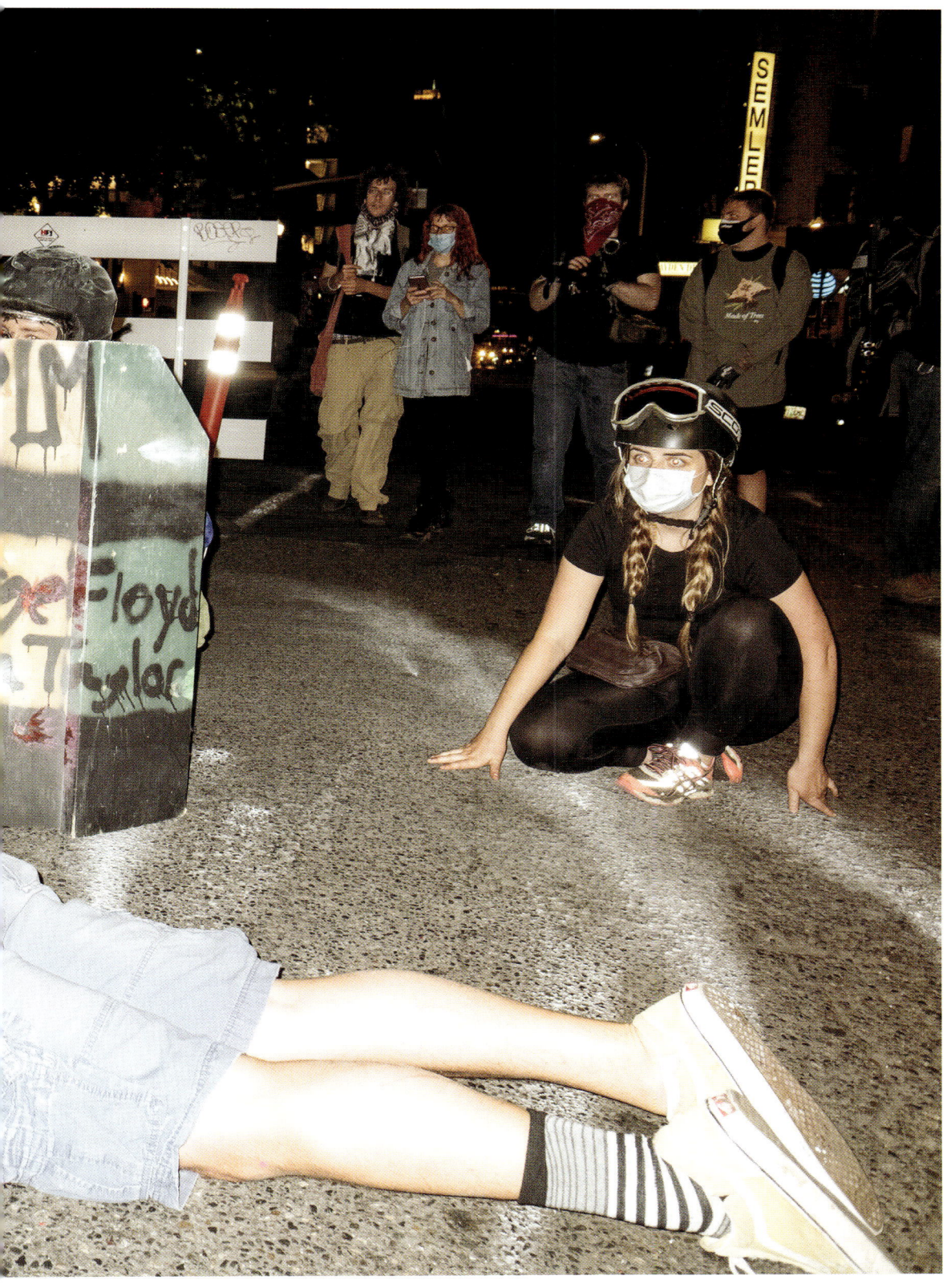

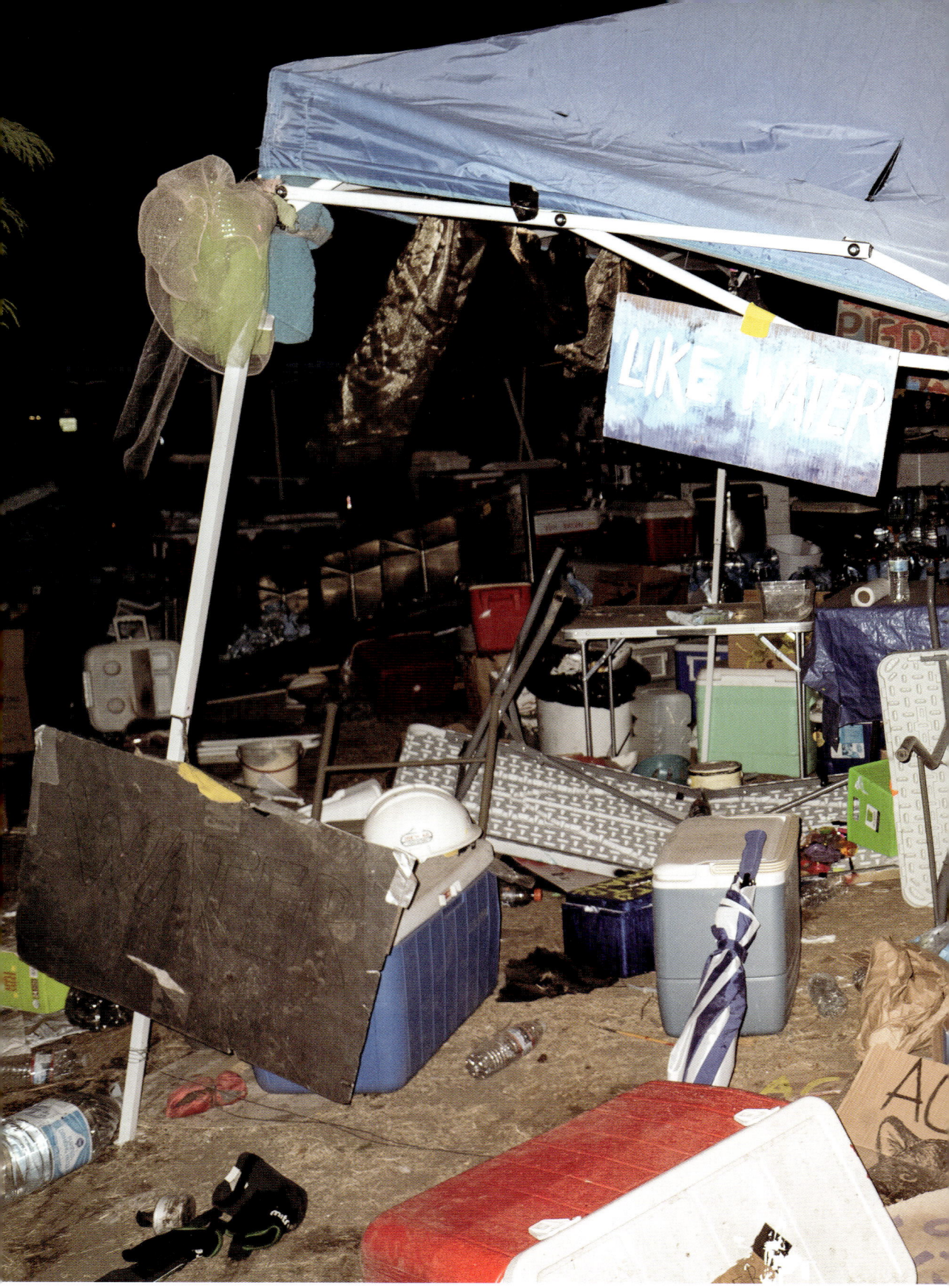

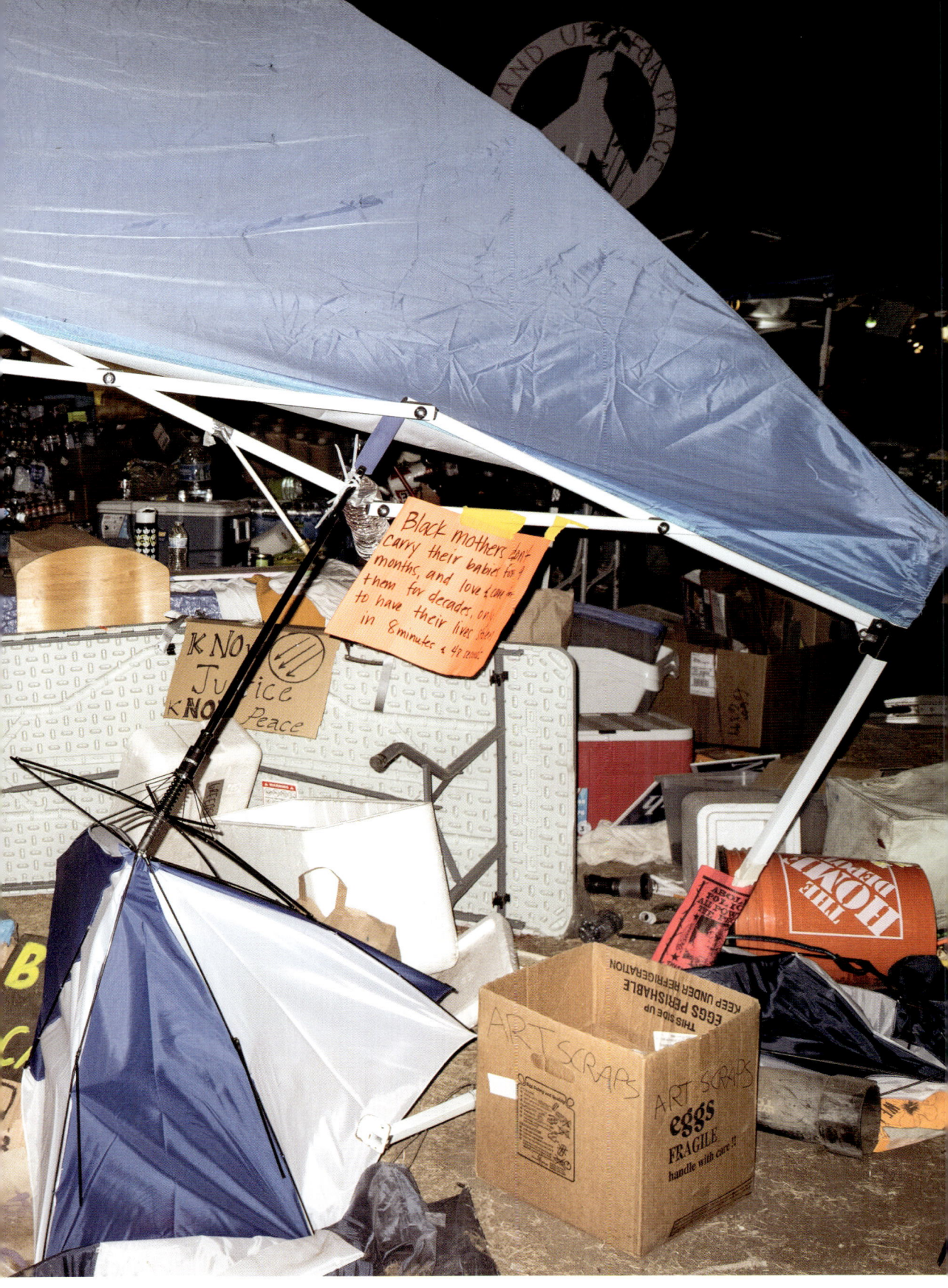

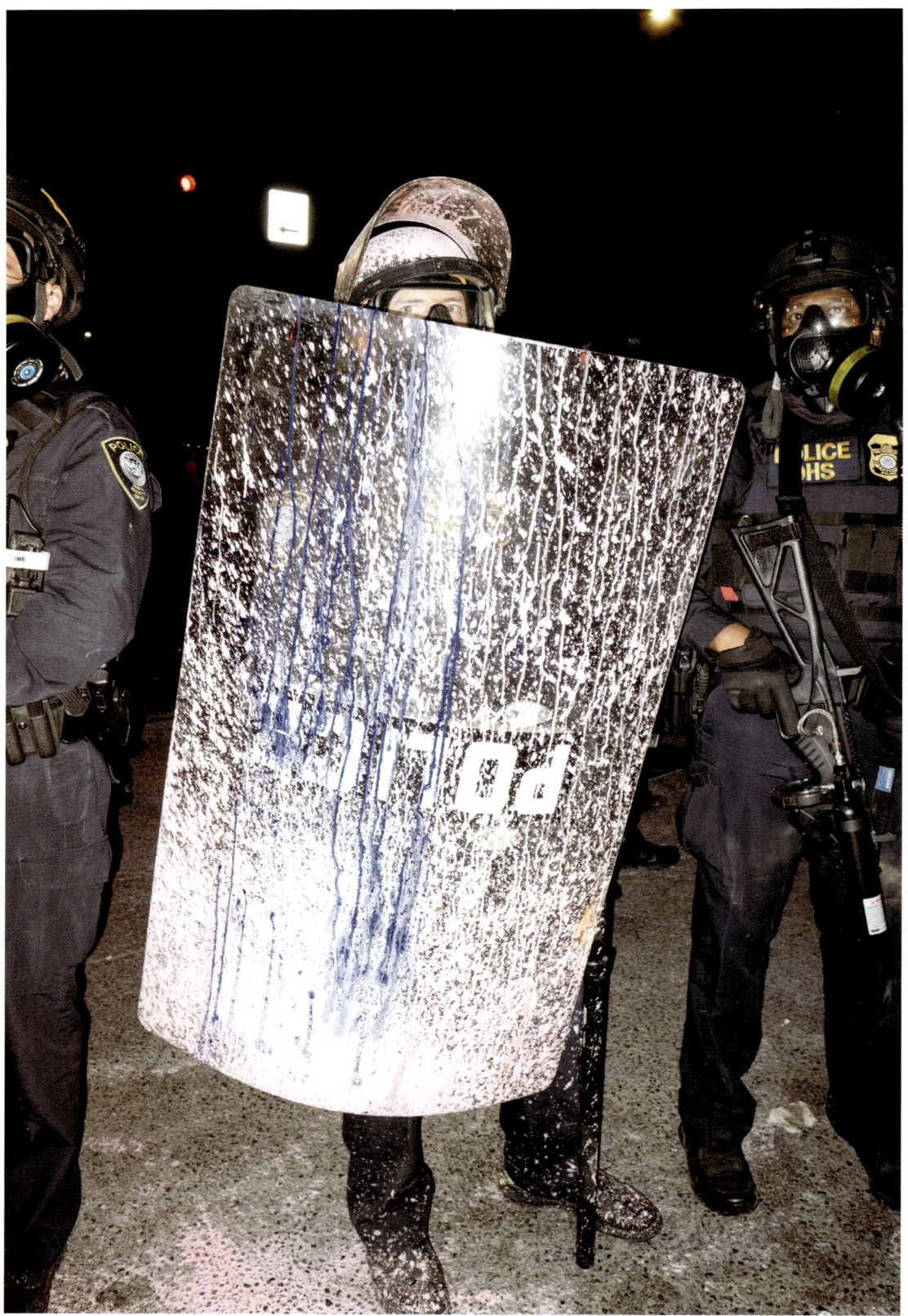

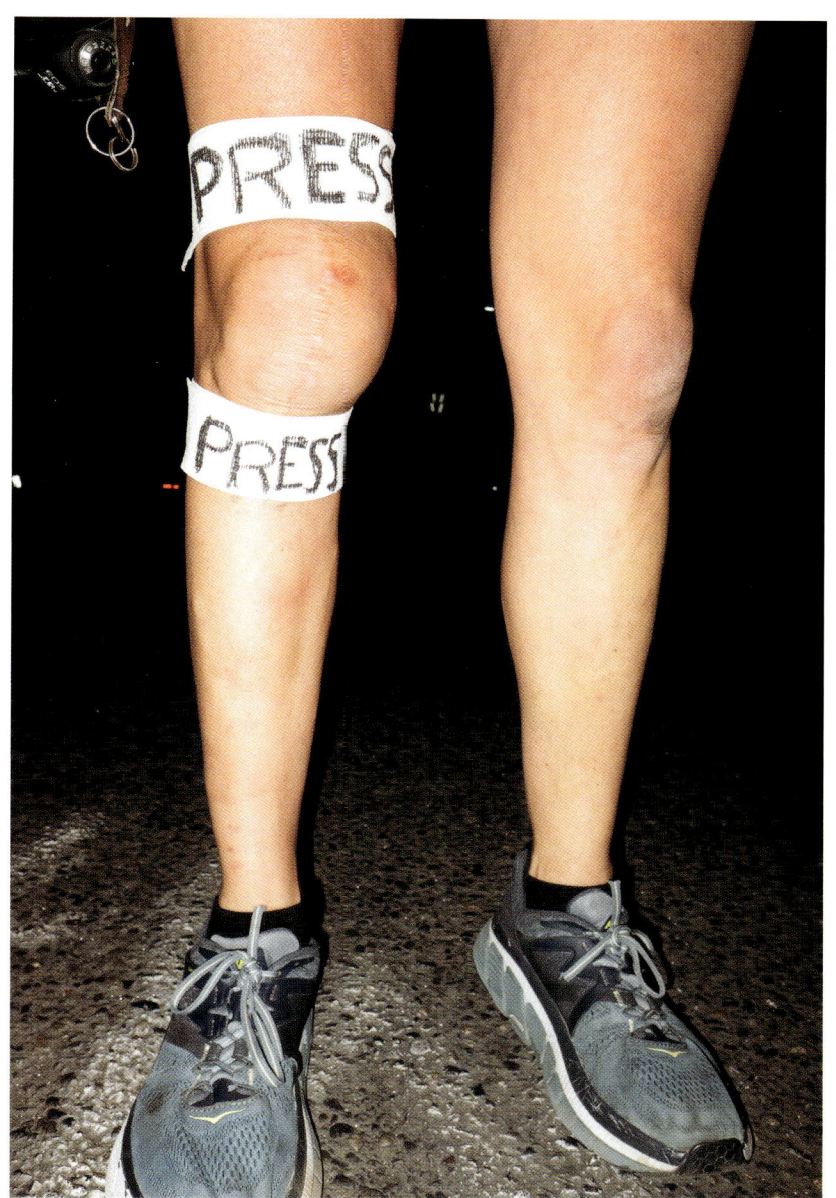

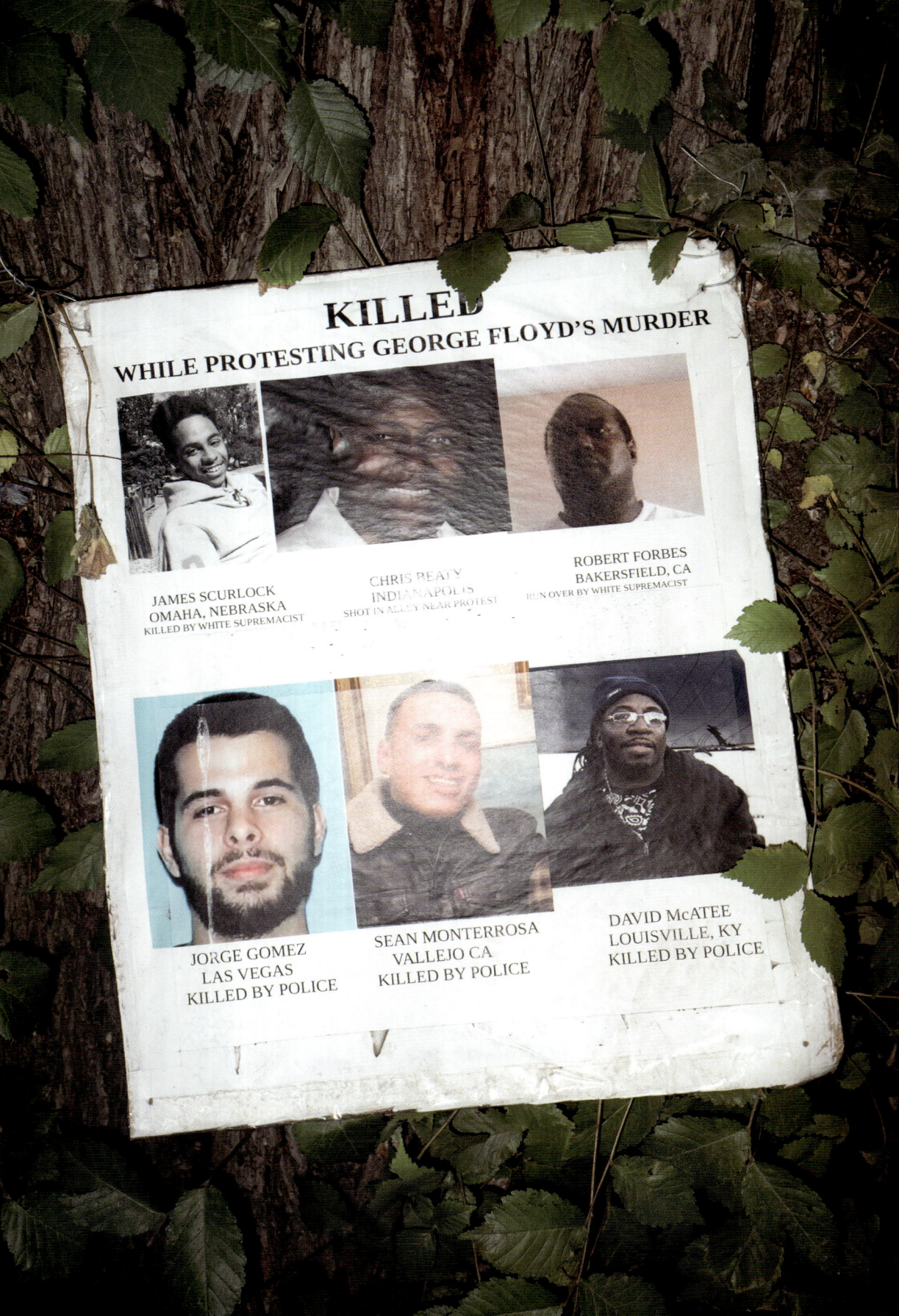

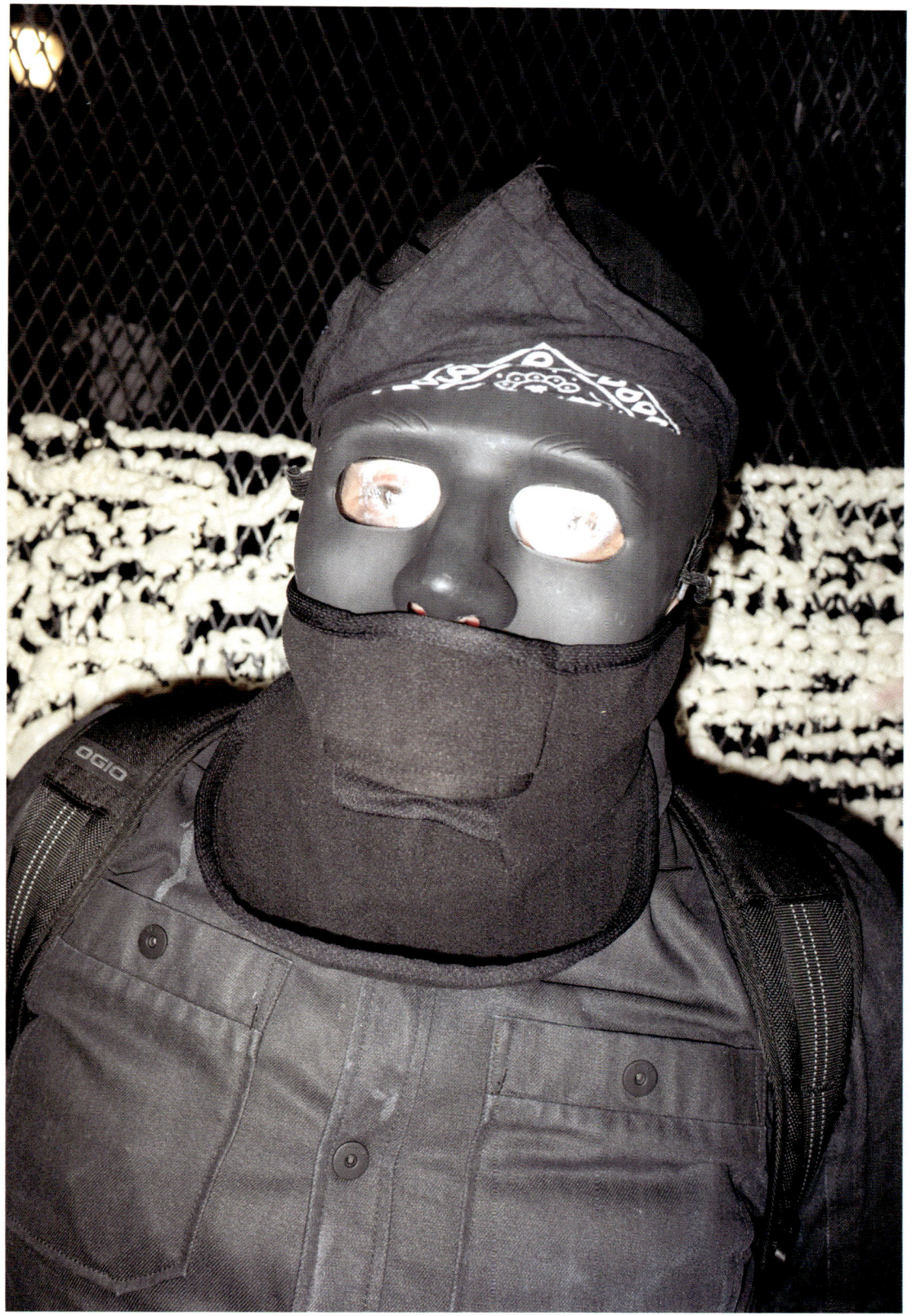

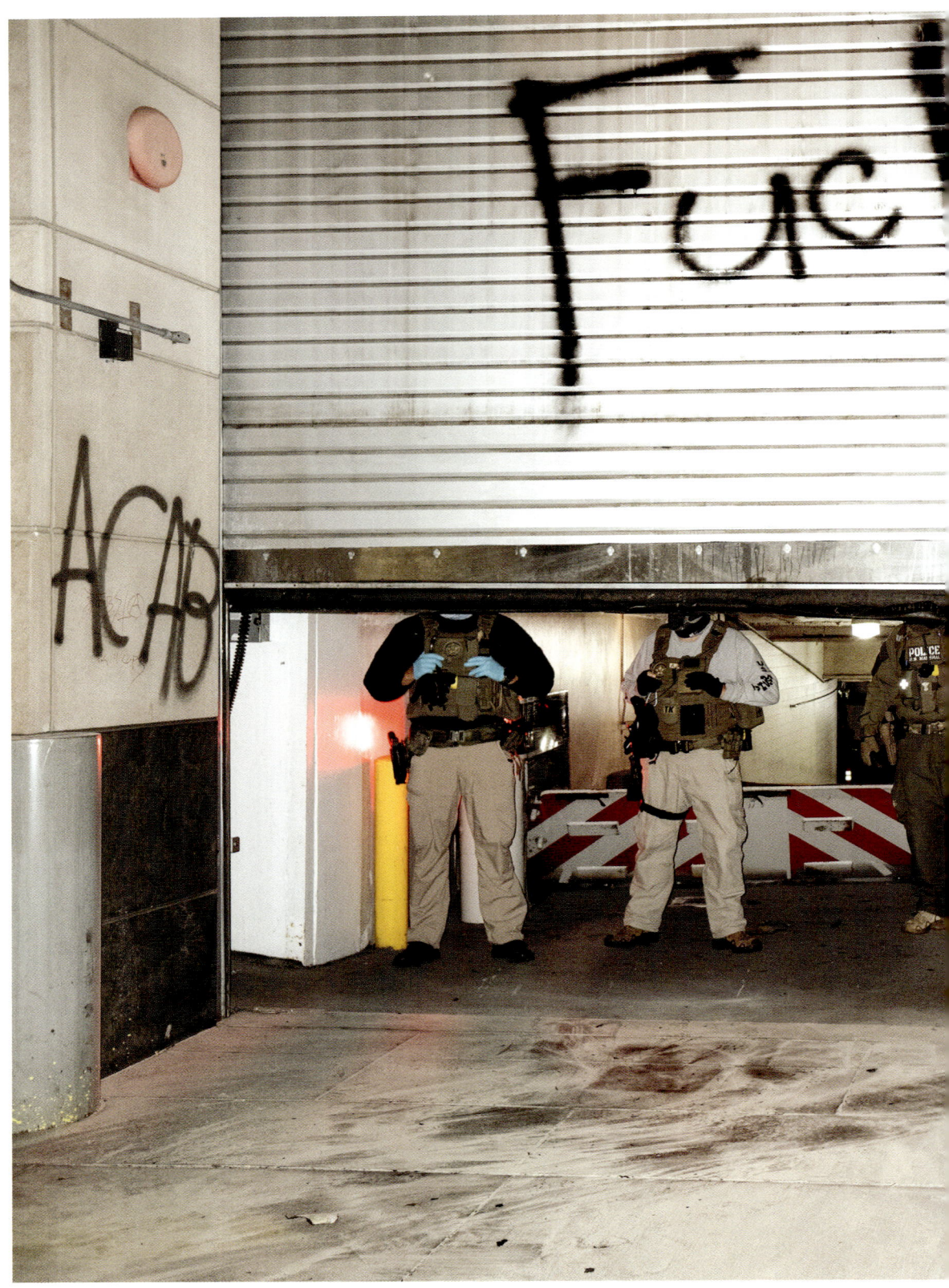

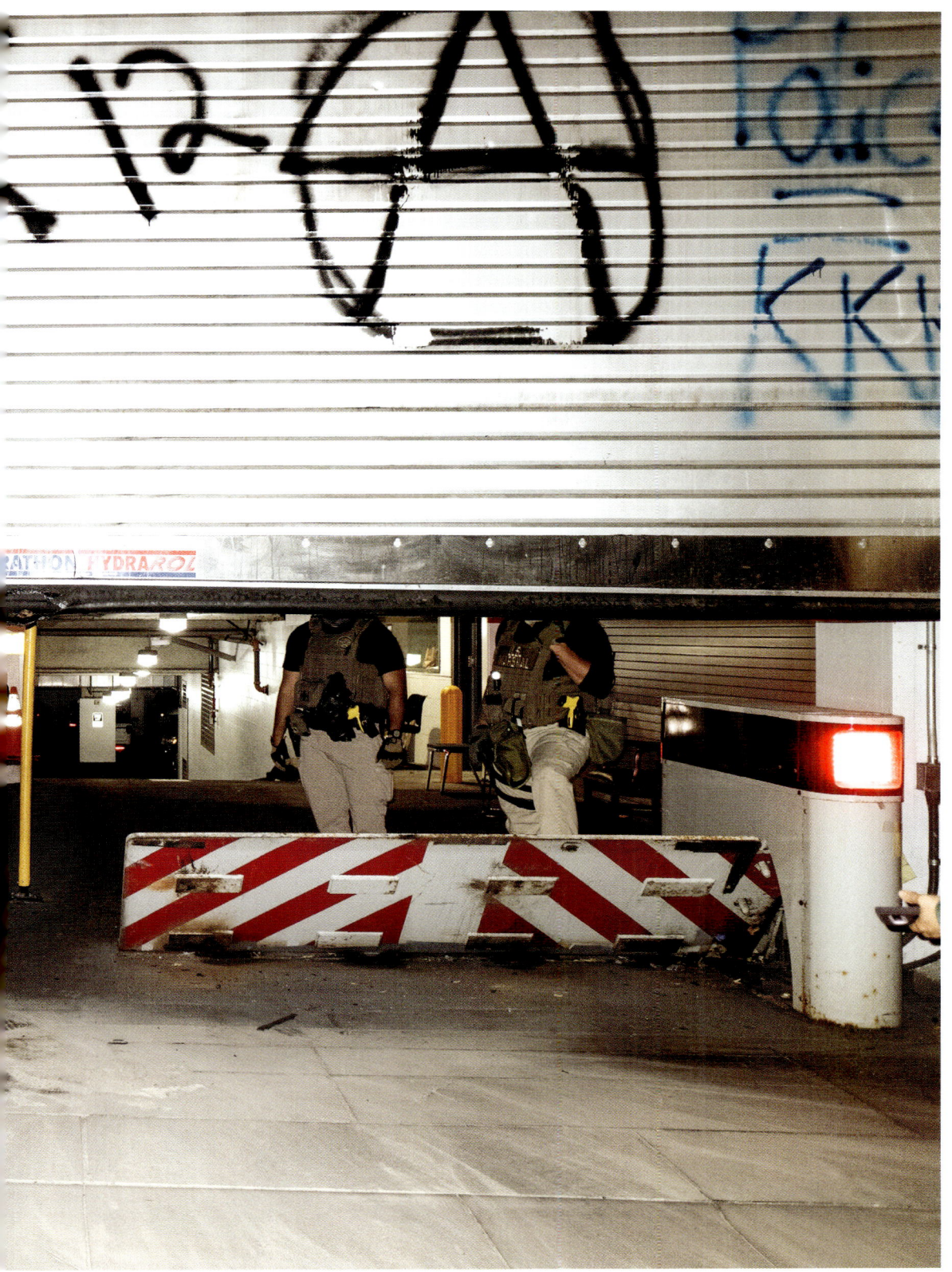

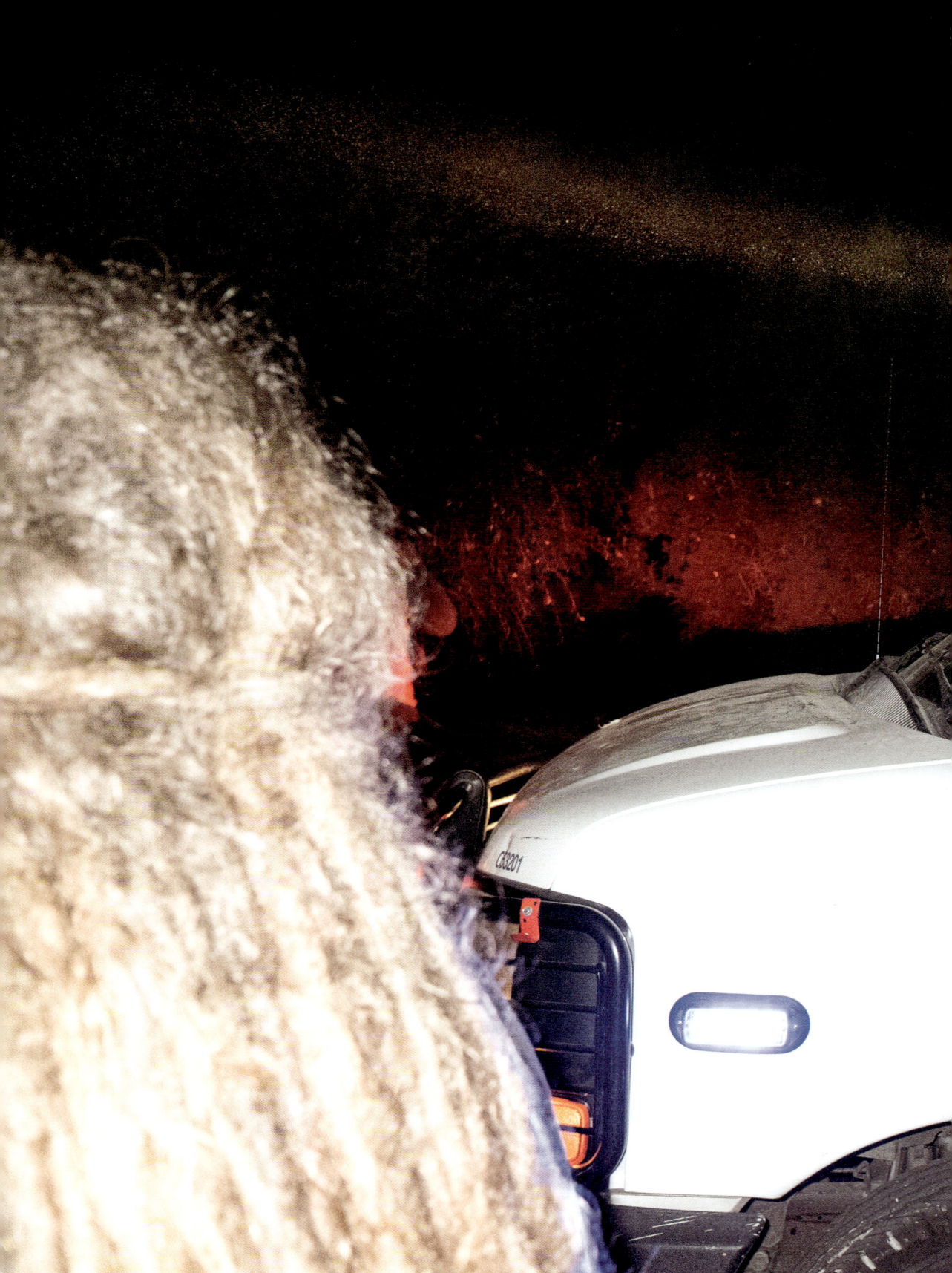

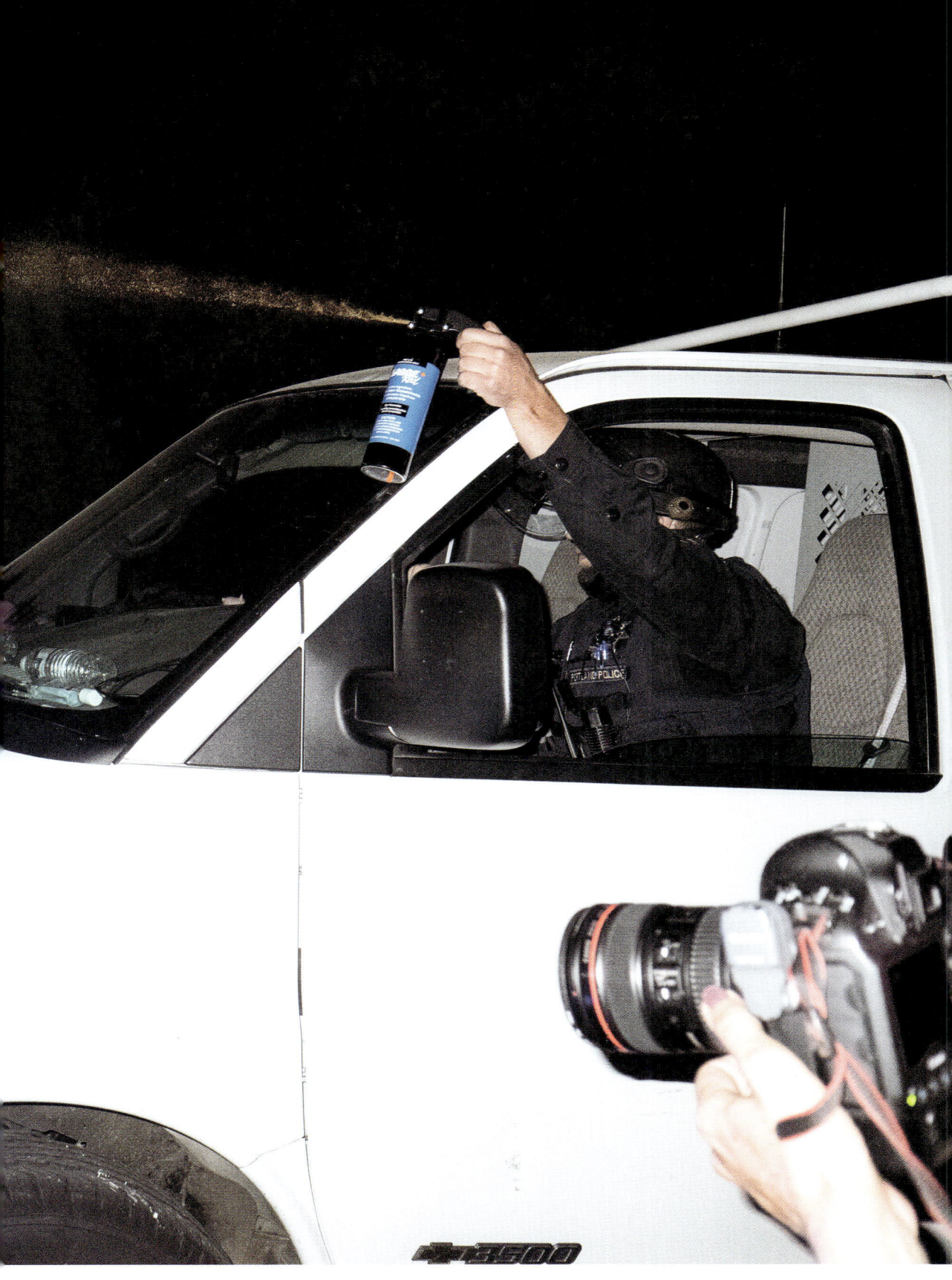

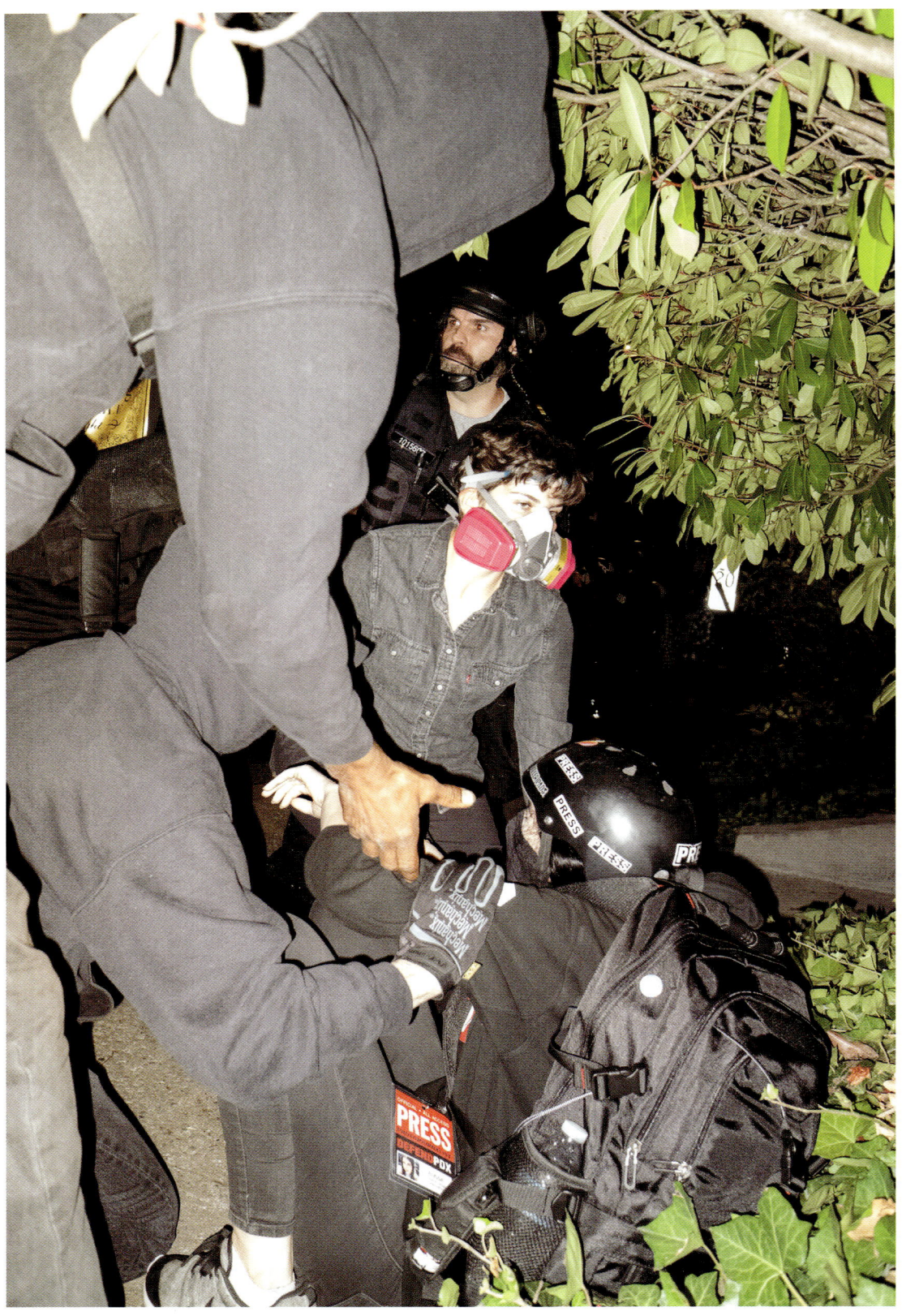

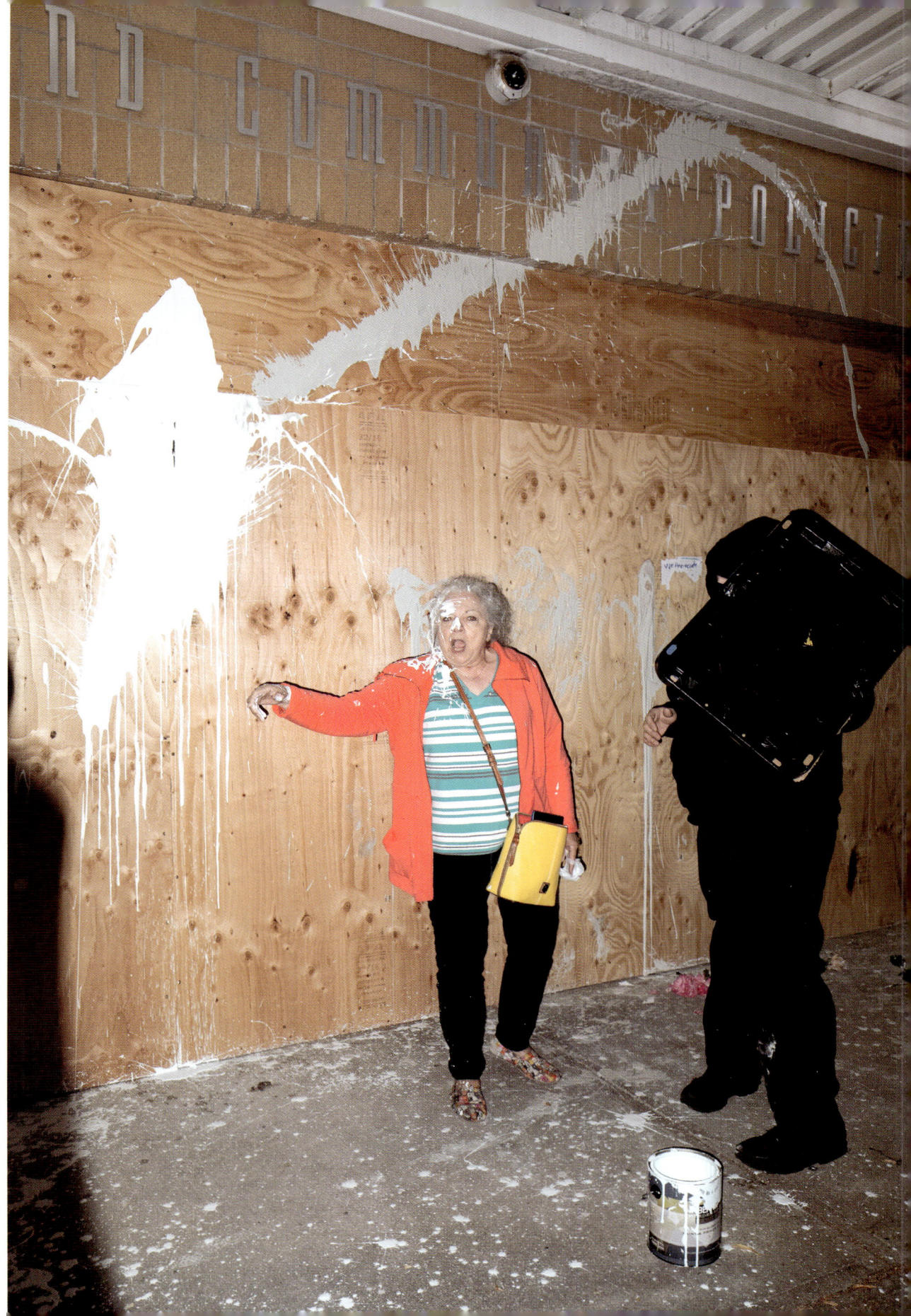

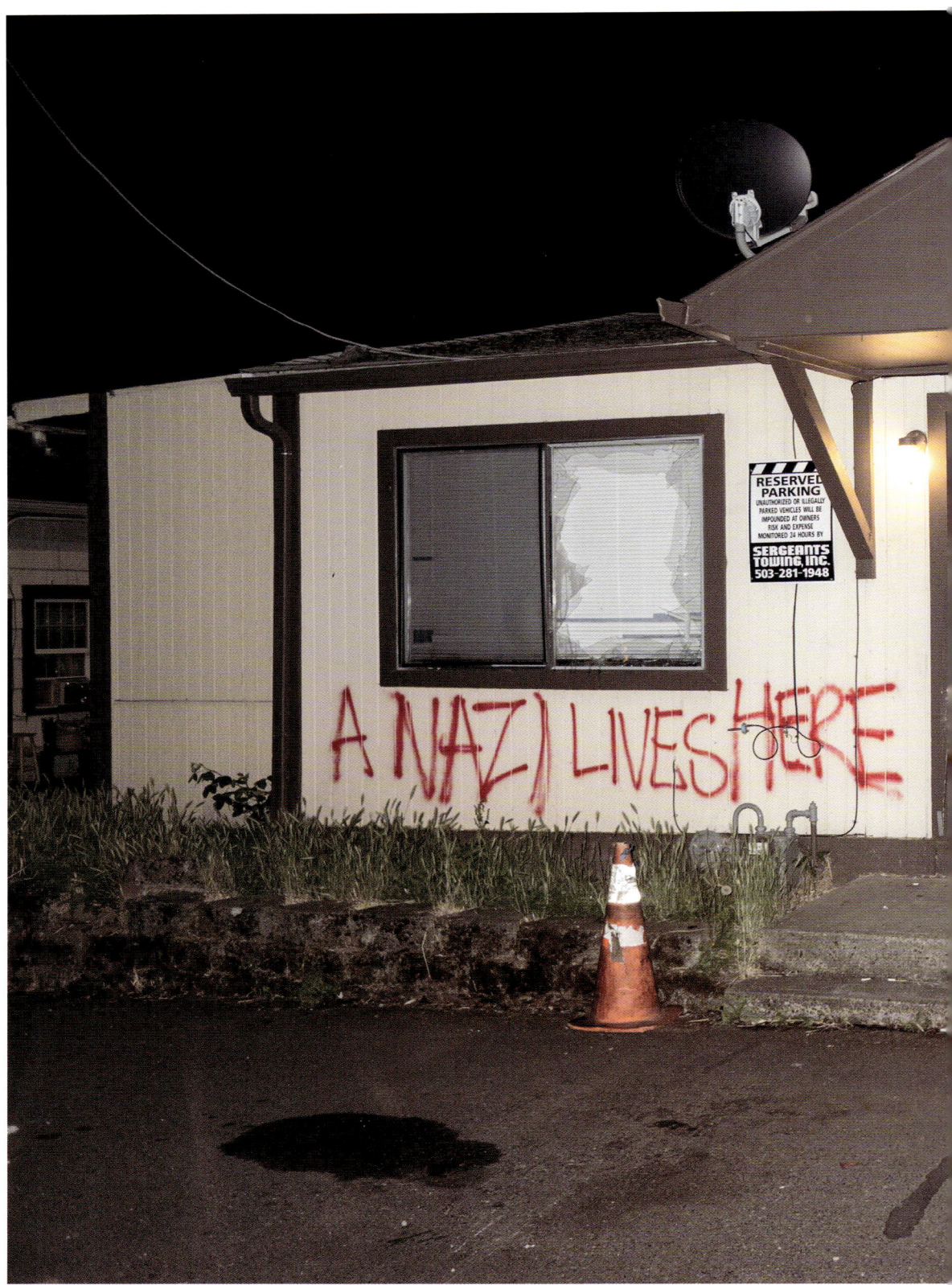

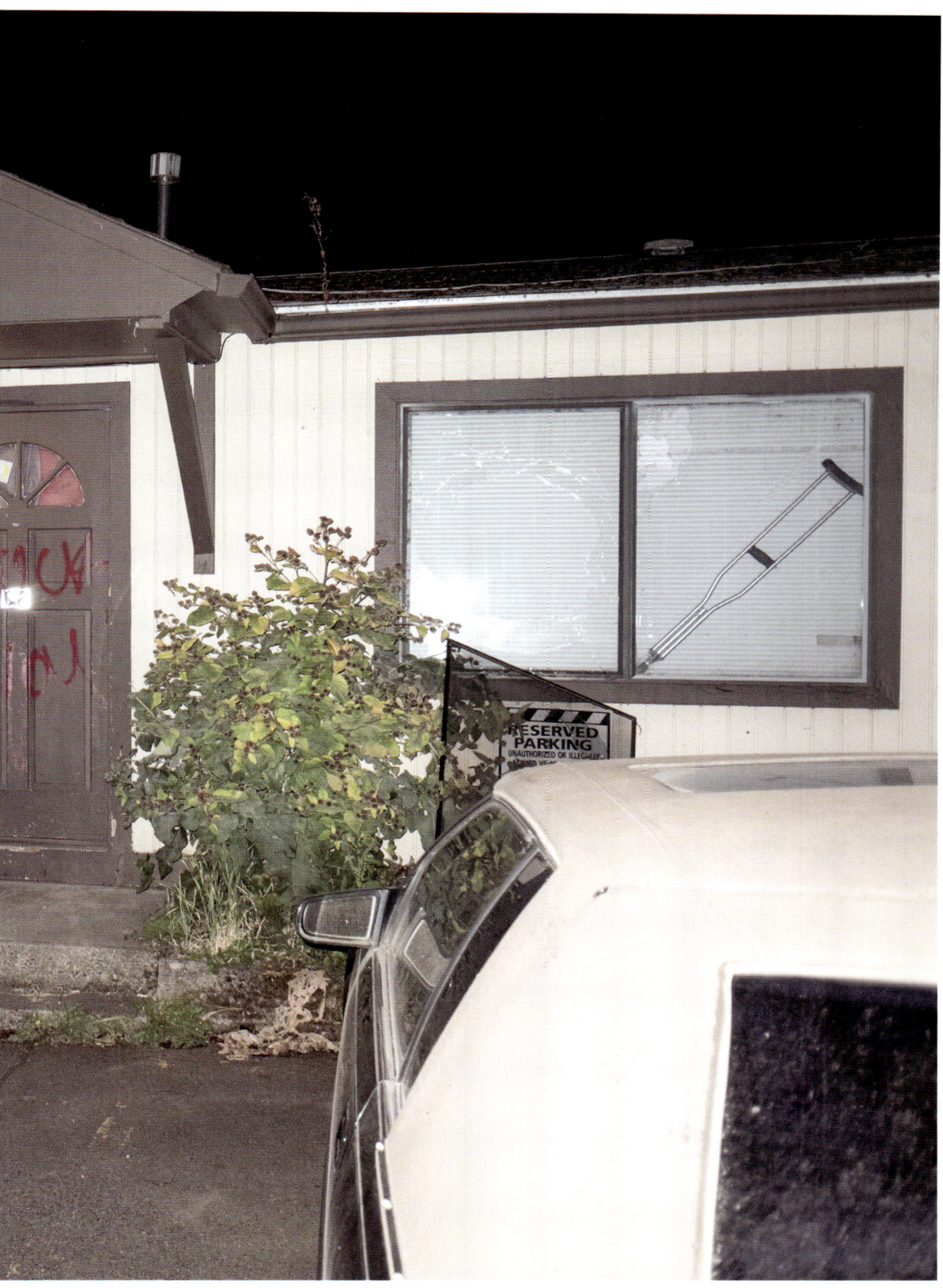

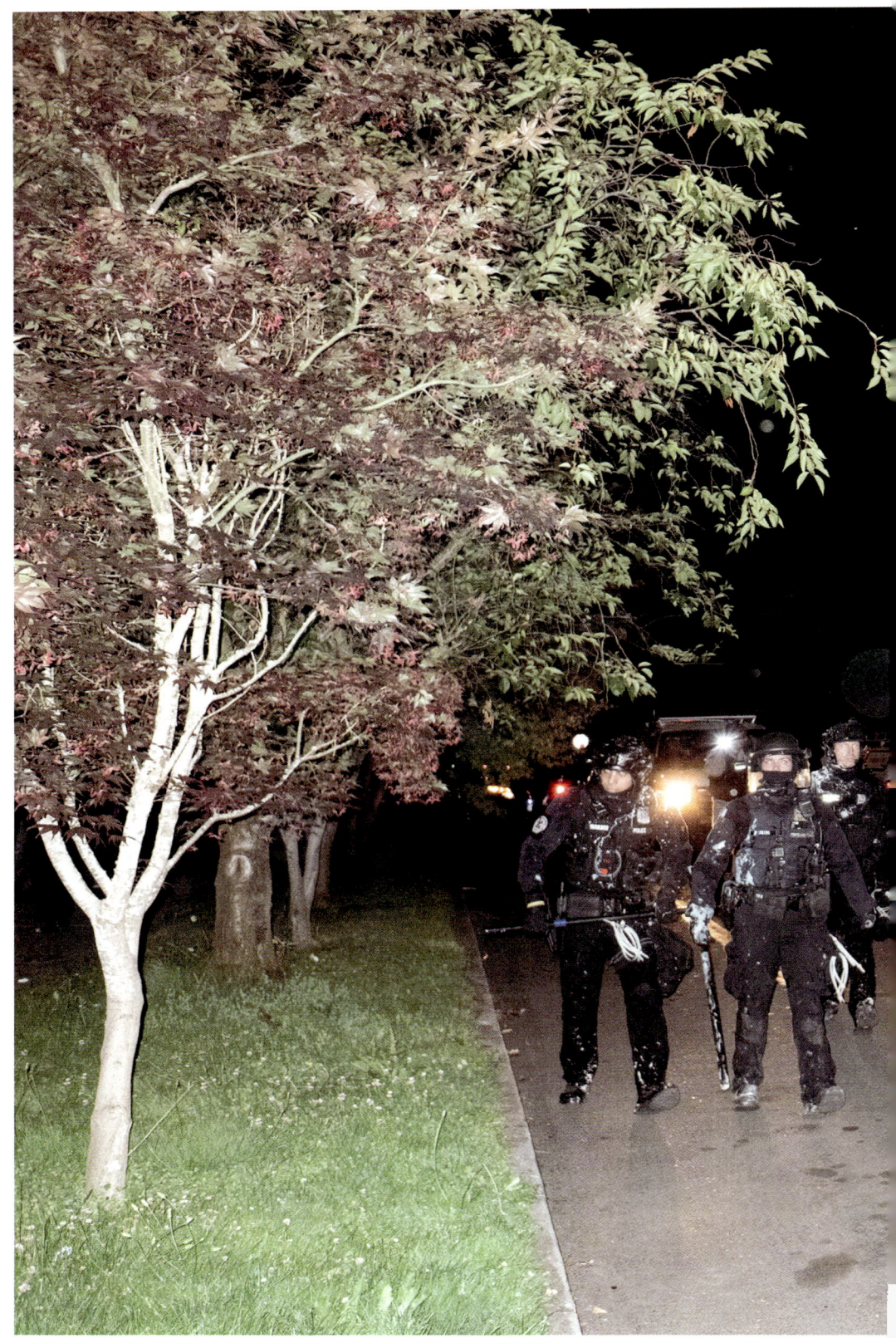

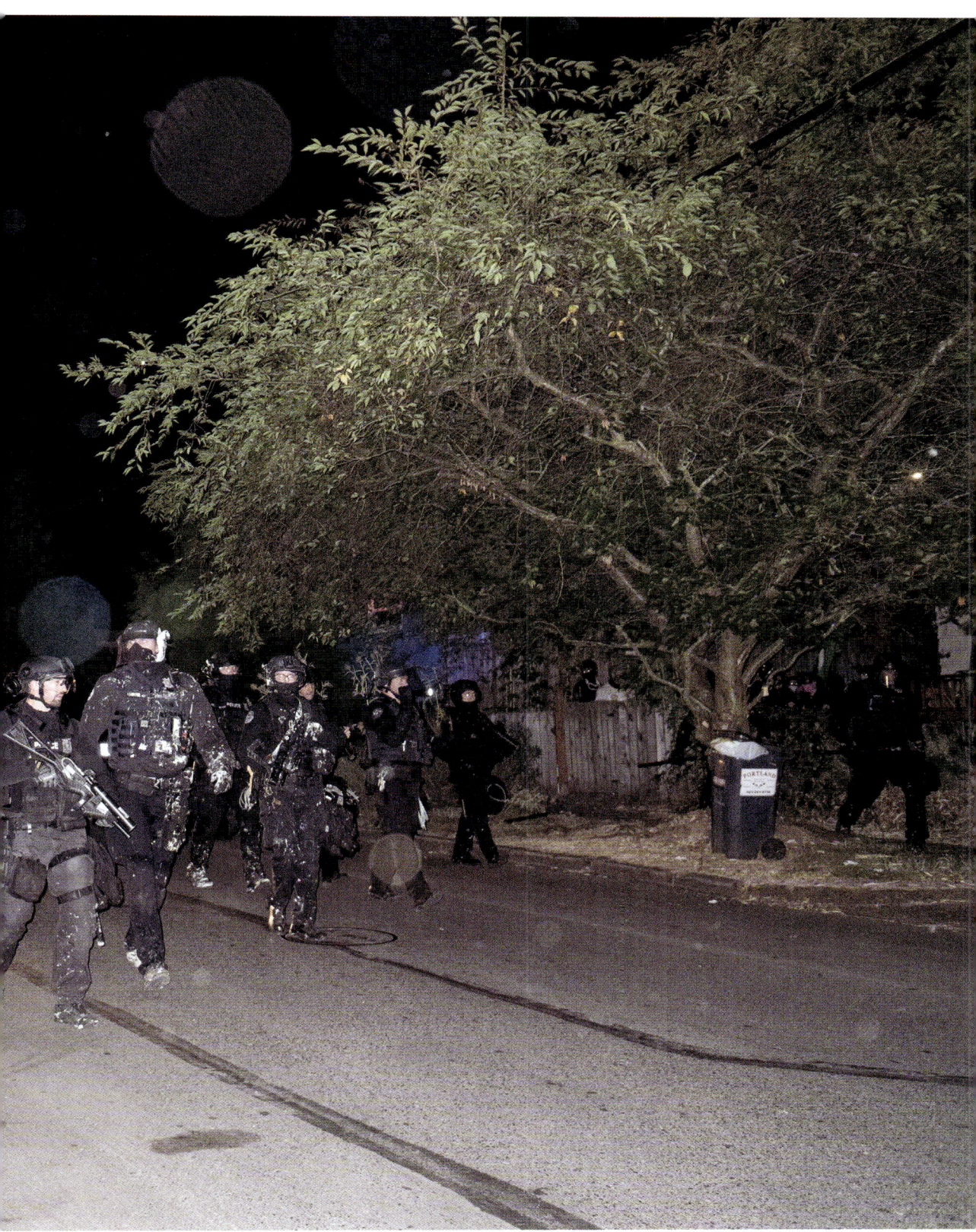

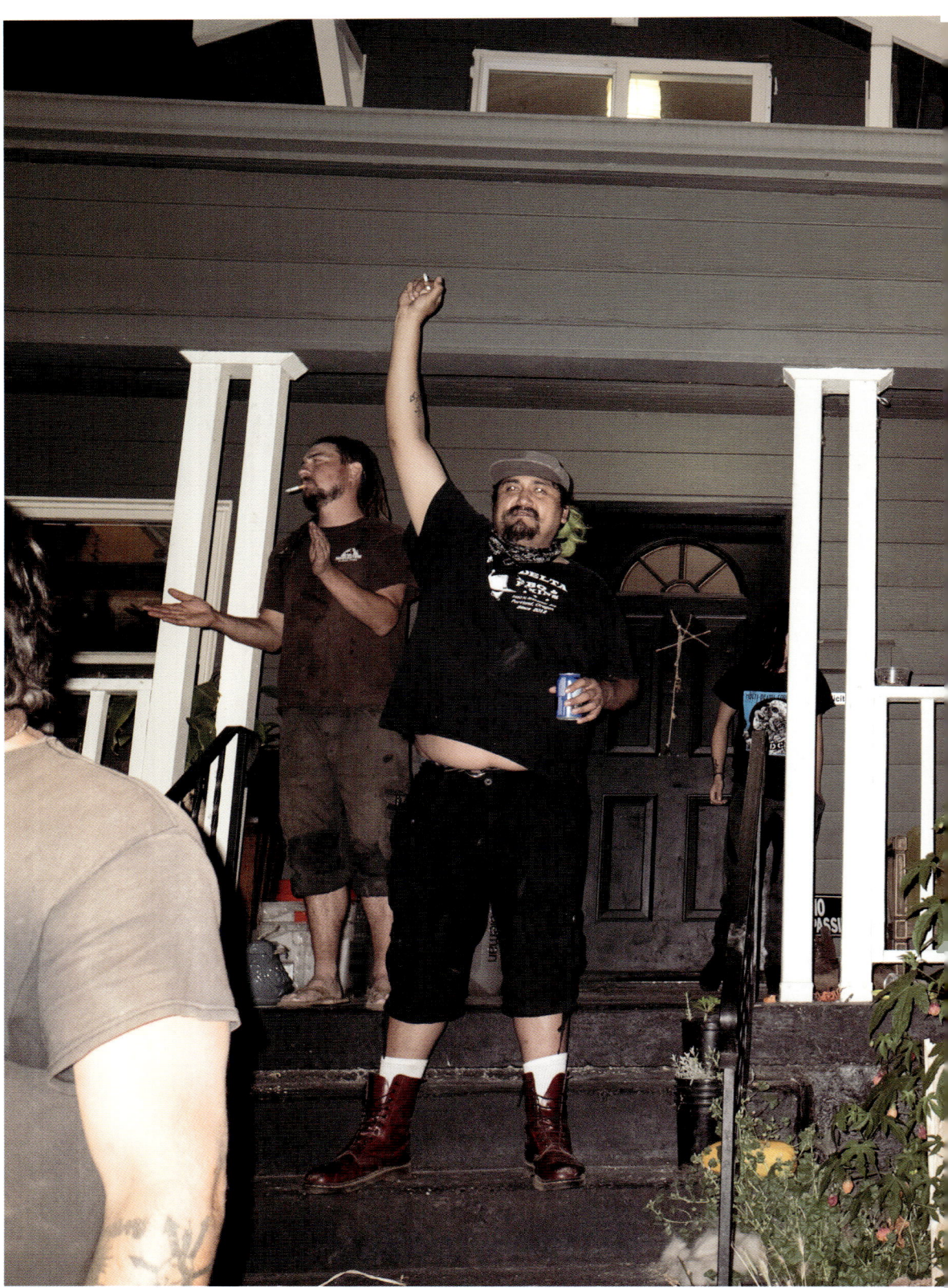

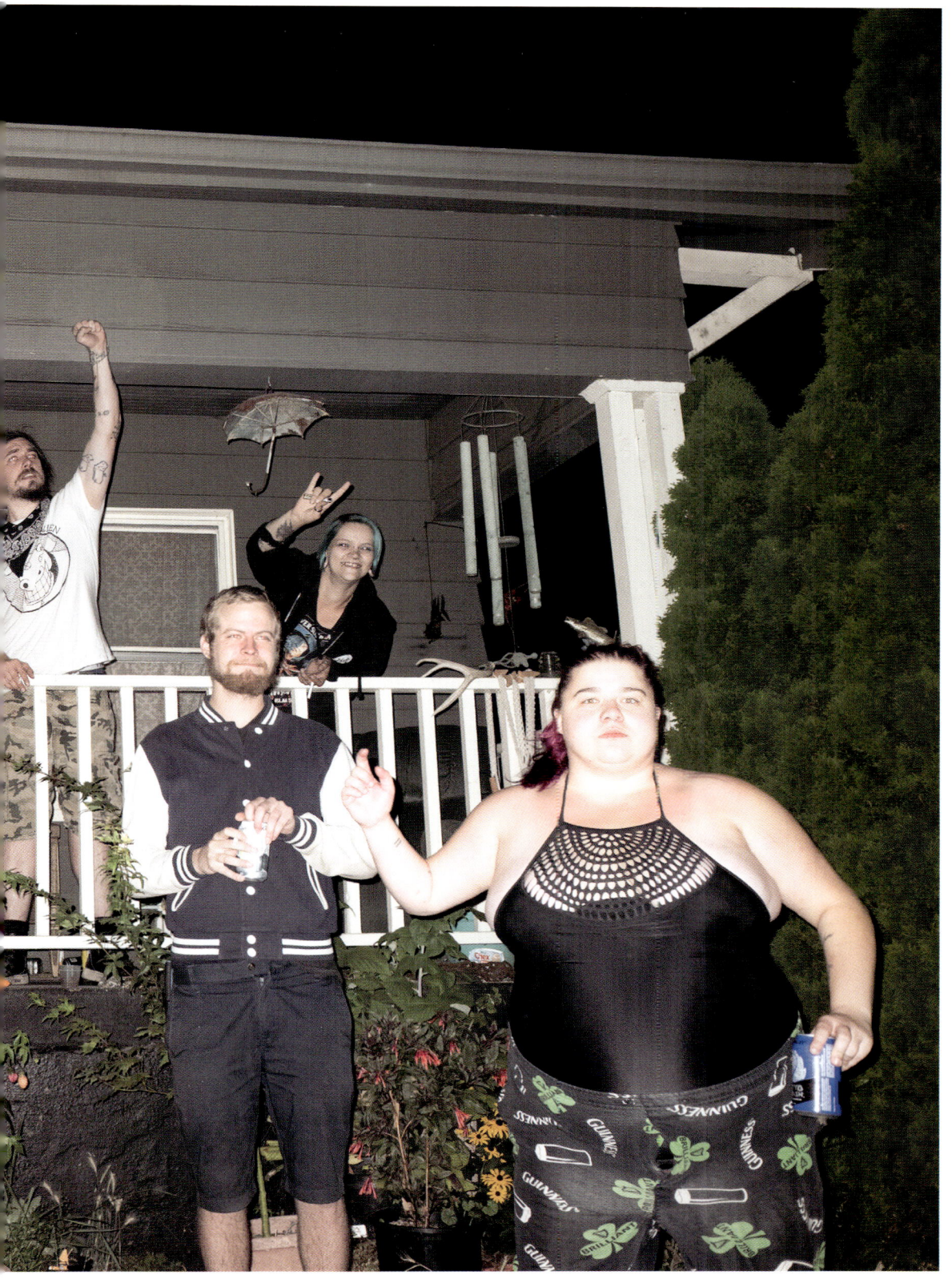

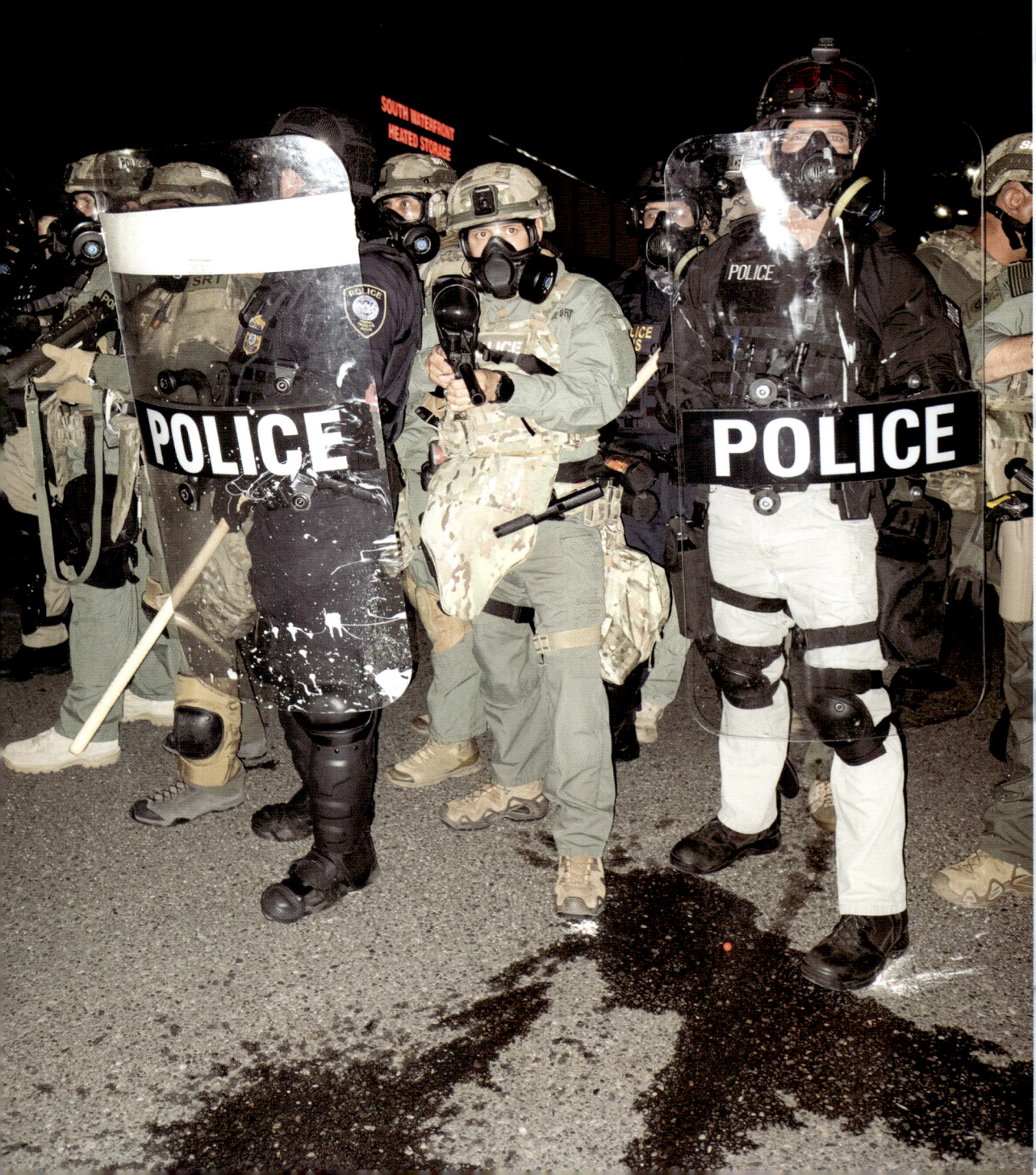

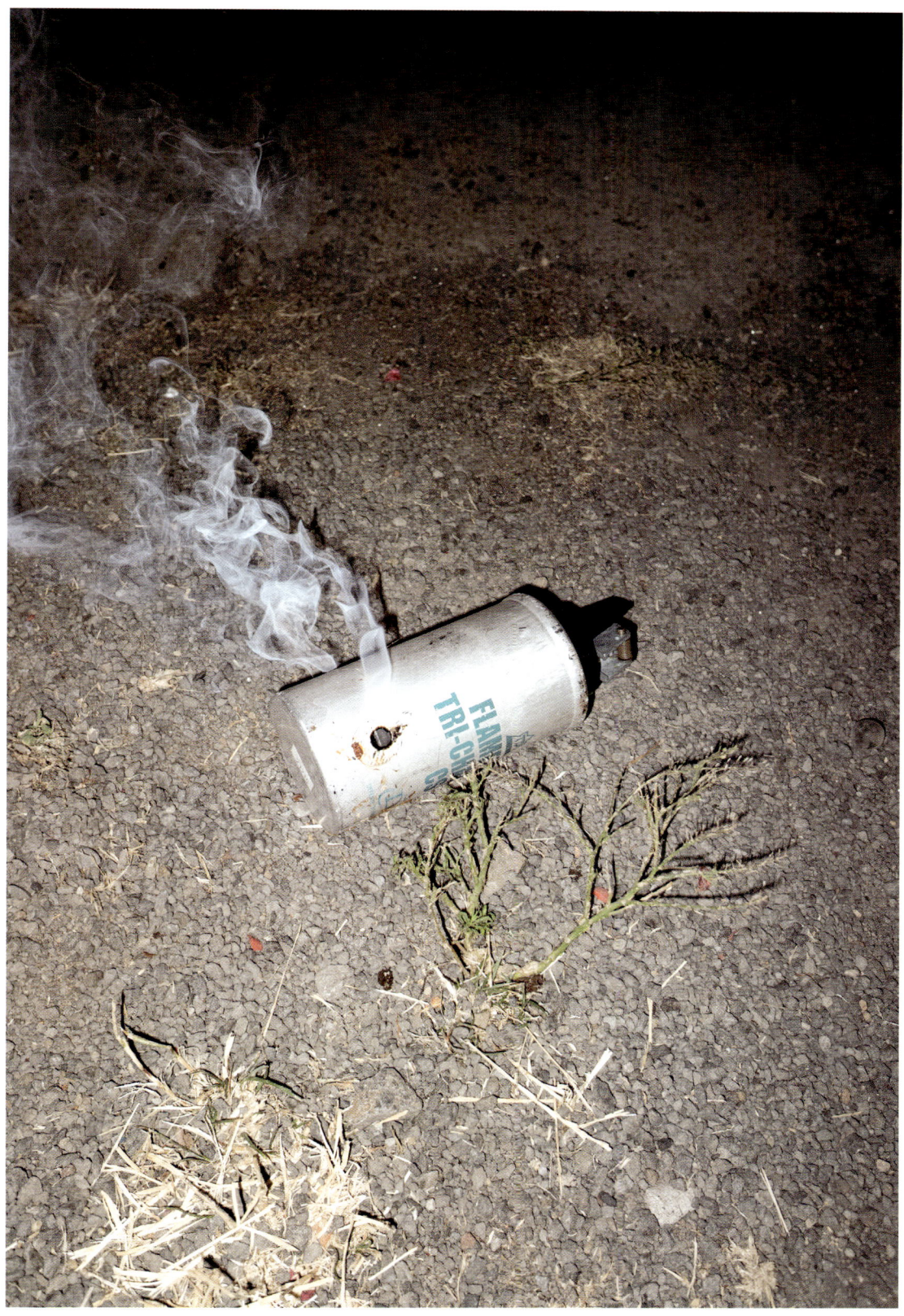

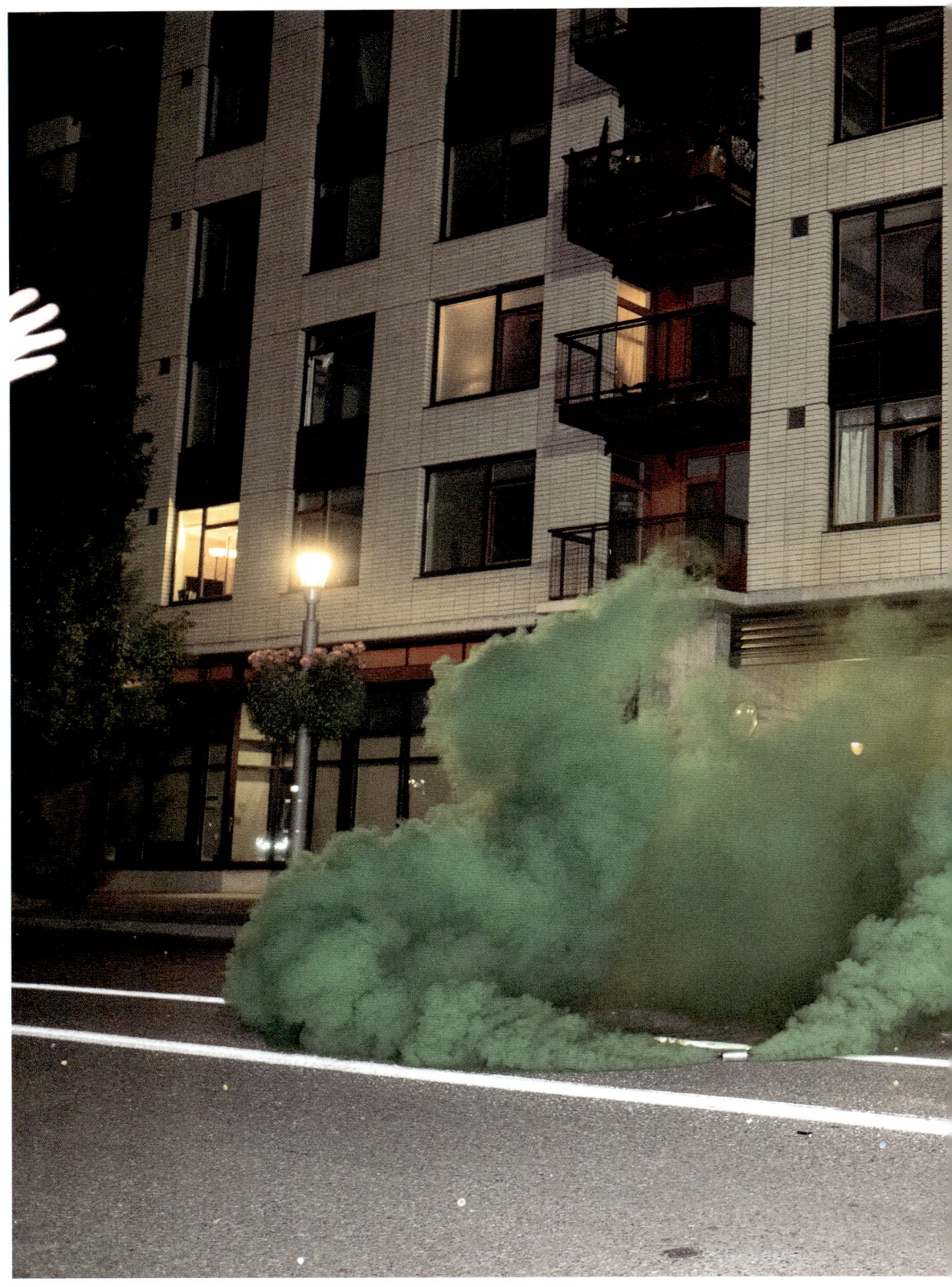

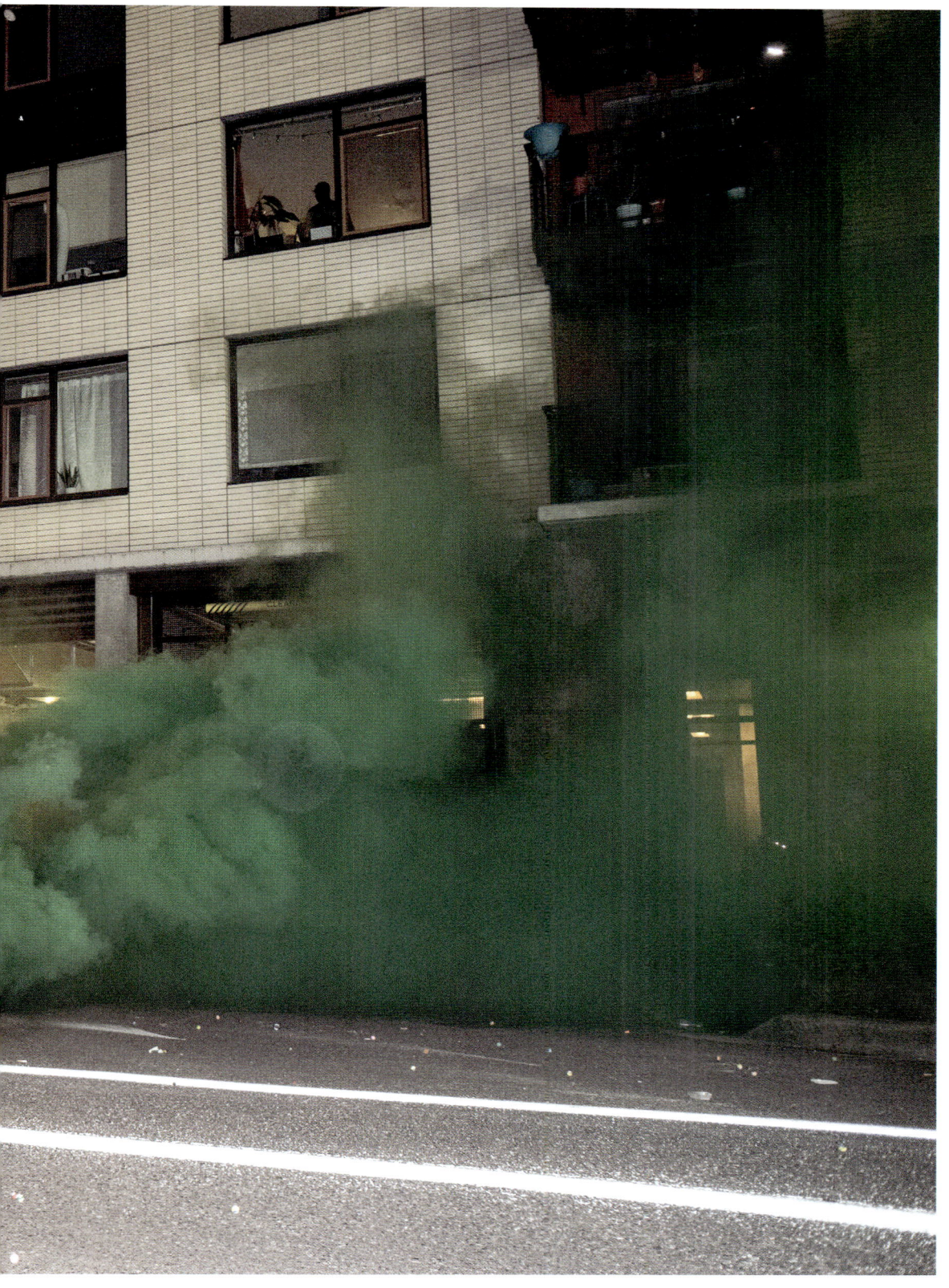

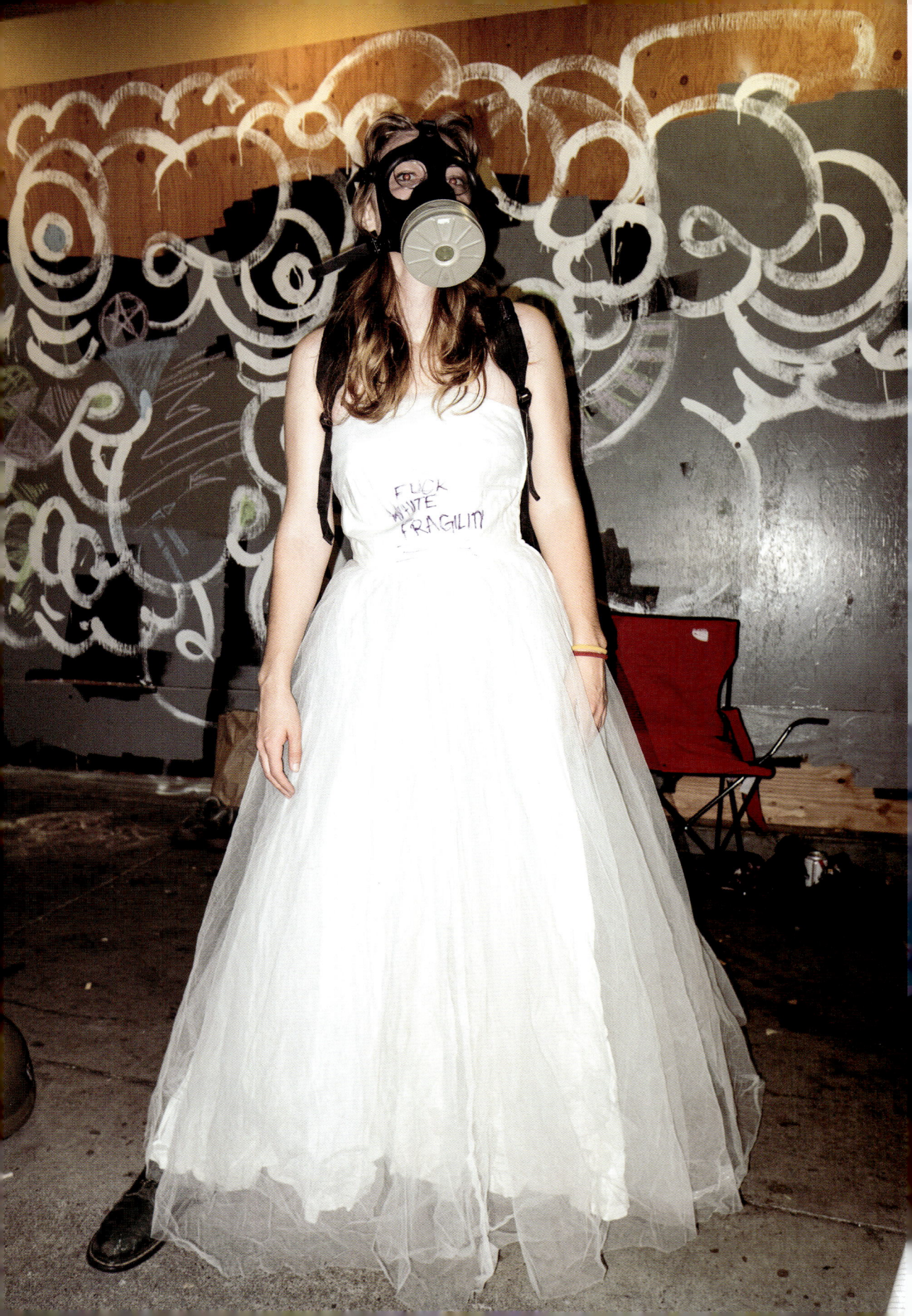

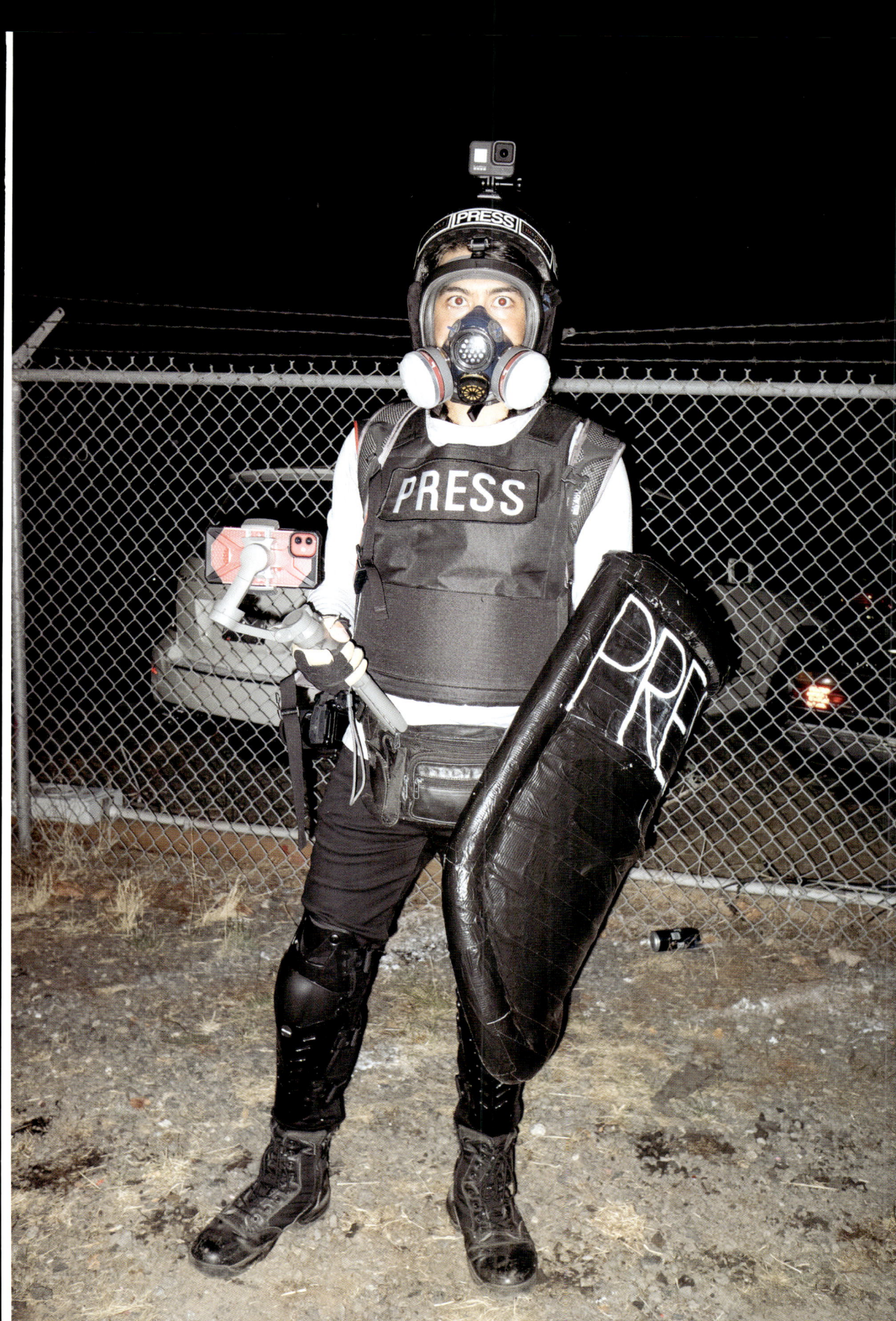

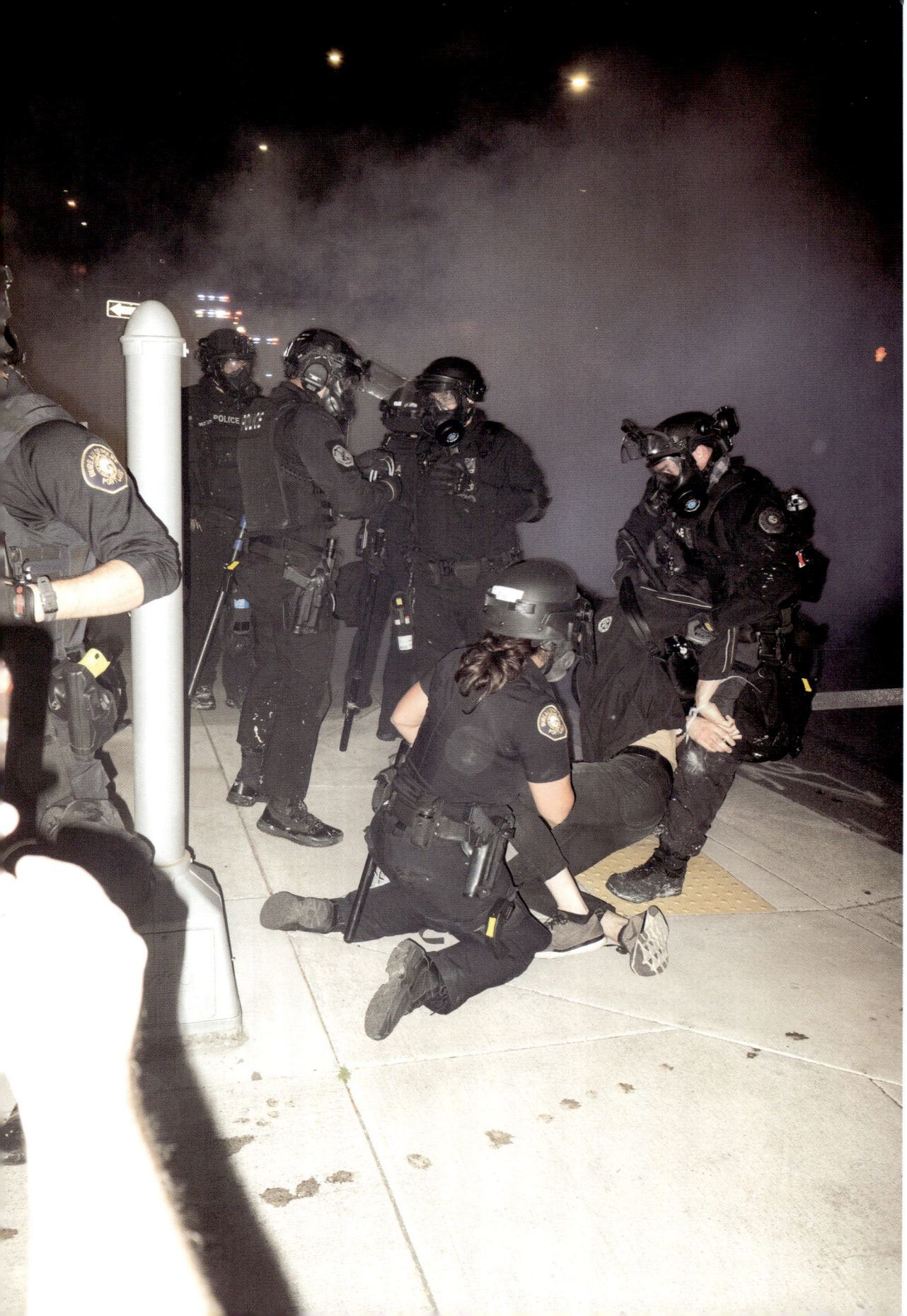

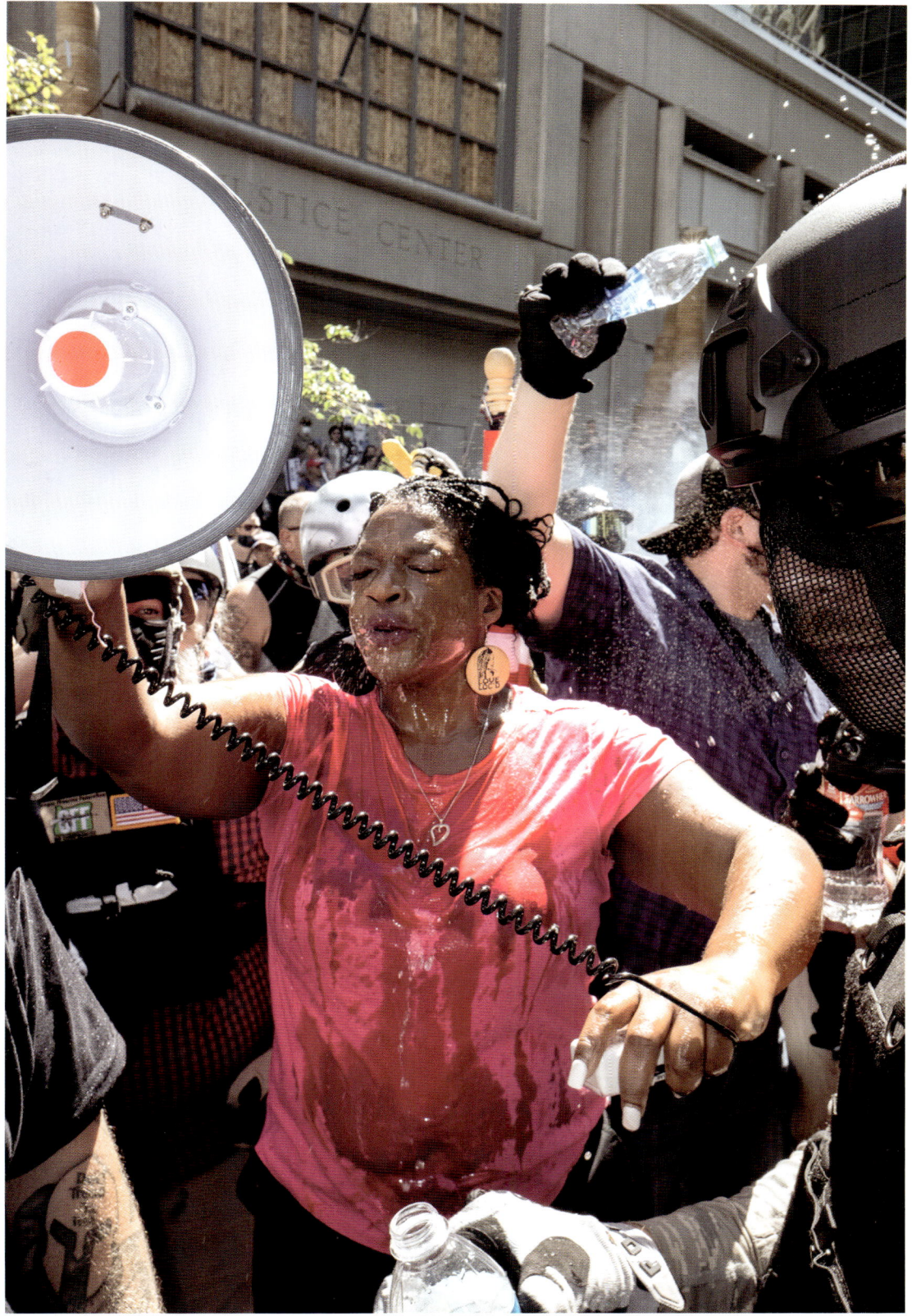

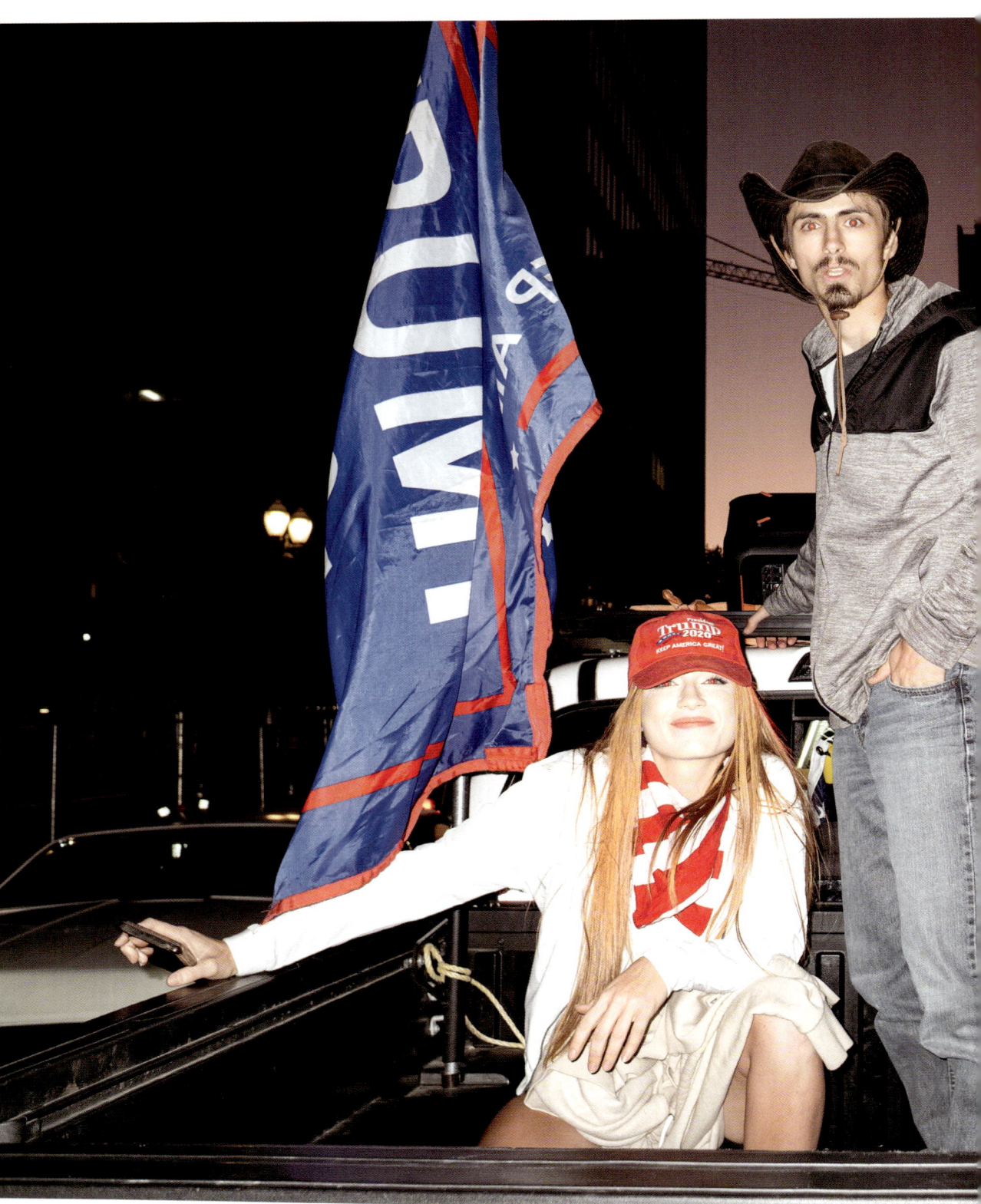

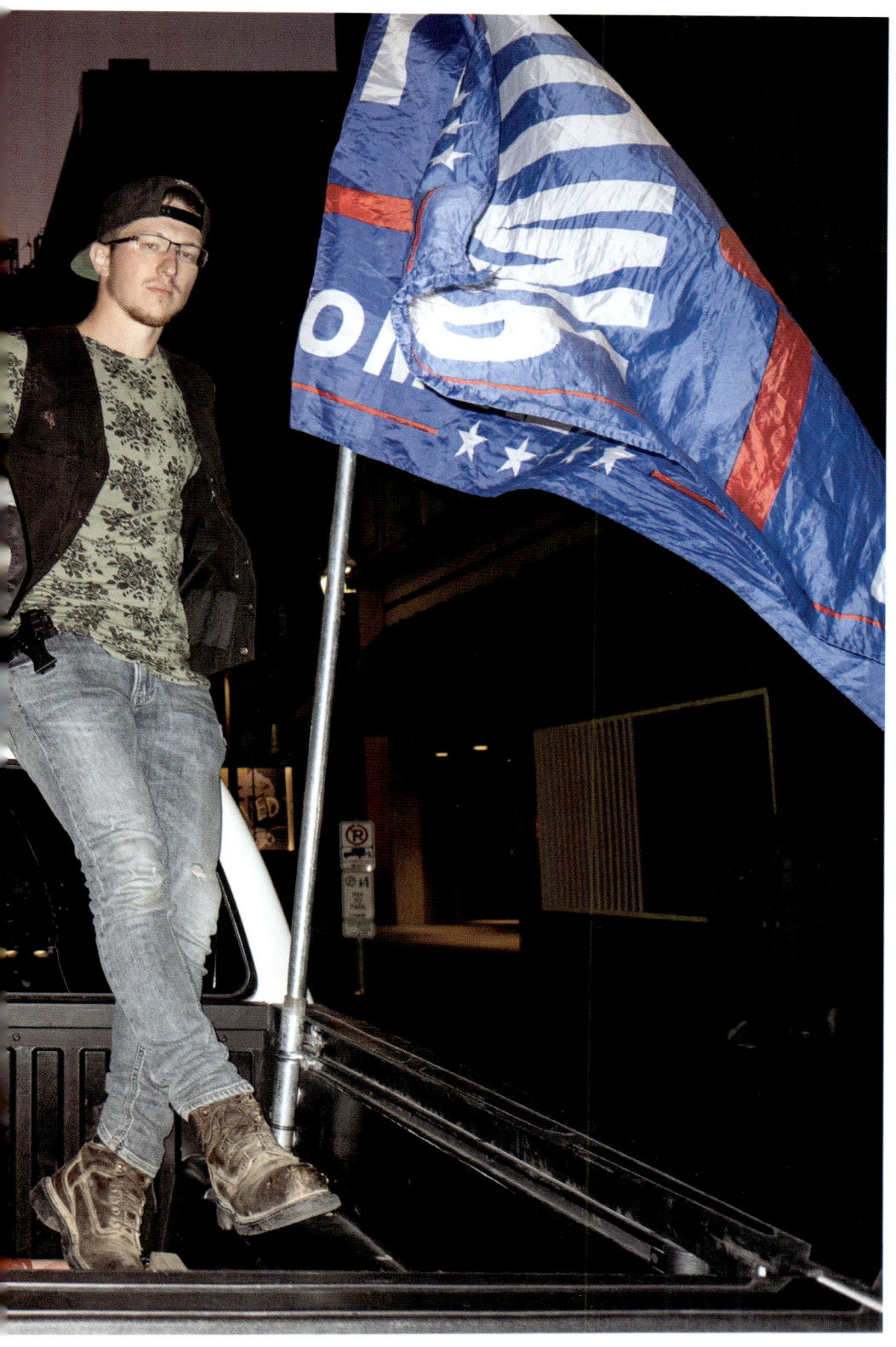

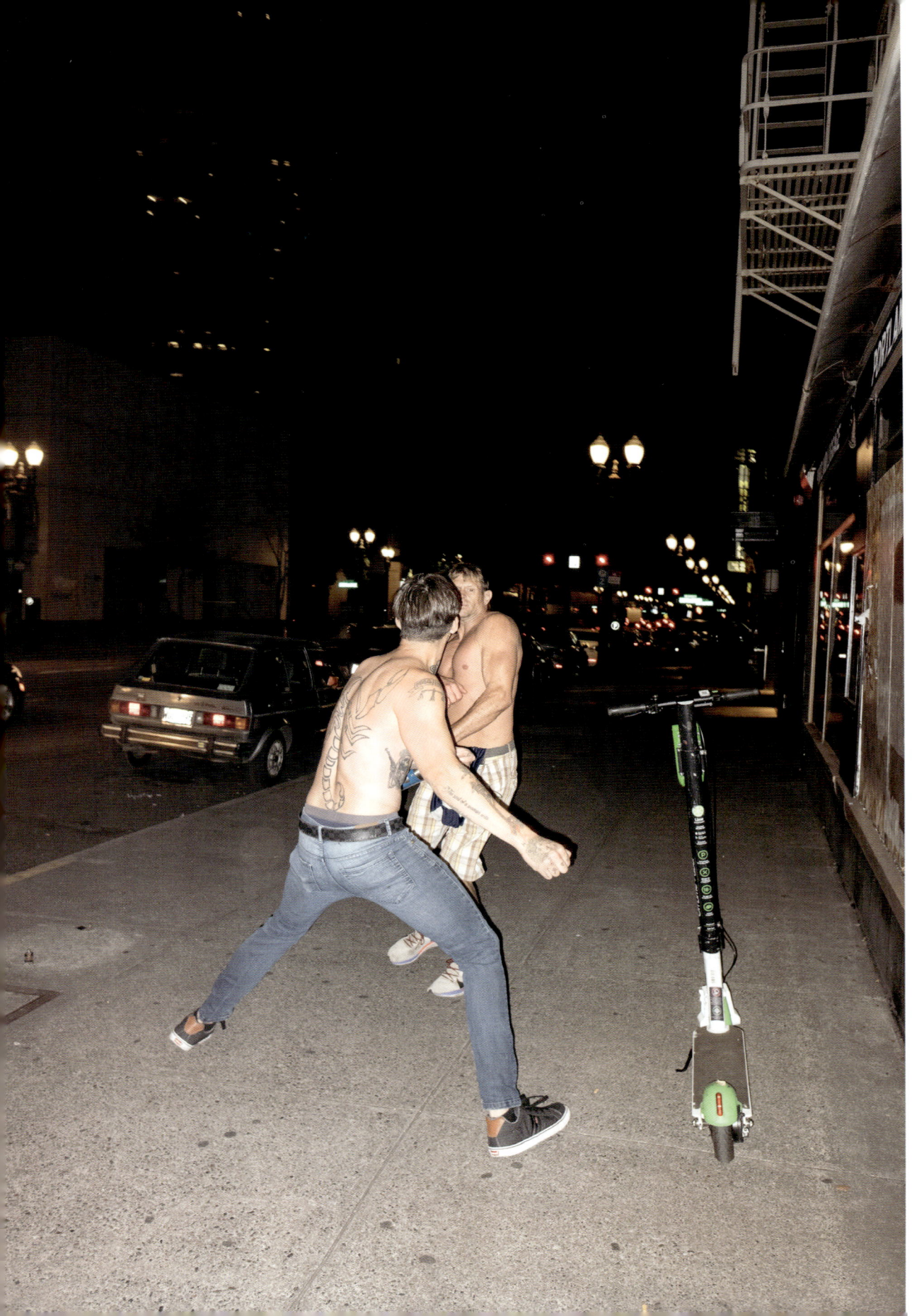

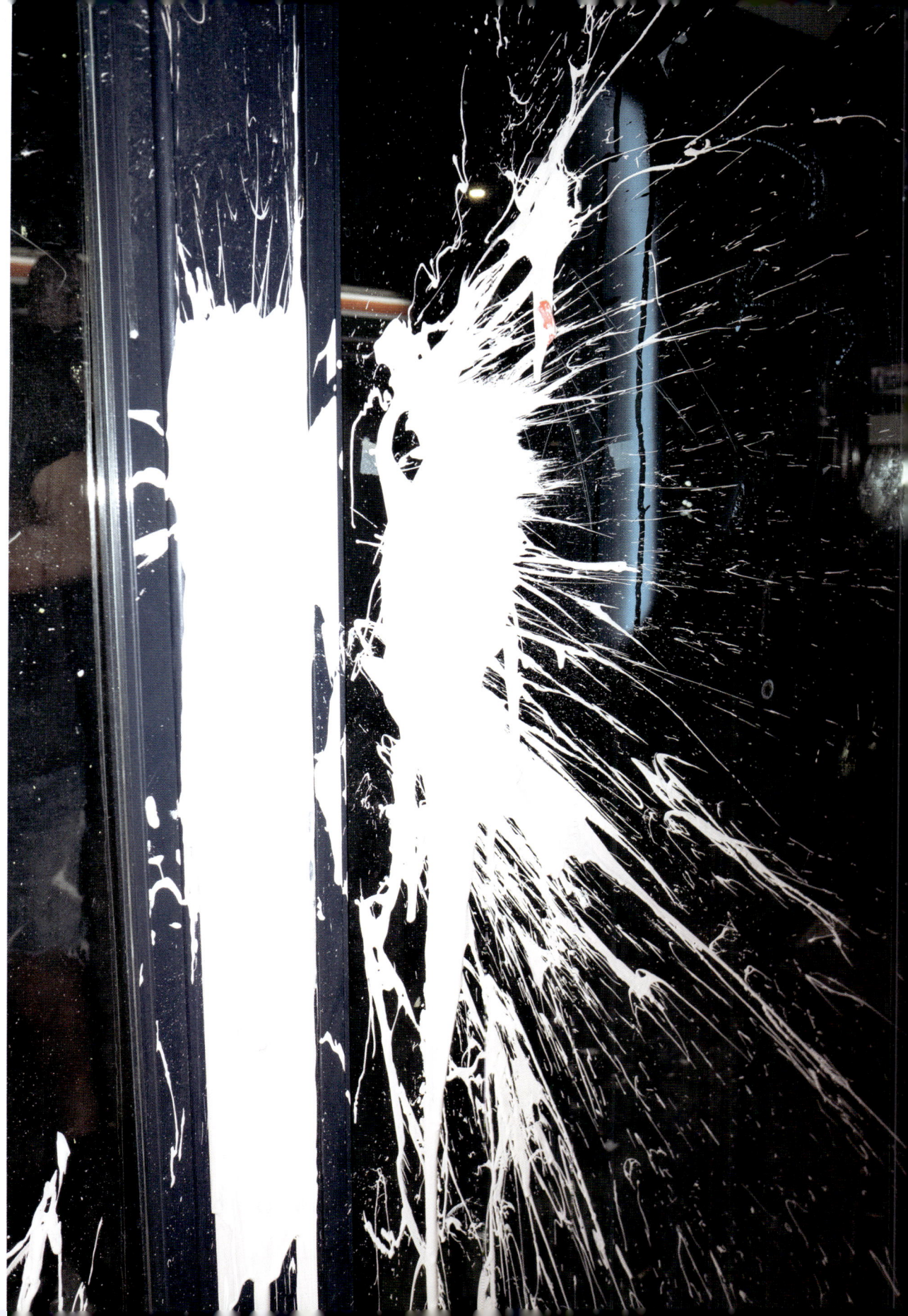

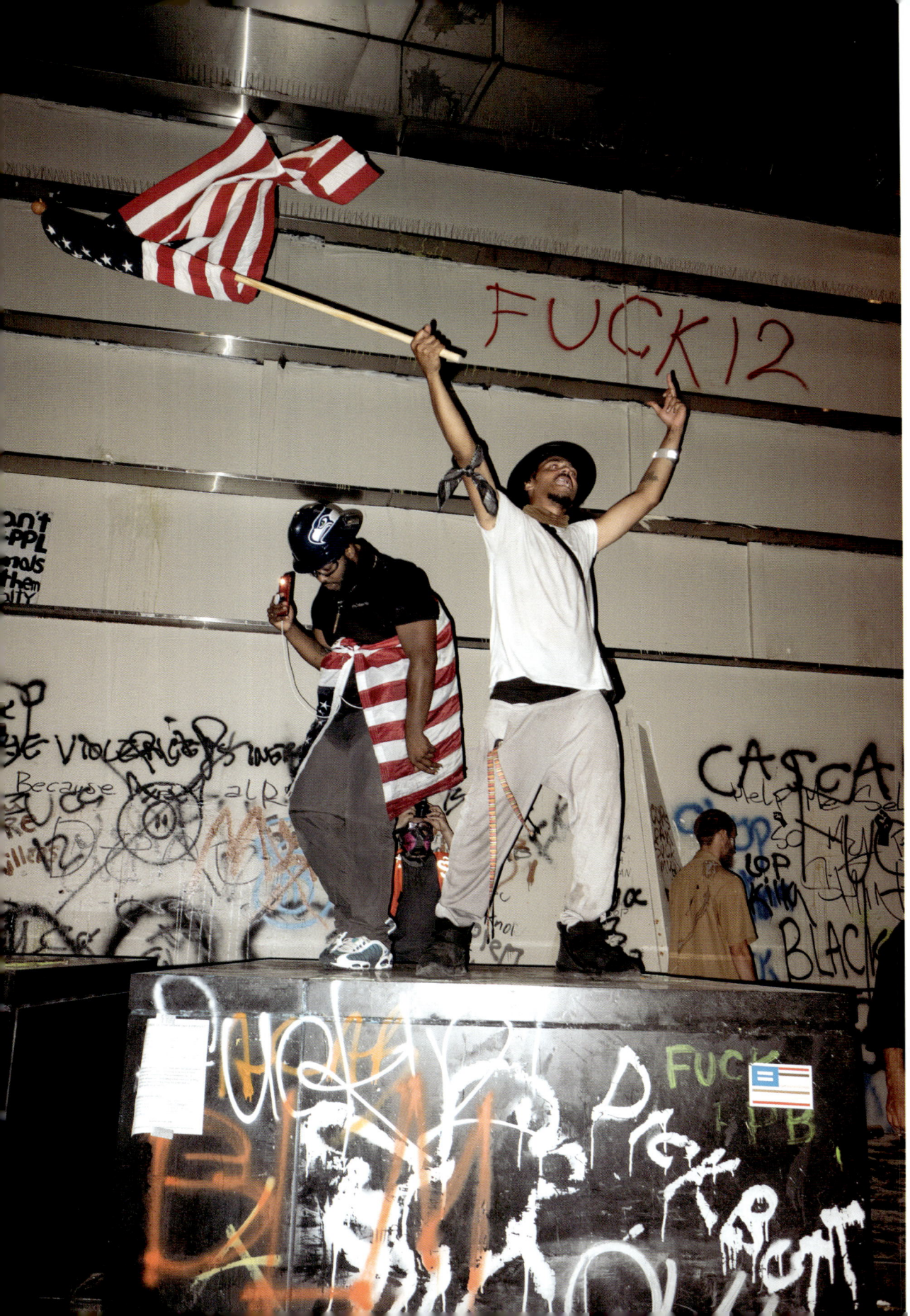

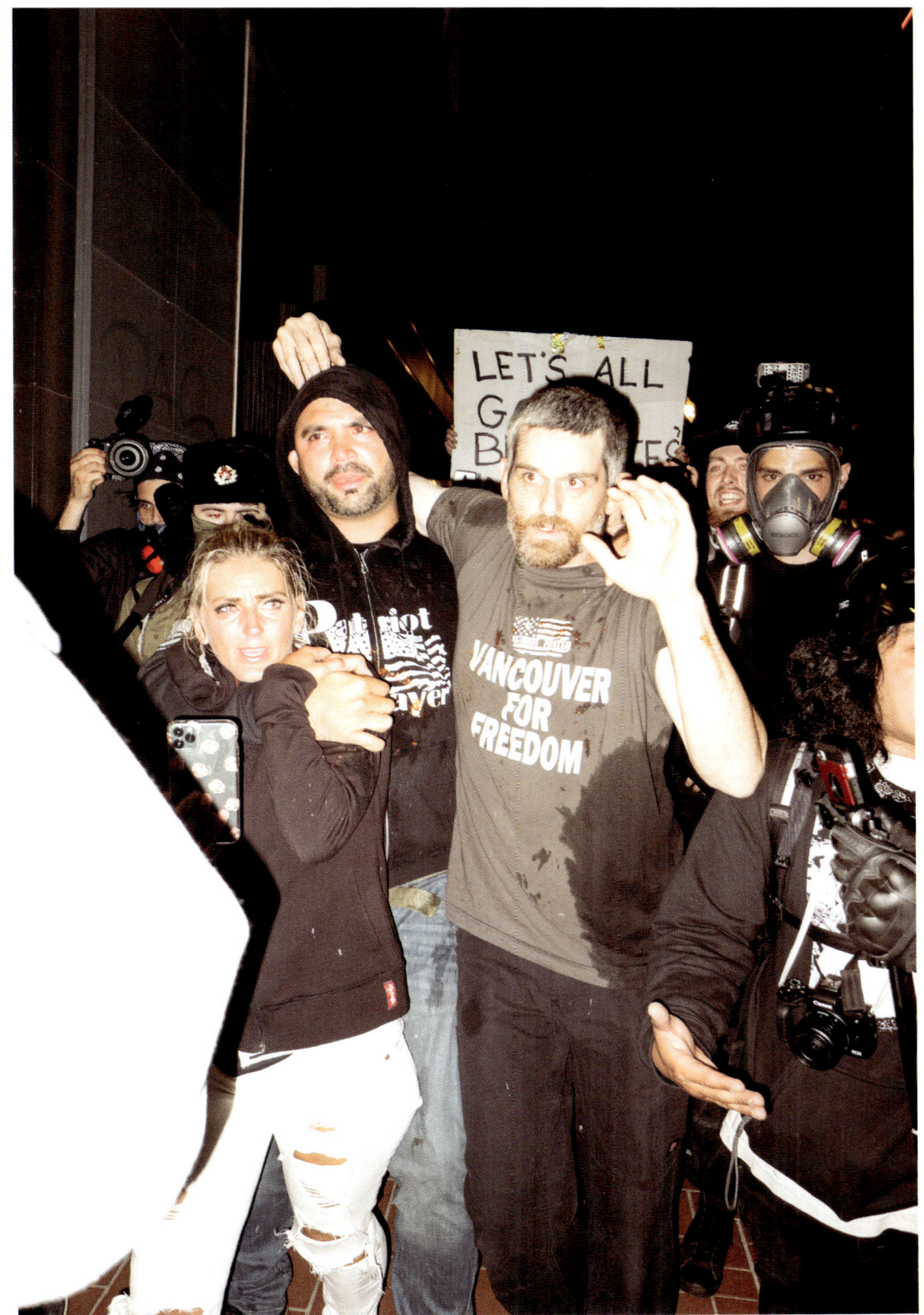

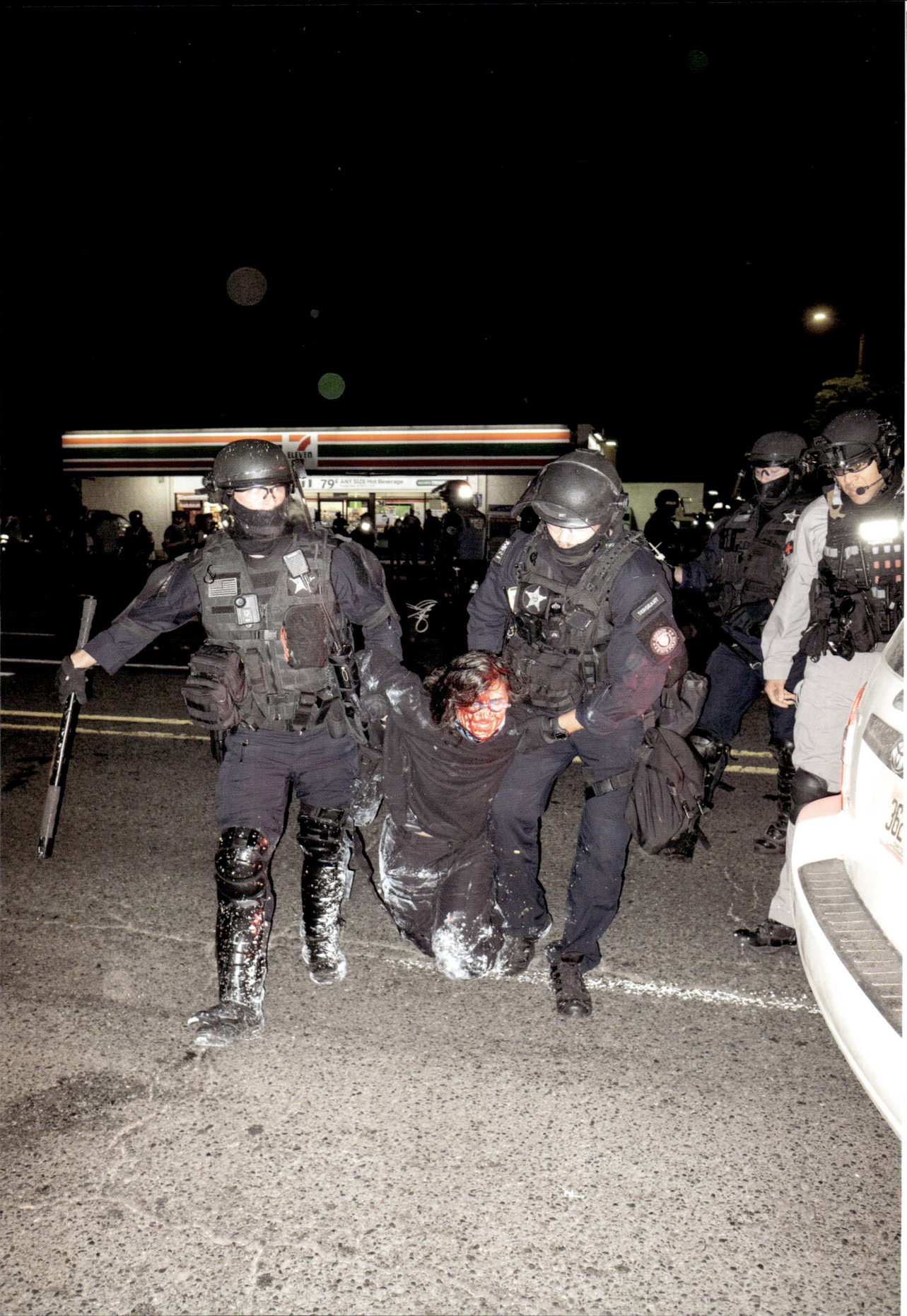

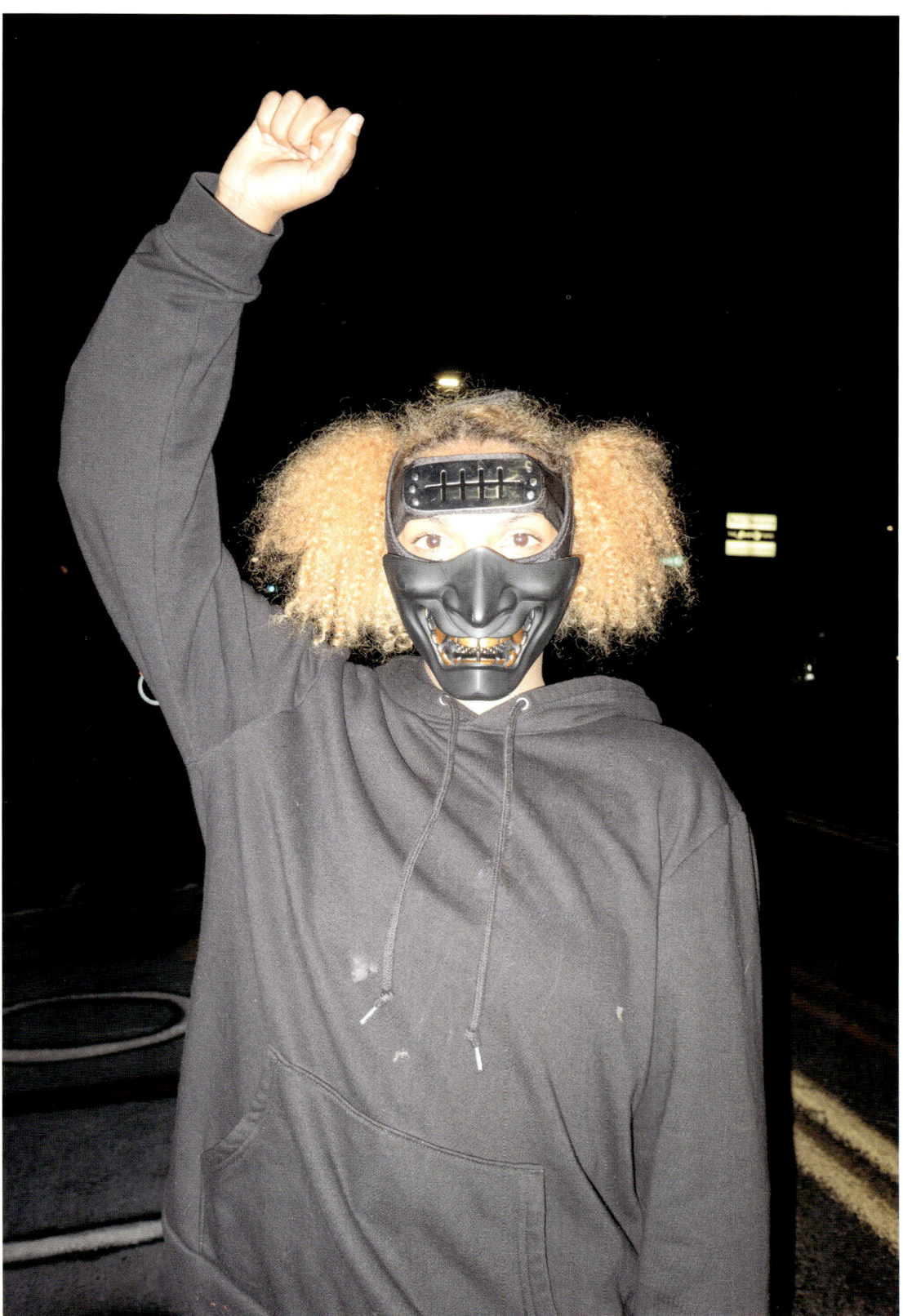

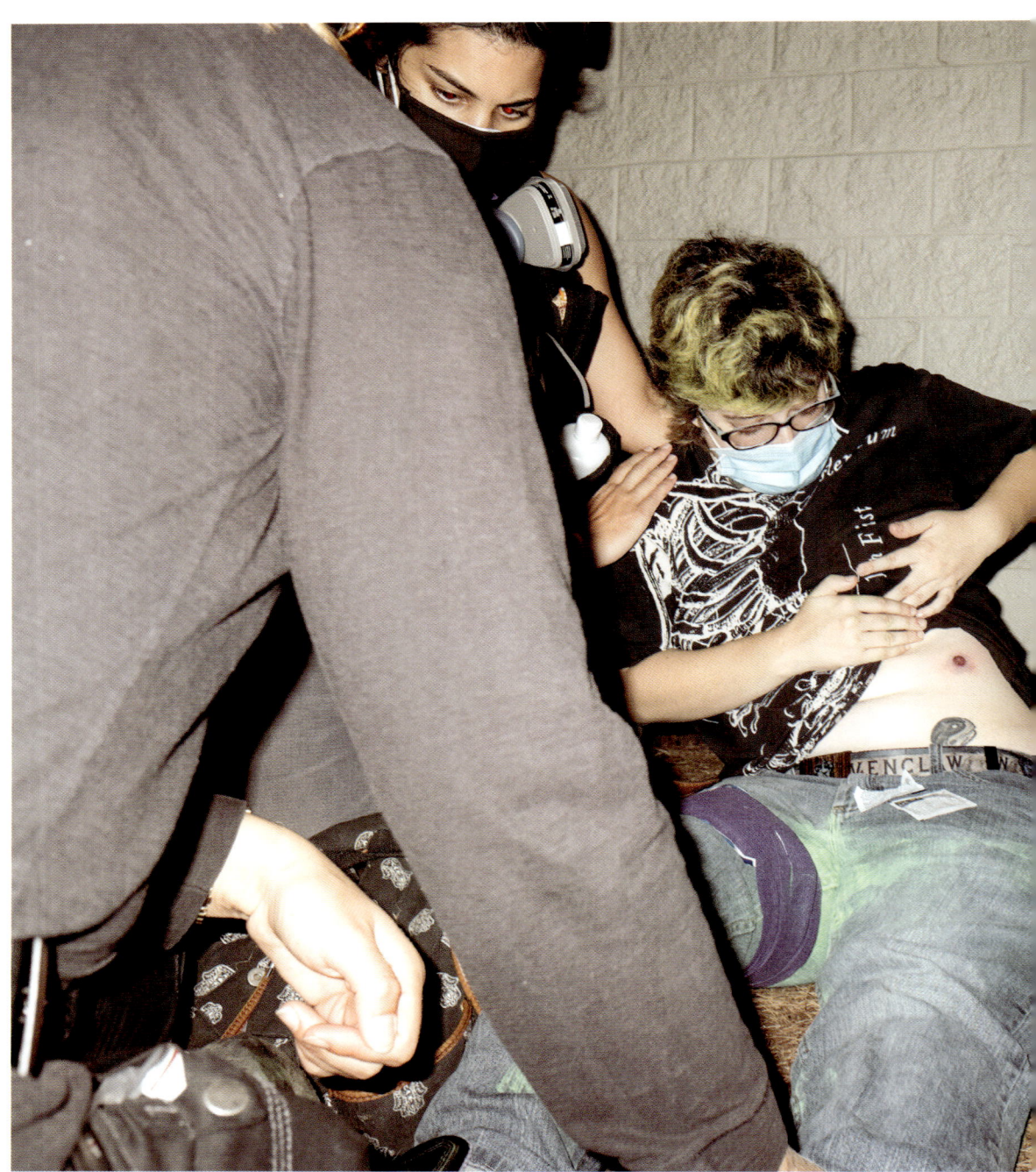

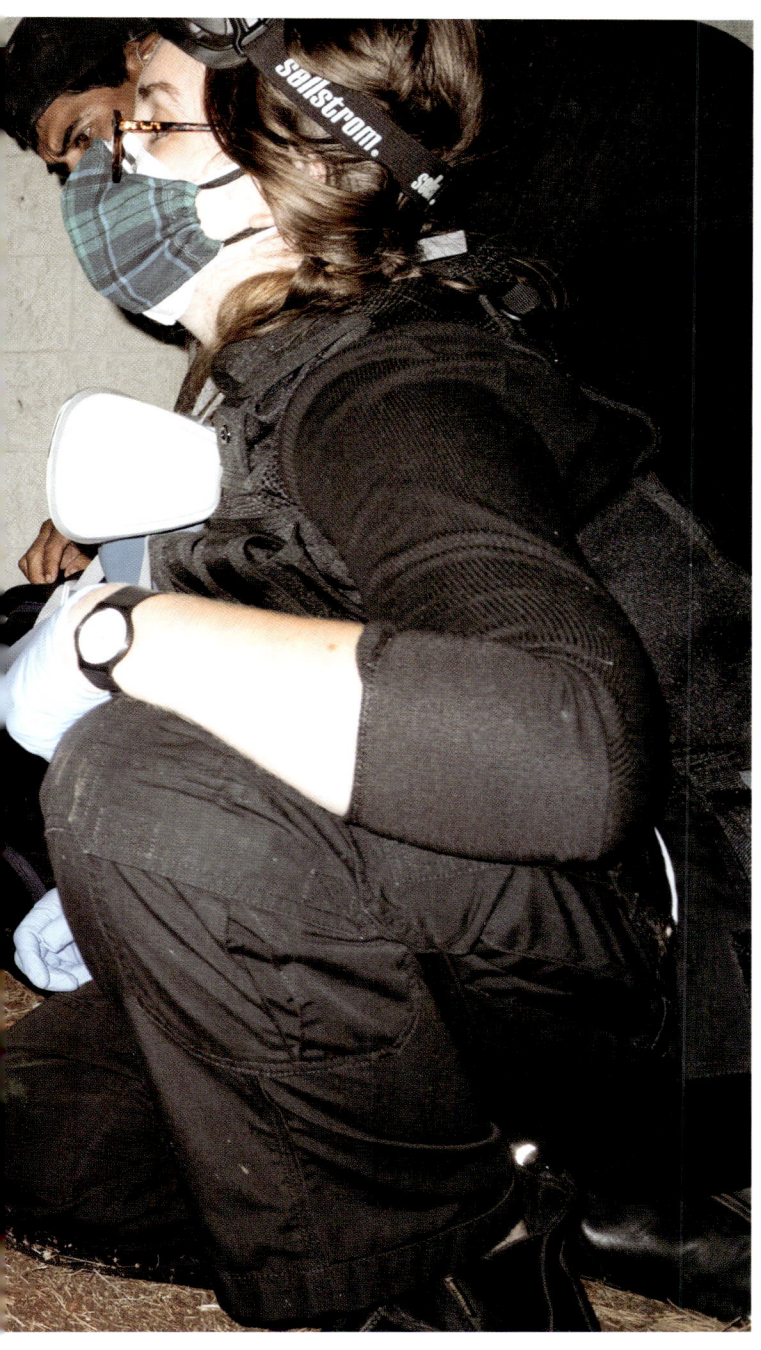

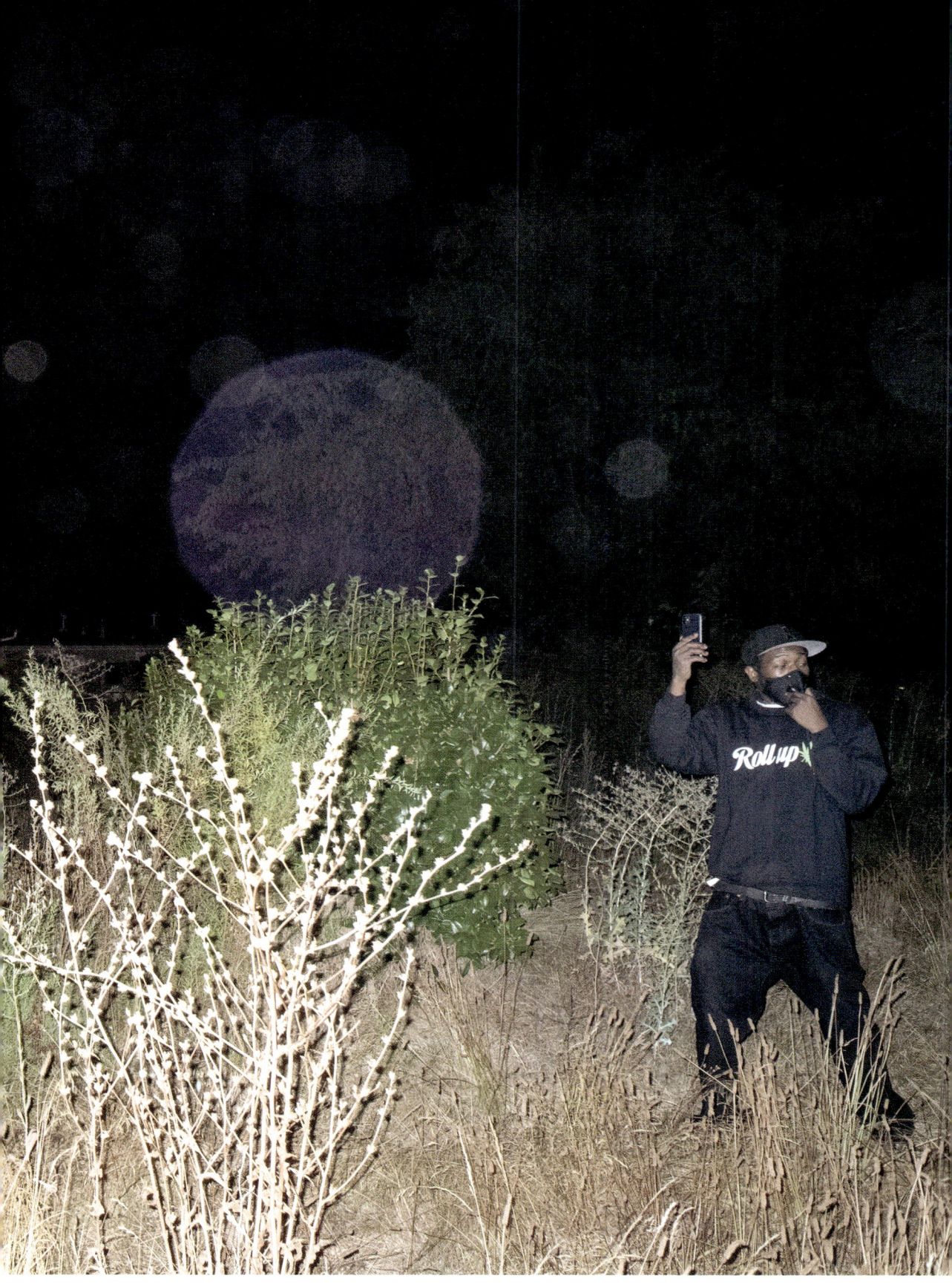

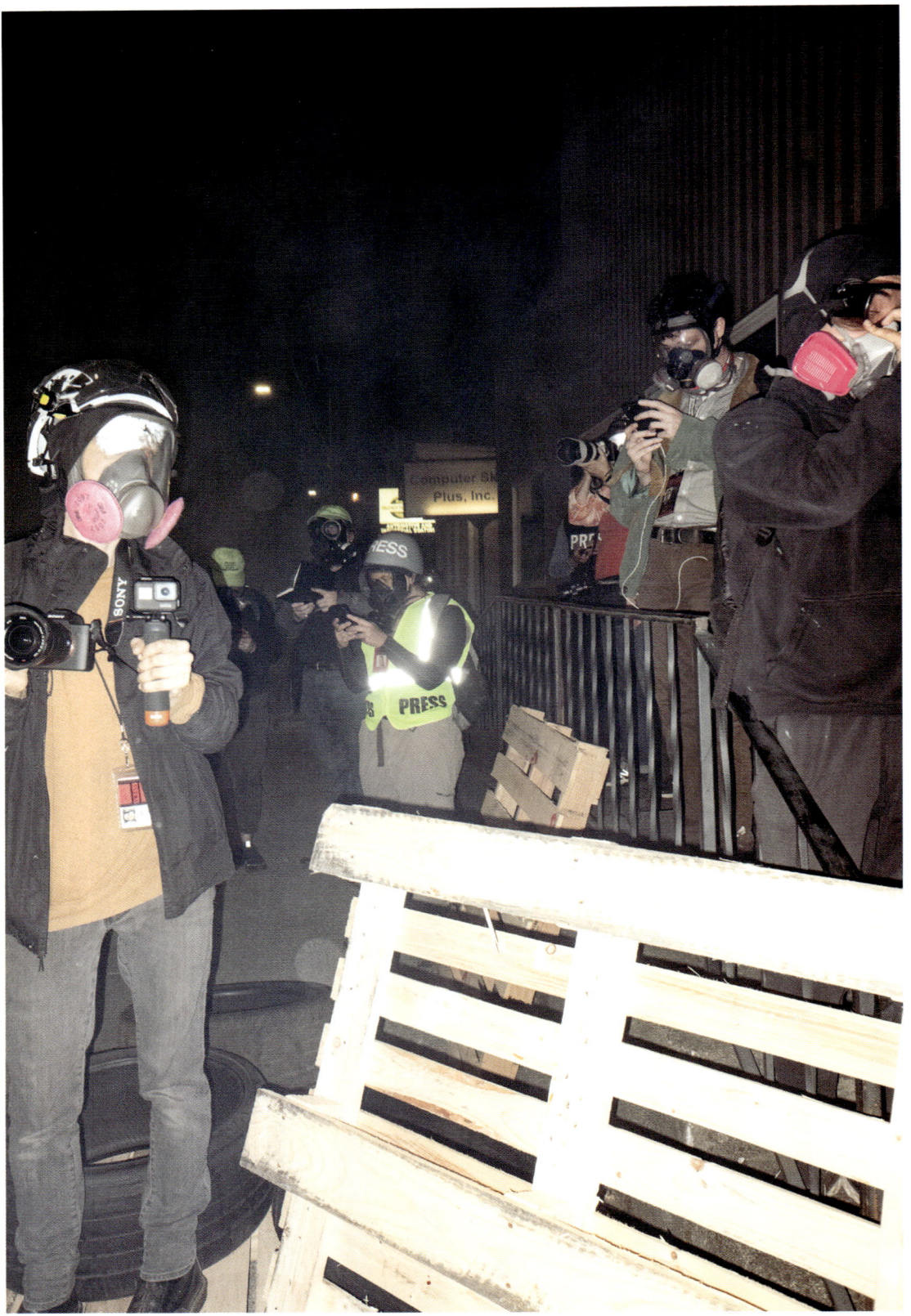

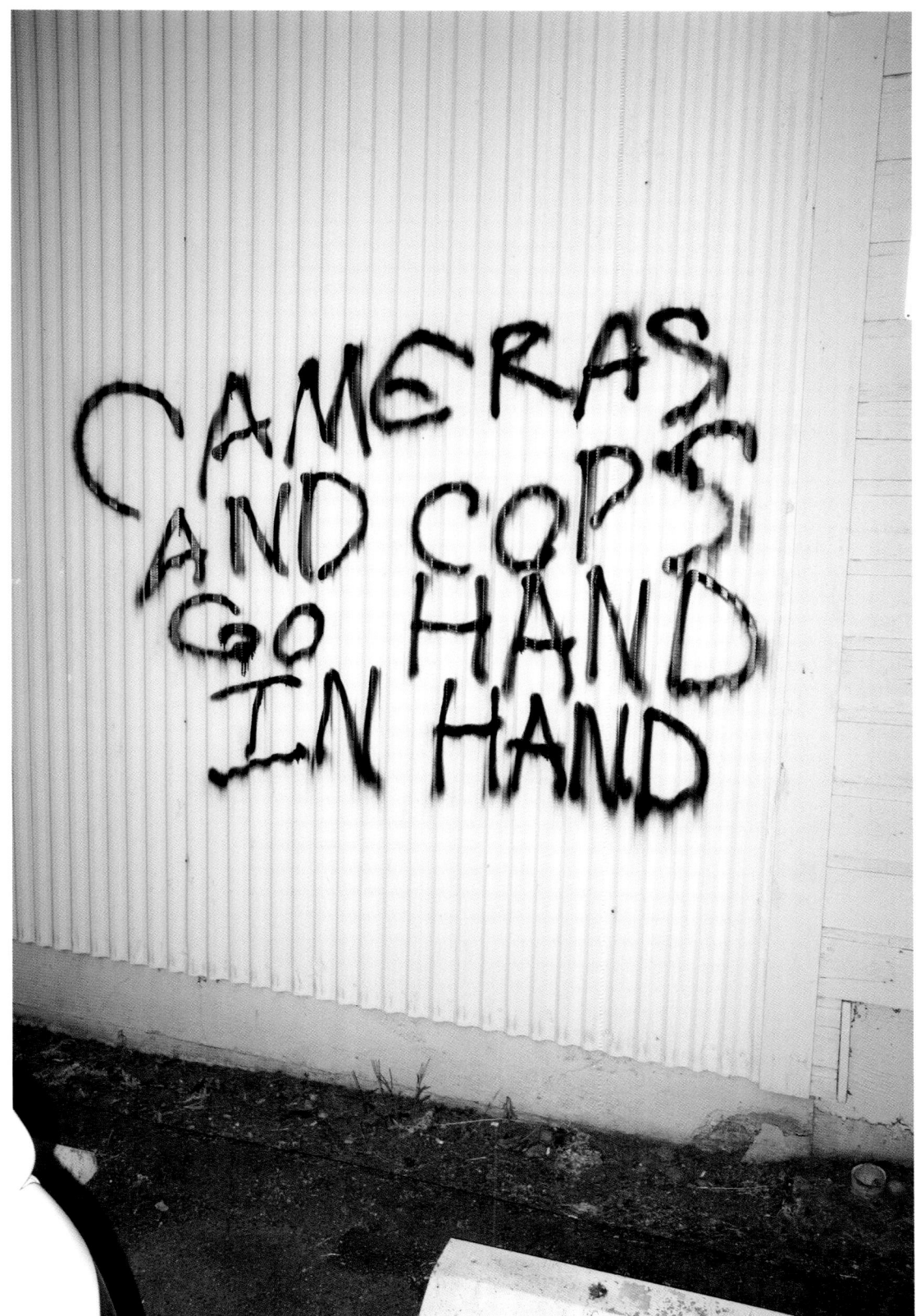

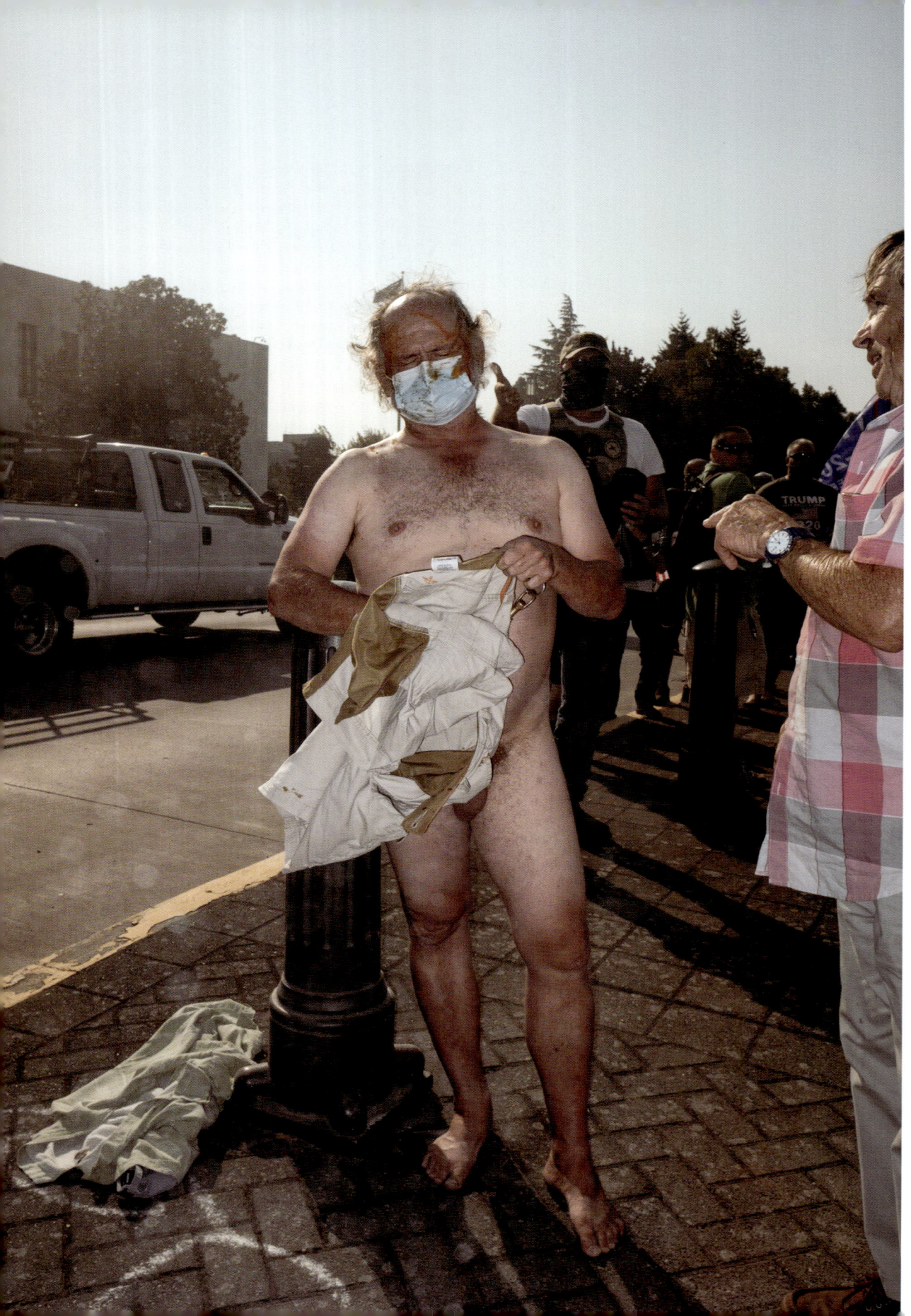

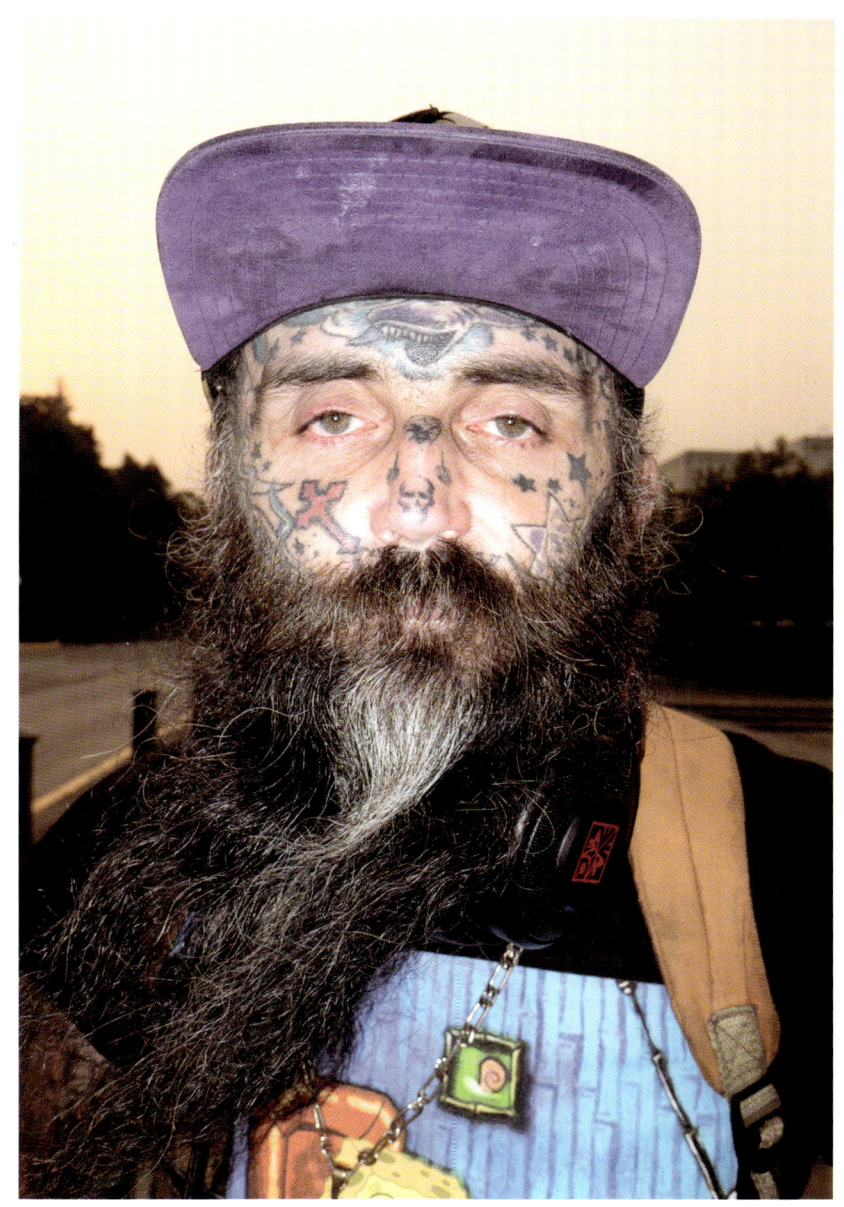

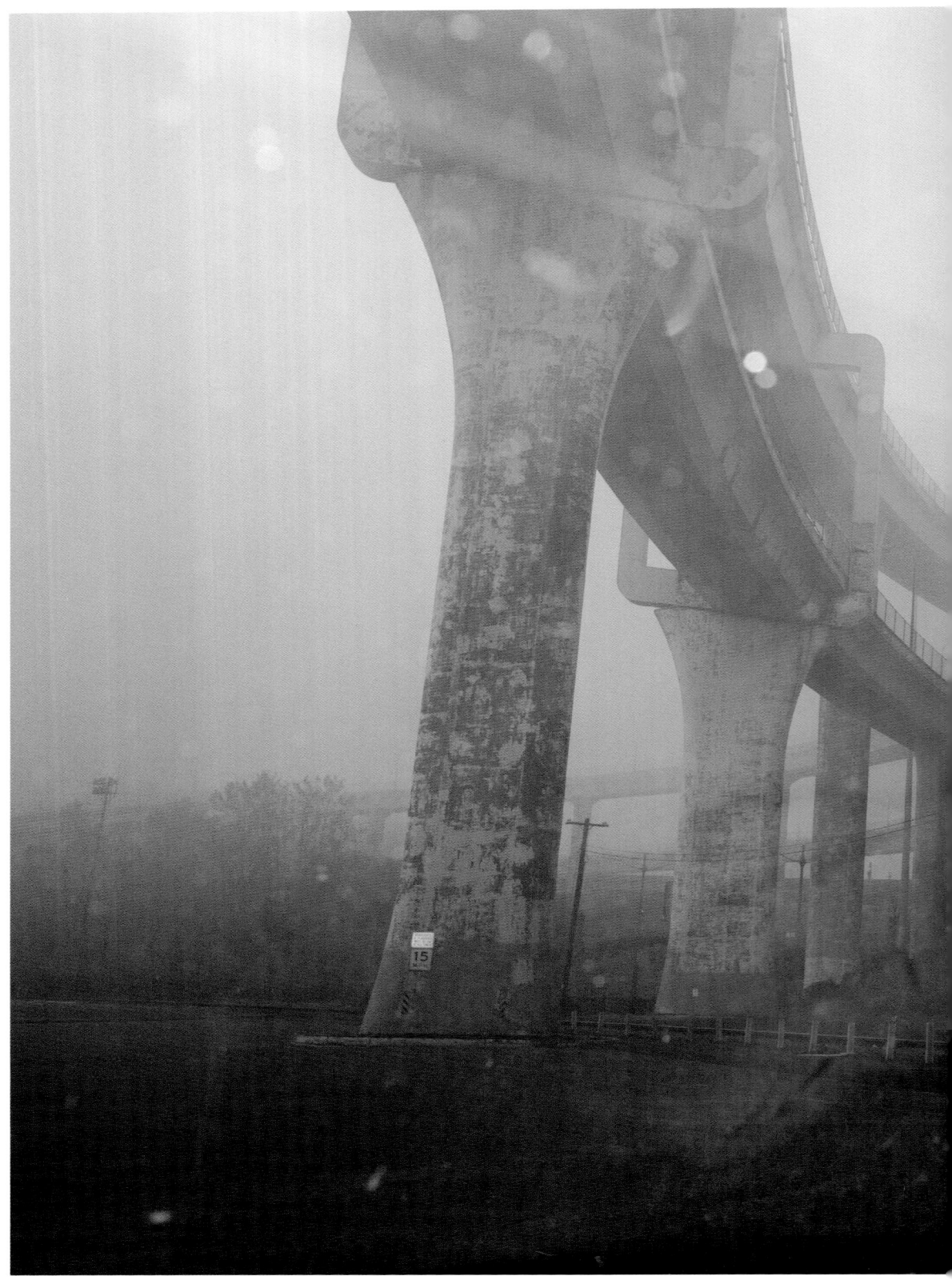

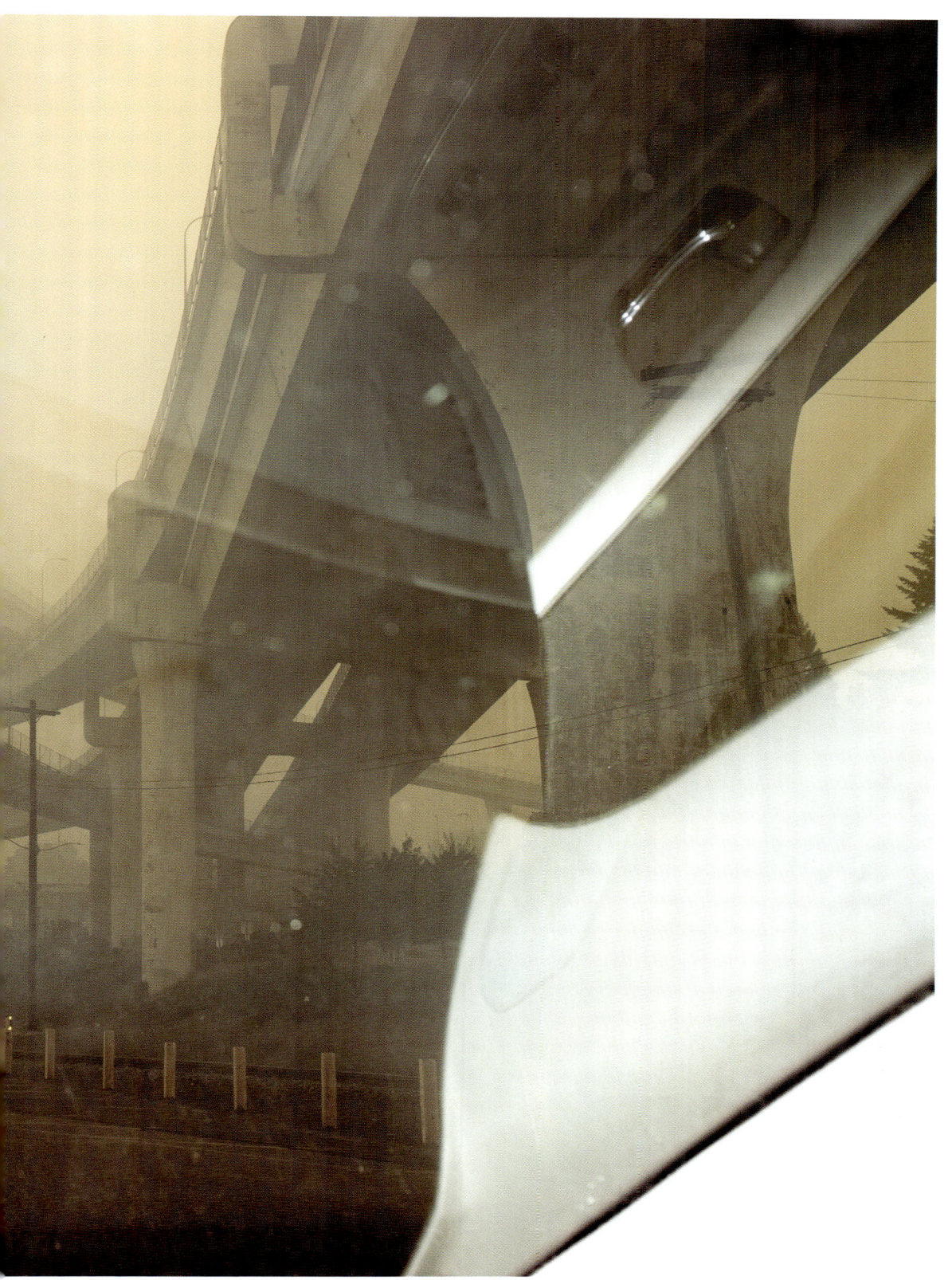

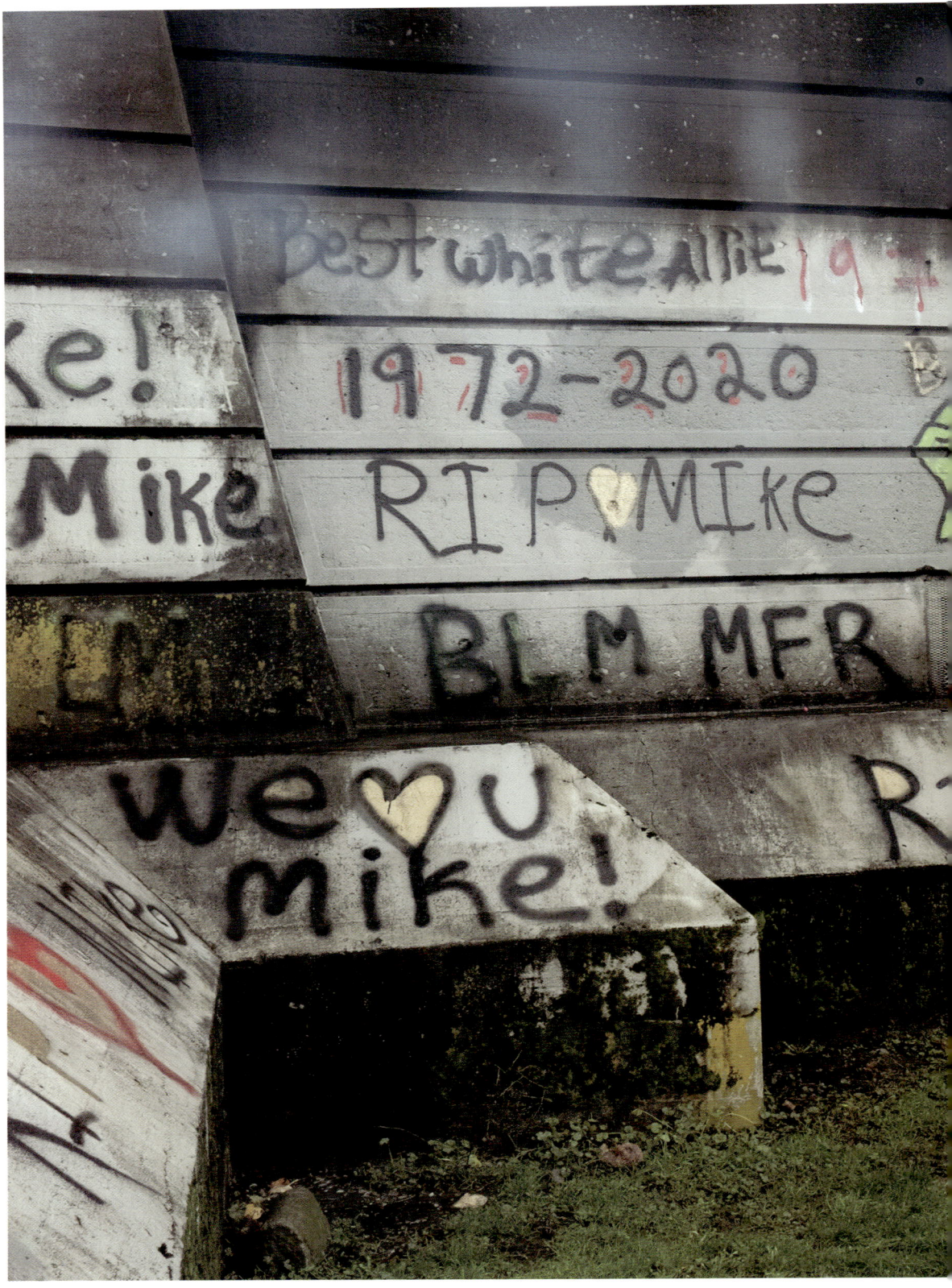

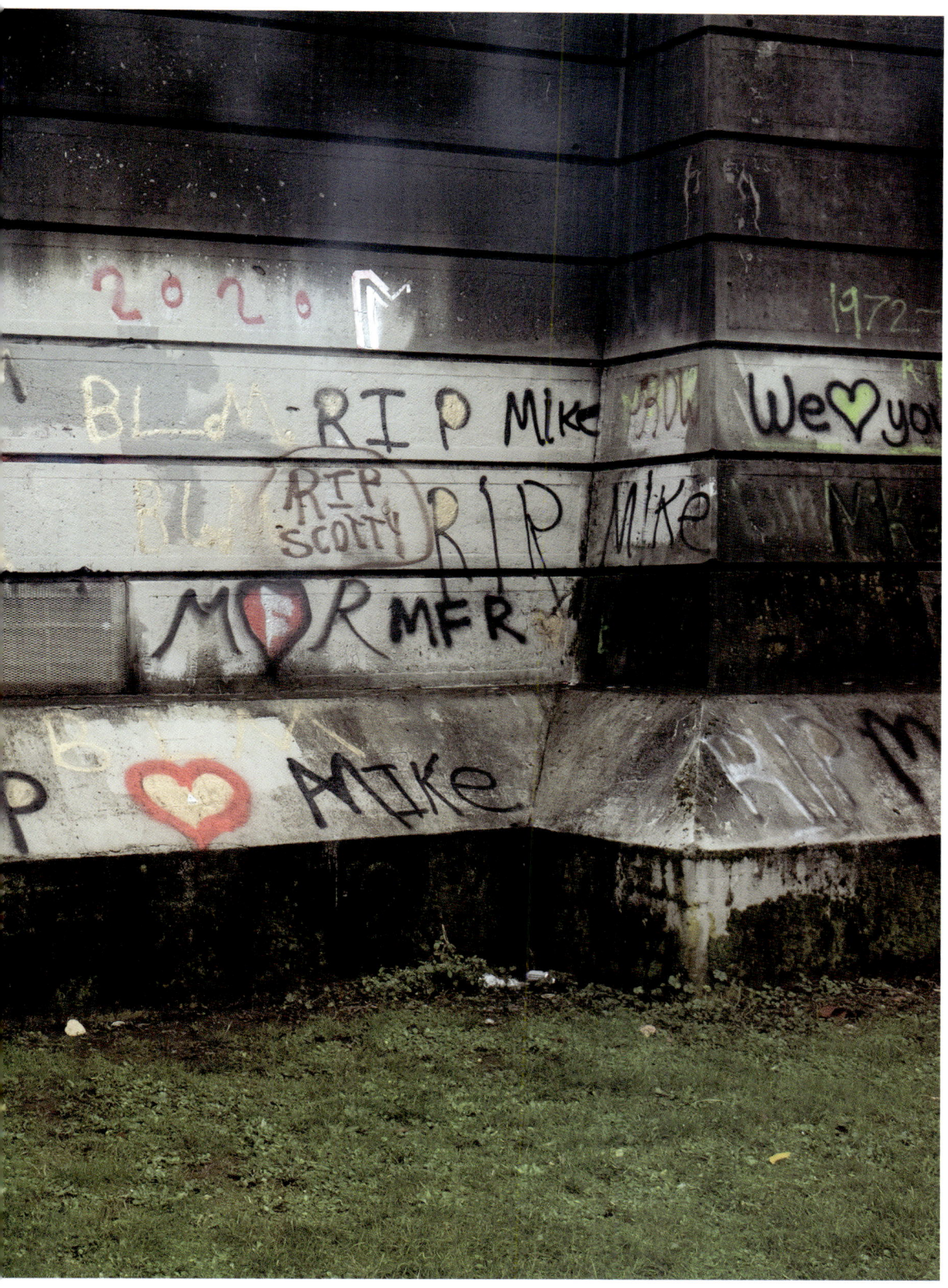

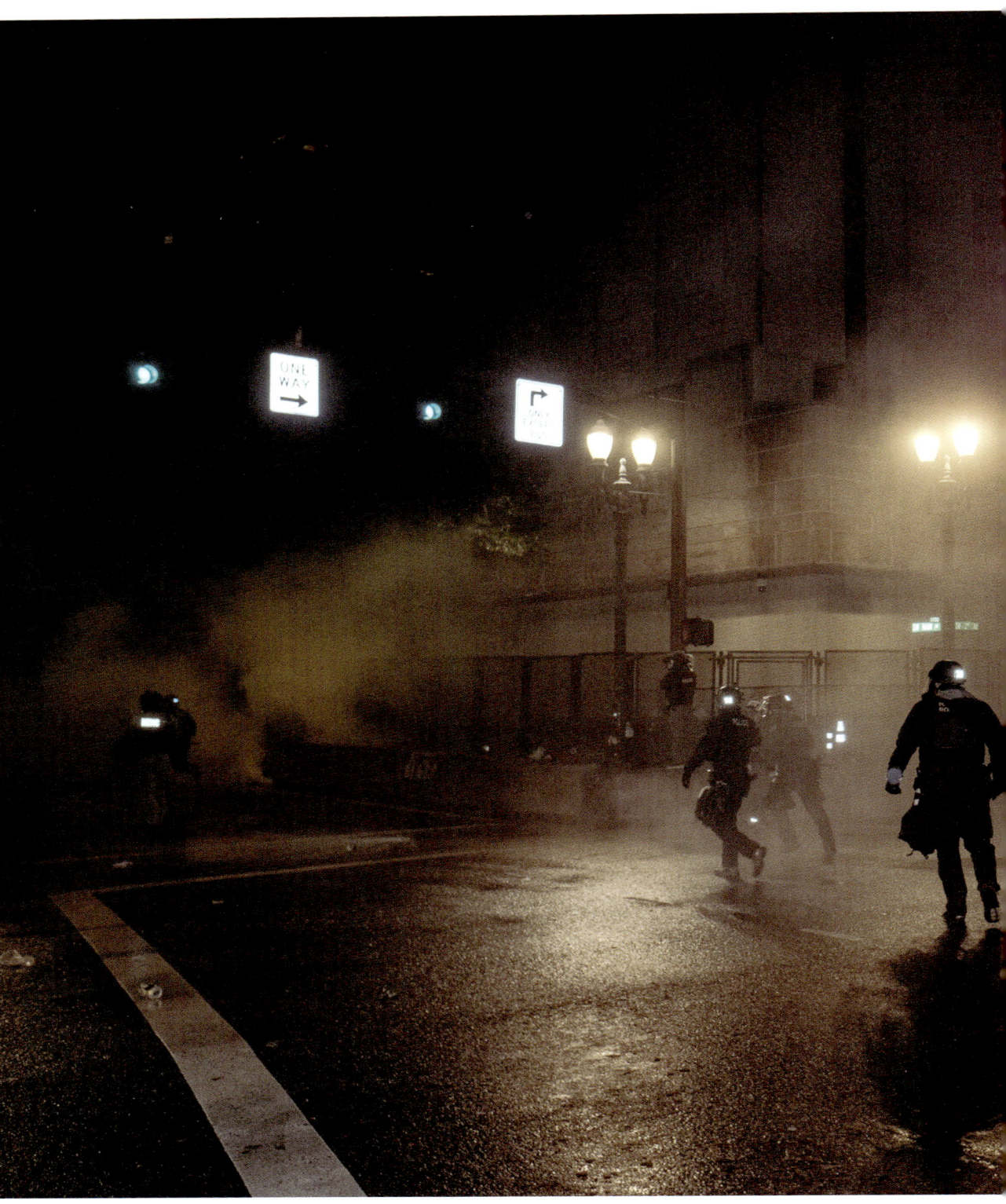

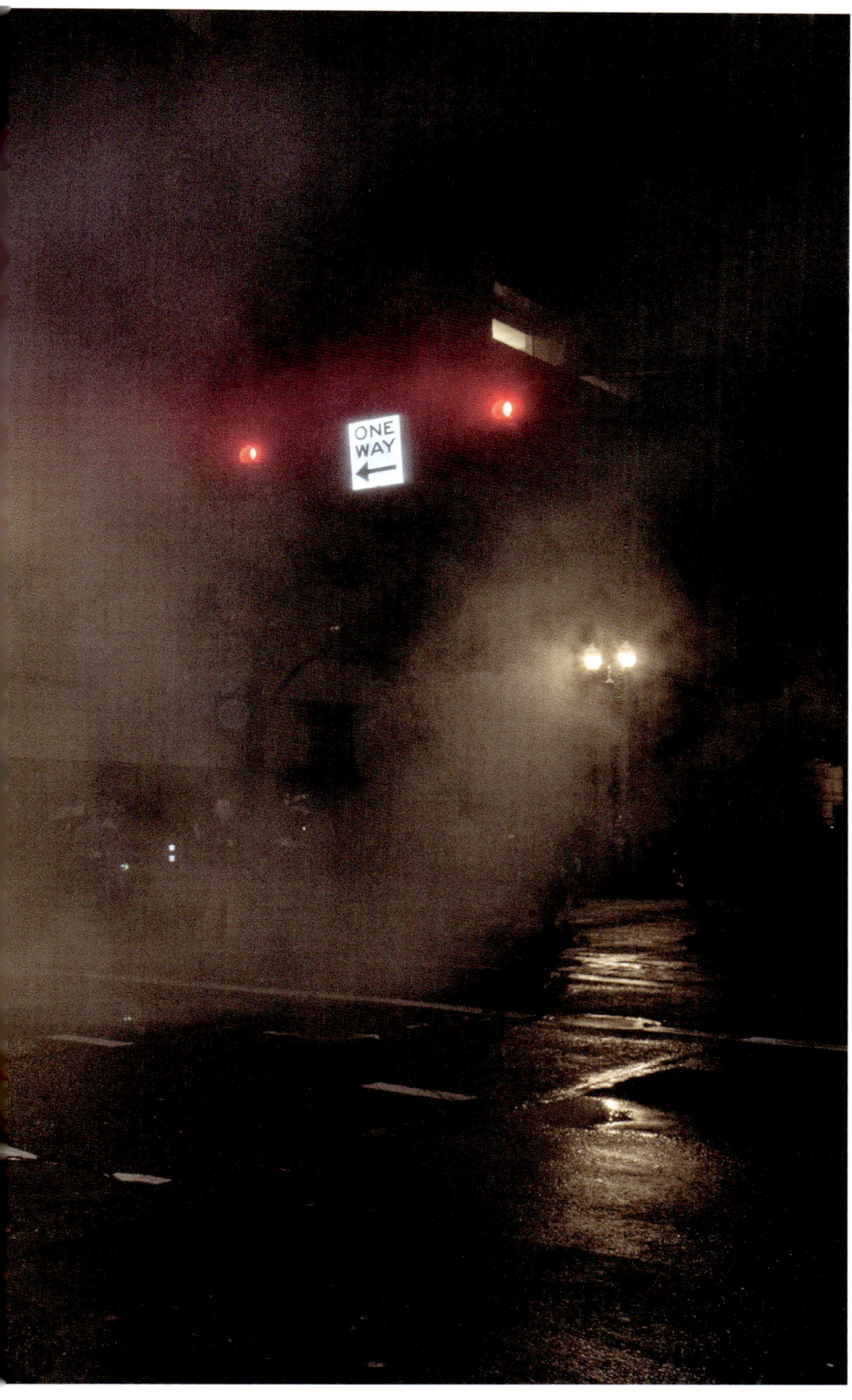

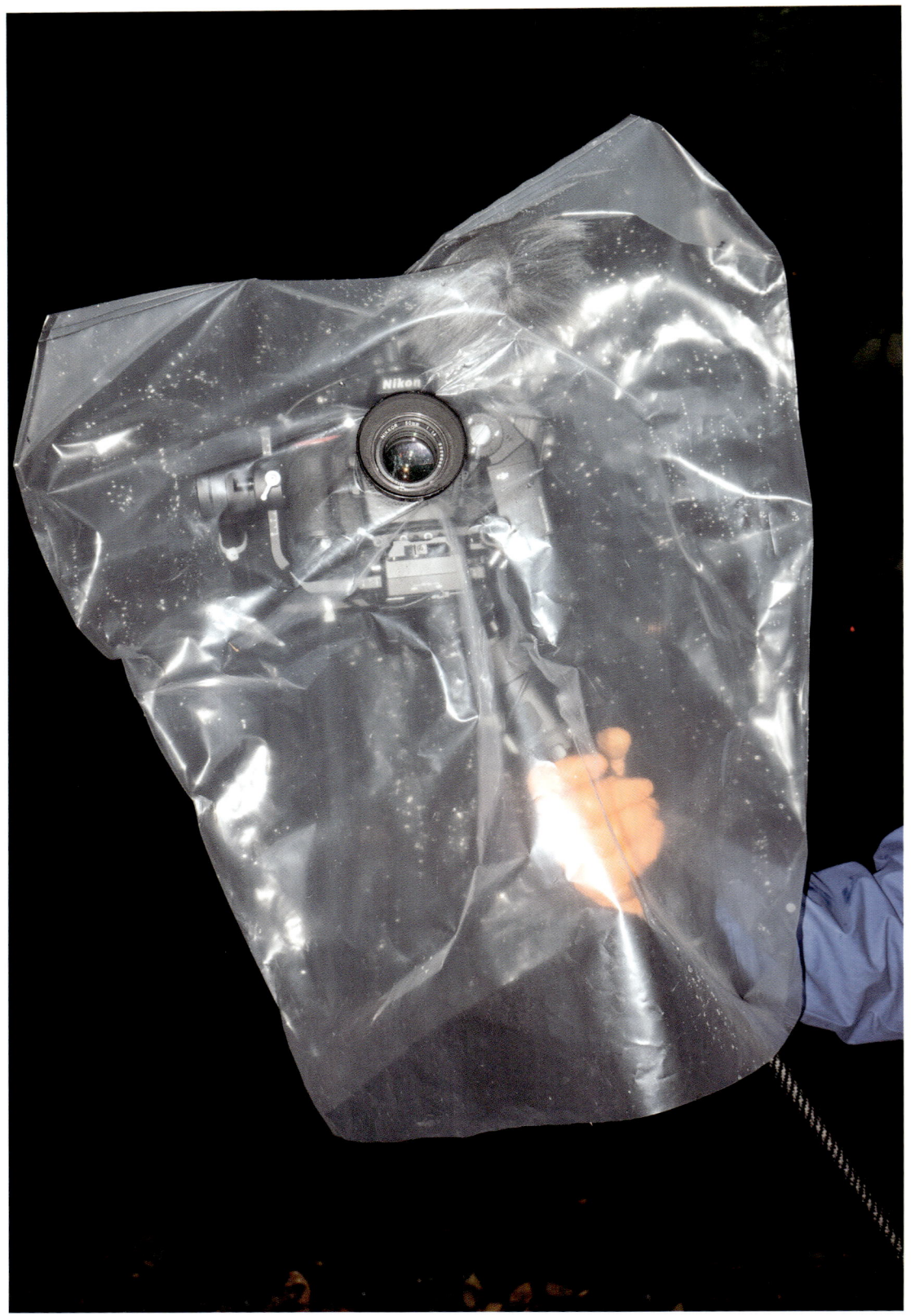

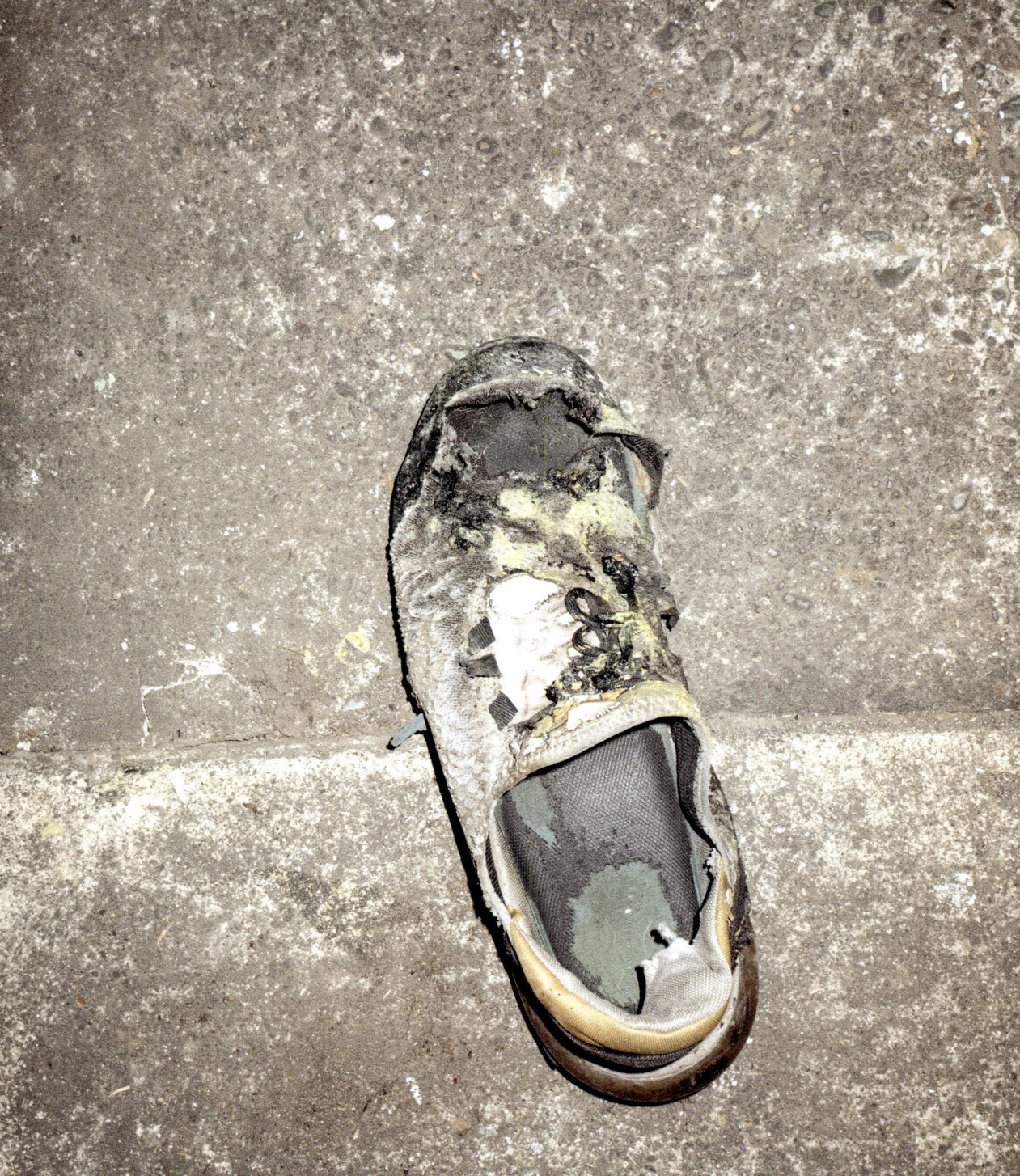

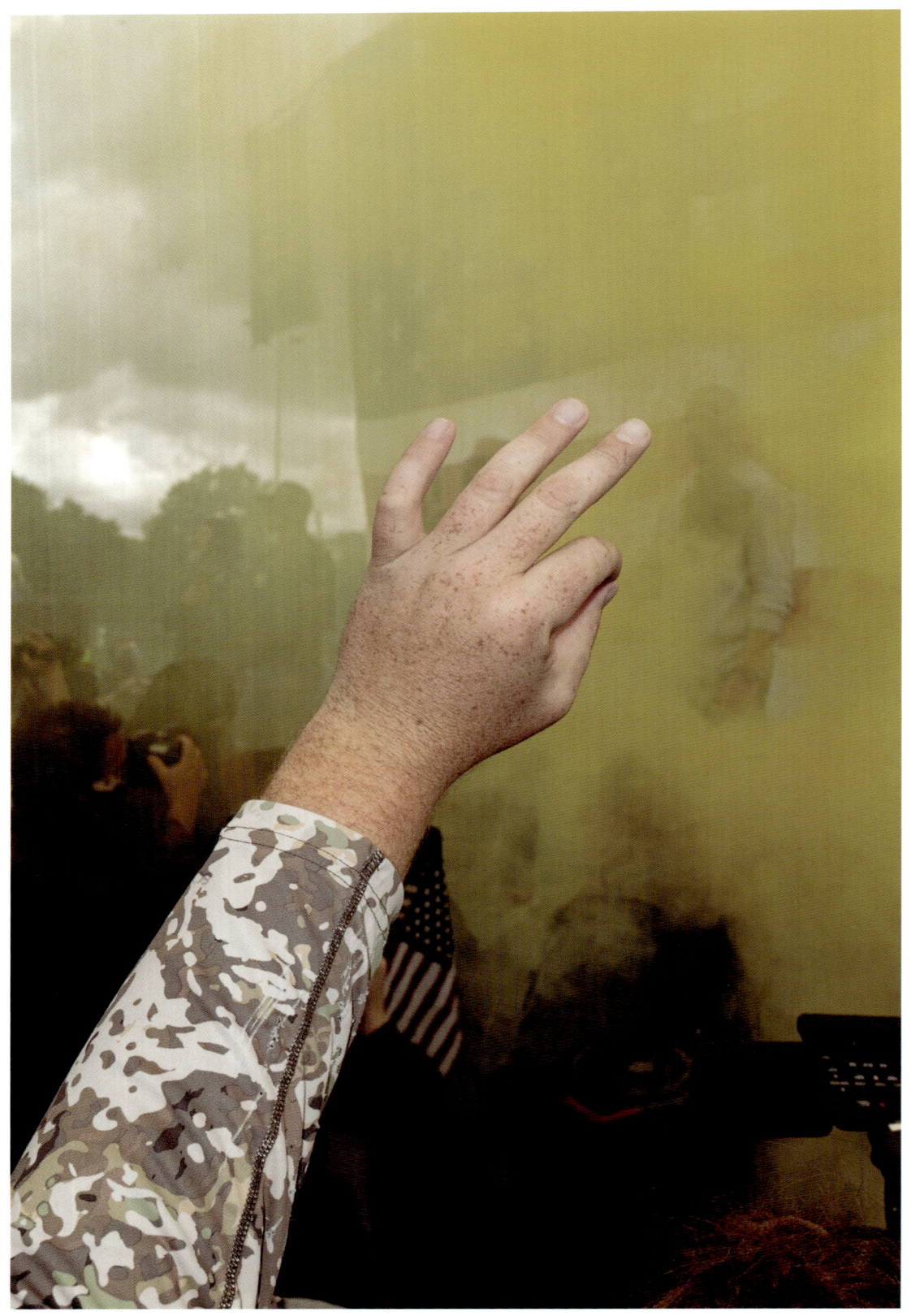

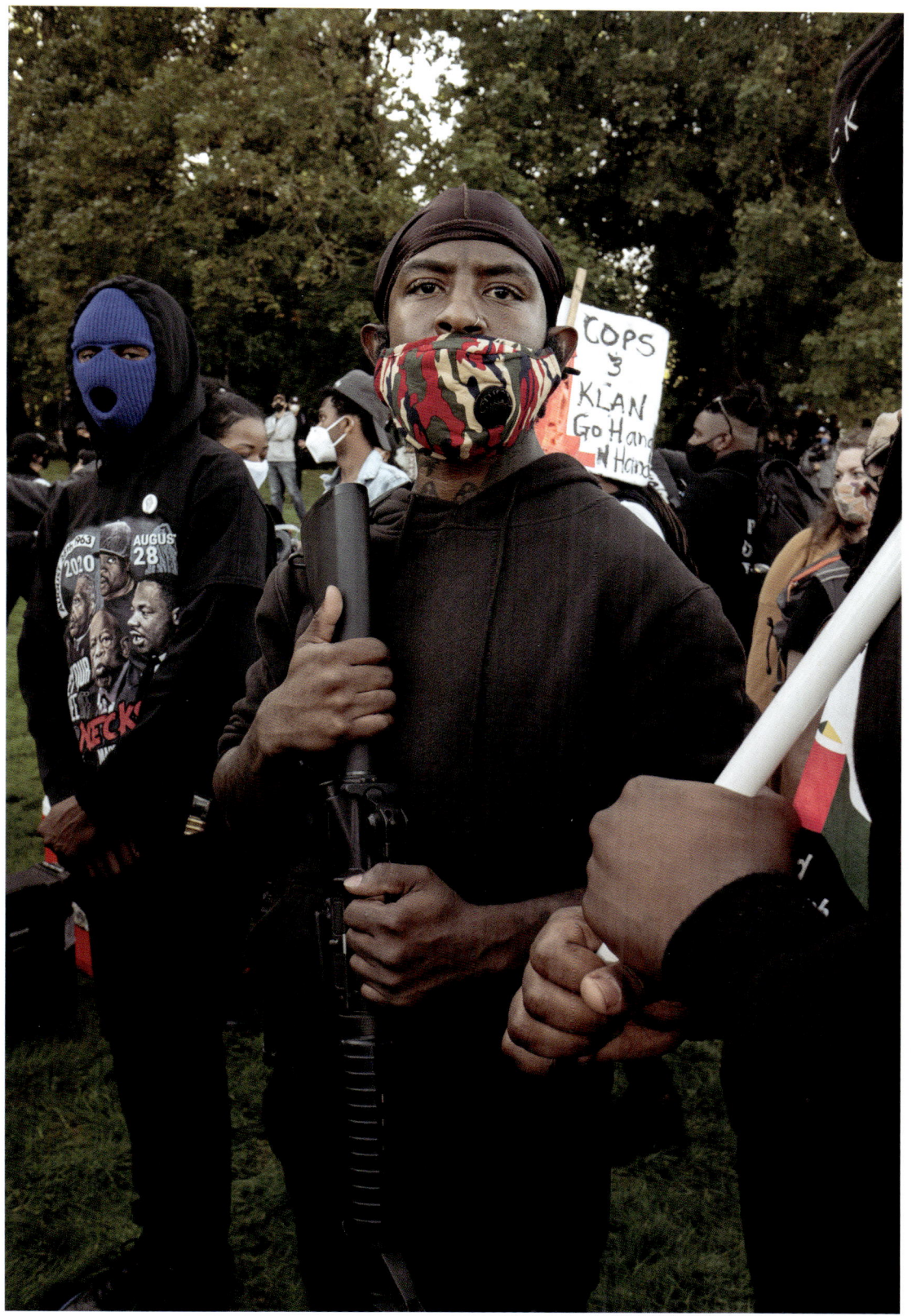

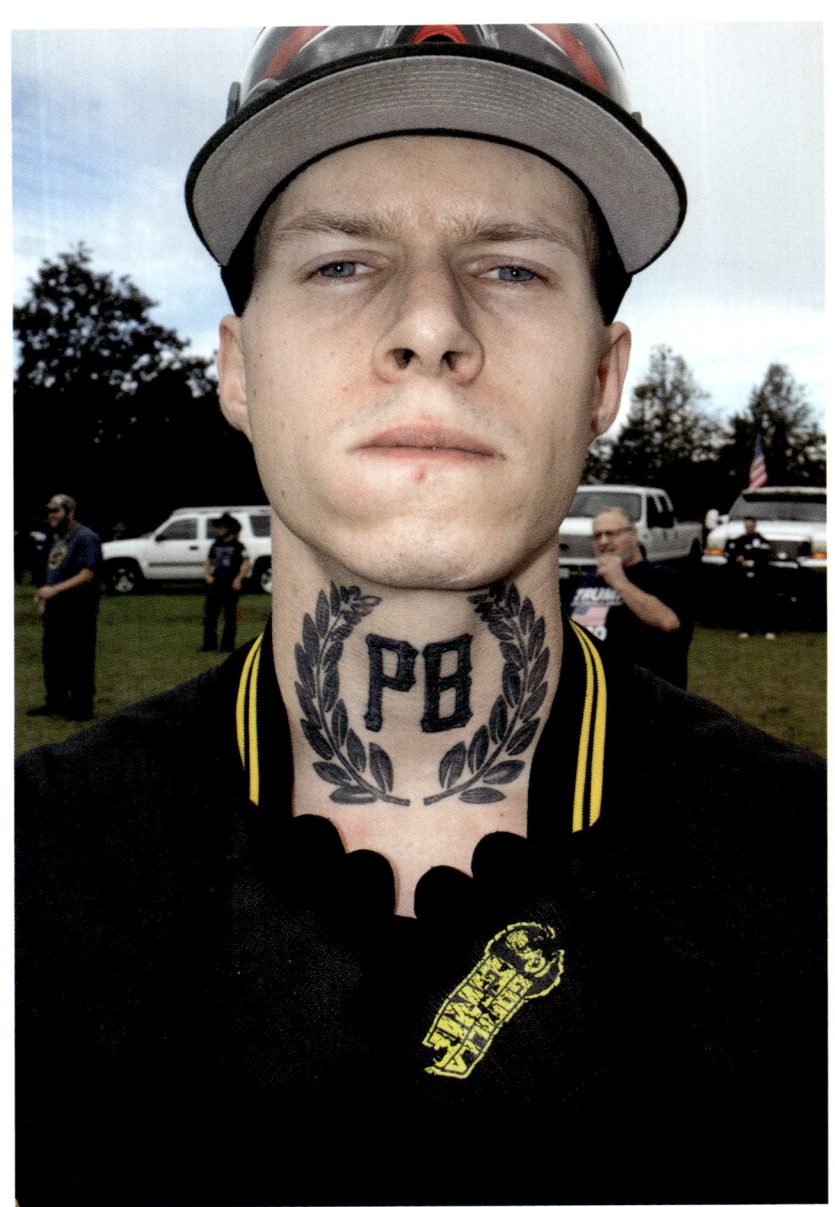

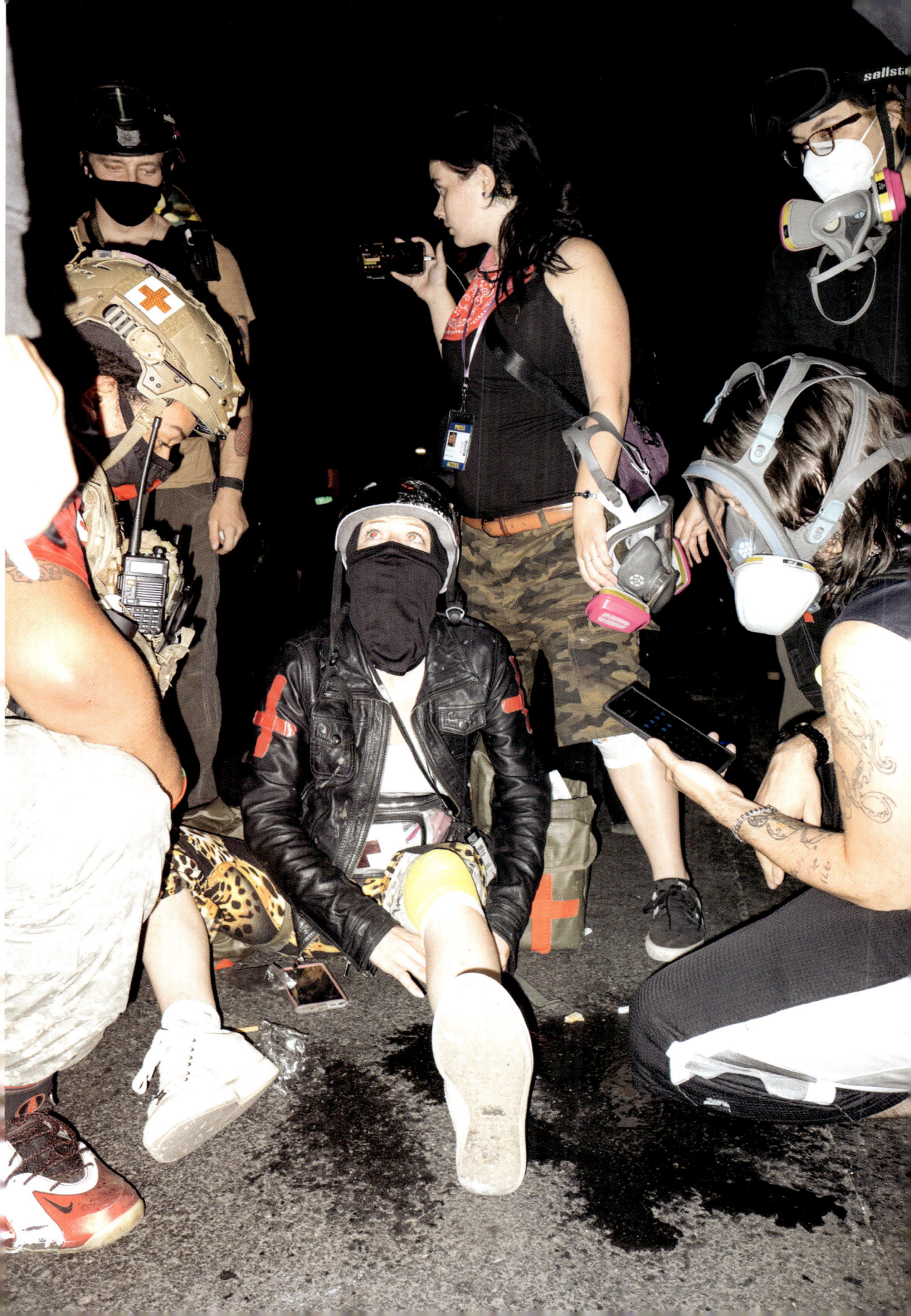

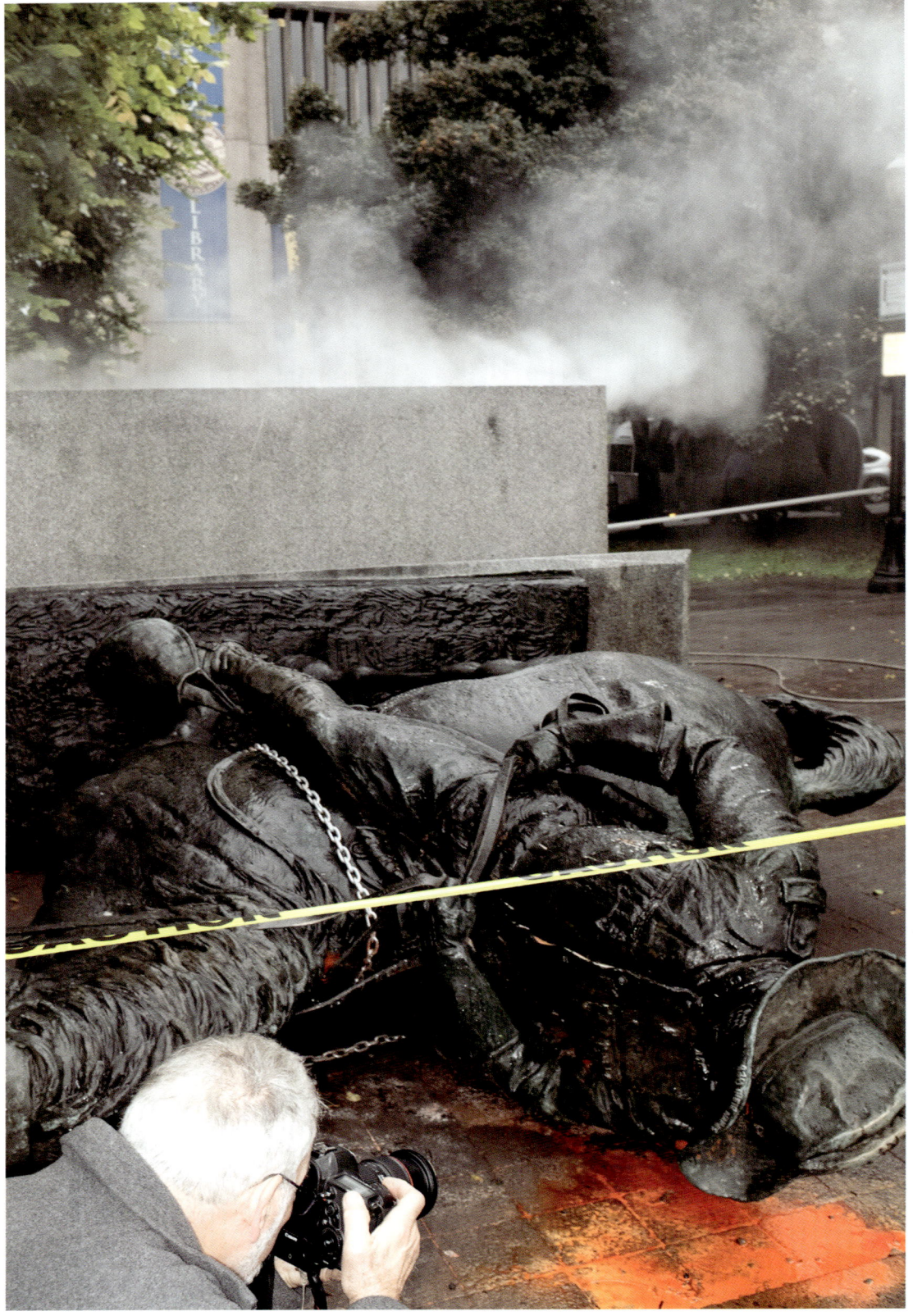

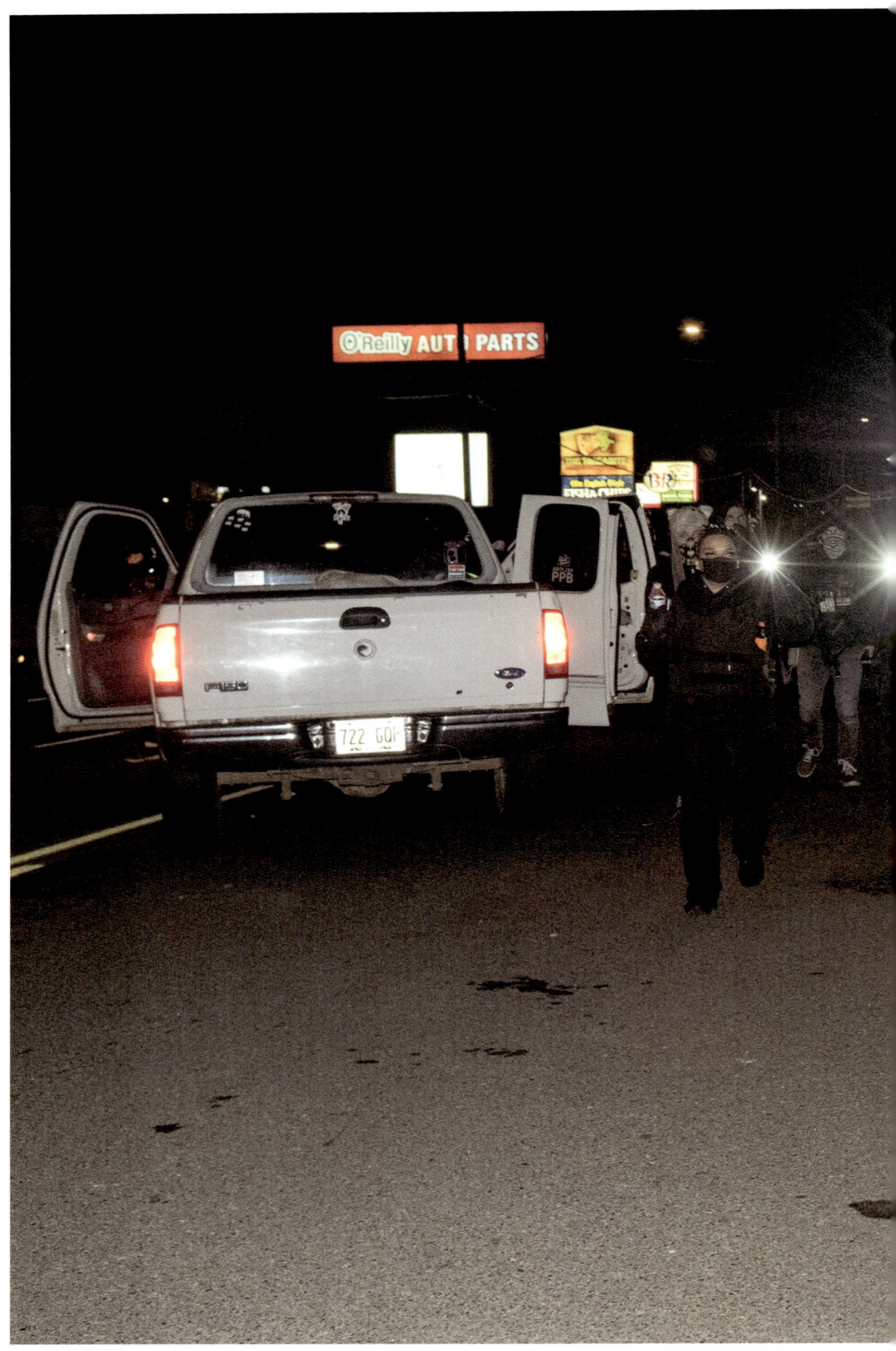

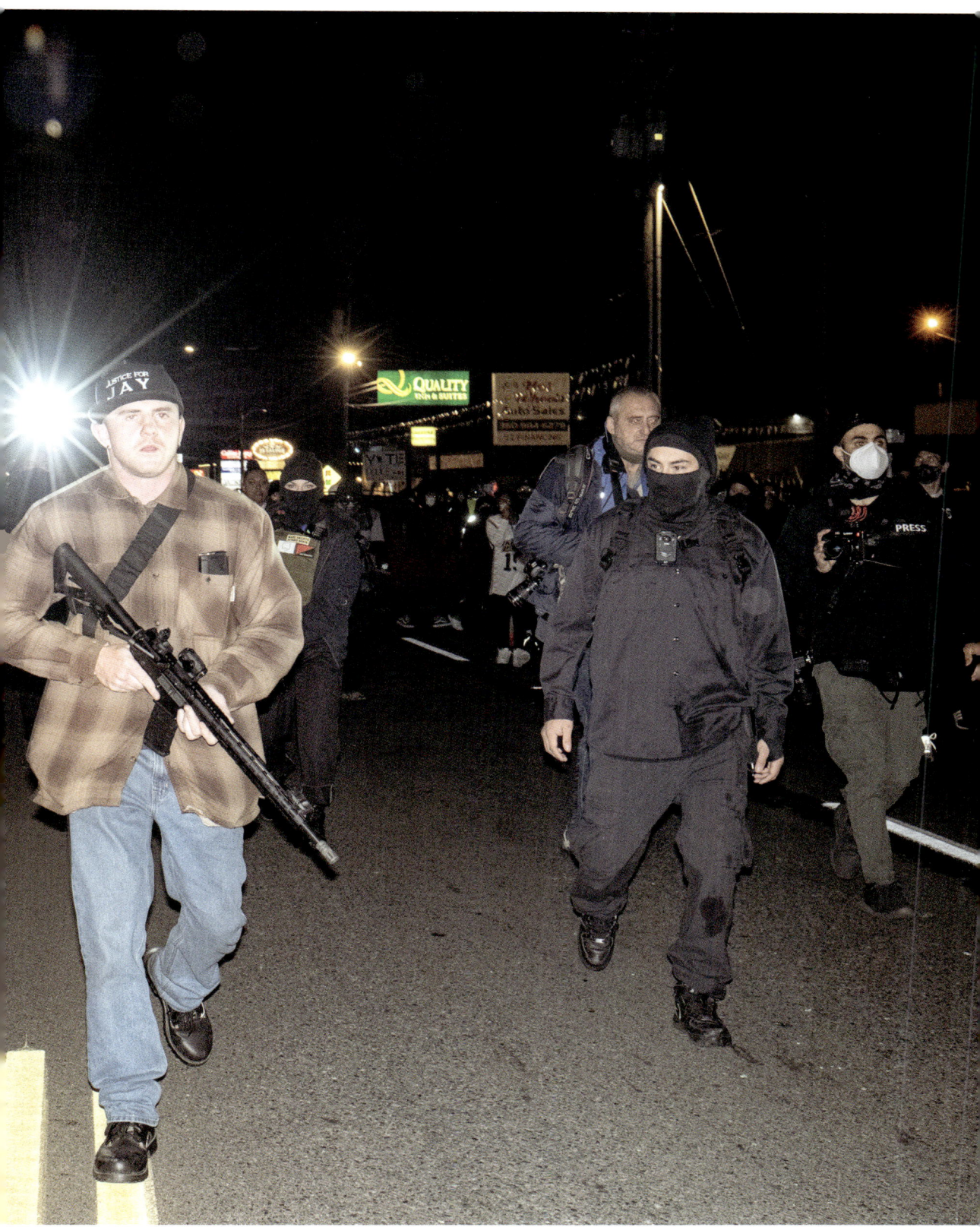

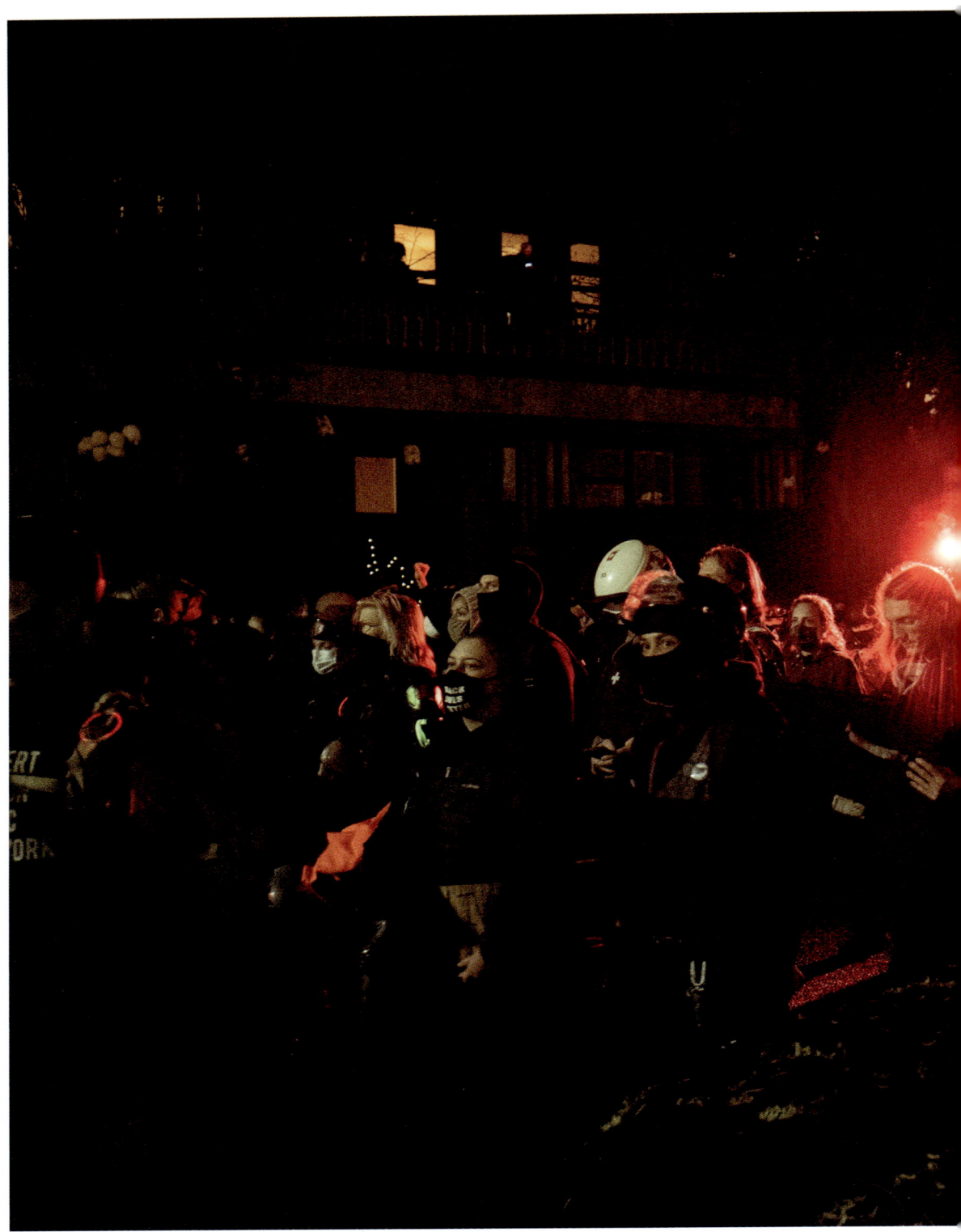

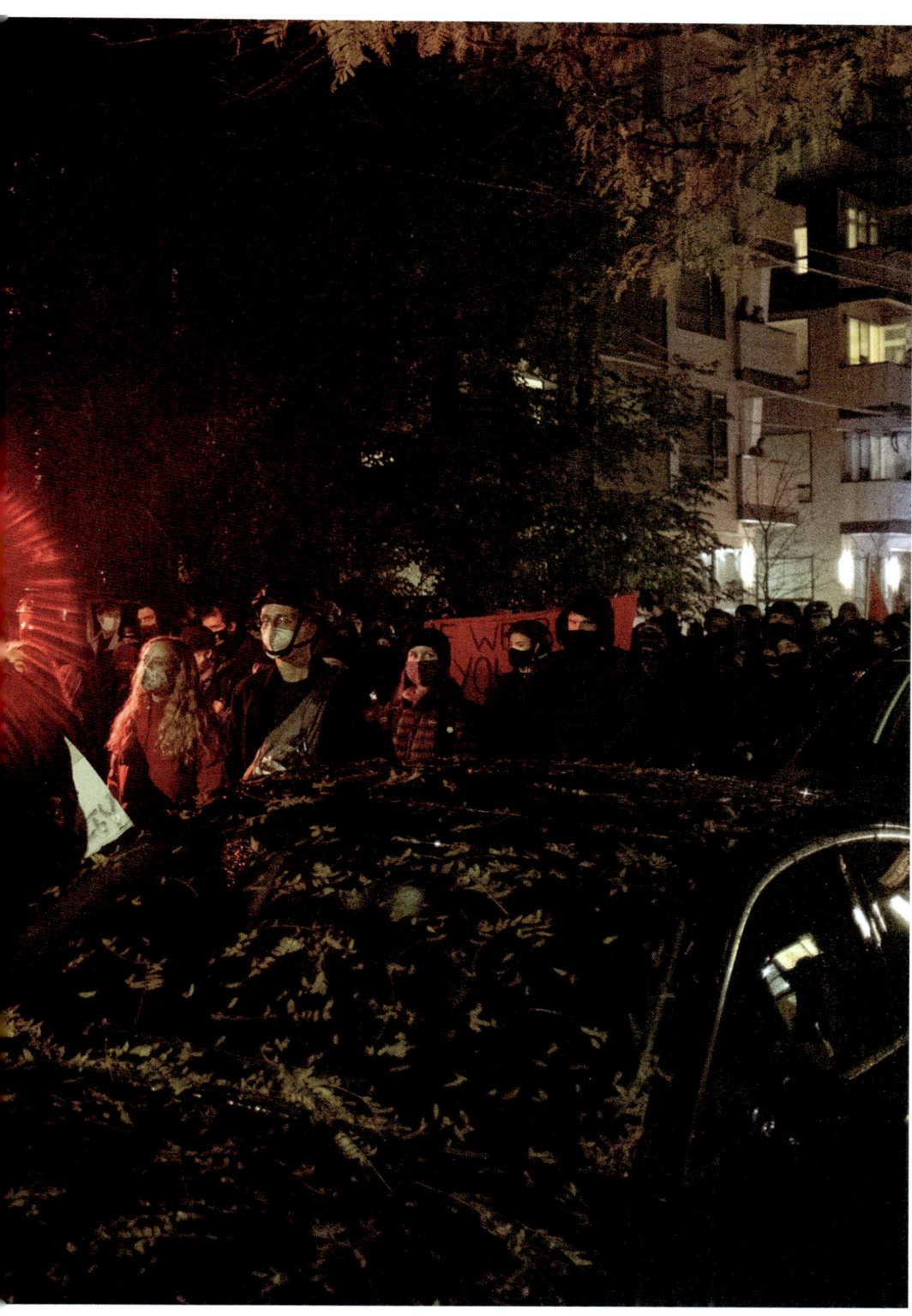

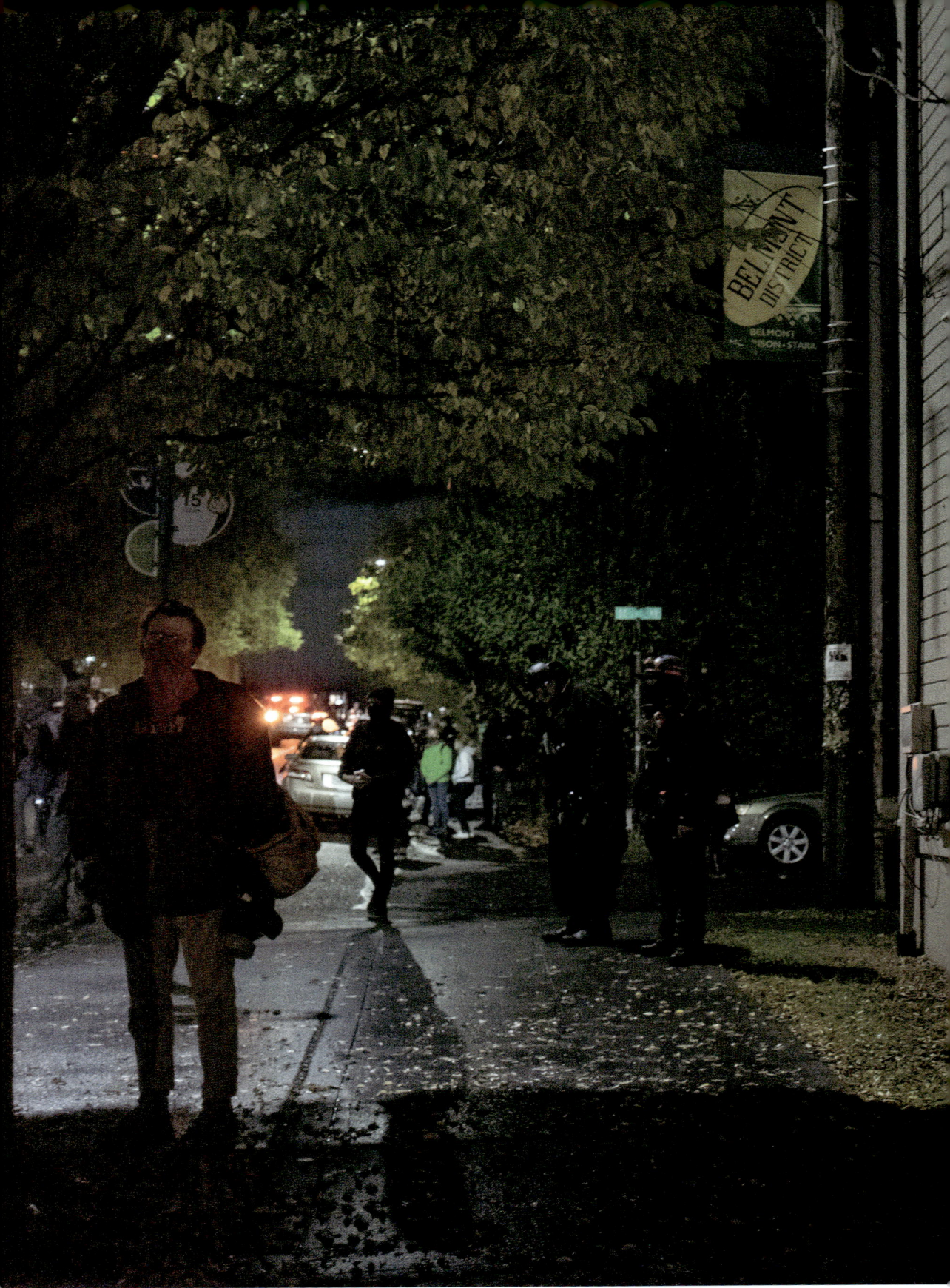

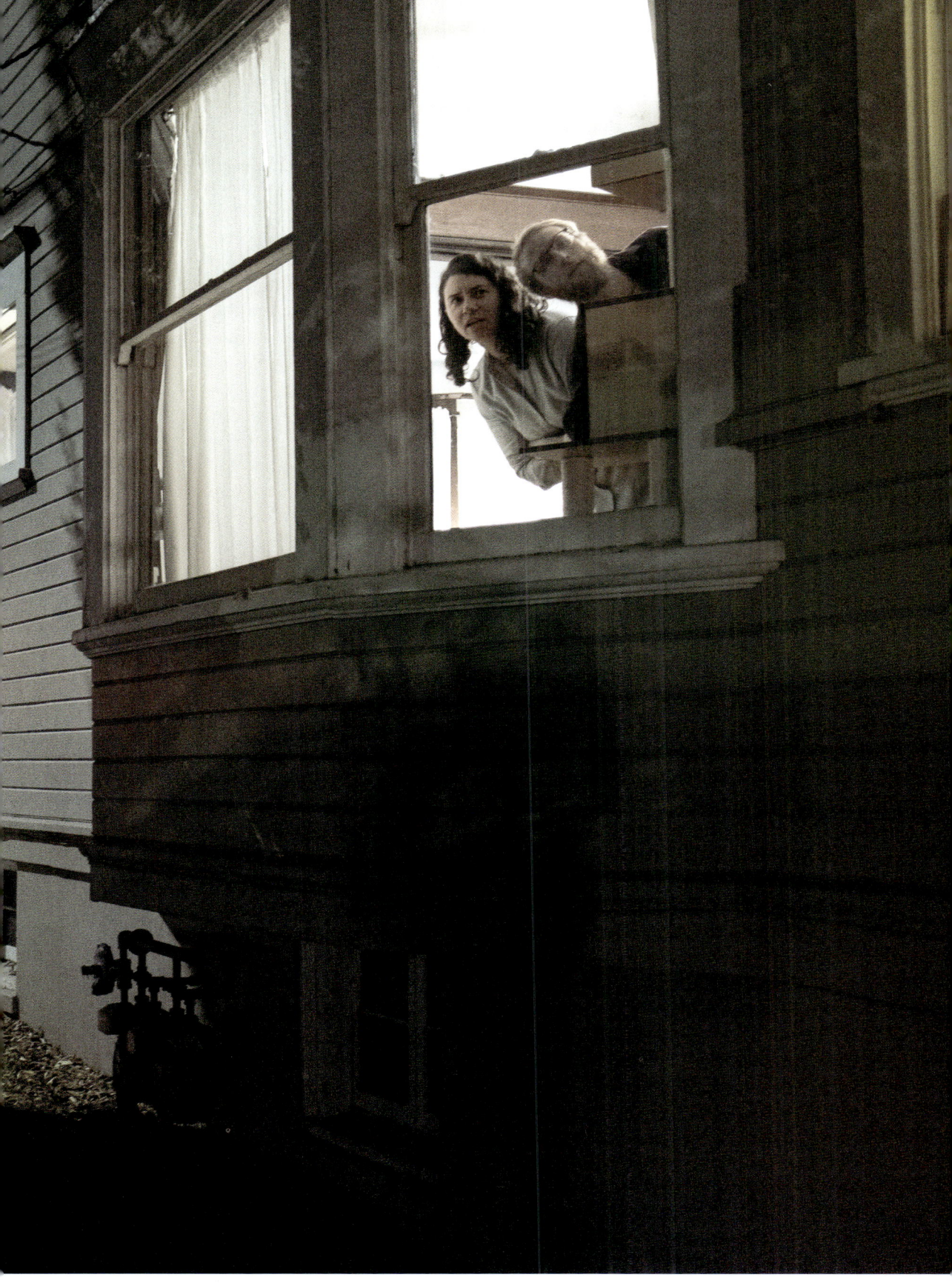

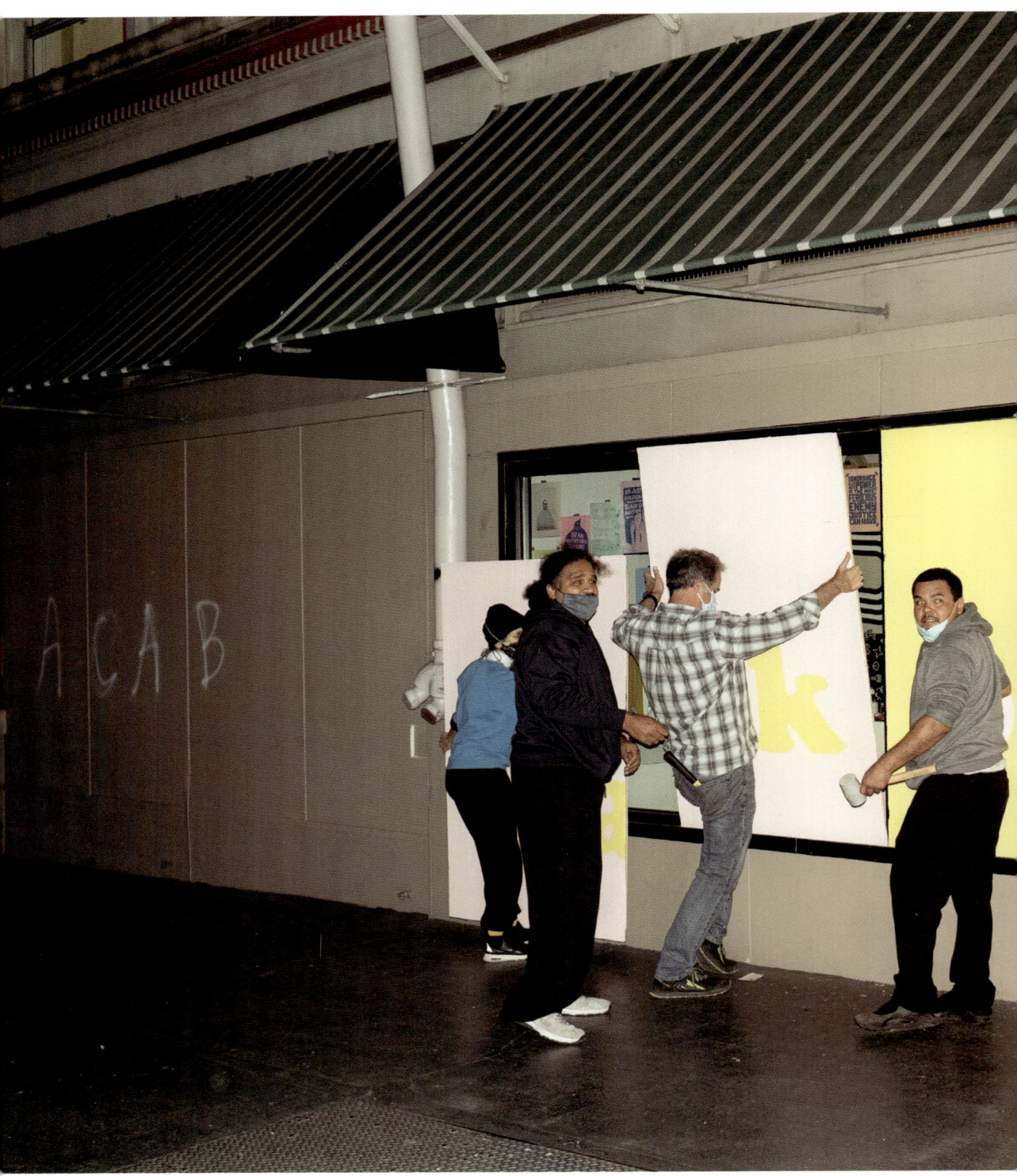

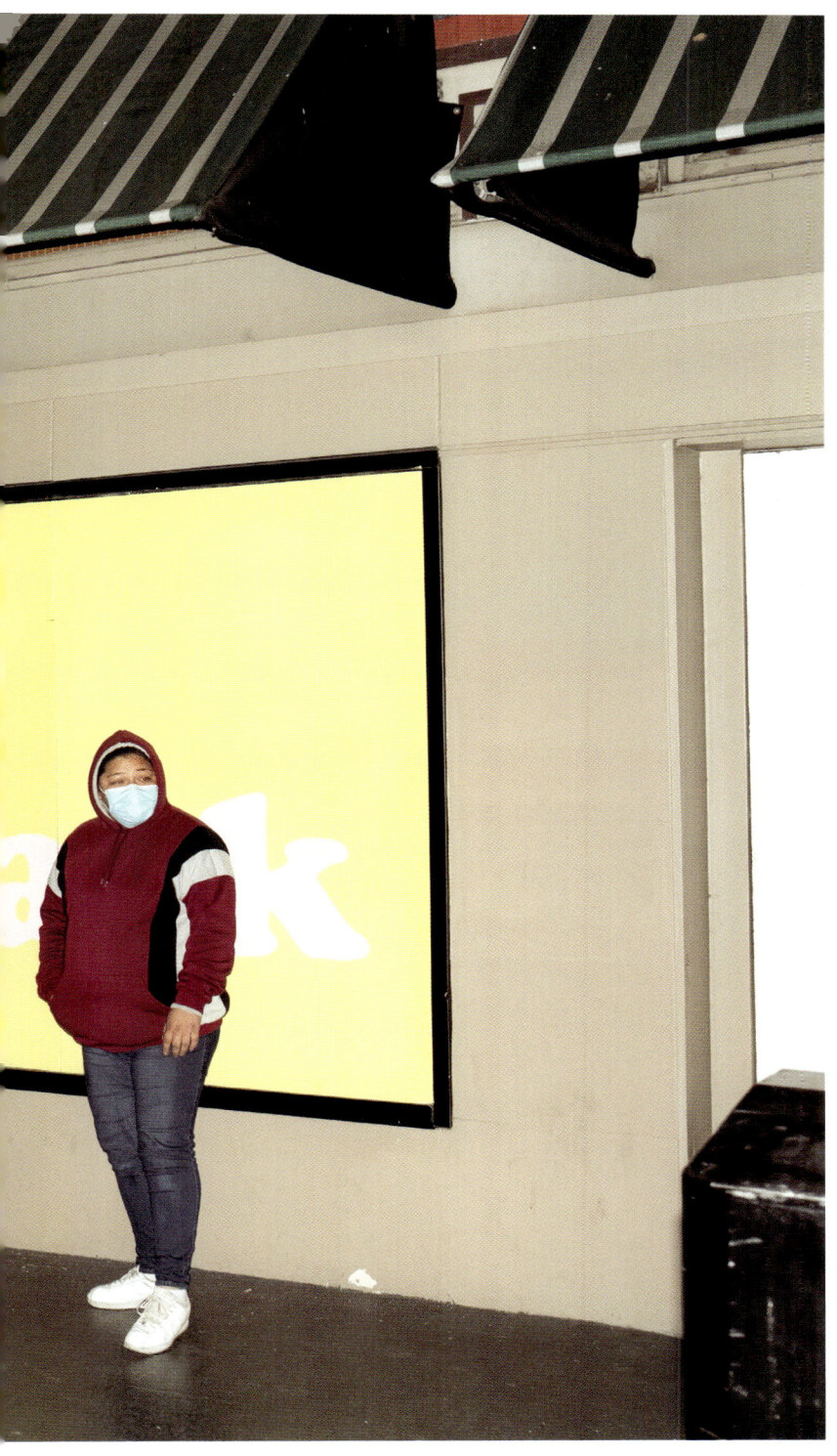

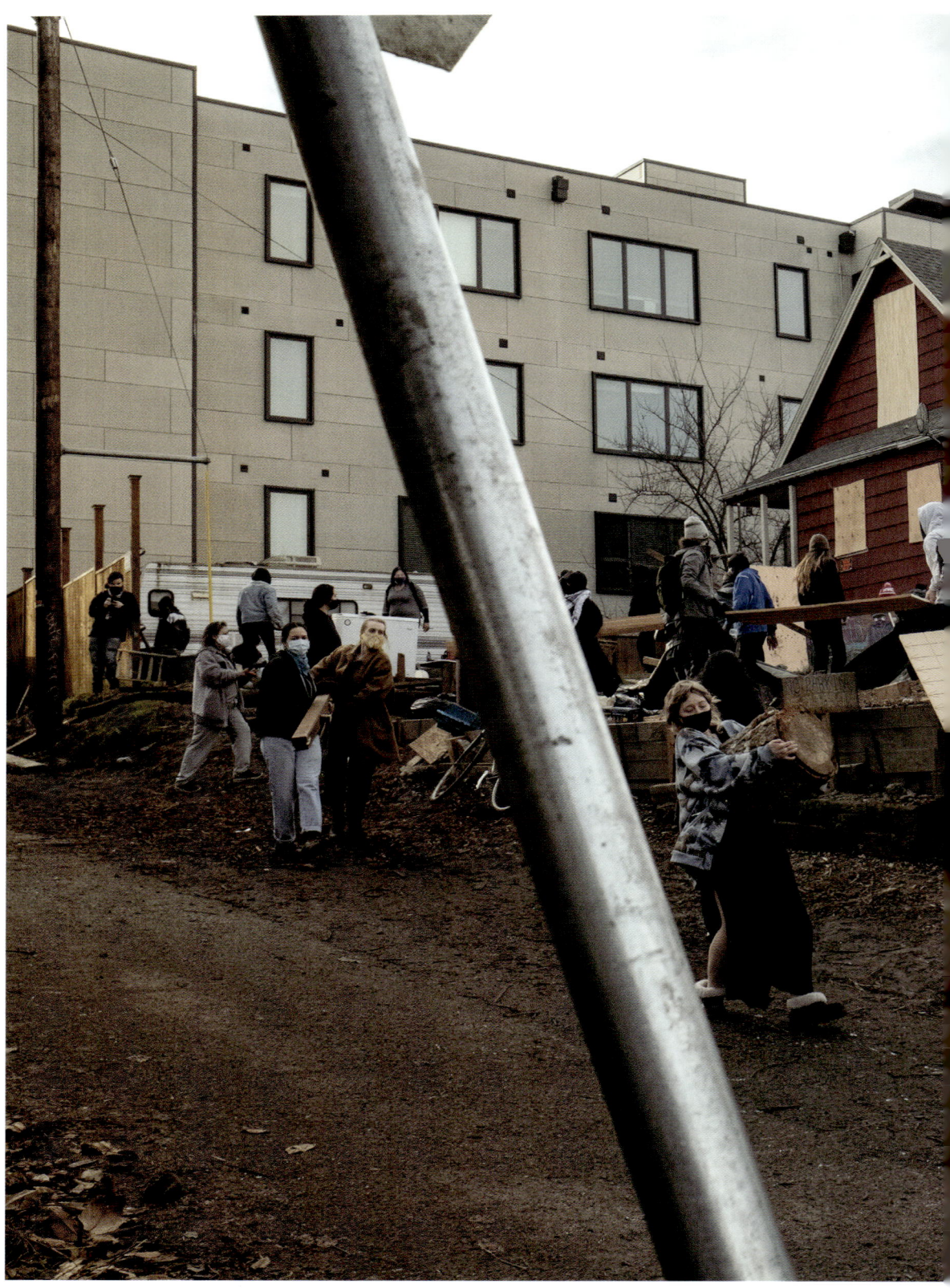

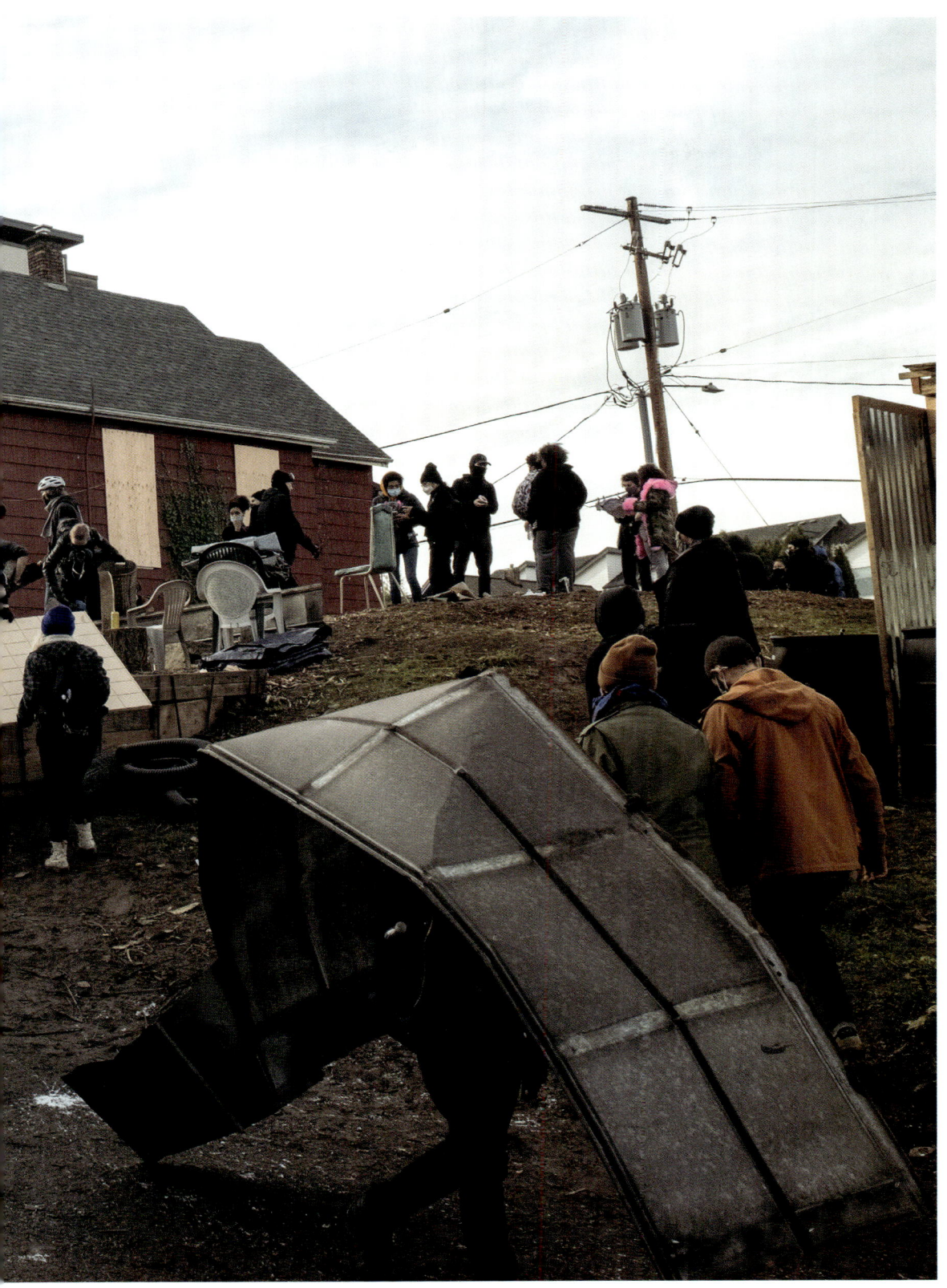

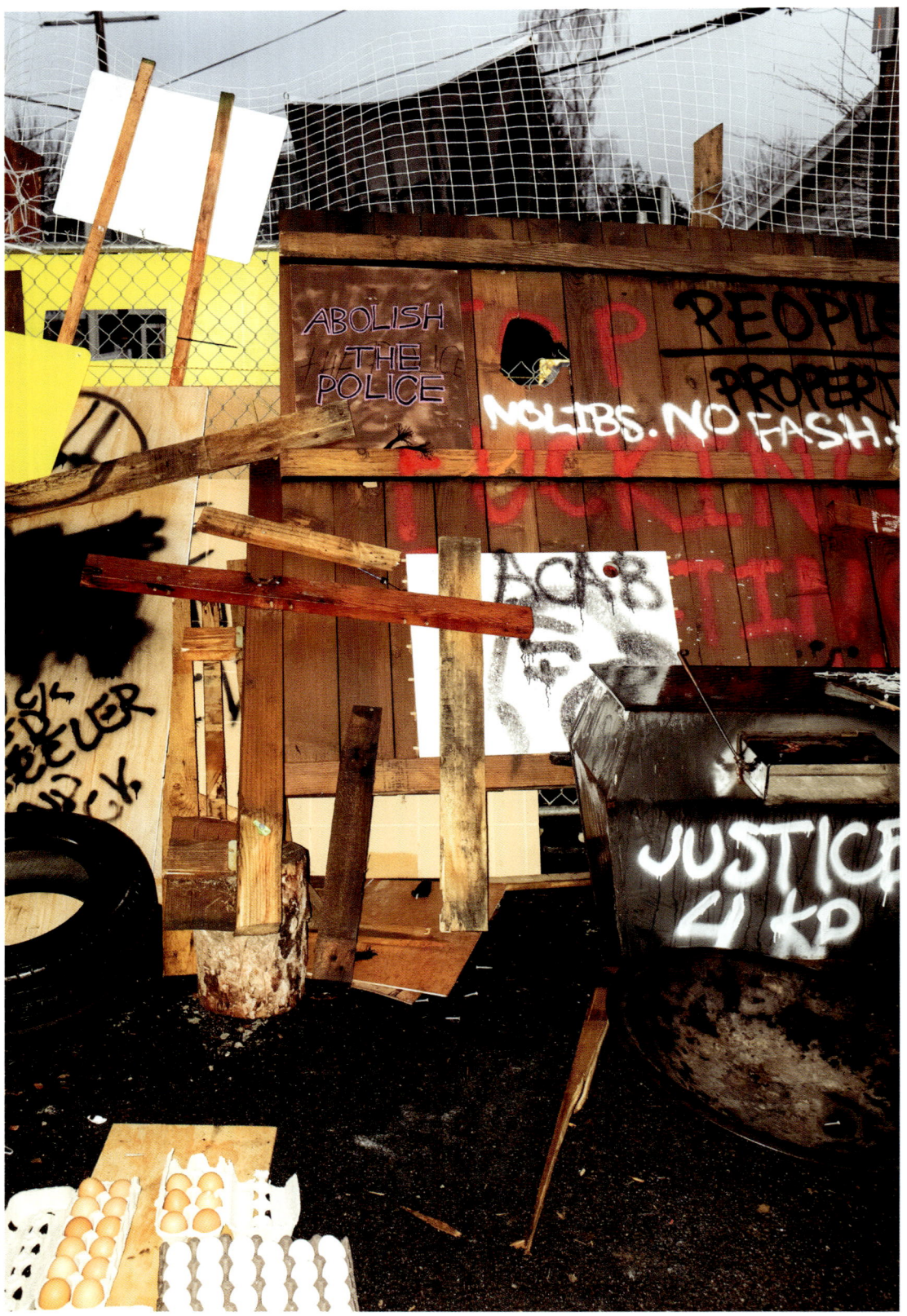

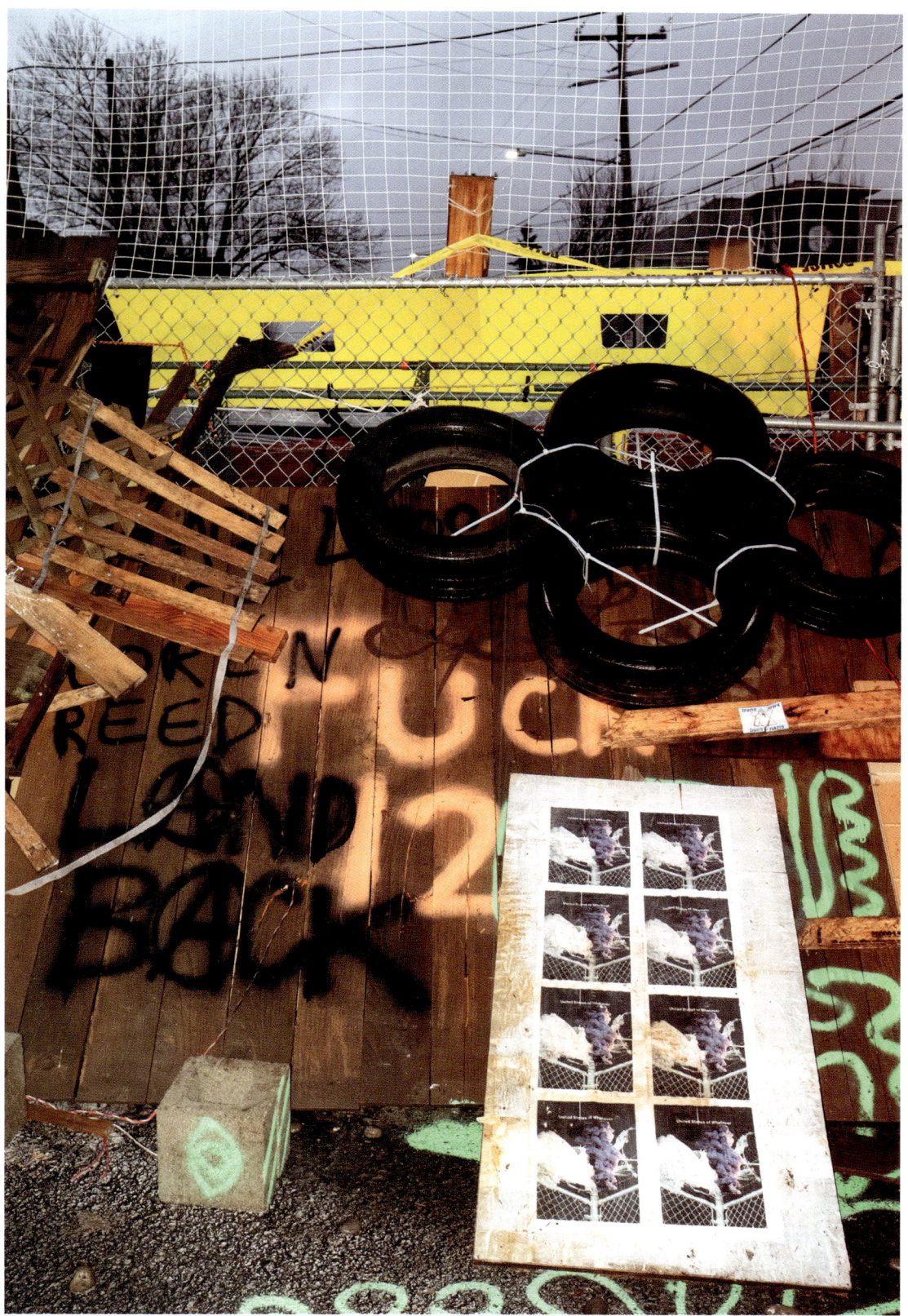

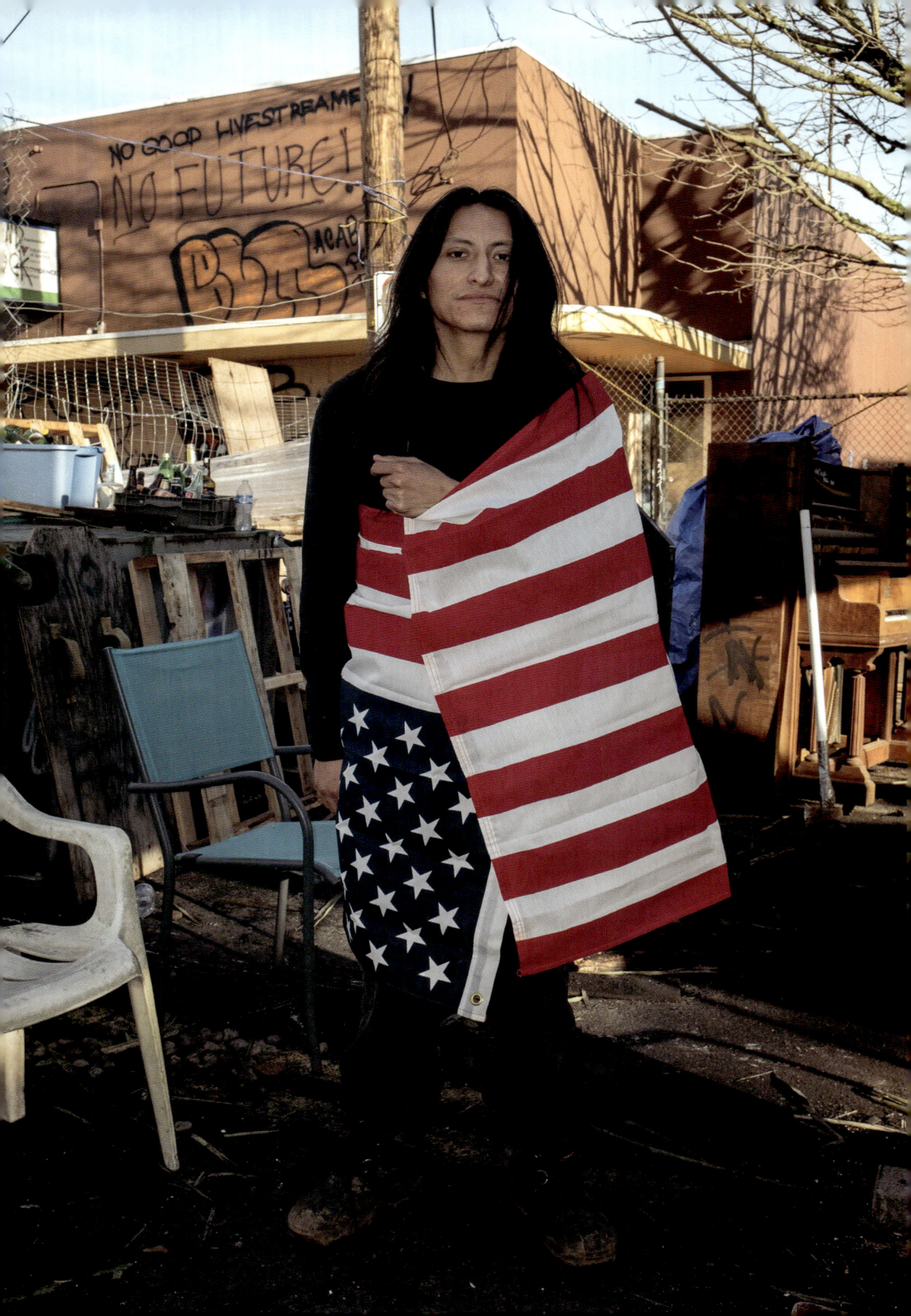

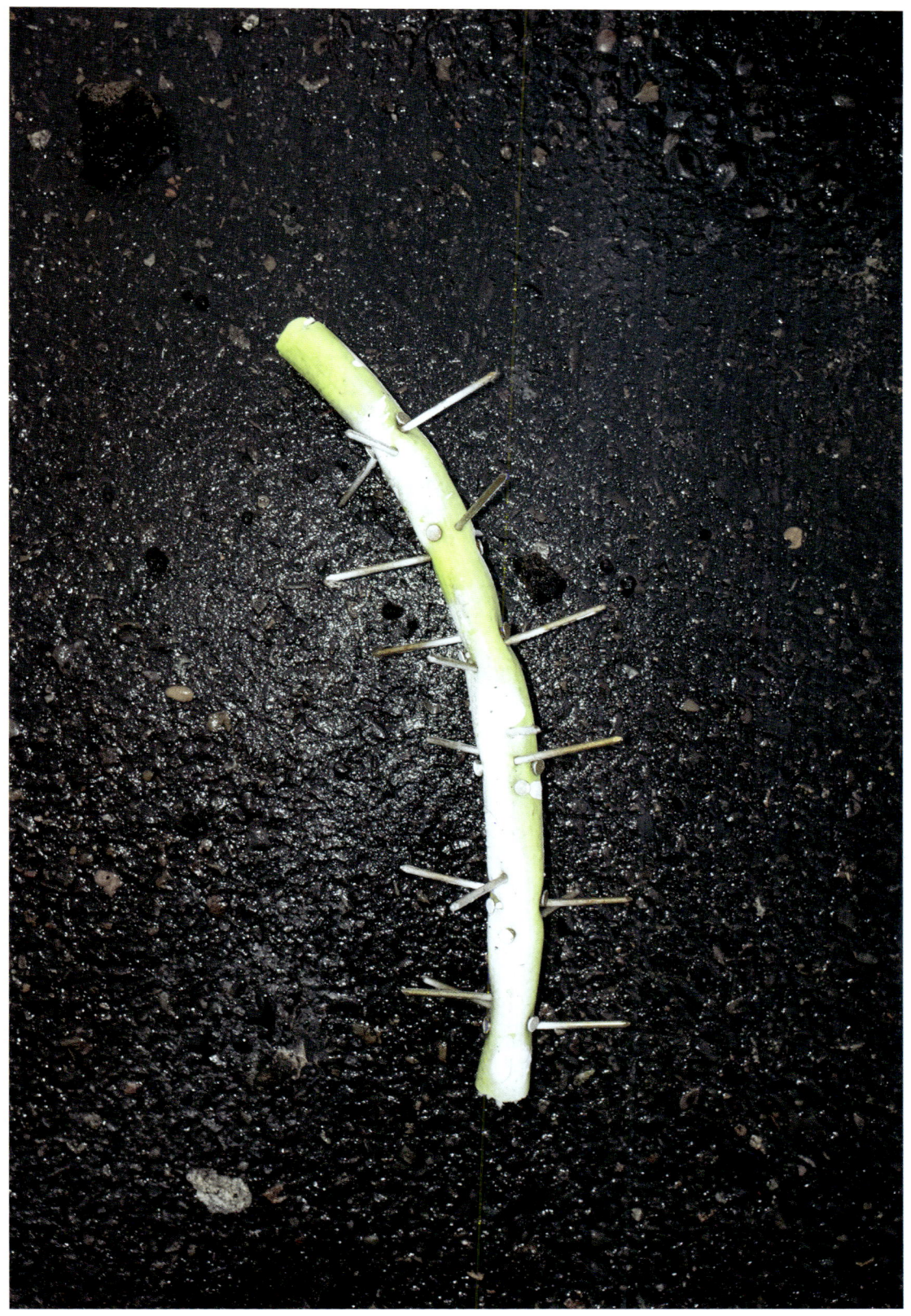

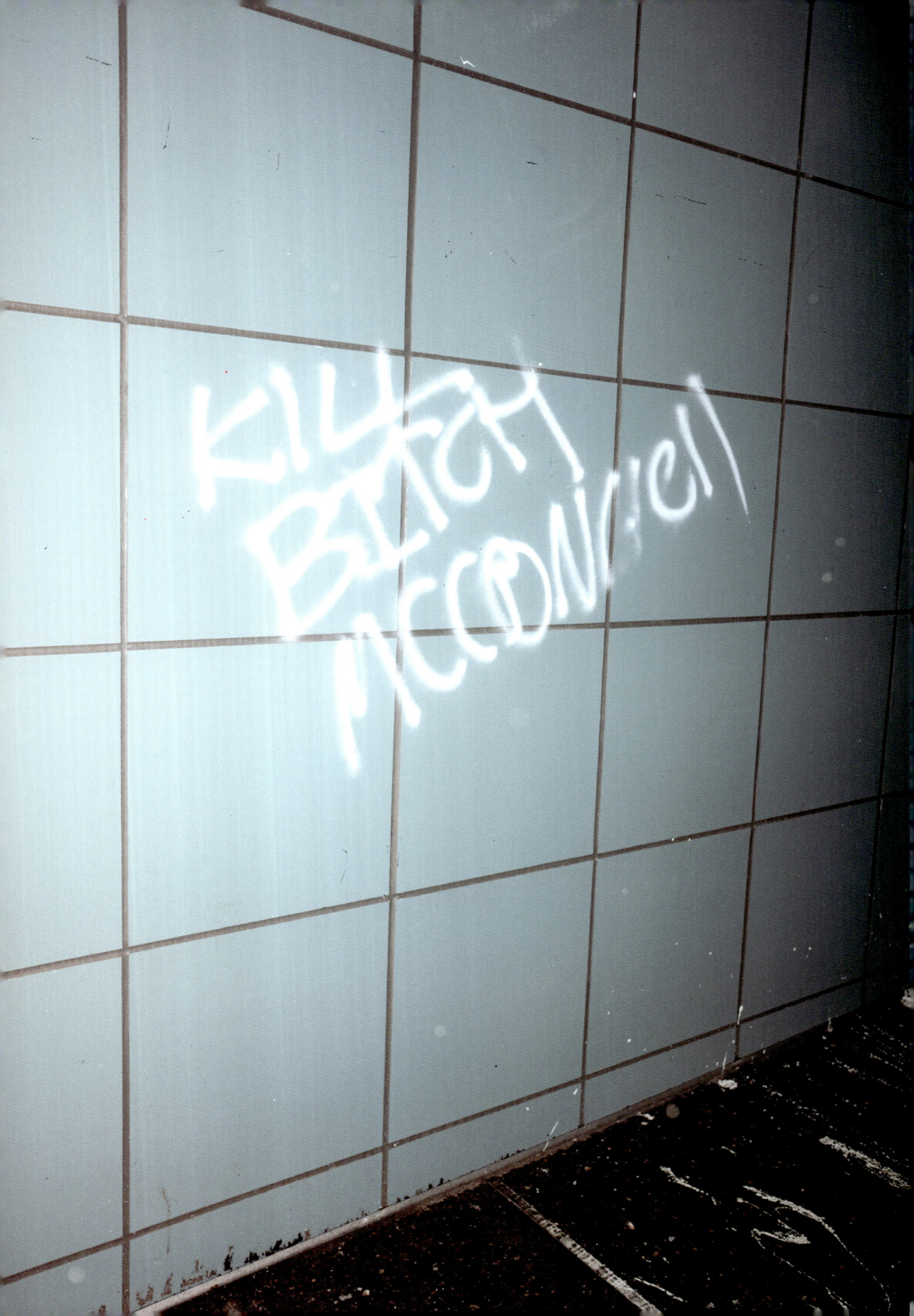

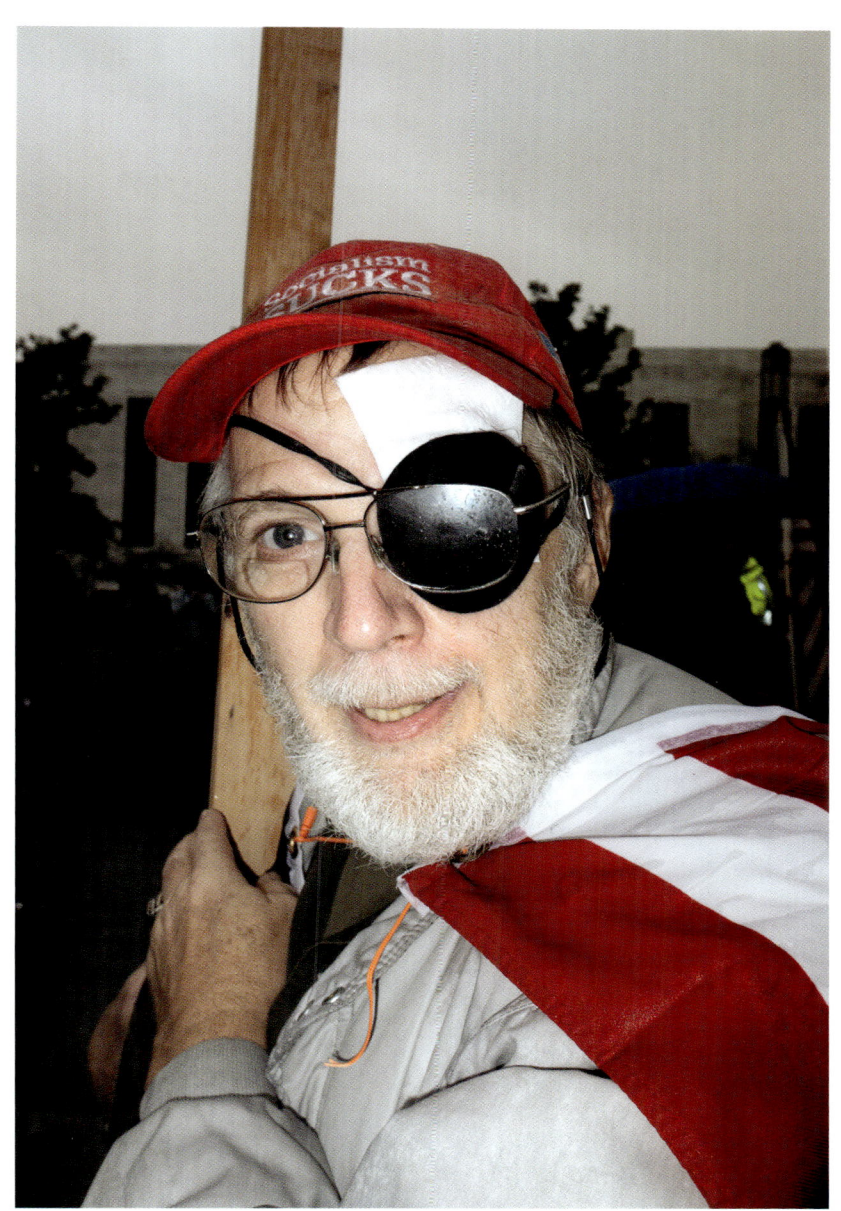

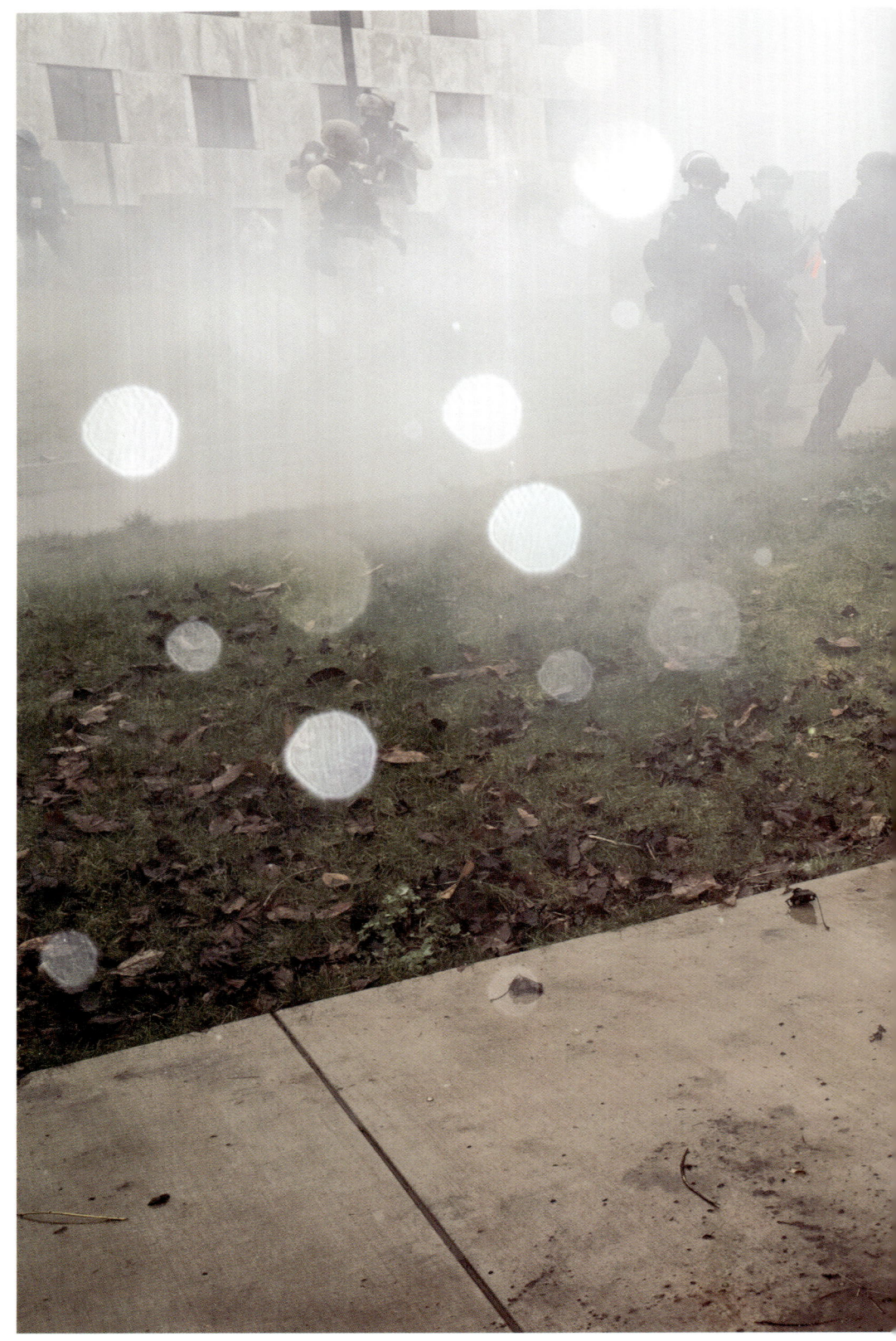

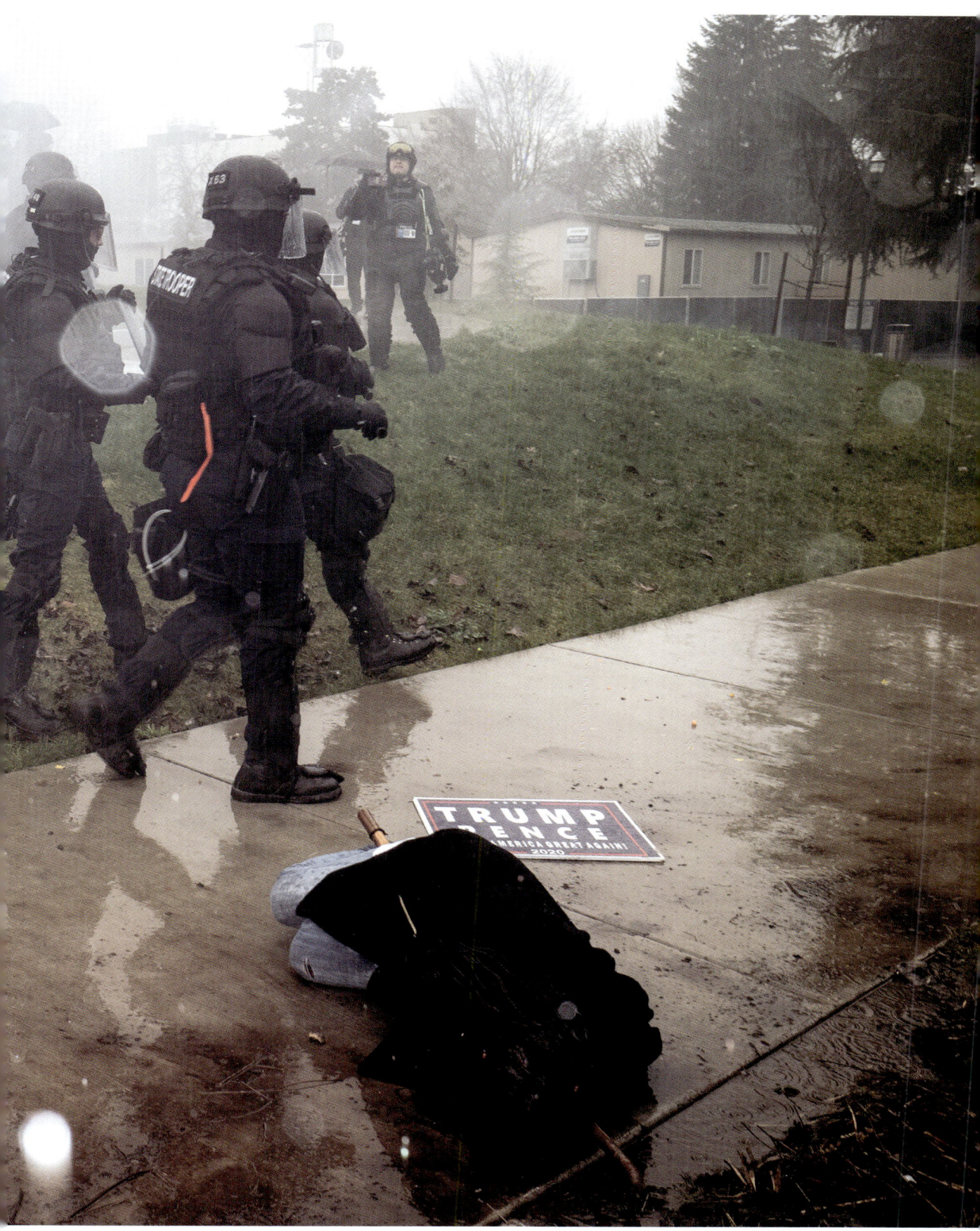

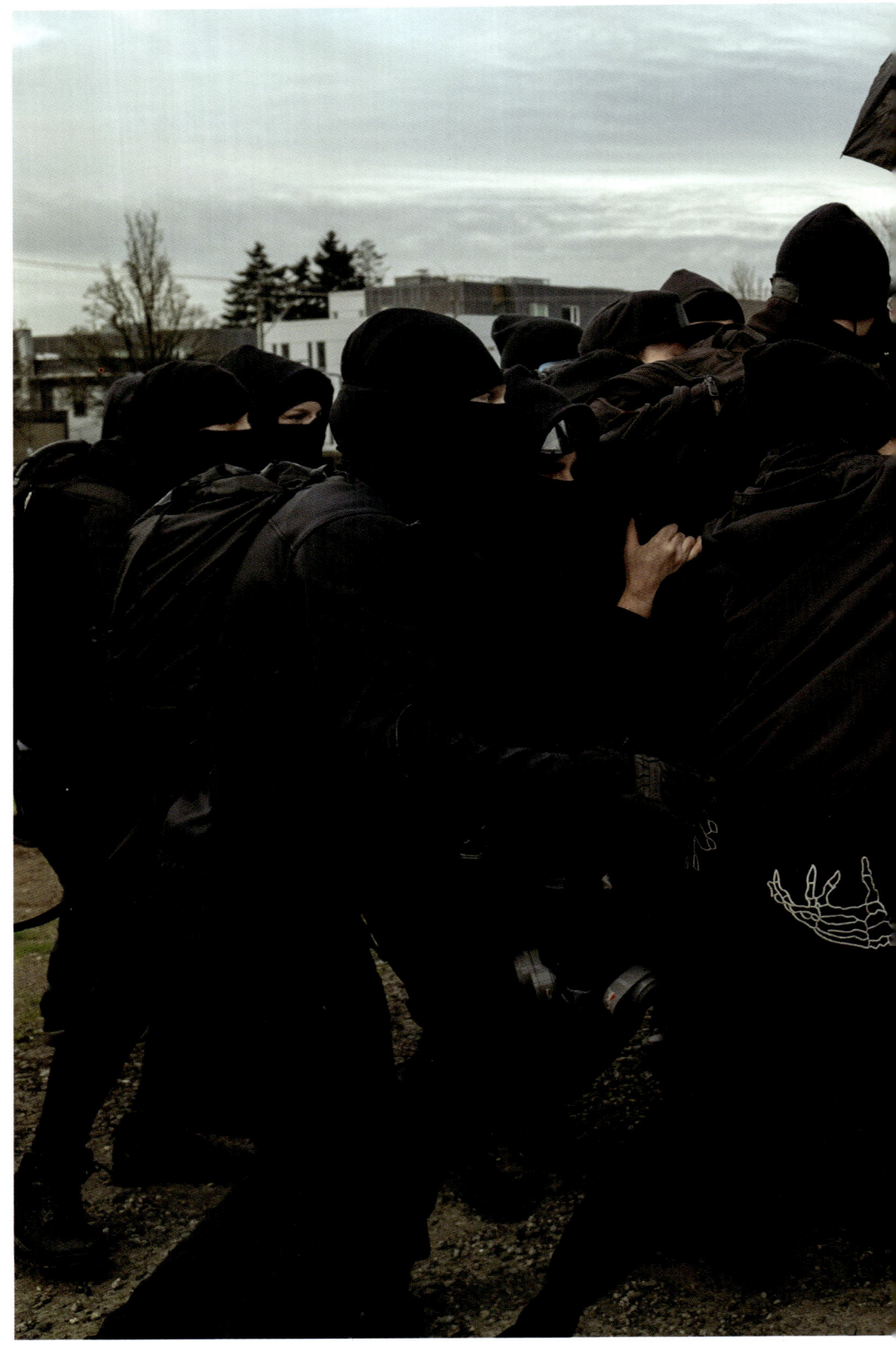

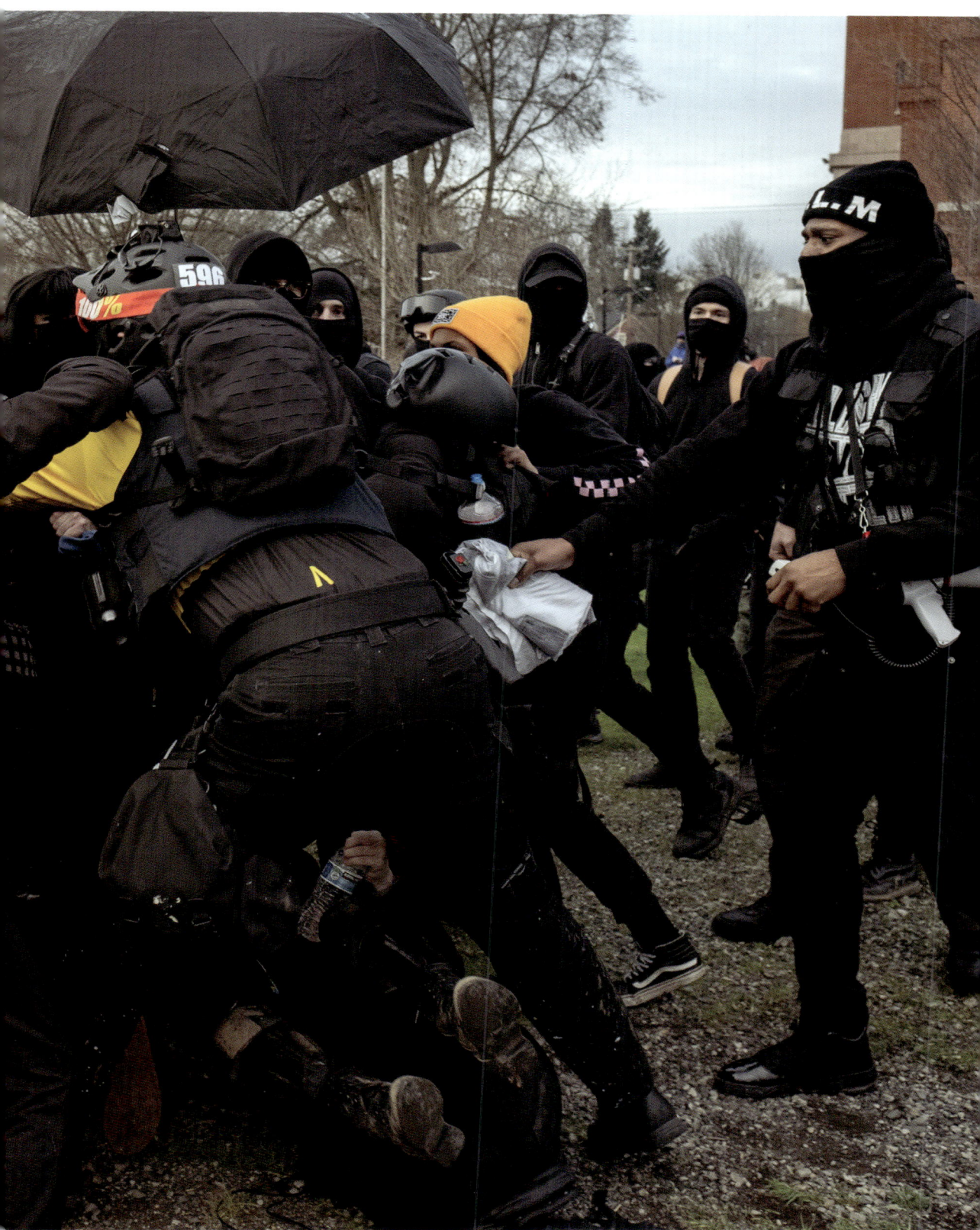

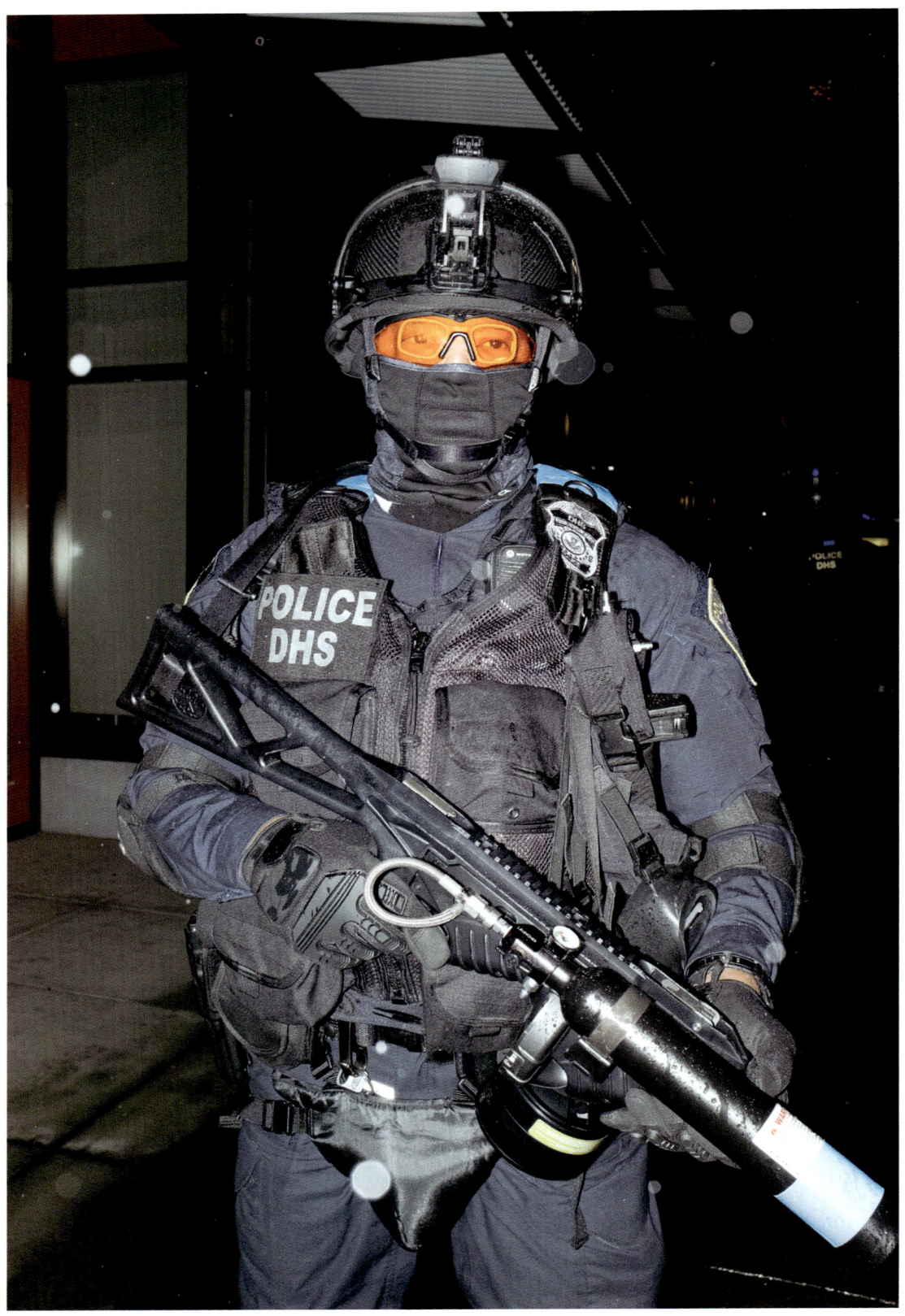

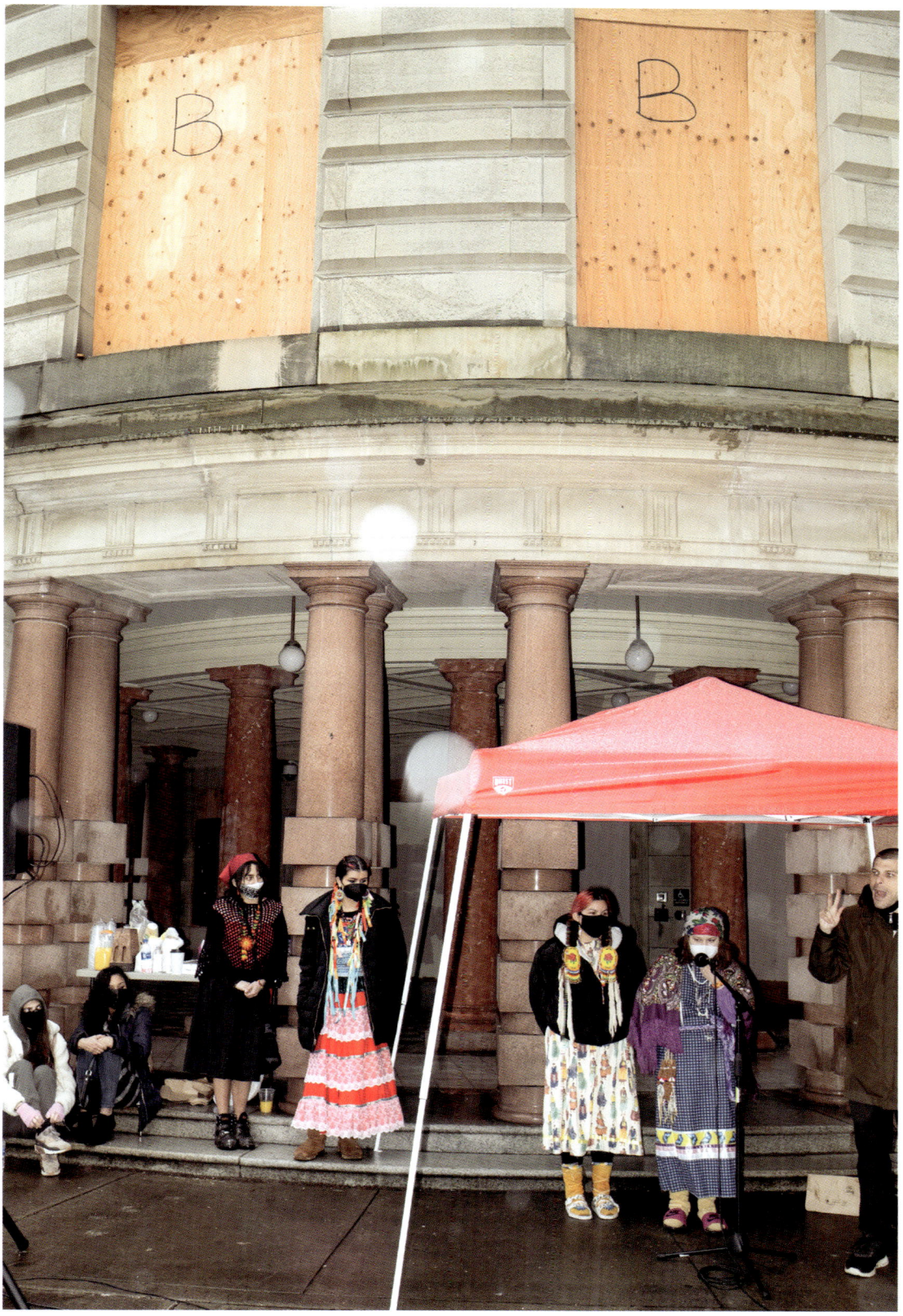

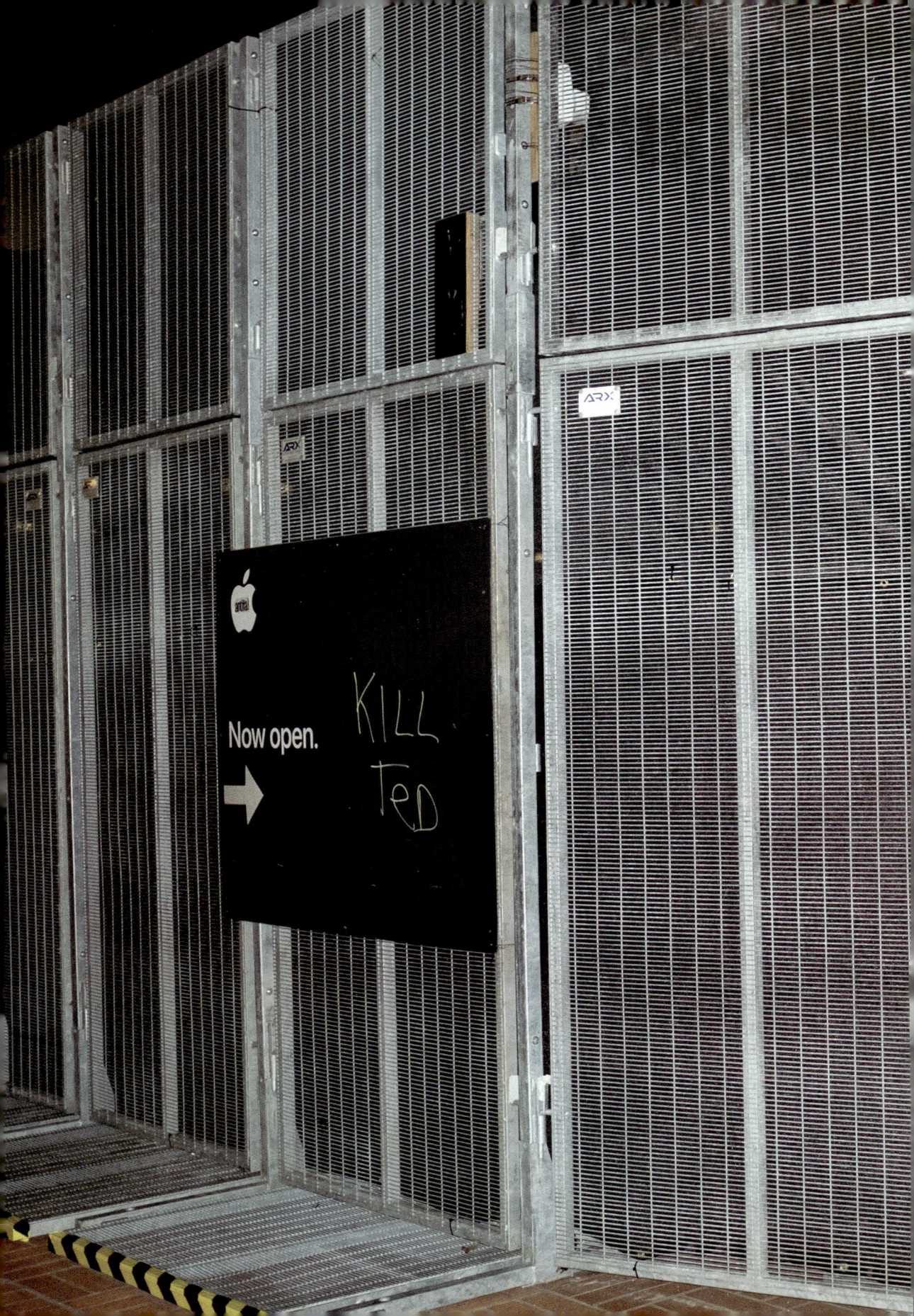

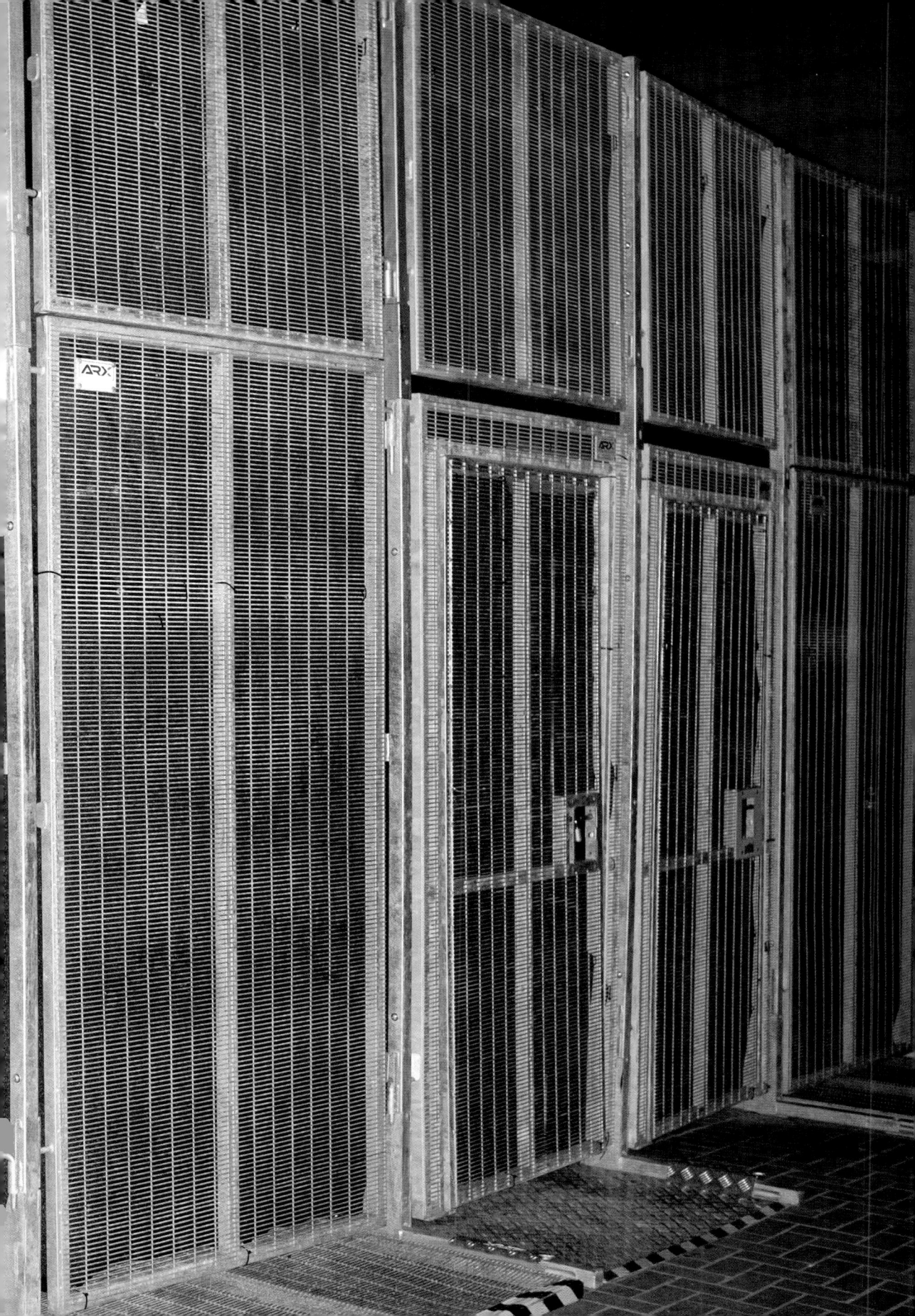

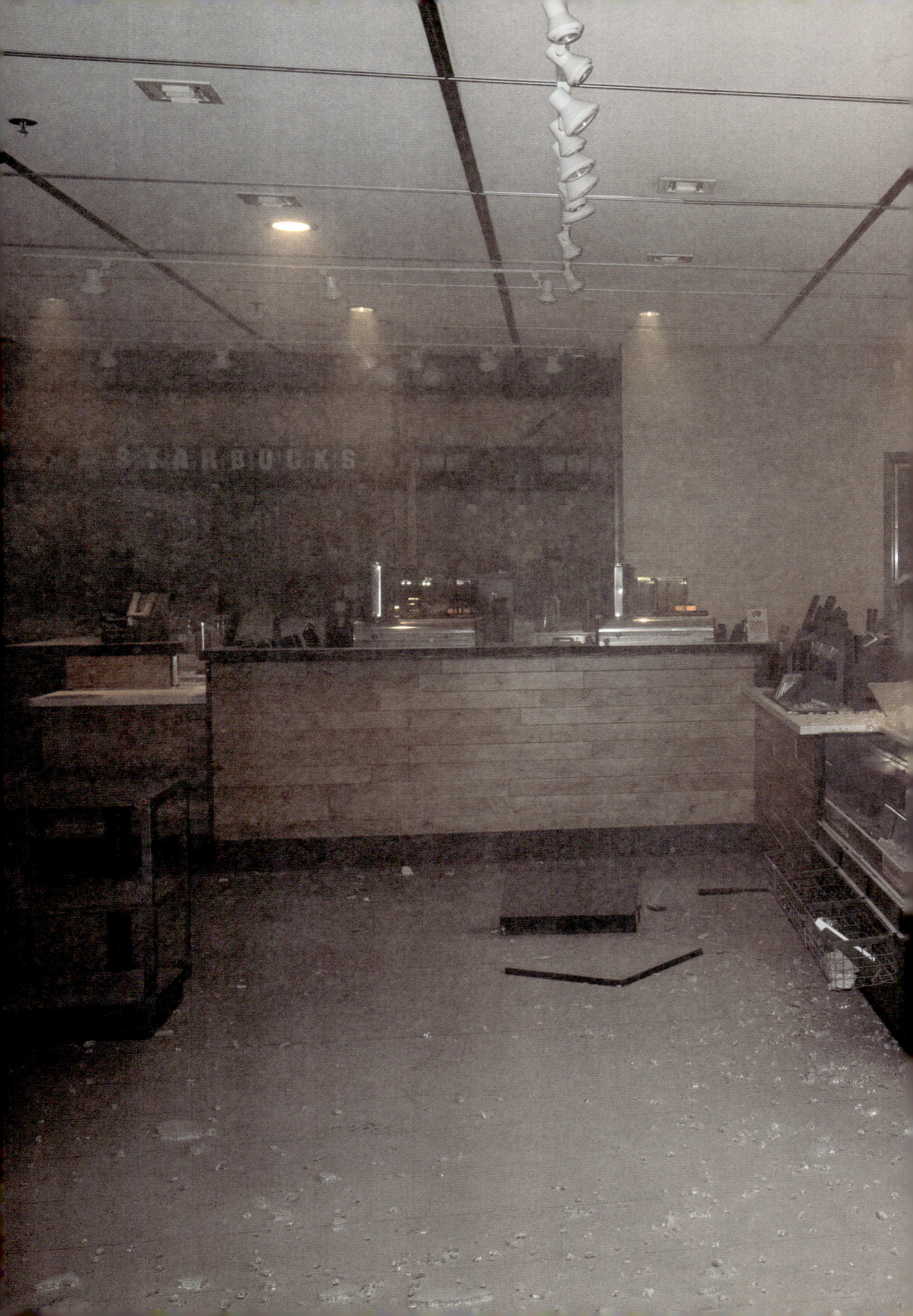

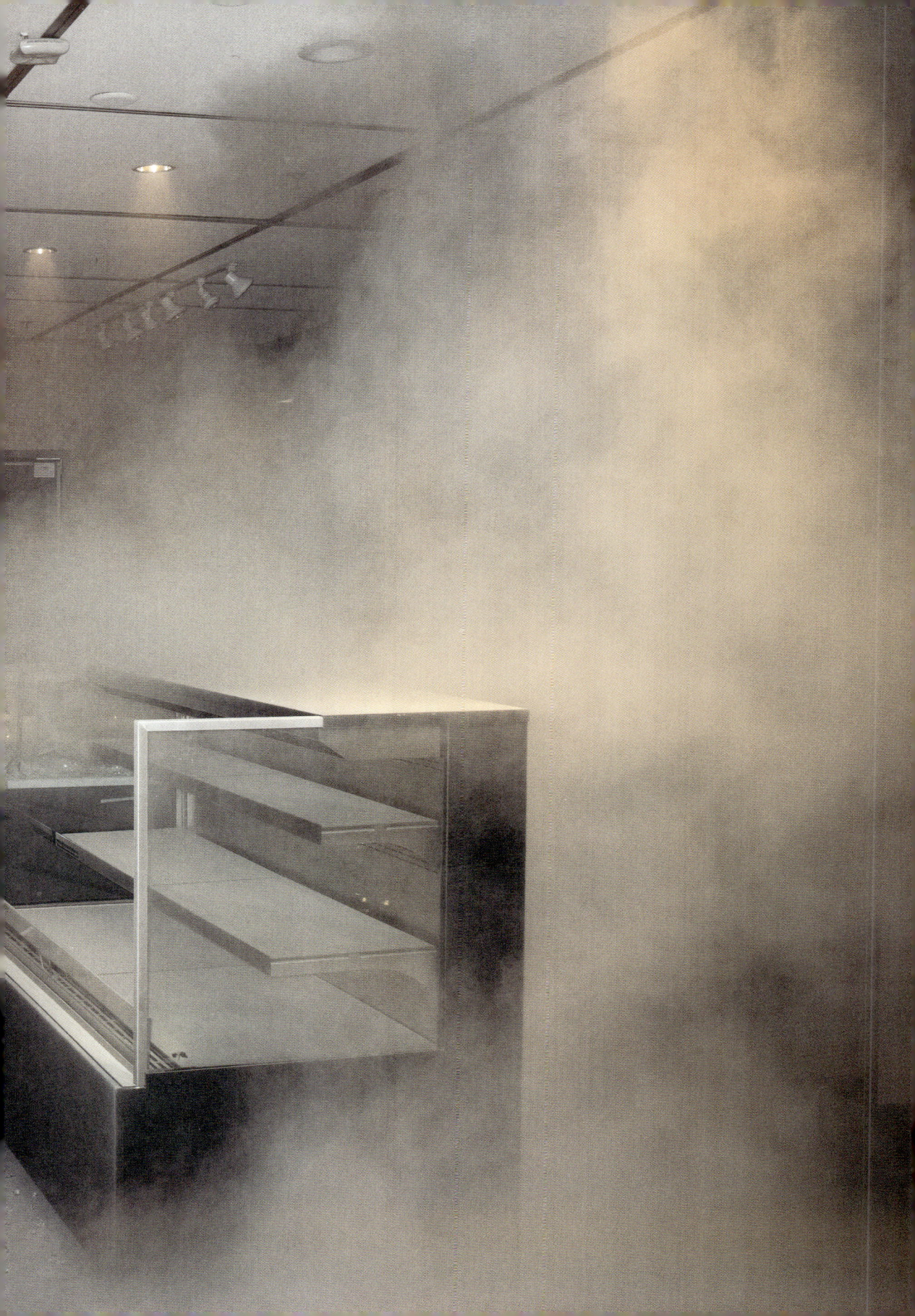

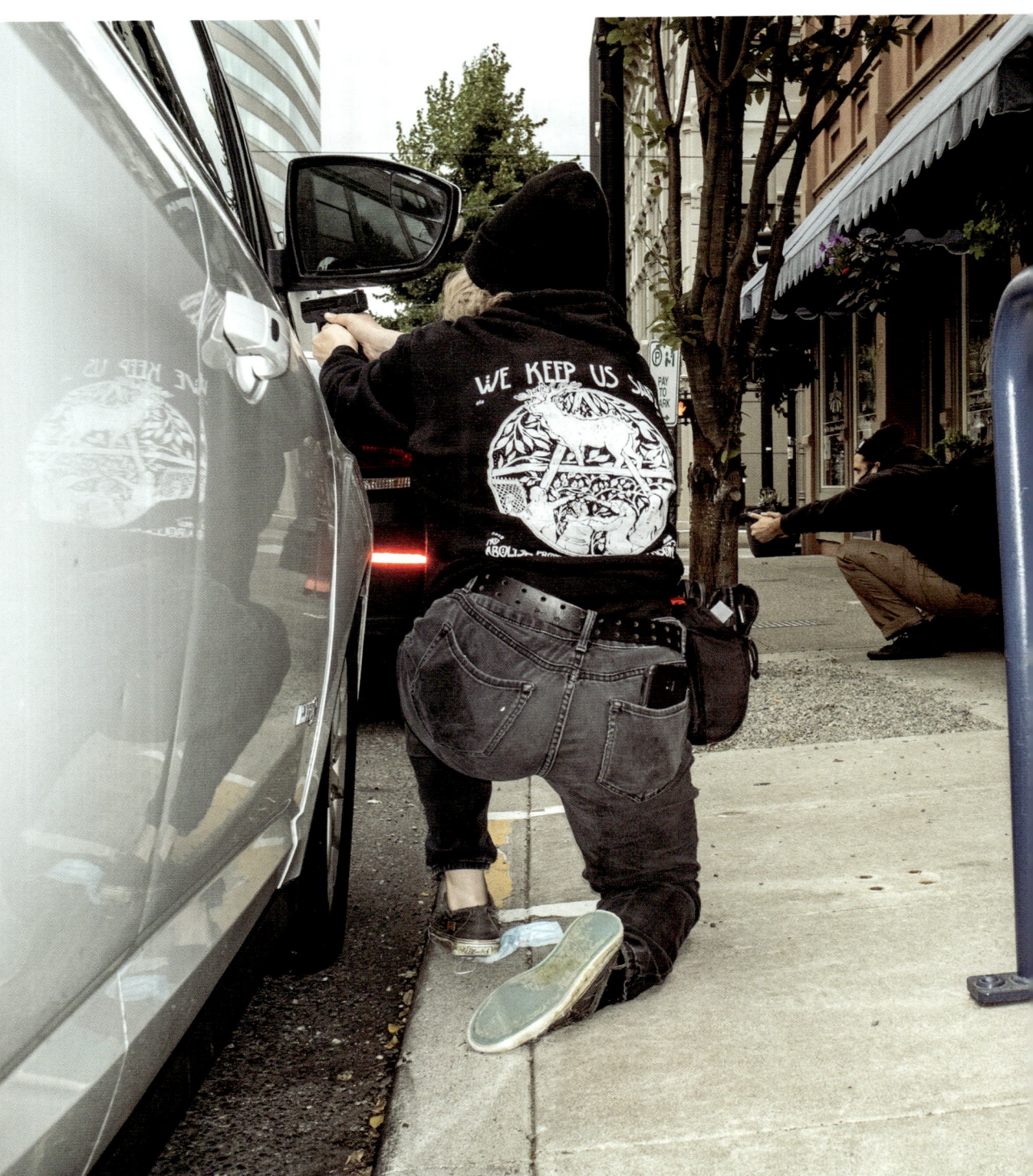

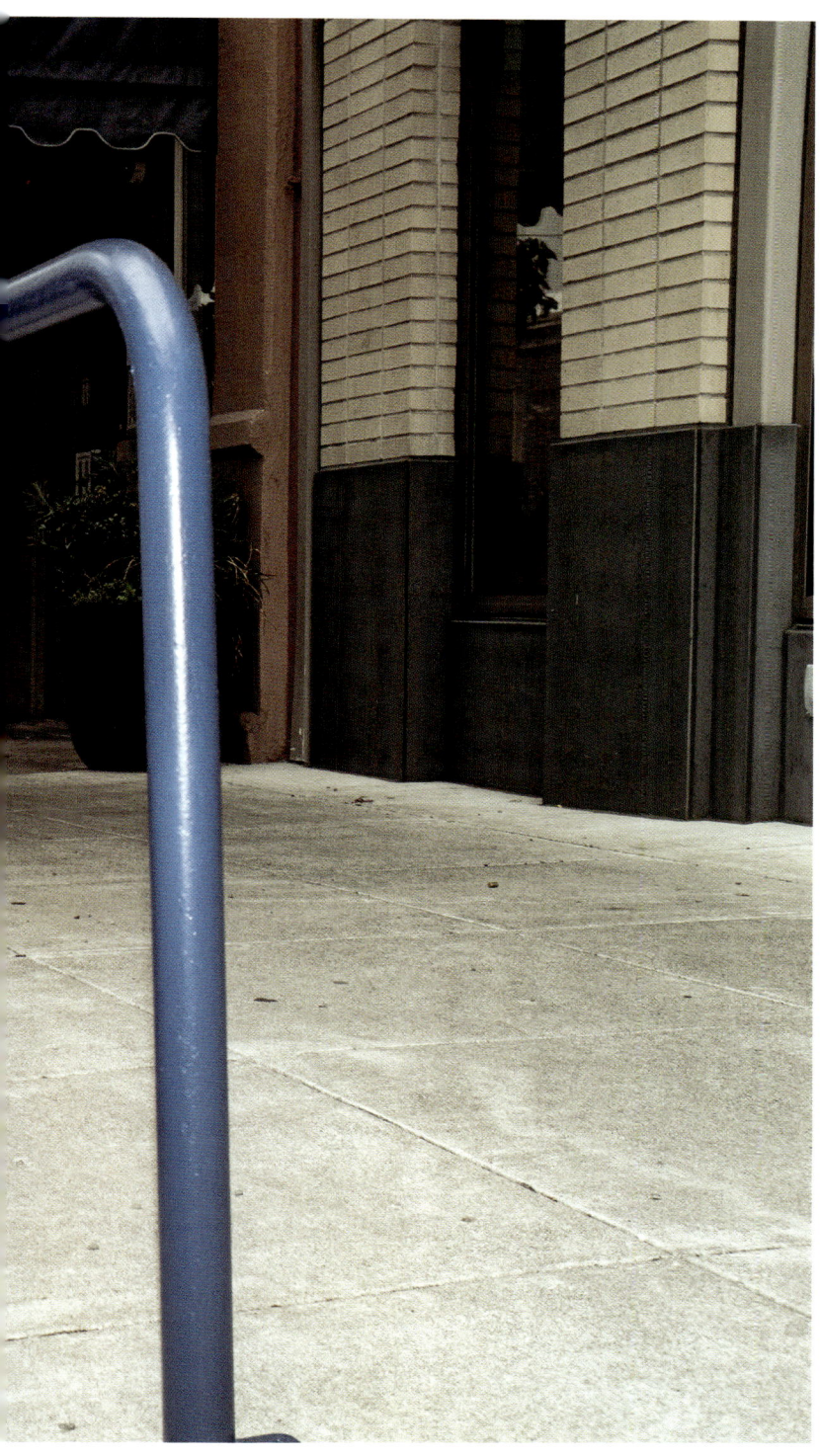

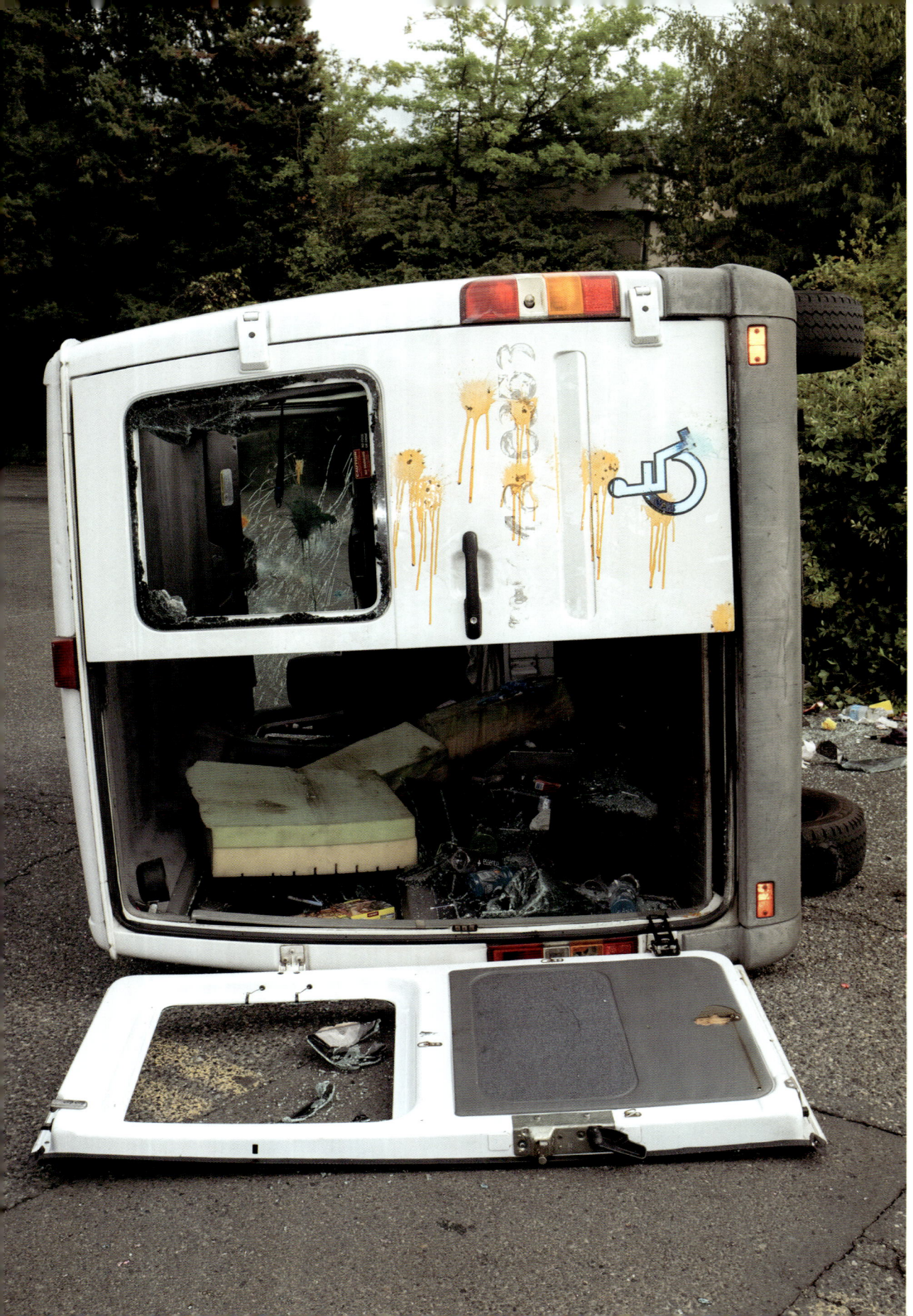

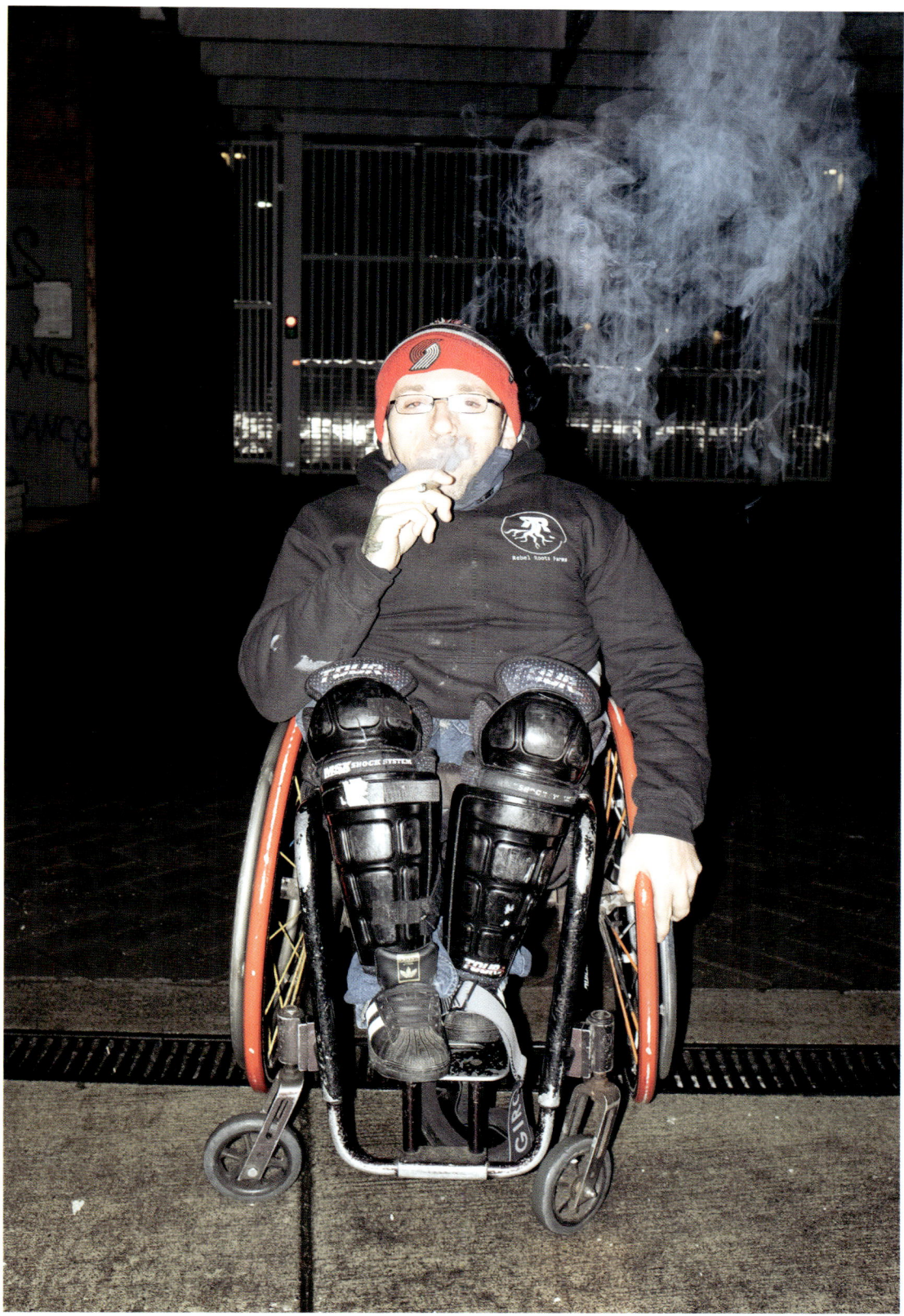

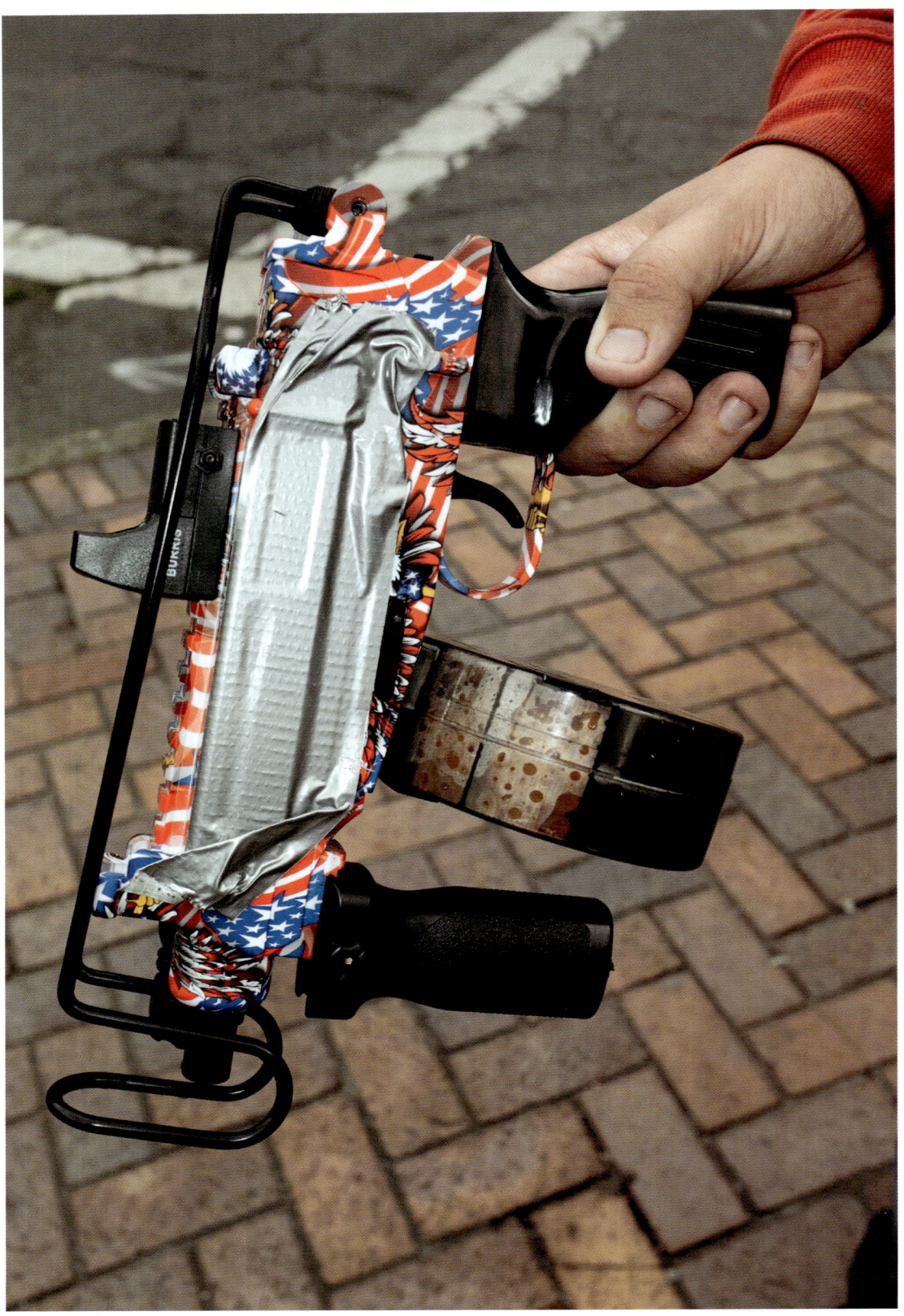

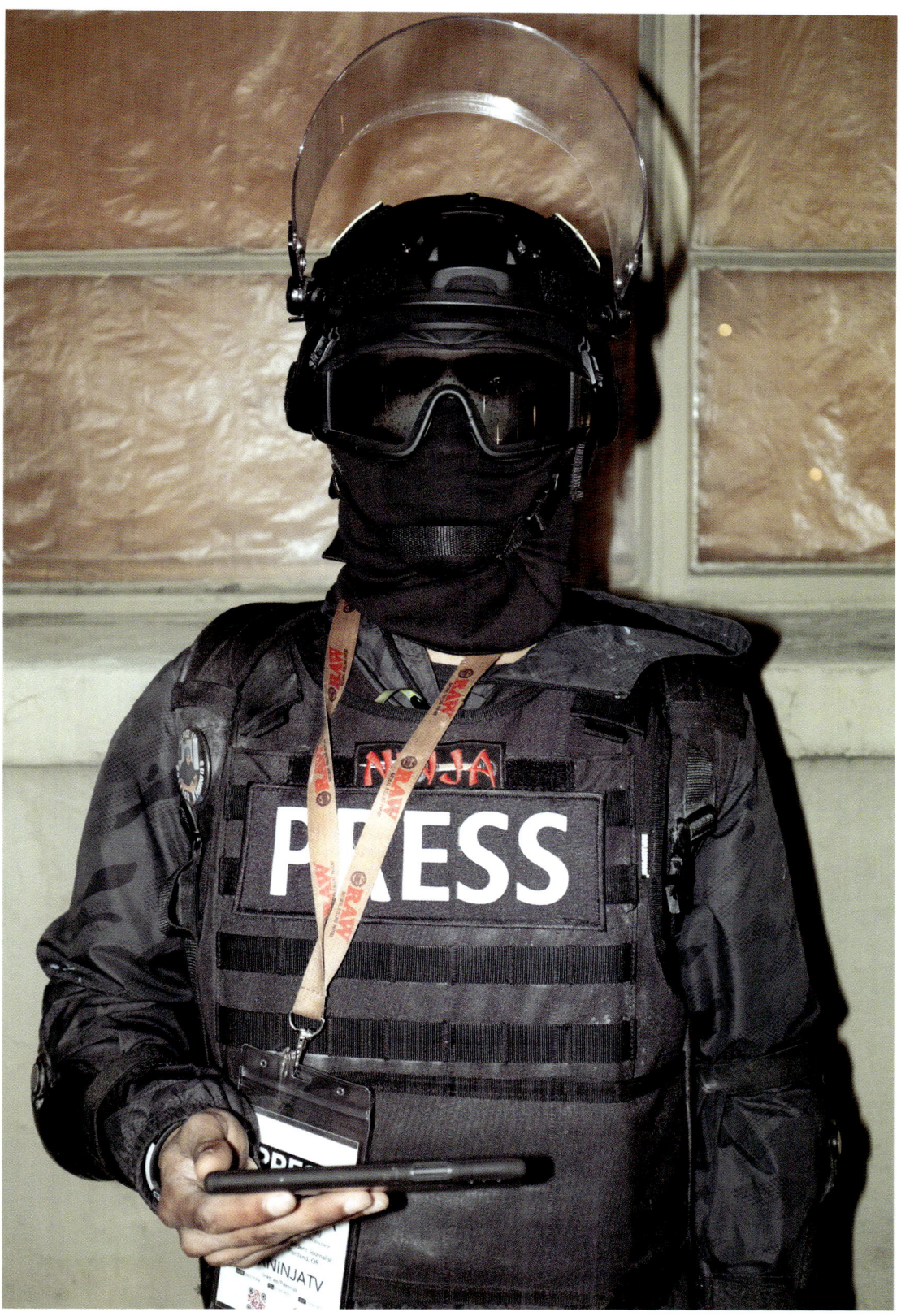

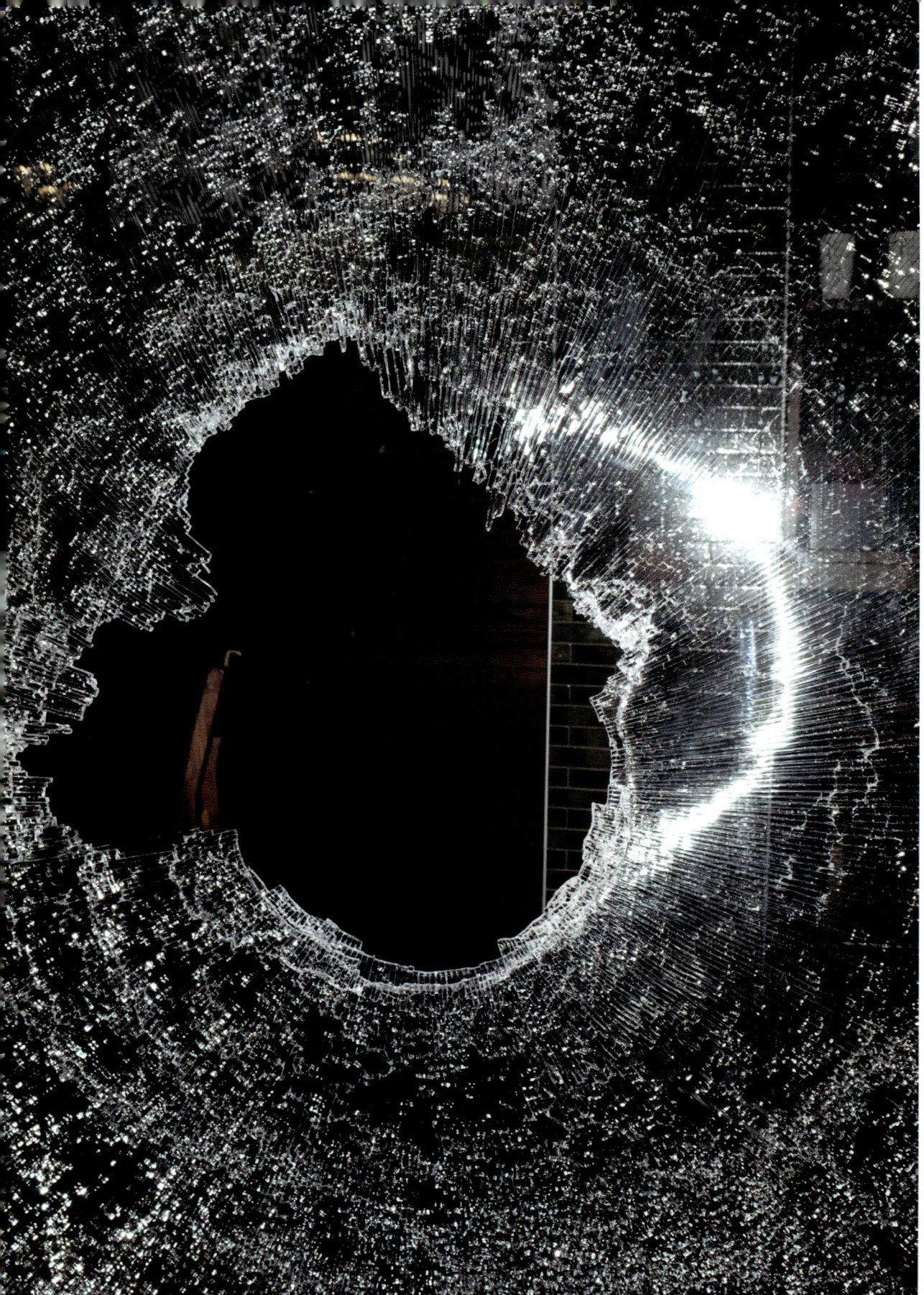

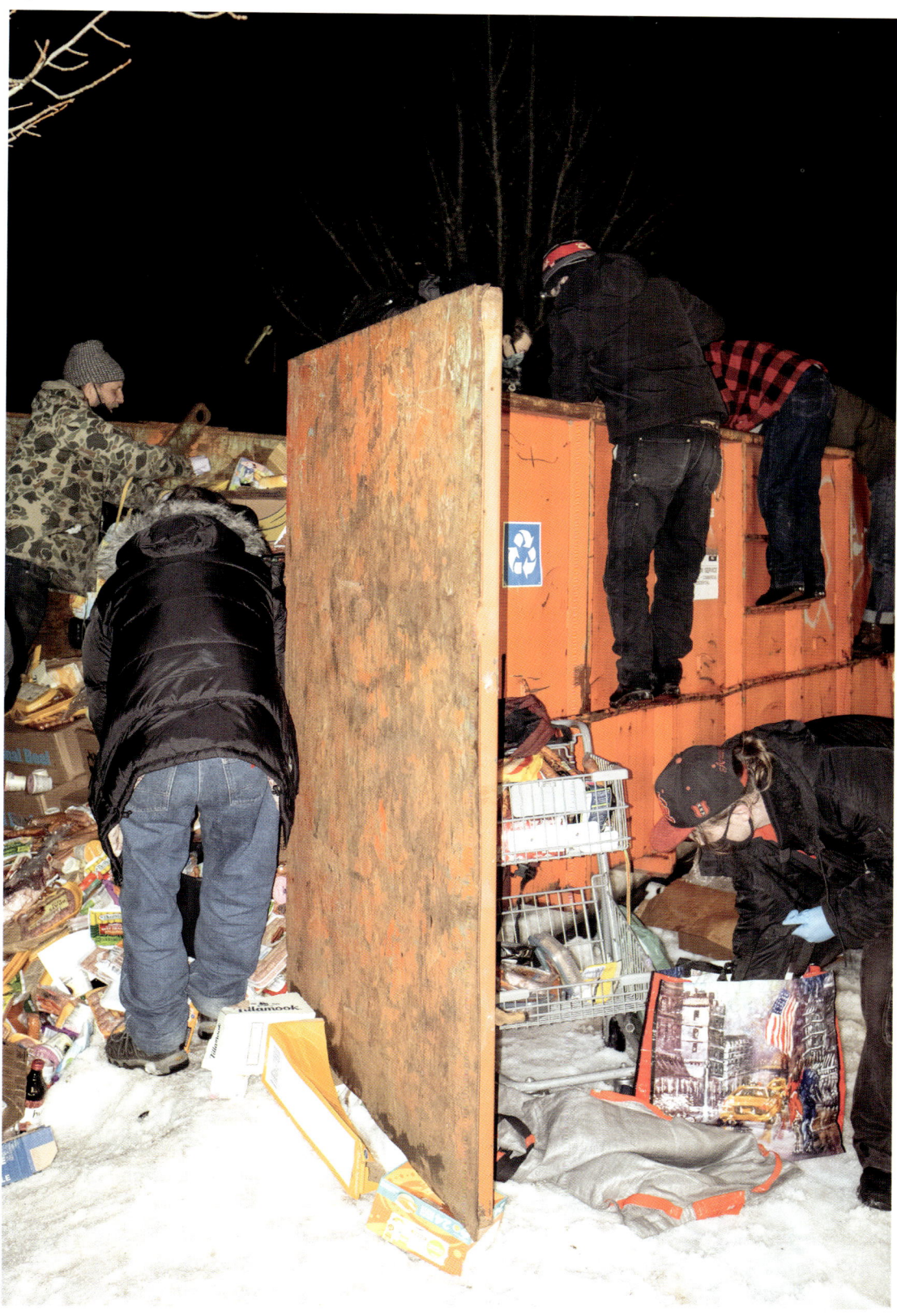

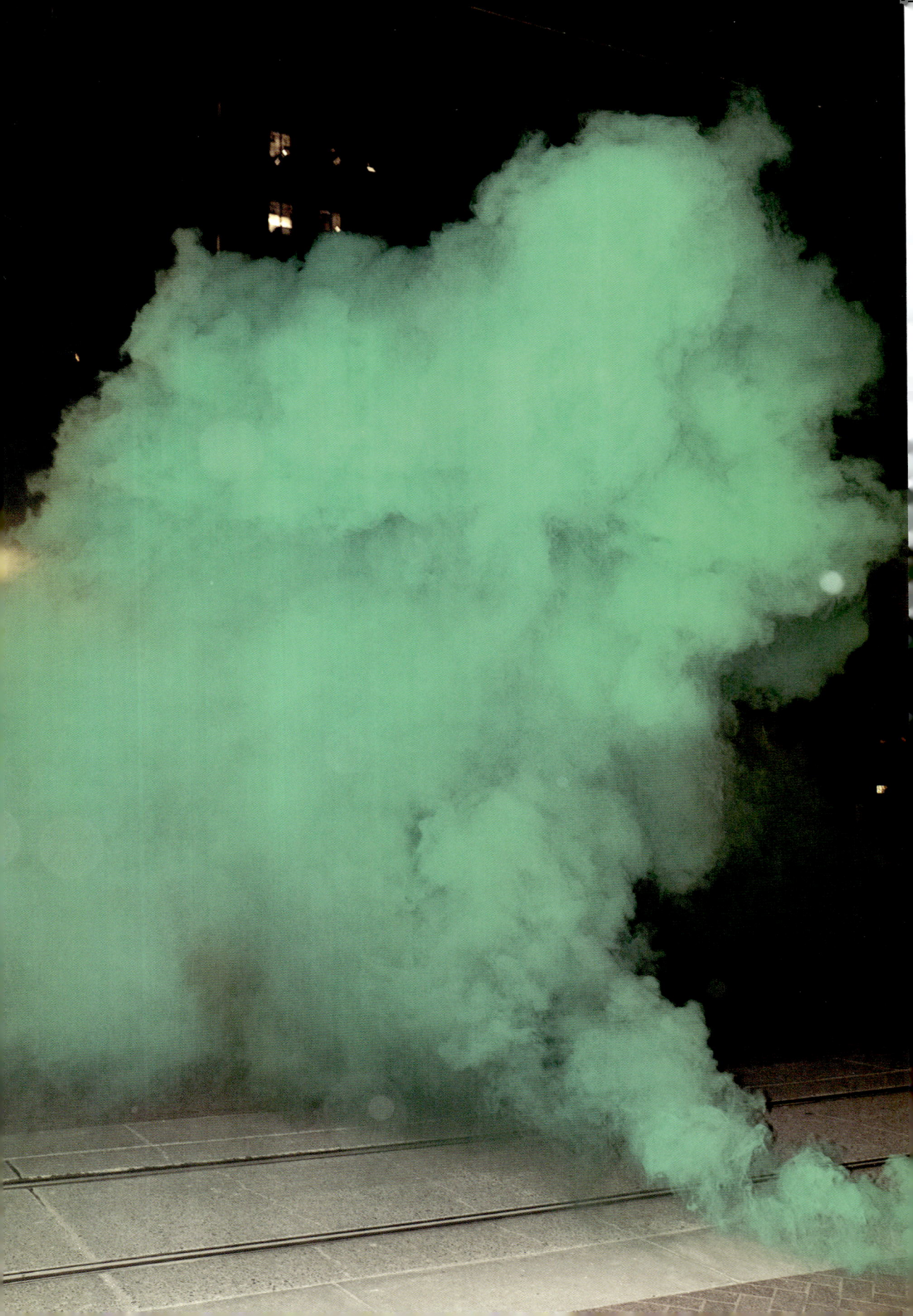

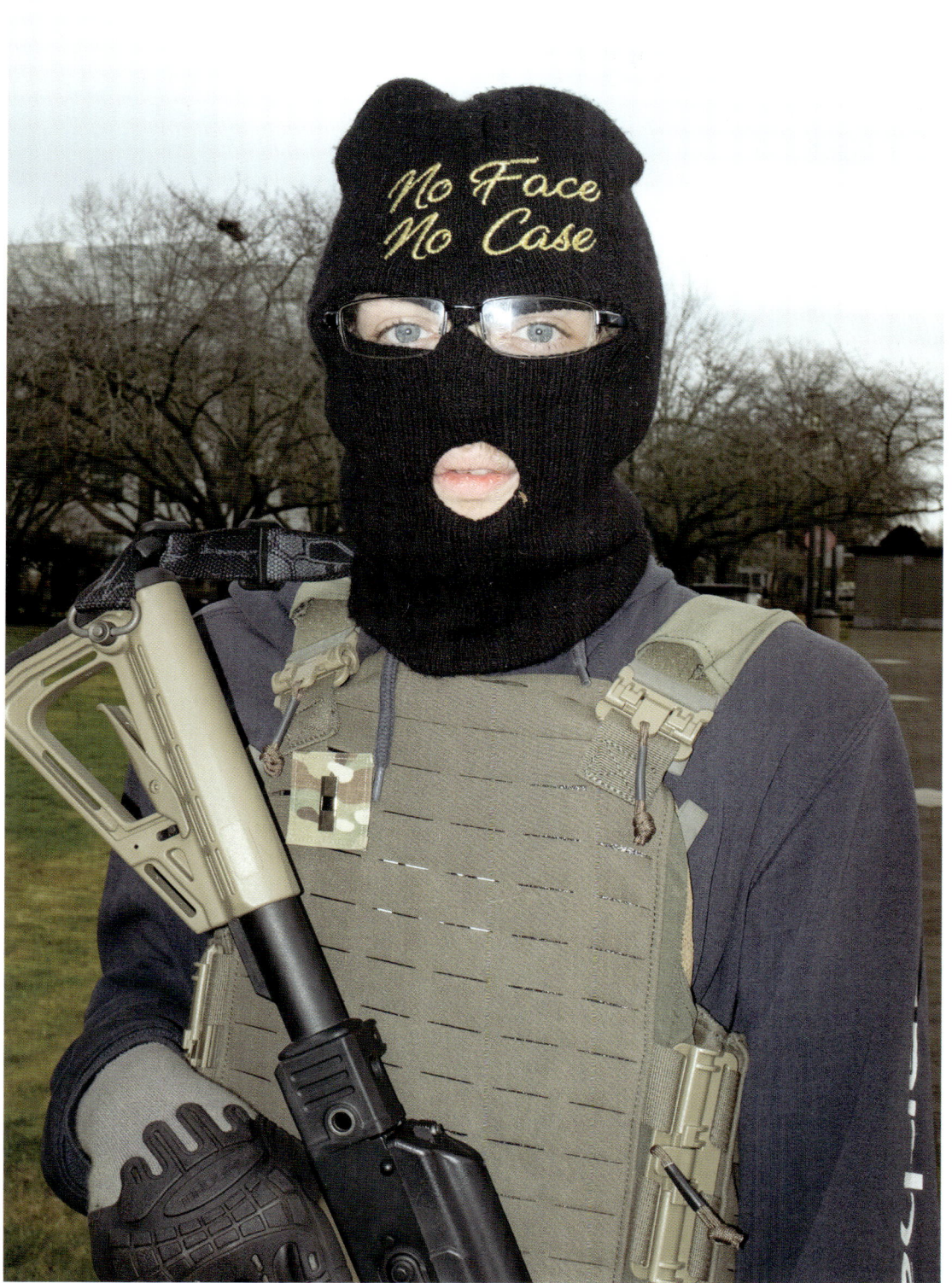

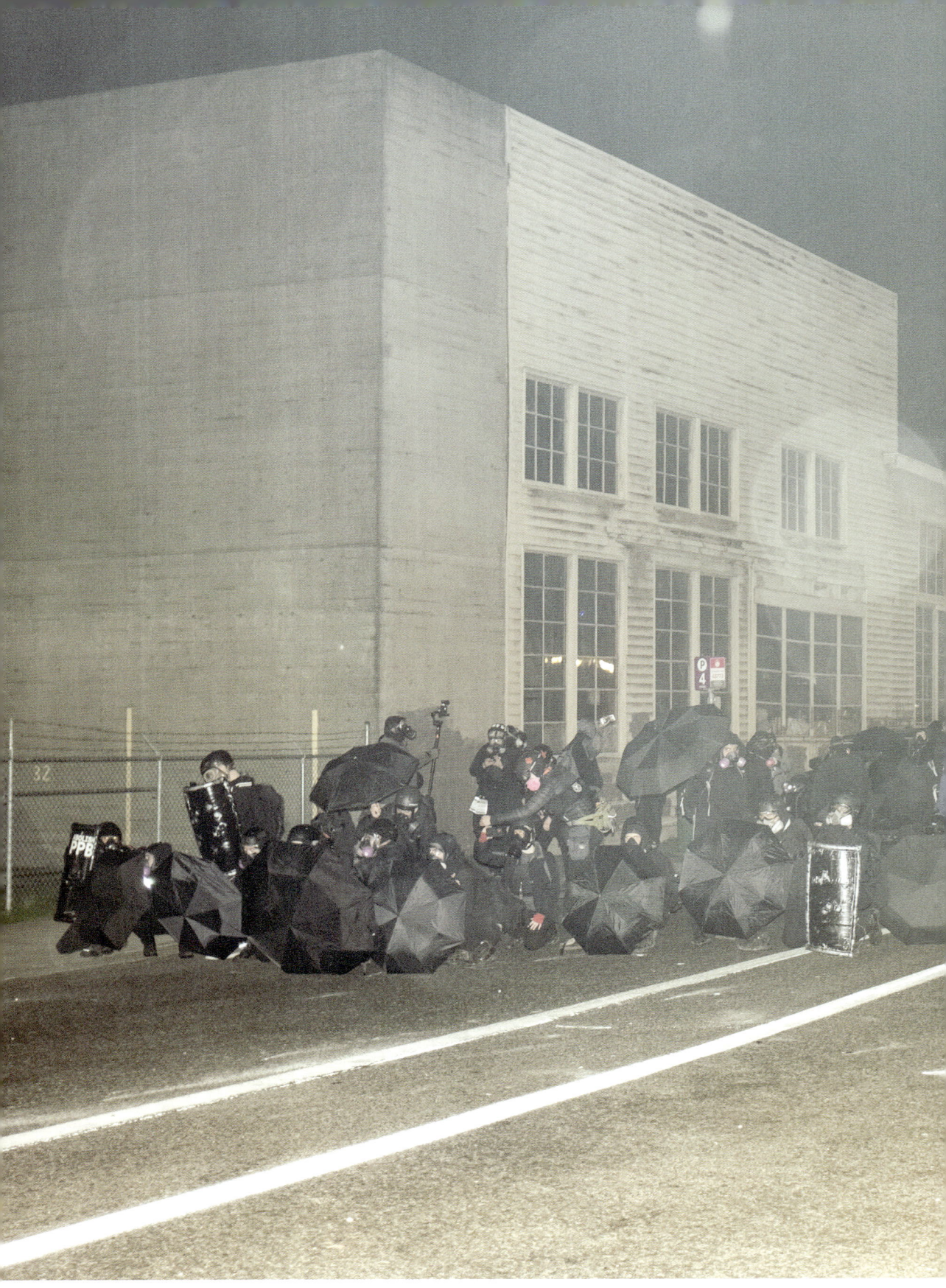

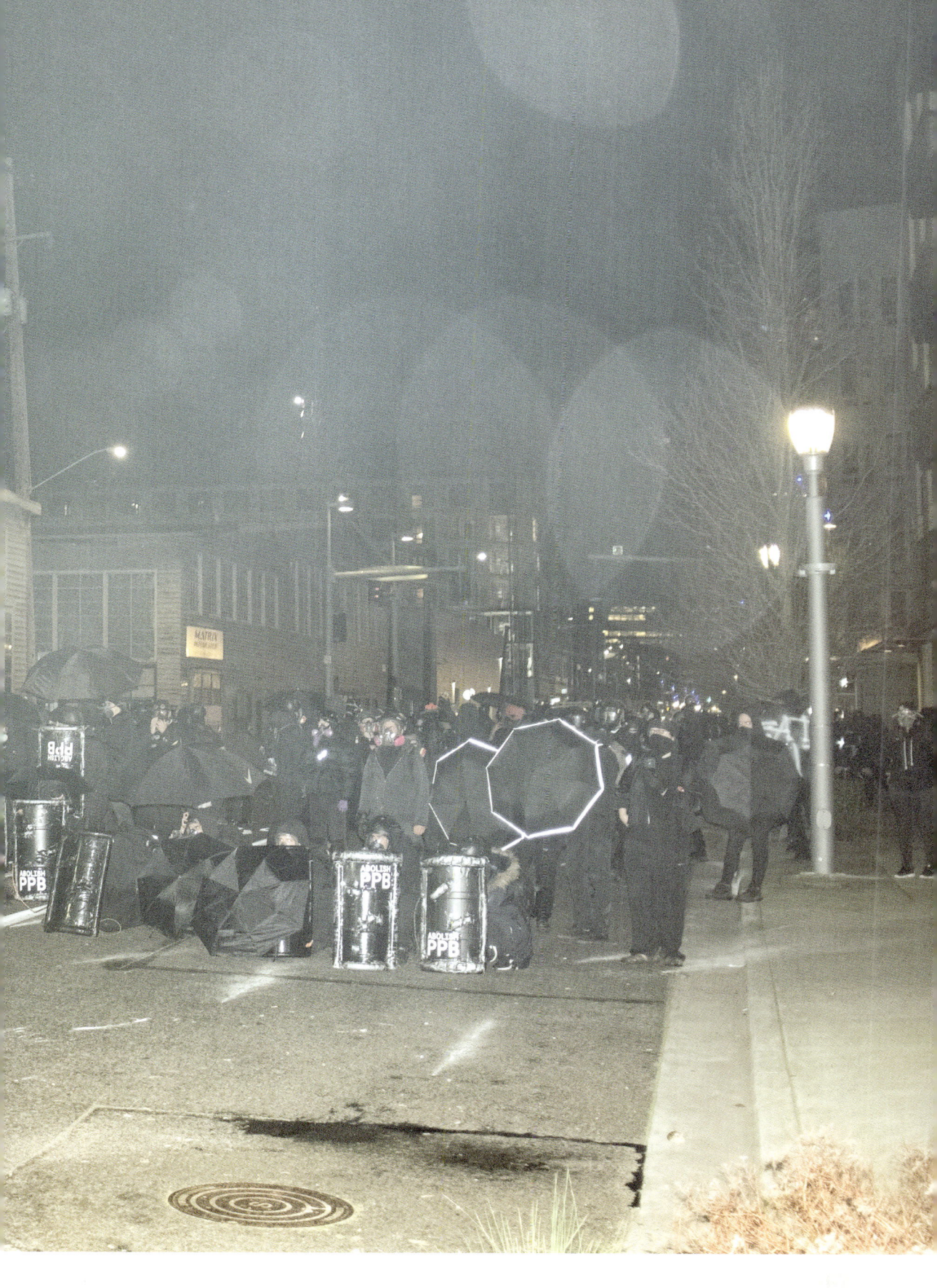

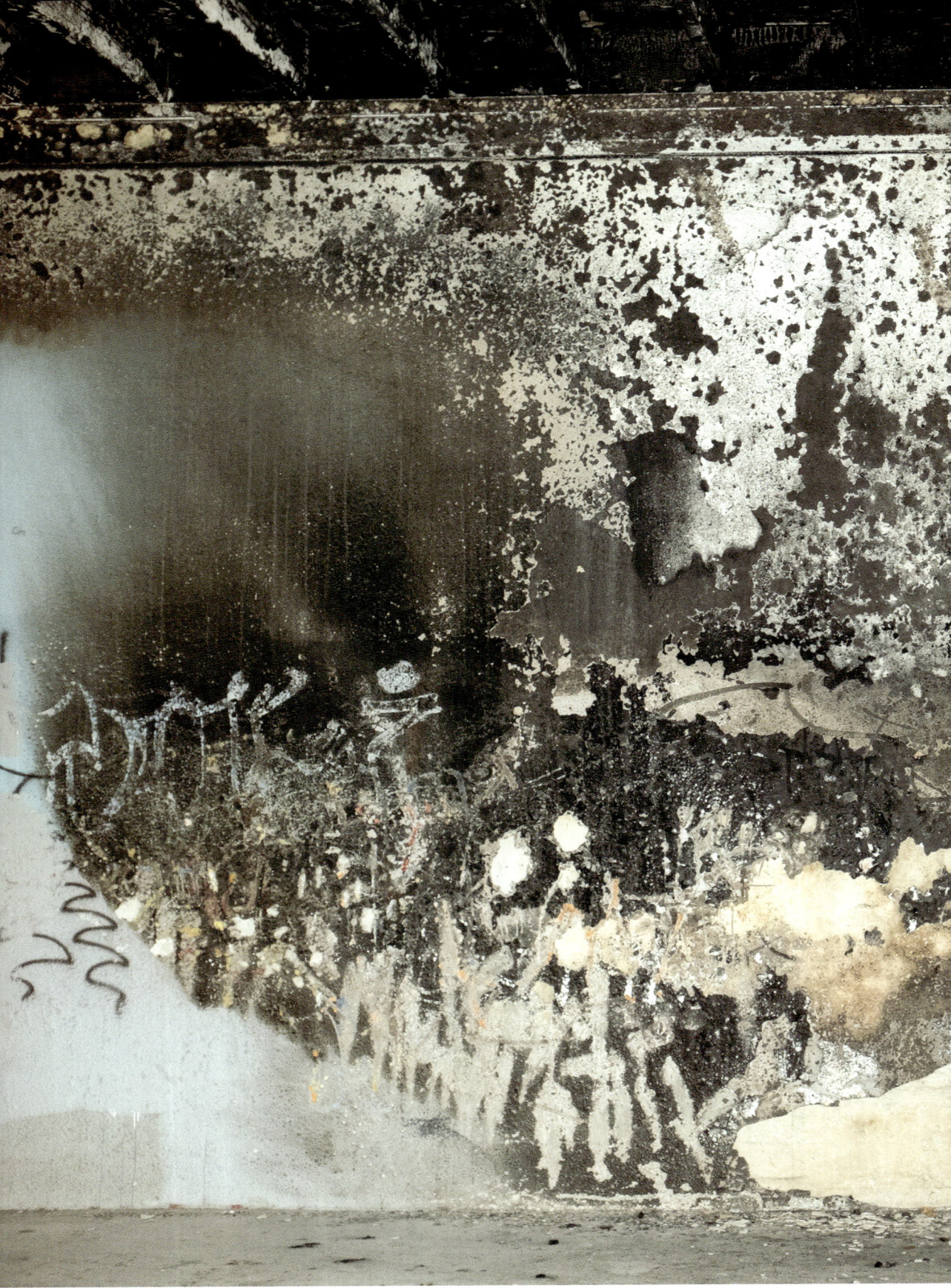

IMAGE CAPTIONS

frontis JUNE 15, 2020
A 1915 bronze statue of Thomas Jefferson lies on the ground after being toppled by protesters at Jefferson High School in Northeast Portland.

vii MAY 30, 2020
Vandalized Louis Vuitton outlet.

2–3 JUNE 5, 2020
Tear gas engulfs a crowd of protesters outside the Multnomah County Justice Center. The government complex, which houses a county jail along with the Portland Police Bureau's Central Precinct, became a focal point of demonstrations after the killing of George Floyd in Minneapolis.

4 JUNE 3, 2020
Protesters and mutual aid supplies converge on *The Promised Land*, a 1993 bronze statue celebrating the arrival of European settlers in Oregon, during nightly demonstrations against police brutality and systemic racism in downtown Portland.

5 JUNE 2, 2020
Demonstrators scale a Starbucks café at Pioneer Courthouse Square.

6 JULY 19, 2020
Antifascist activist Michael Forest Reinoehl shows a fresh Black Lives Matter tattoo on his neck.

7 JUNE 1, 2020
A man at work shows solidarity with marching protesters.

8–9 MAY 30, 2020
Demonstrators protesting the police killing of George Floyd flee smoke bombs and tear gas deployed by law enforcement outside the Multnomah County Justice Center.

10–11 MAY 30, 2020
Looted drugstore.

12   MAY 31, 2020
Protester in reflective jacket.

13   MAY 31, 2020
Pig heads are burned in effigy of police outside the Multnomah County Justice Center.

14   JUNE 6, 2020
Protesters pose for a photo outside the Multnomah County Justice Center.

15   JUNE 6, 2020
Protester with rubber bullet wound.

16   JULY 10, 2020
Protesters pound on a door outside the Mark O. Hatfield United States Courthouse, taunting law enforcement officers stationed inside.

17   MAY 31, 2020
A man armed with an assault rifle guards his vehicle from the threat of rioters after an 8 p.m. curfew went into effect.

18–19   JUNE 10, 2020
The intersection of SW Third and Main Streets after protesters dismantled a section of security fencing surrounding the Multnomah County Justice Center.

20   JUNE 5, 2020
Protest photographer.

21   JUNE 8, 2020
Live streamer's camera rig with improvised weatherproofing.

22   JUNE 15, 2020
Tabloid headlines.

23   JUNE 8, 2020
Activists rally and give speeches in Chapman Square.

24–25   JUNE 15, 2020
Trash fire at Third and Yamhill.

26 JUNE 17, 2020
High-rise denizens peer down from their apartments as protesters gather outside the home of Portland mayor Ted Wheeler.

27 JUNE 15, 2020
Protester with umbrellas.

28 JUNE 26, 2020
A door outside the Portland Police Bureau's North Precinct is barricaded by protesters.

29 JUNE 27, 2020
Protester with swimming goggles on the thirty-first consecutive night of demonstrations after the death of George Floyd.

30–31 JUNE 17, 2020
A man carrying a semi-automatic firearm takes part in a march on the Pearl District residence of Portland mayor Ted Wheeler.

32 JULY 17, 2020
Protesters using colored smoke for cover assemble barricades outside an entrance to the Multnomah County Justice Center.

33 JUNE 27, 2020
Activists send a "Black Lives Matter" placard up a flagpole outside the Multnomah County Justice Center.

34 JUNE 30, 2020
Activists are detained in the street outside the Portland Police Association union office.

35 JUNE 30, 2020
Protesters are confronted by Oregon State Police during demonstrations at the Portland Police Association.

36 JUNE 15, 2020
Broken bank machine.

37 JUNE 30, 2020
Journalist Cory Elia sits in the back of a police car after being arrested at a protest near the Portland Police Association.

38 JULY 5, 2020
Protesters collect unexploded pepper balls used as impact munitions by federal police.

39 JULY 6, 2020
Fake blood on the Multnomah County Justice Center steps.

40–41 JUNE 18, 2020
A 1927 statue of George Washington at the intersection of NE Fifty-Seventh and Sandy Boulevard, toppled from its base by protesters.

42–43 JULY 5, 2020
US Marshals secure Lownsdale Square. Federal officers were deployed to Portland under a Trump administration directive, Executive Order 13933, "On Protecting American Monuments, Memorials, and Statues and Combatting Recent Criminal Violence."

44 JULY 7, 2020
Protesting the feds at SW Madison and Third.

45 JULY 7, 2020
Protesters rally in Chapman Square on the fortieth consecutive night of protest.

46 JULY 7, 2020
The Promised Land, redecorated on day forty. The city later removed the statue for conservation.

47 JULY 10, 2020
A protester takes position on the base of a removed statue during confrontations with federal police.

48–49 JULY 10, 2020
Federal agents pursued by protesters retreat into a side door after making targeted arrests outside the Mark O. Hatfield United States Courthouse.

50 JULY 5, 2020
US Marshals secure the perimeter of Lownsdale Square during protests outside the Mark O. Hatfield United States Courthouse.

51   JULY 16, 2020
           A protester shows where federal police shot him with impact munitions.

52–53   JULY 17, 2020
           Protesters remove a suspected right-wing provocateur from a press conference addressing local outrage over the deployment of federal agents in Portland.

54–55   JULY 17, 2020
           Tear gas deployed by federal police drifts over Terry Schrunk Plaza.

56–57   JULY 16, 2020
           Officers with an ICE Special Response Team assemble outside the Edith Green-Wendell Wyatt Federal Building before launching an offensive against protesters. Department of Homeland Security acting secretary Chad Wolf was in Portland to survey the progress of what he called his "solemn duty to protect federal facilities and those within them."

58   JULY 16, 2020
           A man stands for a portrait after being tear-gassed by federal police.

59   JULY 15, 2020
           Roadblock at the corner of SW Madison and Third, part of the "Chinook Lands Autonomous Territory," where protesters created a temporary police-free zone in Lownsdale Square.

60–61   JULY 17, 2020
           Protesters form a shield line against federal police at Chapman Square.

62–63   JULY 17, 2020
           Using smoke for cover, protesters barricade an entrance to the Multnomah County Justice Center, where law enforcement officers are stationed inside.

64–65   JULY 18, 2020
           US Marshals rush a protester outside the Mark O. Hatfield United States Courthouse.

66–67   JULY 19, 2020
        Protesters take position behind an iron fence surrounding the Mark O. Hatfield United States Courthouse as they prepare to face off with Federal Protective Service officers stationed inside.

68–69   JULY 19, 2020
        Protesters topple a security fence outside the Mark O. Hatfield United States Courthouse.

70   JULY 5, 2020
        Press and protesters mingle in the street outside the Multnomah County Justice Center.

71   JULY 19, 2020
        A protester sports a necklace of squeezable rubber pig toys used to taunt police.

72–73   JULY 26, 2020
        Activists confront federal authorities on SW Third and Taylor.

74–75   JULY 26, 2020
        Mutual aid tents providing food and supplies to protesters are ransacked by federal agents.

76   JULY 26, 2020
        A DHS officer with a paint-splattered shield holds a line against protesters.

77   JULY 30, 2020
        An injured press photographer who was struck in the knee with police impact munitions.

78   JULY 30, 2020
        Protest placard.

79   JULY 26, 2020
        Masked protester outside the Mark O. Hatfield United States Courthouse.

80–81   JULY 31, 2020
        Federal agents guard a rear entrance to the Mark O. Hatfield United States Courthouse.

82–83   AUGUST 5, 2020
          A Portland police officer sprays mace from the driver's seat of his vehicle while attempting to clear protesters from the street.

84   AUGUST 6, 2020
          Demonstrators come to the aid of a reporter who was pushed to the ground during a police offensive outside the East Precinct.

85   AUGUST 6, 2020
          A neighborhood resident argues with protesters after a fire was set and paint splashed across the Portland Police Bureau's East Precinct.

86–87   AUGUST 6, 2020
          A home is vandalized by protesters during altercations with neighbors near the East Precinct.

88–89   AUGUST 14, 2020
          Police sweep a residential North Portland neighborhood for protesters.

90–91   AUGUST 14, 2020
          Residents show support for a passing protest march in North Portland.

92   AUGUST 19, 2020
          Federal agents keep protesters at bay outside an Immigration and Customs Enforcement (ICE) facility in South Portland.

93   AUGUST 26, 2020
          A can of tear gas smolders as protesters are dispersed from outside the ICE building.

94–95   AUGUST 26, 2020
          Hexachloroethane smoke grenades are deployed by federal police outside an ICE facility. HC grenades produce a thick gas of zinc chloride known to be carcinogenic and environmentally harmful.

96   JULY 18, 2020
          Protester in wedding dress and gas mask.

97   AUGUST 19, 2020
          Protest photographer with shield.

98   AUGUST 19, 2020
      Portland police arrest demonstrators near the ICE detention facility in South Portland.

99   AUGUST 22, 2020
      Right-wing activists react during clashes with counter-protesters at a pro-police "No to Marxism in America" rally outside the Multnomah County Justice Center.

100–101   AUGUST 29, 2020
          Trump supporters ride in a caravan "cruise rally" of vehicles parading through downtown Portland.

102   AUGUST 29, 2020
       Two men fight in the street during one night of skirmishes between Trump supporters and counter-protesters.

103   SEPTEMBER 4, 2020
       Projectile paint splattered on a bus shelter near the Portland Police Association.

104   JULY 22, 2020
       Protesters celebrate a police retreat outside the Mark O. Hatfield United States Courthouse.

105   AUGUST 29, 2020
       Joey Gibson (black hoodie), leader of local right-wing group Patriot Prayer, is accosted by counter-protesters during a Trump rally in downtown Portland.

106   SEPTEMBER 4, 2020
       An injured protester is arrested by Oregon State Police outside the Portland Police Association.

107   SEPTEMBER 4, 2020
       Protester at the Portland Police Association.

108–109   SEPTEMBER 4, 2020
          Protest medics tend to a person struck by police impact munitions during demonstrations outside the Portland Police Association.

110–111 SEPTEMBER 5, 2020
A man films confrontations between police and demonstrators near Ventura Park.

112 SEPTEMBER 5, 2020
Members of the press gather on the corner of SE 117th and Stark on the one-hundredth night of protests.

113 SEPTEMBER 5, 2020
Anti-press graffiti, night one hundred.

114 SEPTEMBER 7, 2020
A nude counter-protester is maced and berated by right-wing activists at a Labor Day rally in Salem.

115 SEPTEMBER 7, 2020
Bystander at a Labor Day rally outside the Oregon State Capitol.

116–117 SEPTEMBER 12, 2020
Wildfire smoke under the Fremont Bridge blanketed Portland, effectively halting most protests.

118–119 DECEMBER 12, 2020
Memorials to antifascist activist Michael Forest Reinoehl are painted under the St. John's Bridge three months after he was killed by a US Marshals fugitive task force. Reinoehl was implicated in the shooting death of a Trump supporter during a political rally in downtown Portland.

120–121 SEPTEMBER 23, 2020
Police scramble to subdue protesters after a Molotov cocktail was lobbed at officers outside the Multnomah County Justice Center.

122 SEPTEMBER 23, 2020
Protest photographer's camera rig.

123 SEPTEMBER 5, 2020
The singed left shoe of a protester whose feet caught fire when a Molotov cocktail exploded nearby.

124   SEPTEMBER 26, 2020
An activist flashes the once innocuous "OK" hand sign, now co-opted by the far right, at a Proud Boys rally in Delta Park.

125   SEPTEMBER 26, 2020
Armed community protection volunteers rally in Irving Park.

126   SEPTEMBER 26, 2020
Proud Boy with neck tattoo, Delta Park.

127   SEPTEMBER 4, 2020
A protest medic dresses their own leg injury following a police offensive outside the Portland Police Association.

128   OCTOBER 12, 2020
Theodore Roosevelt, Rough Rider, a 1922 bronze sculpture commissioned after the president's death, lies at the base of its pedestal after being toppled by Indigenous rights activists.

129   OCTOBER 30, 2020
Candles left at a vigil for Kevin Peterson Jr., a twenty-one-year-old Black man killed by police in the parking lot of a US Bank in the Portland suburb of Hazel Dell, Washington.

130–131   OCTOBER 30, 2020
Right-wing activist Chandler Pappas paces through a crowd of mourners following the police killing of Kevin Peterson Jr. Pappas and other armed demonstrators countered the candlelit vigil under the pretense of safeguarding local businesses.

132–133   NOVEMBER 3, 2020
Protesters burn flares while marching in Southeast Portland on Election Day.

134–135   NOVEMBER 3, 2020
Residents watch from their window as protesters march up SE Belmont Street on Election Day.

136–137   NOVEMBER 4, 2020
A downtown Portland business boards its windows in preparation for post-election protests.

138–139　DECEMBER 8, 2020
　　　　Activists salvage available materials to build an eviction blockade outside the Kinney family home in North Portland. The household at 4406 North Mississippi Avenue was successfully defended from eviction by a coalition of community members and housing activists who constructed an elaborate series of barriers around the contested property.

140, 141　DECEMBER 9, 2020
　　　　Inner barrier of the Red House eviction blockade, where antigentrification activists held a five-day standoff with law enforcement, successfully preventing the removal of occupants of a North Portland home.

142　　DECEMBER 12, 2020
　　　　White Rabbit, Red House eviction activist.

143　　DECEMBER 9, 2020
　　　　Improvised caltrops placed near the perimeter of the "Red House on Mississippi" eviction blockade.

144　　DECEMBER 31, 2020
　　　　Anti–Republican party graffiti.

145　　JANUARY 6, 2021
　　　　Man with an eye patch at a pro-Trump "stop the steal" rally outside the Oregon statehouse.

146–147　JANUARY 6, 2021
　　　　An injured woman falls to the ground during skirmishes between Proud Boys, counter-protesters, and law enforcement at a pro-Trump "stop the steal" rally in Salem.

148–149　JANUARY 20, 2021
　　　　Activists scuffle with police at an Inauguration Day "Fuck Biden" rally outside Revolution Hall.

150　　JANUARY 28, 2021
　　　　A Department of Homeland Security agent confronts protesters near the ICE building.

151   FEBRUARY 5, 2021
        Indigenous women activists hold a press conference outside Portland City Hall ahead of federal court arraignments faced by a group of protesters.

152–153 MAY 25, 2021
        Security fencing surrounds an Apple store on the one-year anniversary of George Floyd's death. The computer retailer was looted and vandalized during protests in 2020.

154–155 JANUARY 1, 2021
        Starbucks café, New Year's Eve riot.

156–157 AUGUST 22, 2021
        Left-wing activists exchange gunfire with a man who brandished his handgun at protesters in downtown Portland.

158   AUGUST 22, 2021
        A van belonging to leftist counter-protesters was overturned and ransacked during fighting with Proud Boys and other right-wing activists on NE 122nd Avenue.

159   JANUARY 27, 2021
        Activist Dustin Brandon outside the ICE facility in South Portland.

160   AUGUST 22, 2021
        Antifascist armed with a modified pellet gun.

161   MARCH 12, 2021
        Ninja outside the "kettle."

162   MAY 25, 2021
        Smashed window at a Starbucks café, one year after the police killing of George Floyd.

163   FEBRUARY 16, 2021
        Activists and gleaners salvage food from a supermarket dumpster after power failures forced the business to discard thousands of perishable items.

164   MARCH 11, 2021
       Hexachloroethane smoke is deployed by ICE agents to disperse protesters near Lownsdale Square.

165   JANUARY 17, 2021
       Boogaloo Bois rally.

166–167   JANUARY 20, 2021
           Protesters form a shield line outside the ICE facility on Inauguration Day.

168–169   FEBRUARY 21, 2021
           Burn residue, Creston Park.

ACKNOWLEDGMENTS

Many people helped make this book possible. Thanks to Alice Proujansky, Alan Chin, Sierra Moreno West, and Peter van Agtmael for their early edits and encouragement. Alissa Quart for Word support, and Nick Garcia for publishing the photographs before anyone else would. Invaluable guidance came from RJ Mickelson, Robert Patrick, and Kim Hogeland at OSU Press. Donnell Alexander and Carmen P. Thompson brought the clarity of their words to bear on foggy pictures.

Thanks also to Alexandra Mächler, Mark Murrmann, Kristen Lubben, Balazs Gardi, David Butow, Noelle Flores Théard, Matt Mimiaga, Kenneth Dickerman, Geoffrey Hiller, Susie Smith, B. Ruby Rich, Marcia Allert, Bryan Denton, Deborah Willis, Nick Kahl, Lorie Novak, Joseph Rushmore, Jeb Proujansky, and Blake Andrews.

My fellow Portland photographers and reporters, including but not limited to Justin Yau, Suzette Smith, Beth Nakamura, Dan Steinle, Jordan Gale, Sergio Olmos, Zane Sparling, Laura Jedeed, Nathan Howard, and Mason Trinca.

All the activists and protesters who allowed me to photograph. Thank you for caring enough to do something about it.

SUGGESTED READING

Addae, Angela A., Marisa Chappell, Judson L. Jeffries, and Joseph Lowndes. "Racism, Protest, and Law Enforcement: Historical Context for Contemporary Times." Panel discussion hosted by the Oregon Historical Society and the Oregon Jewish Museum and Center for Holocaust Education, June 20, 2020. www.ohs.org/events/racism-protest-and-law-enforcement.cfm.

Boddie, Ken. "A Brief History of African Americans Killed by PPB." KOIN, June 4, 2020. www.koin.com/news/special-reports/a-brief-history-of-african-americans-killed-by-ppb.

Brown, Richard, and Brian Benson. *This Is Not for You: An Activist's Journey of Resistance and Resilience*. Corvallis, OR: Oregon State University Press, 2021.

Burke, Lucas N., and Judson L. Jeffries. *The Portland Black Panthers: Empowering Albina and Remaking a City*. Seattle: University of Washington Press, 2016.

Cannone, Francheska, Nate Belcik, Macy Franken, Kelly Green, Sarah Harris, Philippe Kerstens, Vicky White, and Katrine Barber. "PDX Protests, Summer 2020: A Syllabus and Timeline." PDXOpen: Open Educational Resources 39, 2021. https://pdxscholar.library.pdx.edu/pdxopen/39.

Cigarran, Jane. "The Case of Cheryl D. James: Institutionalized Racism and Police Violence Against Black Women in Portland, Oregon (1968–1974)," *Oregon Historical Quarterly* 121, no. 1 (2020): 40-67. https://doi.org/10.5403/oregonhistq.121.1.0040.

Crombie, Noelle, and Shane Dixon Kavanaugh. "Behind the Portland Protests: A Troubling Record of Police Killings," *The Crime Report*, August 25, 2020. thecrimereport.org/2020/08/25/behind-the-portland-protests-a-troubling-record-of-police-killings.

Lang, Melissa Cornelius. "'A place under the sun': African American Resistance to Housing Exclusion." *Oregon Historical Quarterly* 119, no. 3 (Fall 2018), 365–375. https://doi.org/10.5403/oregonhistq.119.3.0365.

Perry, Douglas. "'Little Beirut' Legacy: Twenty-One of the Most Memorable Protests in Portland History." *The Oregonian/OregonLive*, April 11, 2016. www.oregonlive.com/living/2016/04/little_beirut_legacy_20_of_the.html.

Serbulo, Leanne C., and Karen J. Gibson. "Black and Blue: Police-Community Relations in Portland's Albina District, 1964–1985." *Oregon Historical Quarterly* 114, no. 1 (2013): 6–37. https://doi.org/10.5403/oregonhistq.114.1.0006.

Thompson, Carmen P., and Darrell Milner, editors. "White Supremacy and Resistance." Special issue, *Oregon Historical Quarterly* 120, no. 4 (Winter 2019). www.ohs.org/oregon-historical-quarterly/back-issues/winter-2019.cfm.